MW01132788

Mapping American Criminal Law

Mapping American Criminal Law

Variations across the 50 States

Paul H. Robinson and Tyler Scot Williams

An Imprint of ABC-CLIO, LLC
Santa Barbara, California • Denver, Colorado

Library of Congress Cataloging-in-Publication Data

Names: Robinson, Paul H., 1948– author. | Williams, Tyler Scot, author.
Title: Mapping American criminal law: variations across the 50 states /
  Paul H. Robinson and Tyler Scot Williams.
Description: Santa Barbara, Calif. : Praeger, an imprint of ABC-CLIO, LLC, 2018. |
  Includes bibliographical references and index.
Identifiers: LCCN 2018001373 (print) | LCCN 2018001875 (ebook) |
  ISBN 9781440860133 (ebook) | ISBN 9781440860126 (hardcopy : alk. paper)
Subjects: LCSH: Criminal law—United States—States.
Classification: LCC KF9219 (ebook) | LCC KF9219 .R63 2018 (print) |
  DDC 345.73—dc23
LC record available at https://lccn.loc.gov/2018001373

ISBN: 978-1-4408-6012-6 (print)
      978-1-4408-6013-3 (ebook)

22 21 20 19 18   1 2 3 4 5

This book is also available as an eBook.

Praeger
An Imprint of ABC-CLIO, LLC

ABC-CLIO, LLC
130 Cremona Drive, P.O. Box 1911
Santa Barbara, California 93116-1911
www.abc-clio.com

This book is printed on acid-free paper ∞

Manufactured in the United States of America

Dedicated to
Sarah Robinson and Abby Williams
for their
unstinting love and support

Contents

Preface

It is common for criminal law scholars from outside the United States to discuss the "American rule" in order to compare it to the rule of other countries.[1] As this volume makes clear, however, there is no such thing as an "American rule." Each of the states, plus the District of Columbia and the federal system, have their own criminal law; there are 52 American criminal codes.

American criminal law scholars know this, of course, but they too commonly speak of the "general rule" as if it reflects some consensus or near consensus position among the states. But the truth is that the landscape of American criminal law is one of almost endless diversity, with few, if any, areas in which there is a consensus or near consensus. Even most American criminal law scholars seem to fail to appreciate the enormous diversity and disagreement among the 52 American jurisdictions.

The best one can do in most instances is to talk of a "majority rule," but even this is extremely difficult business. Every jurisdiction recognizes a person's right to defend himself or herself against unlawful force, for example. But what is the "majority rule" in the United States in the formulation of that defense? Jurisdictions disagree on a wide variety of issues within self-defense, most prominently: (a) What constitutes the "unlawful force" that triggers a right to use defensive force? (b) What temporal requirement must be met for an actor's conduct to be truly "necessary" at that time? (c) What amount of force may be used? (d) When may deadly force be employed? (e) When may an initial aggressor claim self-defense? (f) What is the legal effect, if any, of the defendant provoking the encounter? (g) What is the legal effect of mutual combat on self-defense? (h) Is there a right to resist an unlawful arrest? (i) Is there a duty to retreat from unlawful aggression before using deadly force? There is disagreement among the states on every one of these issues.[2]

Further, as some of us have demonstrated elsewhere, even when the research is done, it is not so easy to construct the majority American rule. To

continue with the self-defense example above, not only do American jurisdictions disagree on each of the self-defense issues listed above, but the pattern
of states making up the majority view on each individual issue varies from
issue to issue. In other words, at the end of the day the "majority rule" for self-
defense in the United States is a rule that no jurisdiction actually adopts.
It is necessarily a composite of the American "majority rule" on each of the
sub-issues.[3]

Unfortunately, there has been little work done to map the enormous diversity among the states, perhaps because it is an extremely burdensome project,
in part for the reasons just noted. Every legal issue requires a major research
project investigating the criminal codes and/or case law of all 52 American
jurisdictions, and a single legal doctrine may have a half-dozen sub-issues
that must each be separately resolved.

Although the paucity of such diversity research is understandable, it is
nonetheless regrettable, for it is the matters of disagreement that often point to
the most interesting issues for scholars. Why is it that there is disagreement
on a particular point? Why hasn't a consensus formed? What are the advantages and disadvantages of the each of the alternative positions such that none
have won the day? Or, is it that the alternative positions have been perpetu-
ated simply out of an ignorance by the legislatures of the disagreements among
the states? That is, does diversity exist not because of genuine disputes about
which position is best but rather because the conflicting positions are not
readily known?

This volume is meant to raise awareness of the enormous diversity among
the states on issues across the criminal law landscape, to document this diversity with a host of specific illustrations on a wide range of issues, to encourage criminal law scholars to investigate these and the many other points of
disagreement that exist among the states, and to encourage each legislature to
look to this new diversity scholarship and to the positions taken by other states
when the legislature sets out to codify or recodify its criminal law (or to
encourage judges to do the same in those jurisdictions that continue to allow
judicial criminal law making[4]).

In each of the next 38 chapters, we examine different areas of American
criminal law and identify the major groupings among the states on an issue
in each area. This is hardly a comprehensive list of the issues on which there are
disagreement; it is only a representative sampling. Indeed, we know of no
area of American criminal law on which there is not disagreement among
the jurisdictions. The only American criminal law universal is its universal
diversity.

Nor are the points of disagreement that we map here the only points of
diversity within each of the issues that we examine. On the contrary, we
commonly pick one particular point of disagreement among the states that

seems particularly interesting or important, but it is commonly only one of many points of interstate disagreement relating to that aspect of criminal law.

For the issue that we take up in each chapter, we group all the American jurisdictions according to the position they take. However, there is such variety in approach that even jurisdictions within the same group commonly take slightly different approaches (which we often attempt to document in the Notes). Thus, even our groupings of states, usually three to seven groups on each issue, understate the extent of American criminal law diversity.

Each chapter provides a map of the United States with each of the states visually coded according to its approach to the issue. These maps, the reader will see, often raise interesting hypotheses about geographic or other state factors that might explain the patterns of agreement and disagreement (red states versus blue states, rural versus urban, rich versus poor, West Coast versus East Coast, etc.). At the end of each chapter we sometimes speculate about the reasons for disagreements, but more importantly, our hope is that the maps will pique the interest of scholars in many disciplines—political scientists, criminologists, criminal law scholars, and sociologists, among others—to investigate alternative hypotheses about why we see the patterns of agreement and disagreement that we see.

Notes

1. For instance, it is common to speak of the "American rule" concerning the duty to rescue and criminal liability for omissions. See, e.g., Peter M. Agulnick and Heidi V. Rivkin, *Criminal Liability for Failure to Rescue: A Brief Survey of French and American Law,* 8 Touro Int'l L. Rev. 93, 95 (1998) (referring to the "American rule" that there is no duty to rescue); Christopher H. Schroeder, *Two Methods for Evaluating Duty to Rescue Proposals,* Law & Contemp. Probs., Summer 1986, at 181 (same); Jay Silver, *The Duty to Rescue: A Reexamination and Proposal,* 26 Wm. & Mary L. Rev. 423, 424 (1985) (same). Likewise, it is common to speak of an "American rule" in the context of the duty to retreat. See, e.g., Garrett Epps, *Any Which Way but Loose: Interpretive Strategies and Attitudes toward Violence in the Evolution of the Anglo-American "Retreat Rule,"* Law & Contemp. Probs., Winter 1992, at 303, 305 (referring to the "American rule" that a person has the right to "stand [her] ground"); Jeannie Suk, *The True Woman: Scenes from the Law of Self-Defense,* 31 Harv. J. L. & Gender 237, 243 (2008) (same); Joseph E. Olson and David B. Kopel, *All the Way Down the Slippery Slope: Gun Prohibition in England and Some Lessons for Civil Liberties in America,* 22 Hamline L. Rev. 399, 465 (1999) (same). The phrase is often invoked by the courts. In the duty to retreat context, see, e.g., Cooper v. United States, 512 A.2d 1002, 1005 (D.C. 1986) (noting that jurisdictions which follow the "American rule" permit a person to "stand [her] ground") and Gillis v. United States, 400 A.2d 311, 312 (D.C. 1979) (same).

2. Paul H. Robinson, Matthew Kussmaul, Camber Stoddard, Ilya Rudyak, and Andreas Kuersten, *The American Criminal Code: General Defenses,* 7 J. LEGAL ANALYSIS 37, 51–57 (2015).

3. For a statement of such a majority rule for self-defense, see Robinson et al., supra note 2, at 50.

4. See Chapter 4, concerning the legality principle, for a list of such jurisdictions.

Acknowledgments

We are very much indebted to many people for their help with this book, especially Silvana Burgese, Sudeshna Dutta, Kelly Farraday, and Nesha Patel of Penn Law's staff for their endless help in the preparation of the manuscript. We also thank Altumash N. Mufti, University of Pennsylvania School of Law Class of 2017, for his research assistance, and Penn Law's Dean Ted Ruger for his generous support for our work. Our excellent editor, Kevin Hillstrom, also deserves our sincere thanks.

PART 1

Preliminary Issues: Punishment Theory and Legality

CHAPTER ONE

Distributive Principles of Criminal Law

What do we seek to achieve by imposing criminal liability and punishment? What principles should govern? These may seem like academic questions, but they are not. One cannot rationally and thoughtfully draft or interpret a criminal code, draft sentencing guidelines, or impose a criminal sentence without knowing the answers to these questions. A drafter of criminal code or sentencing guidelines must make hundreds if not thousands of choices in formulating criminal law rules, and sentencing judges must make a large number of discretionary judgments in determining the amount and method of punishment to impose in a given case. And each of these decisions can be affected by the principle that the criminal justice system has adopted for distributing criminal liability and punishment.

Should criminal liability and punishment rules be set to match an offender's moral blameworthiness for the offense—his *just deserts*? Or should they be set to maximize the general *deterrent* effect of a criminal sentence on other potential offenders? Or should liability and punishment be set according to whether this offender will be dangerous in the future and seek to *incapacitate* him or her during the time of greatest dangerousness?

Which of these principles a jurisdiction adopts as its guide in imposing criminal liability and punishment will have a dramatic effect because each of these alternative principles will generate a quite different distribution. Each will impose a different amount of criminal liability and punishment on a different set of people. Consider two examples.

Should a jurisdiction adopt an insanity defense? If incapacitating dangerous offenders is the criminal law's primary goal, then it certainly should not have such a defense because the people shown to be dangerously mentally ill

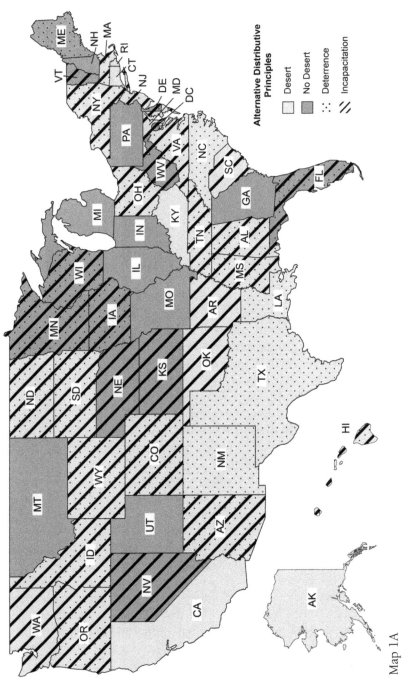

Alternative Distributive Principles

Desert
No Desert
Deterrence
Incapacitation

Map 1A

are exactly the people over which the criminal justice system wants to take control. Punishing insane offenders would also send a useful general deterrent message to other (noninsane) potential offenders, demonstrating how serious the system is about punishing violators. A desert principle, in contrast, would insist on exculpating offenders whose insanity renders them blameless.[1]

Another example illustrates that while deterrence and incapacitation principles may agree on the insanity defense issue, they commonly disagree with one another. Where an attempt fails by chance—the intended victim bends down to tie his shoe at the moment before the assailant's bullet is about to strike his head—the incapacitation principle would punish the failed attempt the same as a successful attempt because the assailant is equally dangerous in both cases, while a deterrence principle would want to punish the attempt less seriously than the completed offense so as to maintain a continuing threat of additional punishment to deter a follow-up attempt. If the failed attacker is already fully liable, why wouldn't he try again?

If desert were the distributive principle in the attempted murder case, it is unclear what the result would be under deontological desert: moral philosophers are divided over whether the resulting death should increase the actor's punishment where his conduct and culpability are identical. On the other hand, under what one might call "empirical desert," the result is clear: ordinary people essentially universally agree that the resulting harm should increase punishment, that murder should be punished more seriously than attempted murder.

There are hundreds of issues like the insanity defense and the significance of resulting harm about which alternative principles differ in their distribution of criminal liability and punishment.

Every jurisdiction in the United States, through constitutional provision, statutory provision, state sentencing commission policy, or appellate court opinion, gives some indication of the principle or principles that should be used in constructing, interpreting, or applying its criminal liability and sentencing rules.[2] States are free to adopt any distributive principle or combination of principles that they choose; there is no federal constitutional limitation on their choice. As Justice Anthony Kennedy wrote in an Eighth Amendment case before the U.S. Supreme Court, "there are a variety of legitimate penological schemes based on the theories of retribution, deterrence, incapacitation, and rehabilitation, and the Eighth Amendment does not mandate the adoption of any one such scheme."[3] And, as Map 1A makes clear, states have exercised this right to choose in a wide variety of ways.

Desert as a Distributive Principle

Thirty states, designated with light shading on the map—Alabama, Alaska, Arizona, Arkansas, California, Colorado, Connecticut, Hawaii, Idaho, Kentucky, Louisiana, Maryland, Massachusetts, Mississippi, New Jersey, New Mexico, New

York, North Carolina, North Dakota, Ohio, Oklahoma, Oregon, Rhode Island, South Carolina, South Dakota, Tennessee, Texas, Virginia, Washington, and Wyoming[4]—have determined that an offender's desert, sometimes called "retributive justice," should serve as one of those guiding purposes.

The principle is expressed in a variety of ways. Many jurisdictions hold that sentencing should provide "just punishment,"[5] or "deserved" punishment,[6] or simply that punishment should satisfy or do "justice."[7] Occasionally, desert is expressed in terms of "fairness," as in a sentencing policy that directs courts to administer "fair" punishment.[8] Two jurisdictions express desert in terms of "personal responsibility" and "accountability for one's actions."[9] One jurisdiction expresses desert in terms of "merited" punishment.[10] Finally, a host of states simply refer to "punishment" as a goal in itself,[11] a reference to desert by implication. (This is consistent with the empirical evidence that ordinary people think of "punishment" in desert terms rather than other distributive principle terms.[12])

The remaining 21 jurisdictions, designated with medium shading on the map—Delaware, District of Columbia, Georgia, Florida, Illinois, Indiana, Iowa, Kansas, Maine, Michigan, Minnesota, Missouri, Montana, Nebraska, Nevada, New Hampshire, Pennsylvania, Utah, Vermont, West Virginia, and Wisconsin[13]—have not set desert as a part of their guiding principle for determining criminal liability and punishment.

Deterrence as a Distributive Principle

Twenty-six states, those with a dots overlay on the map—Alabama, Arizona, Colorado, Delaware, Florida, Hawaii, Idaho, Iowa, Louisiana, Maine, Massachusetts, Minnesota, Mississippi, New Jersey, New Mexico, New York, North Carolina, North Dakota, Ohio, Oregon, South Dakota, Tennessee, Texas, Virginia, Wisconsin, and Wyoming[14]—have set or included deterrence as a guiding principle for their criminal code or sentencing policy. This is nearly always expressed by explicitly using the term "deterrence."

Incapacitation as a Distributive Principle

Thirty-two jurisdictions designated with an overlay of diagonal lines on the map—Alabama, Arizona, Arkansas, Colorado, Delaware, District of Columbia, Florida, Hawaii, Idaho, Iowa, Kansas, Maryland, Massachusetts, Minnesota, Mississippi, Nebraska, Nevada, New Jersey, New York, North Dakota, Ohio, Oklahoma, Oregon, South Carolina, South Dakota, Tennessee, Vermont, Virginia, Washington, West Virginia, Wisconsin, and Wyoming[15]—have included incapacitation of the dangerous as part of their guiding principle. This principle is expressed in a variety of ways. Only two states—Ohio and Virginia—actually use the word "incapacitation" outside of the case law. Many statutes provide that sentencing should serve the purpose of "confinement," when necessary to prevent further crime.[16] The same sentiment is often expressed as "remov[ing]" dangerous offenders from society.[17] Many statutes express the goal in terms of "protection" of the public, such as providing imprisonment "when required [for] public protection."[18] Incapacitation is also expressed in terms of punishment that targets "dangerous," violent, or repeat offenders, those whose freedom "continues to threaten public safety."[19]

Rehabilitation as a Correctional Policy

Forty-two jurisdictions—Alabama, Alaska, Arkansas, California, Colorado, Connecticut, Delaware, District of Columbia, Florida, Georgia, Hawaii, Idaho, Illinois, Indiana, Iowa, Kansas, Kentucky, Louisiana, Maine, Maryland, Massachusetts, Minnesota, Mississippi, Missouri, Montana, New Hampshire, New Jersey, New York, North Carolina, North Dakota, Ohio, Oklahoma, Oregon, South Carolina, South Dakota, Tennessee, Texas, Utah, Vermont, Washington, Wisconsin, and Wyoming—have adopted rehabilitation as a general purpose of their criminal code or sentencing policy. This is often expressed in terms of "rehabilitation"[20] or "reformation,"[21] but occasionally in terms of "correctional" treatment[22] or simply "treatment."[23] Some statutes speak of "improvement" of the offender, suggesting that punishment should "offer the offender an opportunity to improve himself."[24] States may be very specific about correctional programming, for instance, providing that sentences should provide the defendant with "educational or vocational training."[25] Finally, a number of states express rehabilitation in terms of reducing the rate of "recidivism" or the "risk of reoffending."[26]

Although rehabilitation is a popular purpose, it stands in a quite different position than the distributive principles of desert, deterrence, and incapacitation discussed above (which is why it has not been included on the map). There is no jurisdiction that has ever sought to use rehabilitation of the offender as its central principle in deciding who should be punished and how much. Rather, it is classically used not as a *distributive principle for criminal liability and punishment* at all but rather as a matter of *correctional policy*.[27] That is, no state sets its length of prison term according to that which will be needed to rehabilitate the offender—no prison for those who do not need rehabilitation or cannot be rehabilitated; and a lengthy prison sentence, even for a minor offense, for those who need rehabilitation that will take some time. But most states, such as the 42 explicitly mentioning rehabilitation in one form or another, do want to take the opportunity to rehabilitate an offender during whatever term of imprisonment or noncustodial control has been set by reference to one of the three primary alternative distributive principles of desert, deterrence, or incapacitation of the dangerous.

Restorative Justice as an Adjudicative Process

A number of states have in one way or another expressed the importance of what some have termed "restorative justice," which emphasizes restoring the offender to the community by encouraging the offender to repair broken relationships and satisfy debts, particularly those caused by the criminal conduct. This may be expressed as "restoration,"[28] "healing,"[29] "restitution,"[30] or simply "restorative justice."[31]

However, restorative justice is not a distributive *principle* for criminal liability and punishment but rather an alternative adjudication and sentencing *process*, one which commonly involves bringing together the offender, the victim, their family and friends, and members of the community to decide or recommend an appropriate disposition of the case. There are a great variety of restorative processes, some involving larger groups and some smaller groups. What they have in common is an open discussion, out of the glare of official court rules, where the entire group—some form of this process is called a "sentencing circle"—can try to develop an appropriate disposition that will help to both reintegrate the offender and make whole the victim.

Such restorative processes can be very useful and effective, but they are not "distributive principles" for criminal liability and punishment. It is rather the shared judgments of justice of those people in the sentencing circle that will shape the disposition, not any sort of articulated principle.[32] As a practical matter, restorative processes are likely to generate results that track a principle of empirical desert: the empirical evidence is clear that ordinary people think about criminal liability and punishment in desert terms,[33] but nothing in the restorative processes typically demands adherence to this or any other distributive principle.

Variations on a Desert Distributive Principle and Related Rules

Ordinary people's strong support for a desert distributive principle may be part of the explanation for why the American Law Institute (ALI) approved the first-ever amendment to its Model Penal Code in which it dropped the approach of its original 1962 draft that had encouraged states to consider a laundry list of distributive principles. The Model Penal Code was extremely influential and became the basis for recodifications in three-quarters of the states in the decades following its promulgation. It is the original approach of the Model Penal Code that probably accounts for the range of distributive principles cited by so many jurisdictions, as represented in Map 1A. In its 2007 amendment, however, the Model Penal Code rejects this laundry-list approach in favor of a revised Section 1.02(2) that sets desert as a dominant distributive principle that can never be violated.[34]

How do the American jurisdictions differ in their commitment to the desert principle? As Map 1A shows, 30 of the states adopt desert as a distributive principle, although as the map also shows, many of those states also recognize alternative distributive principles that can conflict with desert. Without designating desert as the dominant principle, then, desert may be sacrificed to promote general deterrence or incapacitation of the dangerous.

Map 1B shows the extent of each American jurisdiction's commitment to the desert principle. In some instances, desert is not recognized as a distributive principle but some component of desert is given formal approval, such as requiring proportionality between the seriousness of the offense and the offender's punishment. In some jurisdictions, while not committing to the distributive principle of desert, the authorities at least speak to the endpoint of the desert continuum: they expressly provide that blameless offenders ought to be protected from criminal liability and punishment.

Desert Distributive Principles: Deontological and Empirical

Twenty states, designated with no shading on the map—Arizona, Arkansas, California, Colorado, Idaho, Kentucky, Louisiana, Maryland, Mississippi, New Mexico, North Carolina, Ohio, Oregon, Rhode Island, South Carolina, South Dakota, Tennessee, Texas, Virginia, and Wyoming[35]—have determined that desert is a guiding purpose of the criminal code or sentencing policy.

Ten other states, shown with no shading but an overlay of dots—Alabama, Alaska, Connecticut, Hawaii, Massachusetts, New Jersey, New York, North Dakota, Oklahoma, and Washington[36]—similarly adopt desert as a distributive principle but specifically refer to desert as reflected in shared judgments of the community. As noted above, this has been referred to as "empirical desert" in order to distinguish it from the notion of "deontological desert" derived from moral philosophy. Empirical desert is most reliably based on the research of social psychologists who seek to determine the governing principles that ordinary people have in their heads and use in determining their judgments of justice, as compared to deontological desert, which is derived from logical reasoning, classically by moral philosophers. (Empirical research has shown that there is an enormous amount of agreement on basic principles of justice across demographics, at least with regard to the core of wrongdoing.[37])

A jurisdiction's adoption of empirical desert as a distributive principle is expressed in a number of ways. Some codes state that punishment is the public's "condemnation" of, or its "appropriate response" to, the offender's conduct.[38] Sometimes empirical desert is expressed in terms of holding the offender "accountable" to the community[39] or of vindicating public norms.[40] Some jurisdictions simply state that punishment ought to "promote respect for the law."[41]

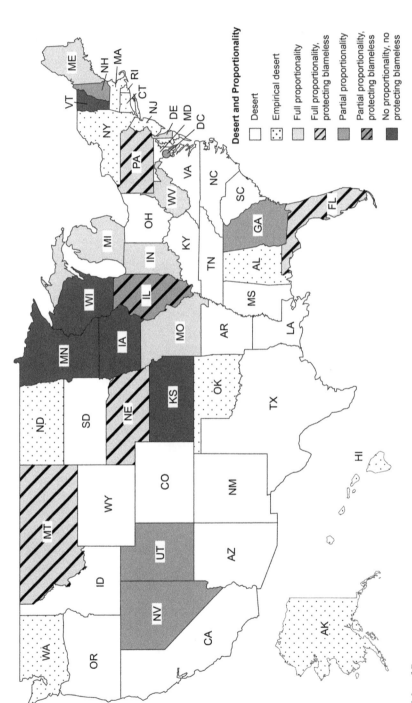

Desert and Proportionality

- Desert
- Empirical desert
- Full proportionality
- Full proportionality, protecting blameless
- Partial proportionality
- Partial proportionality, protecting blameless
- No proportionality, no protecting blameless

Map 1B

The remaining 21 jurisdictions do not openly recognize desert as a distributive principle. However, most of them at least recognize some component of desert—that is, recognize either a principle of proportionality between the seriousness of the offense and the seriousness of the punishment, or make some effort to protect the blameless from criminal liability and punishment, or both.

The Principle of Full Offense Proportionality

Seven states, shown with light shading on the map—Delaware, Indiana, Maine, Michigan, Missouri, New Hampshire, and West Virginia[42]—do not include justice or desert as a guiding principle. However, they have adopted a principle of proportionality between the seriousness of the punishment and the seriousness of the offense. (A desert distributive principle would go further and would take into account not just the seriousness of the offense harm but also the offender's culpability, excuses, and mitigations. In other words, a desert principle would require proportionality between not just the offense harm but the *overall blameworthiness of the offender* and the seriousness of the punishment.)

A common way of expressing the adoption of such an offense proportionality requirement is to call for punishment to "differentiate" between "serious and minor offenses,"[43] or that punishment be "proportioned"[44] or "commensurate"[45] with the nature or harm of the offense.

Full Offense Proportionality Plus Protecting the Blameless

Four states, designated with light shading and an overlay of diagonal lines—Florida, Montana, Nebraska, and Pennsylvania[46]—go beyond an offense proportionality rule to also specifically adopt a provision that a blameless person should be exempt from punishment. Such a provision only adopts the endpoint of the desert principle: it protects the blameless from punishment but does not require that the extent of punishment should otherwise track the extent of an offender's blameworthiness.

States in this category commonly "limit the condemnation of conduct as criminal when it is without fault"[47] or "safeguard conduct that is without fault from being condemned as criminal."[48] Although the states in this group fall short of a full desert principle, they do better in approximating desert than any other nondesert group.

A Partial Offense Proportionality Principle

Four jurisdictions, shown with medium shading on the map—District of Columbia, Georgia, Nevada, and Utah[49]—have adopted a weaker form of the offense proportionality rule, stating that punishment simply ought to take account of the "seriousness,"[50] "severity,"[51] or "gravity"[52] of the offense.[53] That is, the directive is satisfied simply by taking account of the offense seriousness in some way; it does not require that the punishment be proportionate to the offense seriousness.

Partial Offense Proportionality Plus Protecting Blameless

One state, Illinois, with medium shading on the map plus an overlay of diagonal lines, has adopted a partial offense proportionality rule[54] and a provision that the system ought to avoid punishing blameless offenders.[55] By explicitly providing for the protection of blameless persons, Illinois does better than the group immediately above but still leaves itself far away from a desert principle.

No Proportionality and No Protection of the Blameless

Five states, designated with black shading on the map—Iowa, Kansas, Minnesota, Vermont, and Wisconsin[56]—have not adopted desert, justice, offense proportionality, or even protection of the blameless as a distributive principle.

Observations and Speculations

It seems clear from the maps above that most jurisdictions have not yet caught up with the ALI's adoption, in its 2007 amendment to the Model Penal Code, of desert as the inviolate distributive principle. Why this gap between the historically influential ALI and current authorities in the states?

Part of the responsibility no doubt falls on the ALI itself. From its initial promulgation in 1962 until its amendment in 2007, even the Model Penal Code urged states to adopt a laundry list of alternative distributive principles that allowed code and sentencing guideline drafters and individual sentencing judges to sacrifice just deserts to promote other distributive principles, typically crime control through general deterrence or incapacitation of the dangerous.

But the intervening years have revealed much about the limitations of deterrence and incapacitation principles, as well as revealing the crime control benefits of a criminal law that promotes justice rather than sacrifices it to deterrent and incapacitation goals. There is an enormous literature on the subject, but some of the key findings might be summarized this way.[57]

Generally, deterrence has the potential to be an enormously efficient crime control mechanism. By punishing a single offender, one can send a deterrent threat to hundreds or even thousands of potential offenders that could be just the thing to change their mind about committing a contemplated offense. General deterrence does work at least in the sense that having a criminal justice system that imposes punishment for violations is likely to have an effect on people's decisions to commit crimes. What does not work is using general deterrence to formulate criminal law and sentencing rules—that is, to use it as a distributive principle for criminal liability and punishment, such as to decide whether to provide an insanity defense, whether to grade attempts the same as the substantive offense, or hundreds of other specific criminal code or sentencing decisions.

For general deterrence to work effectively as a distributive principle, at least three conditions must be present. First, the intended target must know about the deterrence-based rule—the treatment of the insanity defense and the grading attempts. But the reality is that the target audience rarely knows the law. Second, even if they do know the law, the target audience must be rational calculators who will take that information into account and alter their conduct to most effectively promote their own interests. Yet, the reality is that most in the target audience are commonly highly irrational in their thinking because of the influence of drugs, alcoholism, impulsiveness, mental or emotional disturbance, or a host of other factors. Finally, even if the target audience knows the law and are rational calculators, they will not be deterred by the threat of criminal punishment unless their calculations lead them to conclude that the costs of the contemplated offense outweigh the benefits. Yet the conviction and punishment rates are so low and the threatened punishment so remote that, in comparison to the immediate benefit of the contemplated offense—such as a robbery that will produce the money to immediately buy drugs—the target audience is more likely to conclude that the benefits of the offense outweigh the costs.[58]

Making a general deterrence distributive principle even less attractive is the fact that there is already a general deterrent effect in the punishment threatened by a desert distributive principle. If a deterrence-based principle is to provide significantly greater deterrent effect, it can do so only by means of deviating from desert, as in doing injustice, which the empirical desert research shows can incrementally undercut effective crime control. Thus, even if one could gain some greater deterrent effect by doing injustice, which may be a rare opportunity, even that greater deterrent effect may be outweighed by the system's loss of crime control effectiveness that comes from its loss of moral credibility with the community.

In contrast, an incapacitation distributive principle does in fact work. Putting an offender in prison, for example, will prevent the offender from committing other offenses—at least against persons not in prison. The problem, however, is that clinicians have a limited ability to reliably predict who will in fact be dangerous in the future. Making things worse, the "criminal justice" system seems to feel obliged to look like it is doing justice for past offenses rather openly admitting that it is a preventive detention system whose only focus is future offenses. Thus, it tends to cloak its preventive detention to look like criminal justice by focusing not so openly on clinical assessments of future dangerousness but instead on factors like past criminal record. In most sentencing guidelines, for example, an offender's prior criminal history may count for much more of the resulting sentence than the offense actually committed, on a theory that past criminality predicts future criminality. Unfortunately, that focus further weakens the accuracy of the future dangerousness prediction. The ultimate effect is seriously high false-positive rates—predictions of future dangerousness that are in fact false—that have the effect of wasting correctional expenditures and unjustifiably intruding in the lives of the detainees.[59]

At the same time, empirical studies have suggested that there is not just a deontological virtue in following a desert distributive principle—doing justice is good in itself that requires no other justification—but also that it has a significant crime control benefit. Criminal justice systems that are seen as regularly doing injustice or regularly failing to do justice, especially when these deviations from desert are predictable results of the system's criminal law rules, are systems that are likely to provoke subversion and resistance. In contrast, a criminal justice system that earns a reputation as being devoted to doing justice above all else—to giving people the punishment they deserve, no more and no less—is a system that is likely to inspire greater cooperation, acquiescence, and deference. And, perhaps most importantly, a system that has earned a reputation for moral credibility—as being a reliable authority of what is and is not truly condemnable—is a system that is more likely to lead people to internalize its norms. It is also a system that has the power of its moral credibility to help shift community norms when needed.[60]

Notice that these crime control benefits of a desert distribution flow not from a distributive principle of deontological desert derived from the reasoning of moral philosophers. Instead, the crime control benefits of a desert distribution flow from criminal law building moral credibility *with the community*, primarily by setting criminal liability and punishment distributive rules that track the shared judgments of justice of ordinary people.[61] As noted earlier, this "empirical desert" is recognized as a distributive principle only in 10 states. And even then, most of those states allow other distributive principles to be promoted at the expense of empirical desert.

Although the case for desert as the dominant distributive principle is strengthening, it will no doubt take a long time for these truths to percolate down into the political conversations that influence the formulation of the distributive principles that govern criminal codes, sentencing guidelines, and the calculations of individual sentencing judges.

Notes

1. For a more detailed discussion of how these alternative distributive principles differ, see Paul H. Robinson, *Distributive Principles of Criminal Law: Who Should Be Punished How Much?* at 7–20 (Oxford 2008).

2. Ala. Code § 13A-1-3; Ala. Code § 12-25-2; Alaska Stat. Ann. § 11.81.100; Alaska Const. art. I, § 12; Ariz. Rev. Stat. Ann. § 13-101; Ariz. Rev. Stat. Ann. § 13-101.01; Ark. Code Ann. § 16-90-801; Cal. Penal Code § 1170; Colo. Rev. Stat. Ann. § 18-1-102; Colo. Rev. Stat. Ann. § 18-1-102.5; Conn. Gen. Stat. Ann. § 54-300; Del. Code Ann. tit. 11, § 201; Del. Code Ann. tit. 11, § 6502; D.C. Code Ann. § 3-101; Fla. Stat. Ann. § 775.012; Ga. Code Ann. § 16-1-2; Haw. Rev. Stat. Ann. § 706-606; Idaho Code Ann. § 19-2521; 720 Ill. Comp. Stat. Ann. 5/1-2; Ind. Const. art. I, § 18; Ind. Const. art. I, § 16; Iowa Code Ann. § 901.5; Kan. Stat. Ann. § 21-6601; Ky. Rev. Stat. Ann. § 532.007; La. Stat. Ann. § 15:321; Me. Const. art. I, § 9; Me. Rev. Stat. tit. 17-A, § 1151; Md. Code Ann., Crim. Proc. § 6-202; Mass. Gen. Laws Ann. ch. 211E, § 2; Mich. Comp. Laws Ann. § 769.33a; Minn. Stat. Ann. § 609.01; Minn. Stat. Ann. § 364.01; Mo. Ann. Stat. § 558.019; *Missouri Sentencing Advisory Commission—Purpose and Goals,* Missouri Sentencing Advisory Commission (last accessed Sept. 13, 2017), http://www .mosac.mo.gov/page.jsp?id=45401 (stating that official purpose of sentencing commission is to ensure "proportionality of punishment"); Mont. Code Ann. § 45-1-102; Mont. Const. art. II, § 28; Neb. Rev. Stat. Ann. § 28-102; Neb. Const. art. I, § 15; Nev. Rev. Stat. Ann. § SB 451, § 6; N.H. Const. Pt. 1, art. XVIII; N.H. Rev. Stat. Ann. § 651:61-a; N.J. Stat. Ann. § 2C:1-2; N.Y. Penal Law § 1.05; N.C. Const. art. XI, § 2; N.C. Gen. Stat. Ann. § 164-42.1; N.C. Gen. Stat. Ann. § 164-41; N.D. Cent. Code Ann. § 12.1-01-02; Ohio Rev. Code Ann. § 2929.11; Ohio Rev. Code Ann. § 181.24; Okla. Stat. Ann. tit. 22, § 234; Okla. Stat. Ann. tit. 22, § 1514; Or. Rev. Stat. Ann. § 161.025; Or. Const. art. I, § 15; 18 Pa. Stat. and Cons. Stat. Ann. § 104; R.I. Const. art. I, § 8; 12 R.I. Gen. Laws Ann. § 12-19.3-1; Tenn. Code Ann. § 39-11-101; Tenn. Code Ann. § 40-35-102; Tenn. Code Ann. § 40-35-103; Tex. Penal Code Ann. § 1.02; Utah Code Ann. § 76-1-104; Vt. Stat. Ann. tit. 13, § 7030; Va. Code Ann. § 17.1-801; Wash. Rev. Code Ann. § 9A.04.020; Wash. Rev. Code Ann. § 9.94A.010; W. Va. Const. art. III, § 5; State v. Broughton, 196 W. Va. 281, 292, 470 S.E.2d 413, 424 (1996) (internal quotations and citations omitted) (interpreting the constitutional requirement of proportionality to include incapacitation); Wyo. Const. art. I, § 15; Bear Cloud v. State, 2012 WY 16, ¶ 63, 275 P.3d 377, 402 (stating that the four legitimate goals of penal sanctions are retribution, deterrence, incapacitation, and rehabilitation). Five states—Mississippi, New Mexico, South Carolina, South Dakota, and Wisconsin—have not codified general purposes as to criminal law or sentencing, either by statute, commission policy, or constitutional provision. For these jurisdictions, court decisions guide sentencing policy. See Taggart v. State, 957 So. 2d 981, 994 (Miss. 2007) (adopting principles of rehabilitation, retribution, "separation from society," and deterrence); State v. Kirby, 2003-NMCA-074, ¶ 28, 133 N.M. 782, 789, 70 P.3d 772, 779 ("[T]he traditional aims of punishment [are] retribution and deterrence."); State v. Jones, 2010-NMSC-012, ¶ 35, 148 N.M. 1, 10, 229 P.3d 474, 483 ("[U]nlike the adult criminal justice system, with its focus on punishment and deterrence, the juvenile justice system reflects a policy favoring the rehabilitation and treatment of children."); State v. Tucker, 324 S.C. 155, 174, 478 S.E.2d 260, 270 (1996) (recognizing incapacitation and

rehabilitation as proper goals of sentencing); State v. Fletcher, 322 S.C. 256, 260, 471 S.E.2d 702, 704 (Ct. App. 1996) (recognizing "punishment" per se as a proper goal of sentencing); State v. Talla, 2017 S.D. 34, ¶ 14, 897 N.W.2d 351, 355 (stating that retribution, deterrence, incapacitation, and rehabilitation are legitimate penological goals); State v. Setagord, 211 Wis. 2d 397, 416, 565 N.W.2d 506, 514 (1997) (holding that the primary considerations in assigning punishment are the offender's rehabilitative needs and the interests of deterrence and incapacitation).

3. Harmelin v. Michigan, 501 U.S. 957, 959, 111 S. Ct. 2680, 2683, 115 L. Ed. 2d 836 (1991) (Kennedy, J., concurring in part).

4. See supra note 2.

5. Alabama ("just and adequate punishment"), Arizona ("just and deserved punishment"), Connecticut ("just punishment"), Hawaii ("just punishment"), Massachusetts ("punish the offender justly" and "provide just punishment"), Virginia ("just criminal penalties"), and Washington ("punishment which is just"). See supra note 1.

6. Arizona ("just and deserved punishment"), Colorado ("a sentence [the offender] deserves"), and Tennessee ("justly deserved"). See supra note 2.

7. North Carolina ("satisfy justice"), Oklahoma (do "justice"), and Rhode Island ("do justice to the victim [and] the offender"). See supra note 2.

8. Connecticut ("fair, just, and equitable") and Maryland ("fair and proportional"). See supra note 1.

9. Oregon ("personal responsibility, accountability for one's actions") and Kentucky ("hold offenders accountable"). See supra note 2.

10. North Dakota ("merited punishment"). See supra note 2.

11. California, Colorado, Idaho, Louisiana, Ohio, Oklahoma, and Texas. See supra note 2.

12. See Paul H. Robinson, *Intuitions of Justice and Utility of Desert,* Part I (The Nature of Judgments about Justice) (Oxford 2013); Robinson, *Distributive Principles of Criminal Law,* supra note 1, Chapters 7 and 8.

13. See supra note 2.

14. See supra note 2.

15. See supra note 2.

16. Alabama, Delaware, Florida, Minnesota, New Jersey, New York, North Dakota, and Oregon. See supra note 1.

17. Arizona ("remove from society persons whose conduct continues to threaten public safety"), Arkansas ("protect the public by restraining offenders"), and Tennessee ("[restrain] repeat offenders"). See supra note 1.

18. Alabama, Colorado ("provide [punishment] when required in the interests of public protection"), Hawaii, Iowa, Massachusetts, Nevada, Ohio, Oklahoma ("incarceration [is] a punishment and . . . a means of protecting the public"), and Vermont (courts should consider "the risk to self, others, and the community at large presented by the defendant"). See supra note 2.

19. District of Columbia (punish with "due regard for the . . . dangerousness of the offender"), Hawaii ("protect the public from further crimes of the

defendant"), Idaho (imprisonment imposed when there is an "undue risk [that] defendant will commit another crime"), Iowa ("protection of the community from further offenses by the defendant and others"), Kansas (goal "that dangerous offenders shall be correctively treated in custody for long terms as needed"), Maryland (imprisonment for "violent" or "career" criminals), Massachusetts ("protect the public from further crimes of the defendant"), Nebraska ("subject to public control persons whose conduct indicates that they are disposed to commit crimes"), Nevada (target offenders with "predatory or violent nature," who "must receive sentences which reflect the need to ensure the safety and protection of the public"), New Jersey ("subject to public control persons whose conduct indicates that they are disposed to commit offenses"), Ohio ("protect the public from future crime by the offender"), Tennessee ("[restrain] repeat offenders"), Virginia ("due regard . . . to the dangerousness of the offender"), and Washington ("reduce the risk of reoffending by offenders in the community"). See supra note 2.

20. Alabama, Alaska, Arkansas ("rehabilitation and restoration to the community"), California, Colorado, Connecticut ("rehabilitation and reintegration"), Delaware ("rehabilitation and restoration [as] useful, law-abiding citizens within the community"), District of Columbia, Florida ("opportunity for rehabilitation"), Georgia, Illinois, Iowa, Louisiana, Maine, Minnesota, Missouri, New Hampshire, New Jersey, New York, North Dakota, Ohio, Oklahoma, Oregon, South Carolina ("rehabilitation and restoration"), South Dakota, Tennessee, Texas, Utah, and Wisconsin (address "rehabilitative needs"). See supra note 2.

21. Indiana, Montana, New Hampshire, North Carolina, Oregon, and Wyoming. See supra note 1.

22. Hawaii ("correctional treatment"), Idaho ("correctional treatment"), Kansas ("[corrective] treat[ment]"), and Maryland ("[correction] options . . . for appropriate criminals"). See supra note 1.

23. Vermont. See supra note 2.

24. Kentucky ("improv[e] outcomes for . . . offenders") and Washington ("offer the offender an opportunity to improve himself or herself").

25. Hawaii ("provide the defendant with needed educational or vocational training, medical care, or other correctional treatment") and Massachusetts ("provide the defendant with needed educational or vocational training"). See supra note 2.

26. Kentucky ("reduc[e] recidivism and criminal behavior") and Washington ("reduce the risk of reoffending by offenders in the community"). See supra note 2.

27. See generally Robinson, *Distributive Principles of Criminal Law,* supra note 1, Chapter 5 (Rehabilitation).

28. Arkansas, Colorado, and Delaware. See supra note 2.

29. Colorado. See supra note 2.

30. For instance, Alaska, Arkansas, Idaho, Maine, Massachusetts, Missouri, Montana, New Hampshire, New Jersey, North Carolina, Ohio, Oklahoma, and Tennessee have all incorporated restitution into their general purposes statutes. See supra note 2.

31. California, Colorado, and Missouri. See supra note 2.

32. See generally Robinson, *Distributive Principles of Criminal Law*, supra note 1, Chapter 9 (Restorative Justice).

33. See Robinson, *Intuitions of Justice and Utility of Desert*, Part I (The Nature of Judgments about Justice) (Oxford 2013); Robinson, *Distributive Principles of Criminal Law*, supra note 1, Chapters 7 and 8.

34. Robinson, *Distributive Principles of Criminal Law*, supra note 1, Chapter 11.B.

35. See supra note 2.

36. See supra note 2.

37. See Robinson, *Intuitions of Justice and Utility of Desert*, supra note 1, Chapters 1 and 2.

38. Alaska ("community['s] condemnation of the offender"), New Jersey ("condemn conduct [that hurts the] public interests") and New York ("provide appropriate public response to particular offenses"). See supra note 2.

39. Connecticut ("[hold] the offender accountable to the community"). See supra note 2.

40. North Dakota ("ensure the public safety . . . through the vindication of public norms by the imposition of merited punishment") and Oklahoma ("demonstrate . . . that the offender's conduct is unacceptable to society"). See supra note 2.

41. Alabama, Hawaii, Massachusetts, and Washington. See supra note 2.

42. See supra note 2.

43. Delaware. See supra note 1. This formulation is also adopted by a number of desert jurisdictions, including Alabama, Alaska, Arizona, Colorado, Florida, Montana, Nebraska, New York, Oregon, Pennsylvania, and Washington. See supra note 2. But the breadth of the desert principle makes up for the limitations of the proportionality principle by itself.

44. Delaware, Indiana, Maine, Missouri, New Hampshire, and West Virginia. See supra note 2. This formulation is also adopted by some desert jurisdictions, including Alabama, Arizona, Delaware, Maryland, Nebraska, New York, Rhode Island, and Washington. See supra note 2. But the breadth of the desert principle makes up for the limitations of the proportionality principle by itself.

45. This principle is adopted by Arkansas, a desert jurisdiction. Arkansas policy is that punishment ought to be "commensurate" with the nature of the offense, "taking into account factors that may diminish or increase an offender's culpability." See supra note 1. But the breadth of the desert principle makes up for the limitations of the proportionality principle by itself.

46. See supra note 2.

47. Alaska, Arizona, Colorado, and Illinois have adopted the formulation, though none of the four full proportionality states have adopted it. See supra note 2.

48. Florida ("safeguard conduct that is without fault . . . from being condemned as criminal"); Montana ("safeguard conduct that is without fault from condemnation as criminal"); Nebraska ("safeguard conduct that is without fault and which is essentially victimless in its effect from condemnation as criminal"); Pennsylvania ("safeguard conduct that is without fault from condemnation as criminal").

See supra note 2. Some desert states have also adopted a similar provision: North Dakota, Texas, and Washington. See supra note 2.

49. See supra note 2.

50. The District of Columbia ("due regard for the . . . seriousness of the offense"), Georgia ("prescribe penalties which are proportionate to the seriousness of the crimes"), Illinois ("prescribe penalties which are proportionate to the seriousness of offenses"), and Utah ("proportionate to the seriousness of [the] [offense]") use this language. See supra note 2. A number of desert and full proportionality jurisdictions use the language of seriousness: California, Connecticut, Hawaii, Idaho, Massachusetts, Michigan, North Dakota, Ohio, Oregon, Tennessee, Texas, Virginia, and Washington. See supra note 2.

51. Nevada ("[impose] sentences that increase in direct proportion to the severity of [the] crimes and [the] histories of criminality"). See supra note 2.

52. One full proportionality jurisdiction has also adopted this partial proportionality formulation: Maine ("[impose] sentences that do not diminish the gravity of offenses"). See supra note 2.

53. Note that one full proportionality jurisdiction—Pennsylvania—has also adopted a kind of partial proportionality provision, with a purpose to "safeguard offenders against excessive, disproportionate[,] or arbitrary punishment." See supra note 2.

54. See supra note 47.

55. Illinois ("limit the condemnation of conduct as criminal when it is without fault"). See supra note 2.

56. See supra note 2.

57. See generally Robinson, *Distributive Principles of Criminal Law,* supra note 1.

58. Robinson, *Distributive Principles of Criminal Law,* supra note 1, Chapters 3 and 4.

59. Robinson, *Distributive Principles of Criminal Law,* supra note 1, Chapter 6.

60. Robinson, *Distributive Principles of Criminal Law,* supra note 1, Chapter 7.

61. Robinson, *Distributive Principles of Criminal Law,* supra note 1, Chapter 8.

CHAPTER TWO

Habitual Offender Statutes

As Chapter 1 has noted, the most fundamental question facing a criminal law maker is this: What purpose should the criminal law rules seek to achieve? One might think that there is an easy and obvious answer: criminal law rules should be formulated to do justice and avoid future crime. But these two laudable objectives can sometimes conflict.[1]

For example, imagine somebody who is seriously mentally ill to the point of being blameless for his or her offense conduct but who nonetheless remains extremely dangerous. Should the criminal law be formulated so as to take and keep control of this dangerous person, as by abolishing any defense for mental illness? Or, should the criminal law be formulated so as to do justice, thus providing an insanity defense, and not be distracted by a defendant's potential for future criminality?

The same conflict in purposes can arise in the opposite case: where a person is blameworthy for an offense but, perhaps because of the unique circumstances of the offense, there is no possibility of the person committing another offense in the future. Consider the man who has been law abiding all his life but who kills his abusive father, where everyone agrees that the crime was a product of unique circumstances that will never again arise in the man's life. Should the criminal law focus on justice and impose criminal liability and punishment (perhaps somewhat reduced to reflect the special circumstances), or should the criminal law focus on the complete absence of any future dangerousness and avoid imposing any criminal liability and punishment? Should the criminal law's focus be on the past or the future?

This recurring tension between doing justice and controlling dangerous offenders appears in a wide variety of situations that criminal law makers must deal with. One common situation is that of the habitual offender. The offenses that he or she commits may be minor in character, and each would normally deserve an equally minor punishment. For example, an offender might have a record of committing a number of minor property crimes of opportunity, such as petty theft or fraud. In one famous case that went to the U.S. Supreme Court, *Rummel v. Estelle*, the offender's current offense was getting $130 from a bar owner with a promise to fix his air conditioner, which he had no intention of doing.[2]

Jurisdictions began adopting so-called "three strikes statutes," which provide for automatic life imprisonment for an offender who commits a third offense. Rummel was such an offender and received a life sentence. His minor offense would not normally justify anything but a minor punishment, perhaps with a slight bump for what Andrew von Hirsch calls "nose thumbing"; in committing an offense again, after previously having been specifically punished for it, the offender has aggravated the seriousness of his violation by thumbing his nose at societal norms.

But the empirical evidence suggests that nose thumbing is an aggravating factor, like an increase in culpability level or offense harm level. It may increase the deserved punishment for an offense by some proportion, but it is hardly more important than the offense itself, so could hardly have the effect of doubling, tripling, or quadrupling or more that the three-strikes rule does. The rule represents an explicit shift from a focus on what the offender deserves for his or her past offense to a focus instead on controlling future dangerousness— in other words, shifting from justice for a past offense to preventing a future offense, shifting from criminal justice to preventive detention.

In *Rummel*, the U.S. Supreme Court ruled that there is no constitutional violation in this shift; Rummel's life sentence for the $130 air-conditioning fraud was upheld. On the other hand, as three-strikes statutes became popular, with every U.S. jurisdiction adopting some kind of habitual offender statute, many people became uncomfortable with the potential for enormous disparity between the punishment deserved for the past offense and punishment imposed. Many people thought a serious injustice was being done in cases like *Rummel*, and the last several decades have seen a shift away from open-ended three-strikes statutes.

Increasingly, states have narrowed their habitual offender statutes by limiting the kind of offenses that will qualify for three-strikes treatment and by increasing the seriousness of the prior offenses required to trigger three strikes. The most common means of limiting the application of the statute is to require that the offense at hand, and perhaps the past offenses as well, involve the use of violence.

Map 2 indicates the approach on this issue that each state takes.[3]

Life Sentence Only If Offenses Were Violent Crimes

Six jurisdictions, those with no shading on the map—Kansas, Maine, Minnesota, New Hampshire, New Mexico, and Ohio[4]—do not punish habitual offenders with mandatory or discretionary life sentences or sentences of life

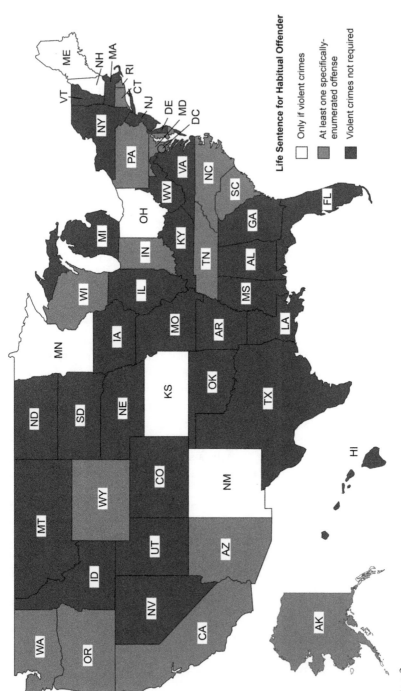

Life Sentence for Habitual Offender

☐ Only if violent crimes

At least one specifically-enumerated offense

Violent crimes not required

Map 2

without parole, except for crimes of violence.[5] In some of these states, the offender's last offense in a series of offenses must have been a violent crime, while in other states, all the offenses in the series must have been violent.[6]

Life Sentence Only If at Least One of the Offenses Was a Specifically Enumerated Offense

Sixteen jurisdictions designated with medium shading on the map—Alaska, Arizona, California, Connecticut, District of Columbia, Indiana, Maryland, North Carolina, Oregon, Pennsylvania, Rhode Island, South Carolina, Tennessee, Washington, Wisconsin, and Wyoming[7]—do not punish habitual offenders with mandatory or discretionary life sentences or sentences of life without parole unless the offender has committed at least one felony offense that the legislature deems particularly serious and thus has targeted for special attention.[8] Unlike crimes of violence, which necessarily involve the use or threat of physical force against another person, these specifically enumerated crimes often include burglary, arson, extortion, online enticement of a minor, or drug offenses.

Repeat-offender statutes vary widely in this category. Some statutes permit or mandate life when the actor commits a series of specifically enumerated offenses. Others permit or mandate life when the triggering offense is a specifically enumerated offense, even where the predicate offenses are not. Some jurisdictions permit or mandate life even where the triggering offense is not a specifically enumerated offense, but the predicate offenses are specifically enumerated offenses.

Life Sentence Even Though None of Prior Offenses Were Violent Crimes

Twenty-nine jurisdictions, shown in black on the map—Alabama, Arkansas, Colorado, Delaware, Florida, Georgia, Hawaii, Idaho, Illinois, Iowa, Kentucky, Louisiana, Massachusetts, Michigan, Mississippi, Missouri, Montana, Nebraska, Nevada, New Jersey, New York, North Dakota, Oklahoma, South Dakota, Texas, Utah, Vermont, Virginia, and West Virginia[9]—punish habitual offenders with mandatory or discretionary life sentences or sentences of life without parole in certain cases where none of the offenses were violent or even specifically enumerated by the legislature. Habitual-offender statutes in these jurisdictions often require life sentences for repeated, serious drug crimes, or certain repeated, nonviolent sexual offenses, or the third or fourth conviction for any felony. In Massachusetts, for example, courts must give the maximum sentence for the third conviction of any felony, which effectively requires life imprisonment for a three-time coin counterfeiter. In Nevada, a fourth-time felon may receive life without parole for any felony.

Observations and Speculations

The narrowing of the three-strikes rule that one sees in the first and even the second groups above are certainly a welcome development for those whose focus is on doing justice, for the narrowing would seem to limit application of the rule to cases of disproportionality between the punishment deserved and the punishment imposed.[10]

But for those who believe that the criminal law ought to be strictly focused on the future and not the past and should not be distracted by notions of justice and injustice, this narrowing of the three-strikes statutes may not be a good thing. Doing justice may be a laudable abstraction, but it is a luxury that we cannot afford if we are to effectively fight crime. As unfortunate as it may be, there can be a natural and irresolvable conflict between doing justice and fighting crime, and the demands of practical necessity require a focus on reducing crime even if it means deviating from just punishment.

Or does it? It is true that for more than a century the classic view has been that the aims of justice and crime control are necessarily, inevitably, and unavoidably in conflict in many cases. The distributive principle that the *utilitarian crime fighters* would use in deciding who should be punished how much is simply markedly different from the distributive principle that the *moral philosopher* would use in deciding who should be punished how much.[11] But the last two decades have seen increasing empirical evidence that doing justice may indeed be the most effective crime control strategy.[12]

The most important development here is the growing appreciation that ordinary people feel strongly that justice should be done and injustice should be avoided and, further, that ordinary people have a relatively nuanced and sophisticated sense of justice, no matter their educational level (or any other demographic). What this means for effective crime control is that each time the criminal law deviates from deserved punishment as ordinary people perceive it, such deviation undermines the system's moral credibility with them, and that, in turn, can seriously undermine their willingness to assist, cooperate, and defer to the system.

A system that has earned a reputation with the community as one that regularly and unnecessarily does injustice or fails to do justice loses the power of social influence that it might otherwise have. Rather than assistance, cooperation, and deference, it inspires resistance, subversion, and defiance. Will witnesses report crimes? Will they help investigators? Will they testify at trial? Will jurors follow their legal instructions? Will people defer to the criminal law in those gray areas where the condemnability of conduct is unsettled? Will the enormous power of stigmatization of criminal conviction be lost? (That is, will people conclude that this or that criminal conviction is just one more example of the criminal law being out of step with the community's judgments of what is condemnable?) Most importantly, perhaps, will people be willing to internalize the societal norms that criminal law promotes?

Ultimately, criminal law's most effective crime control strategy may be to harness the powerful forces of social influence and internalized norms by always trying to do justice and avoid injustice. That is, the criminal justice system ought to be devoted to doing justice, not to please the moral philosophers, but as a strategy of effective utilitarian crime control.

In this light, the narrowing of the three-strikes statutes to diminish the disproportionality between deserved punishment and imposed punishment is a reform that is likely to reduce damage to the system's moral credibility and thus ultimately reduce crime.

Notes

1. See Robinson and Cahill, *Criminal Law,* 2nd ed., 20–26 (Wolters Kluwer 2012).

2. Rummel v. Estelle, 445 U.S. 263 (1980).

3. Except as noted otherwise, research is from Caitlyn Lee Hall, *Good Intentions: A National Survey of Life Sentences for Nonviolent Offenses,* 16 N.Y.U. J. Leg. Pub. Pol'y. 1101 (2013).

4. See, e.g., Kan. Stat. Ann. § 21-6626 (mandating a sentence of life without parole for certain sexually violent triggering offenses where predicate offenses may include any sexually motivated crimes); Ohio Rev. Code Ann. §§ 2901.01, 2929.14, 2929.01 (mandating a life sentence for certain violent crimes where the offender has previously been convicted of crimes defined violent by the legislature); Minn. Stat. Ann. § 609.106 (mandating a sentence of life without parole where triggering offense is first-degree murder under certain conditions and the person has a previous conviction for a "heinous crime," which by statute is limited to certain violent crimes); N.H. Rev. Stat. Ann. § 651:6 (mandating life without parole for a person convicted of two or more aggravated sexual assaults, and life for a person convicted of murder or three sexual assaults); see also Caitlyn Lee Hall, *Good Intentions: A National Survey of Life Sentences for Nonviolent Offenses,* 16 N.Y.U. J. Leg. Pub. Pol'y. 1101, 1136–38 (2013) (listing jurisdictions with habitual-offender statutes that permit or mandate sentences of life or life without parole only when either the triggering offense is a violent crime or the defendant is convicted of a series of violent crimes).

5. Violent offenses, for these purposes, are "offenses that by definition involve the use or threat of physical force against the person of another." Hall, *Good Intentions,* at 1112.

6. See Hall, *Good Intentions,* at 1136–38.

7. See, e.g., Cal. Penal Code §§ 667.75, 667.5, 667 (permitting a life sentence where the offender has been convicted three times of drug offenses related to minors); D.C. Code Ann. §§ 22-1804a, 22-4501, 23-1331 (permitting a life

sentence where the offender has been convicted three times of crimes of violence, which the legislature defined to include arson and burglary); Alaska Stat. Ann. §§ 12.55.125(l), 33.16.090, 12.55.185, 11.41.520 (mandating life without parole where offender has committed an "unclassified or class A felony," such as extortion, and has been previously convicted of two "most serious felonies," which the legislature defined to include arson and online enticement of a minor); see also Caitlyn Lee Hall, *Good Intentions: A National Survey of Life Sentences for Nonviolent Offenses,* 16 N.Y.U. J. Leg. Pub. Pol'y. 1101, 1131–35 (2013) (listing jurisdictions with habitual-offender statutes that permit or mandate sentences of life or life without parole in certain cases where the "triggering" offense or "predicate" offenses include one of a list of offenses deemed particularly serious or violent).

8. In many jurisdictions, the legislature has defined certain offenses as "violent," even though the offense does not necessarily involve the use or threat of physical force against another person. See, e.g., D.C. Code Ann. § 23-1331 (defining "[crime] of violence" to include burglary).

9. See, e.g., Okla. Stat. Ann. tit. 63, § 2-415 (requiring sentence of life without parole for three-time convicted drug traffickers); Nev. Rev. Stat. Ann. § 207.010 (permitting sentence of life without parole for four-time felons); Mass. Gen. Laws Ann. ch. 279, § 25(a), ch. 267, § 17 (directing courts to punish habitual offenders for the maximum term required by law, which in effect mandates a life sentence for a series of nonviolent crimes, including coin counterfeiting); see also Caitlyn Lee Hall, *Good Intentions: A National Survey of Life Sentences for Nonviolent Offenses,* 16 N.Y.U. J. Leg. Pub. Pol'y. 1101, 1126–31 (2013) (listing jurisdictions with habitual-offender statutes that permit or mandate sentences of life or life without parole in certain cases where the offenses are nonviolent).

10. For evidence that three-strikes statutes, as popular as they may be with politicians, conflict with ordinary people's judgments of justice, see Paul H. Robinson, *Intuitions of Justice and Utility of Desert,* 120–28 (Oxford 2013).

11. For a complete discussion of these alternative distributive principles, see Paul H. Robinson, *Distributive Principles of Criminal Law: Who Should Be Punished How Much?* (Oxford 2008).

12. See Robinson, *Intuitions of Justice and Utility of Desert,* Chapters 8–10 (Oxford 2013).

CHAPTER THREE

Death Penalty

The death penalty was essentially a universal among the states in the 1850s, but its history since has been one of limitation and declining use.[1] As Map 3 shows, 20 states have abolished it altogether, while the frequency of its use in the remaining 31 states has been significantly reduced over time.[2]

Much of this change has been prodded by Supreme Court cases that challenged the procedures used to impose the death penalty and more recently cases that sought to limit the offenses for which capital punishment is available. In 1972, the Supreme Court held in *Furman v. Georgia*[3] that the then-current sentencing schemes for imposing the death penalty violated the Eighth Amendment prohibition against cruel and unusual punishment. There was no majority or concurring opinion. Only two justices declared the death penalty to be per se unconstitutional. Four years later, the Court approved the revised Georgia statute in *Gregg v. Georgia*,[4] holding that the death penalty is permissible under certain conditions and procedures.

With limitations on the sentencing procedures established, the Supreme Court undertook to limit the cases in which the death penalty could be imposed: in 1977 barring its use for rape of an adult where there is no death,[5] in 2002 barring it for people with intellectual disabilities,[6] in 2005 barring it for people who were juveniles at time of offense,[7] and in 2008 barring its use for child rape where the victim did not die.[8] These and a number of other decisions have made clear that the Court sees the Eighth Amendment cruel and unusual prohibition as including a requirement of proportionality between the unique seriousness of the penalty and the blameworthiness of the offender: the penalty ought to be reserved for the most blameworthy instances of murder. Although it may prefer to leave such proportionality judgments to the states, the Court seems to intend to oversee these judgments and to enforce a prohibition against disproportionality.[9]

To encourage proportionality, states must identify those specific aggravating factors to murder that may trigger eligibility for the death penalty. It is

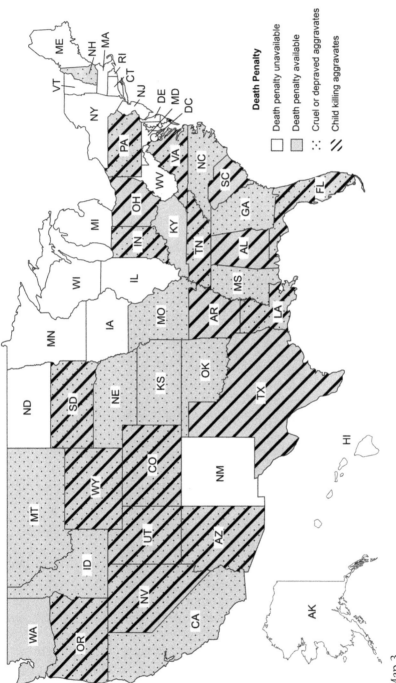

Death Penalty

☐ Death penalty unavailable

▨ Death penalty available

∴ Cruel or depraved aggravates

⁄⁄ Child killing aggravates

Map 3

common for the death penalty sentencing procedures to require that at least one aggravating factor exist before an offender can be eligible for capital punishment: the court "shall not impose sentence of death unless it finds one of the aggravating circumstances enumerated . . . and further finds that there are no mitigating circumstances sufficiently substantial to call for leniency."[10]

Virtually every one of the death penalty states includes among its aggravating factors a murder for hire and a murder during the commission of rape. Beyond that, however, states disagree about what the aggravating factor should be. Map 3 indicates the states that adopt either or both of the two common additional aggravating factors: a cruel and depraved killing or killing a child. A wide variety of other factors are also recognized in various jurisdictions.[11]

Death Penalty Unavailable

Twenty jurisdictions, designated on the map as Death Penalty Unavailable—Alaska, Connecticut, Delaware, District of Columbia, Hawaii, Illinois, Iowa, Maine, Maryland, Massachusetts, Michigan, Minnesota, New Jersey, New Mexico, New York, North Dakota, Rhode Island, Vermont, West Virginia, and Wisconsin[12]—do not have a death penalty statute or have a statute that has been declared facially unconstitutional.

Death Penalty Available

Thirty-one states, designated on the map as Death Penalty Available—Alabama, Arizona, Arkansas, California, Colorado, Florida, Georgia, Idaho, Indiana, Kansas, Kentucky, Louisiana, Mississippi, Missouri, Montana, Nebraska, Nevada, New Hampshire, North Carolina, Ohio, Oklahoma, Oregon, Pennsylvania, South Carolina, South Dakota, Tennessee, Texas, Utah, Virginia, Washington, and Wyoming[13]—have valid death penalty statutes, meaning that a death sentence may be imposed by law.

However, in many of these states the death penalty has not been imposed in years: California, Colorado, Kansas, Montana, Nebraska, Nevada, New Hampshire, North Carolina, Oregon, Pennsylvania, and Wyoming have not carried out an execution in more than 10 years.[14] Imposition of the death penalty has been halted for a variety of reasons. In Pennsylvania, for instance, the governor imposed a moratorium, citing a "flawed system" that is "ineffective, unjust, and expensive."[15]

Aggravation for Cruel or Depraved Killing

The most common aggravating factor, found in 24 of the 31 death penalty states, is a cruel or depraved killing. The factor is found in Arizona, California, Colorado, Florida, Georgia, Idaho, Indiana, Kansas, Louisiana, Mississippi,

Missouri, Montana, Nebraska, Nevada, New Hampshire, North Carolina, Oklahoma, Oregon, Pennsylvania, South Dakota, Tennessee, Utah, Virginia, and Wyoming.[16]

This aggravating factor has been criticized by courts as too vague, standing alone, to properly narrow the class of persons eligible for the death penalty.[17] Nevertheless, the standard is still used in death sentencing.

Aggravation for Killing a Child

Another common aggravating factor found in 18 of the 31 death penalty states is the killing of a child. The factor is found in Alabama, Arizona, Arkansas, Colorado, Florida, Indiana, Louisiana, Nevada, Ohio, Oregon, Pennsylvania, South Carolina, South Dakota, Tennessee, Texas, Utah, Virginia, and Wyoming.[18]

The applicable age of the victim that triggers this aggravating factor ranges from 10 in Texas[19] to 17 in Wyoming,[20] and the modal age is 12 in Colorado, Florida, Indiana, Louisiana, Pennsylvania, and Tennessee.

Observations and Speculations

It is hardly a surprise that the Supreme Court cases—or any thoughtful lawmaker, such as the American Law Institute and its Model Penal Code[21]— would seek to assure a careful procedure for death penalty sentencing. The penalty is unique. It represents the most serious power that government could exercise over an individual. If there is any issue on which one would want the criminal justice system to be thoughtful and careful in its adjudication, this is it.

But the other thrust of the Supreme Court cases is less expected: the interpretation of the Eighth Amendment's cruel and unusual punishment prohibition to include a proportionality requirement. As several of the justices pointed out in dissent, there is little in the language of the Eighth Amendment to suggest a proportionality analysis.[22] On the other hand, a proportionality requirement would seem to many people to be a fundamental and obvious requirement, especially when the state is imposing the ultimate penalty. Recall from Chapter 1 that such a proportionality requirement (requiring proportionality between the seriousness of the penalty and the seriousness of the offender's offense) is a common feature of the general purposes section of modern American criminal codes.

Yet, as obvious and fundamental as a proportionality requirement might seem, it is surprisingly revealing about the criminal law system that adopts it. This is because the blameworthiness proportionality requirement, especially when set as a requirement for the death penalty, as is now constitutionally required throughout the United States, is consistent with some basic principles for distributing criminal liability and punishment but inconsistent with others. In other words, the adoption of a blameworthiness proportionality requirement reveals the most basic principles that drive the criminal law system that adopts such a requirement.

If one were to create a criminal justice system designed to incapacitate dangerous offenders in order to avoid future crime, there is little reason to adopt a requirement of blameworthiness proportionality between the seriousness of the offender's violation and the seriousness of the punishment imposed. If incapacitation of the dangerous was the primary distributive principle for criminal liability and punishment, the focus would be strictly on predictions regarding future criminality, not past criminality. A longer prison term, for example, would be justified only where a future serious offense was predicted, without regard to whether the past offense was major or minor.

In the special context of capital punishment, such a purely prevention-oriented system might logically reserve the death penalty for killings by prisoners already serving a life term. For all other offenders, a life term would seem to provide the necessary incapacitation; the death penalty would be unnecessary.

That there are no American jurisdictions that adopt this approach leads one to conclude, then, that incapacitation of the dangerous—pure future prevention—is not the distributive principle for criminal liability and punishment guiding American jurisdictions.

If one were to create a criminal justice system that used general deterrence as its primary distributive principle, it might well support a principle of proportionality between the seriousness of the punishment and the seriousness of the offense *harm*, but it would have no reason to take into account in making this proportionality balance factors relating to the offender, his or her culpability and capacities, which the Supreme Court cases and the state statutes clearly do. The focus of a general deterrence distributive principle would be to look strictly to the extent of the harm caused. (That is, for efficiency purposes a general deterrence principle might find it appropriate to invest more punishment dollars, as with longer prison terms, in order to avoid more serious offenses in the future.)

Yet, in practice, we see that the blameworthiness proportionality principle applied in the death penalty cases looks well beyond just the seriousness of the offense harm and does indeed examine the culpability and capacities of the offender. The death penalty is constitutionally barred for cases of lower culpability—reckless or negligent killings, as opposed to intentional killings—and is barred for offenders with excusing conditions, such as immaturity or mental illness. A general deterrence distributive principle would ignore these factors.

It should also be noted that a distributive principle of general deterrence would almost never want to use this ultimate penalty. The problem is, once an offender commits an offense to which the death penalty attaches, all general deterrence from committing further offenses instantly evaporates. Once the attacker has killed the intended victim, for example, if the death penalty now attaches the person might as well go ahead and kill all the witnesses as well. A distributive principle of general deterrence will be constructed to always have some additional penalty available to serve as a continuing threat to deter an offender from committing additional offenses.

Again, the adoption of the blameworthiness proportionality requirement as an apparently fundamental principle reveals that general deterrence, like incapacitation of the dangerous, cannot be the dominant distributive principle driving American criminal law.

In contrast, requiring proportionality between the punishment imposed and the blameworthiness of the offense is entirely consistent with desert as a distributive principle. Indeed, blameworthiness proportionality is the core essence of a desert distributive principle, which requires that a case of greater blameworthiness receive more punishment than a case of lesser blameworthiness. (And it turns out that both moral philosophers and ordinary people have nuanced judgments about such relative blameworthiness.[23])

At the same time, nothing in modern desert theory requires the use of capital punishment at all. The endpoint of the punishment continuum could be set at life or fixed number of years, and it would not offend a desert distributive principle. For that principle cares primarily about blameworthiness proportionality, not absolute punishment.[24] (The old notion of "an eye for an eye" as a justification for the death penalty for murder represents a conception of desert—"vengeful desert" it has been called—that no living desert theorist would support. It is a notion of desert that exists only as a strawman kept on stage by those who wish to promote general deterrence or incapacitation of the dangerous as distributive principles, and feel obliged to discredit a desert distributive principle in order to do that.[25])

Indeed, it has been argued that a strict application of the blameworthiness proportionality principle would mean that in practice the death penalty would never be imposed even though it is technically available. As the uniquely most egregious punishment, the blameworthiness proportionality principle would require that it be held in reserve for the use in the uniquely most egregiously blameworthy offense. If one can imagine an offense more blameworthy than the offense at hand, which is probably always possible, then the case at hand cannot deserve the uniquely most egregious punishment.[26]

To summarize, a desert distributive principle doesn't require use of the death penalty at all and, if it is used, would reserve it for the most egregious case. Thus, the abolition of capital punishment in 20 states and the modern American trend toward reduced frequency of executions in death penalty states is consistent with desert being the dominant distributive principle in the United States. (And there is little reason to believe that modern American legal academia would want to disapprove of this result.[27])

Notes

1. See Furman v. Georgia, 408 U.S. 238, 337 (1972). By 1917, 12 states had abolished the death penalty. Id. at 349. For a helpful history of capital punishment in the United States, see *Furman*, 408 U.S. 333–42.

2. See *Prisoners Executed under Civil Authority in the United States, by Year, Region, and Jurisdiction, 1977–2016*, Bureau of Justice Statistics (Apr. 27, 2017), https://www.bjs.gov/content/data/exest.csv.

3. 408 U.S. 238 (1972).

4. 428 U.S. 153 (1976).

5. Coker v. Georgia, 43 U.S. 584 (1977).

6. Atkins v. Virginia, 536 U.S. 304 (2002).

7. Roper v. Simmons, 543 U.S. 551 (2005).

8. Kennedy v. Louisiana, 554 U.S. 407 (2008).

9. See Solem v. Helm, 463 U.S. at 290–92. See generally Paul H. Robinson and Michael T. Cahill, *Criminal Law*, 2nd ed., 76–78 (Wolters Kluwer 2012).

10. Model Penal Code § 210.6(2). See, e.g., Ga. Code Ann. § 17-10-30 ("In all cases of other offenses for which the death penalty may be authorized, the judge shall consider, or he shall include in his instructions to the jury for it to consider, any mitigating circumstances or aggravating circumstances otherwise authorized by law. . . ."); Utah Code Ann. § 76-3-207.

11. For instance, many states include murder for the purpose of avoiding lawful arrest or prosecution, e.g., Kan. Stat. Ann. § 21-6624; Okla. Stat. Ann. tit. 21, § 701.12; Tenn. Code Ann. § 39-13-204; Wyo. Stat. Ann. § 6-2-102, murder where the victim was a police officer, e.g., Ala. Code § 13A-5-40; La. Stat. Ann. § 14:30; Mo. Ann. Stat. § 565.032; N.C. Gen. Stat. Ann. § 14-17, and murder where the victim was a witness in a criminal trial, e.g., Colo. Rev. Stat. Ann. § 18-1.3-1201; Ind. Code Ann. § 35-50-2-9; Va. Code Ann. § 18.2-31.

12. Some state statutes were held invalid by state courts. See, e.g., N.Y. Crim. Proc. Law § 400.27 (providing death penalty); People v. LaValle, 3 N.Y.3d 88, 817 N.E.2d 341 (2004) (declaring state statute facially invalid); Del. Code Ann. tit. 11, § 4209 (providing death penalty); Rauf v. State, 145 A.3d 430 (Del. 2016) (declaring state statute facially invalid). Others, such as New Jersey, New Mexico, Illinois, Connecticut, and Maryland, recently repealed their death penalty statutes through the legislative process. See Jonathan Ross, *The Marriage of State Law and Individual Rights and a New Limit on the Federal Death Penalty*, 63 Clev. St. L. Rev. 101, 127–28 (2014).

13. Ala. Code Ann. § 13A-5-40; Ariz. Rev. Stat. § 13-751; Ark. Code Ann. § 5-4-601; Cal. Penal Code § 190; Colo. Rev. Stat. Ann. § 18-1.3-1201; Fla. Stat. Ann. § 921.141; Ga. Code Ann. § 17-10-30; Idaho Code Ann. § 19-2515; Ind.

Code Ann. § 35-50-2-9; Kan. Stat. Ann. § 21-6624; Ky. Rev. Stat. Ann. § 507.020; La. Stat. Ann. § 14:30; Miss. Code. Ann. § 97-3-21; Mo. Ann. Stat. § 546.720; Mont. Code Ann. § 45-5-102; Neb. Rev. Stat. Ann. § 28-105; Nev. Rev. Stat. Ann. § 200.030; N.H. Rev. Stat. Ann. § 630:1; N.C. Gen. Stat. Ann. § 14-17; Ohio Rev. Code Ann. § 2929.02; Okla. Stat. Ann. tit. 21, § 701.10; Or. Rev. Stat. Ann. § 163.105; 18 Pa. Stat. and Cons. Stat. Ann. § 1102; S.C. Code Ann. § 16-3-20; S.D. Codified Laws § 23A-27A-1; Tenn. Code Ann. § 39-13-202; Utah Code Ann. § 76-3-206; Va. Code Ann. § 19.2-264.2; Wash. Rev. Code Ann. § 9.82.010; Wyo. Stat. Ann. § 6-2-101.

14. See *Prisoners Executed under Civil Authority in the United States, by Year, Region, and Jurisdiction, 1977–2016*, Bureau of Justice Statistics (Apr. 27, 2017), https://www.bjs.gov/content/data/exest.csv.

15. Mark Berman, *Pennsylvania's Governor Suspends the Death Penalty*, Wash. Post. (Feb. 13, 2015), https://www.washingtonpost.com/news/post-nation/wp/2015/02/13/pennsylvania-suspends-the-death-penalty/?utm_term=.8385becadd2a.

16. Ariz. Rev. Stat. § 13-751; Cal. Penal Code § 190.2; Colo. Rev. Stat. 18-1.3-1201; Fla. Stat. § 921.141; O.C.G.A. § 17-10-30; Idaho Code Ann. § 19-2515; Ind. Code Ann. § 35-50-2-9; Kan. Stat. Ann. § 21-6624; La. Rev. Stat. Ann. 14:30; Miss. Code Ann. § 97-3-19; Mo. Rev. Stat. § 565.032; Mont. Code Ann. § 46-18-303; Neb. Rev. Stat. Ann. § 29-2523; Nev. Rev. Stat. Ann. § 200.030; N.H. Rev. Stat. 630:5; N.C. Gen. Stat. § 14-17; 21 Okla. Stat. § 701.12; Or. Rev. Stat. § 163.115; 42 Pa. Cons. Stat. § 9711; S.D. Codified Laws § 22-16-4; Tenn. Code Ann. § 39-13-204; Utah Code Ann. § 76-3-207; Utah Code Ann. § 76-3-202; Va. Code Ann. § 18.2-31; Wyo. Stat. Ann. § 6-2-102.

17. See, e.g., Godfrey v. Georgia, 446 U.S. 420 (1980) (plurality opinion) (reviewing aggravating factor, that the crime was "outrageously or wantonly vile, horrible and inhuman," and concluding that "almost every murder" could be characterized in this manner).

18. Ala. Code § 13A-5-40; Ariz. Rev. Stat. § 13-751; Ark. Code Ann. § 5-10-101; Colo. Rev. Stat. 18-1.3-1201; Fla. Stat. § 921.141; Ind. Code Ann. § 35-50-2-9; La. Rev. Stat. Ann. 14:30; Nev. Rev. Stat. Ann. § 200.030; Ohio Rev. Code Ann. § 2903.01; Or. Rev. Stat. § 163.115; 42 Pa. Cons. Stat. § 9711; S.C. Code Ann. § 16-3-20; S.D. Codified Laws § 22-16-4; Tenn. Code Ann. § 39-13-204; Tex. Penal Code Ann. § 19.03; Utah Code Ann. § 76-3-207; Utah Code Ann. § 76-3-202; Va. Code Ann. § 18.2-31; Wyo. Stat. Ann. § 6-2-102. In Ohio, the defendant must have "purposely" caused the death of a child under 13. See Ohio Rev. Code Ann. § 2903.01. In Utah, the aggravating factor is that the murder was committed in the course of child abuse, which as a practical matter would likely include every case where the victim of murder was a child. See Utah Code Ann. § 76-5-109.

19. Tex. Penal Code Ann. § 19.03.

20. Wyo. Stat. Ann. § 6-2-102.

21. Model Penal Code § 210.6, Sentence of Death for Murder; Further Proceedings to Determine Sentence, promulgated in 1962, served as a model for the

U.S. Supreme Court's suggestions for the kind of death penalty sentencing procedures that would pass constitutional muster.

22. See Atkins v. Virginia, 536 U.S. 304, 337 (2002) ("Today's decision . . . find[s] no support in the text or history of the Eighth Amendment.") (Scalia, J., dissenting).

23. See Paul H. Robinson, *Intuitions of Justice and the Utility of Desert*, Chapters 1–2 (Oxford 2013).

24. See Paul H. Robinson, *Distributive Principles of Criminal Law: Who Should Be Punished How Much?* Chapters 7–8 (Oxford 2008).

25. See Paul H. Robinson, *Competing Conceptions of Modern Desert: Vengeful, Deontological, and Empirical*, 67 Cambridge Law Journal 145 (2008).

26. See Robinson et al., *Codifying Shari'a: International Norms, Legality & the Freedom to Invent New Forms*, 2 Journal of Comparative Law (British) 1, 17–18 (2007).

27. The only amendment to the Model Penal Code since its promulgation by the American Law Institute more than half century ago seems to suggest that modern American legal academia joins in that conclusion. The amendment rejects the laundry list of the purposes of sentencing contained in the original Model Penal Code and substitutes a rule that sets desert as the dominant principle, which can never be violated. See Paul H. Robinson, *The ALI's Proposed Distributive Principle of "Limiting Retributivism": Does It Mean in Practice Anything Other Than Pure Desert?* 7 Buffalo Criminal Law Review 3 (2003).

CHAPTER FOUR

Legality Requirement

Criminal law serves to protect people from the most serious wrongs and also holds the greatest power we give to government to intrude into people's lives, even imposing imprisonment or death. For these reasons, it is argued that it is particularly important that criminal law be fair and effective, and that the definition of offenses, defenses, and the principles of liability and punishment ought to be the product of the most democratic of the branches, the legislative branch.

Specifically, criminal law should make clear to people beforehand exactly what conduct is prohibited, or required or tolerated, upon threat of criminal punishment. And when there is a violation of the law's rules of conduct, criminal liability and punishment ought to be imposed consistently and uniformly for all defendants. It ought to depend on what the offender has done and his or her culpability, not on the particular decision maker who decides the case.[1]

For all these reasons, criminal law commits itself to what is called "the legality principle," which requires that criminal offenses and liability rules be defined by the legislature with clarity and precision and announced beforehand, and that the rules be specific and unambiguous enough to provide uniformity in application.

The legality principle is not itself a legal rule but rather an umbrella concept under which huddle a variety of doctrines including, for example, the constitutional prohibition against vague statutes and ex post facto laws, as well as the traditional practice of interpreting any ambiguity in criminal offense in favor of the defendant—called "the rule of strict construction" or "the rule of lenity." Further, most modern American criminal codes explicitly abolish common-law offenses (that is, offenses created by judges) and allow prosecution only for offenses codified by the legislature.

The effect of the legality principle doctrines is to bar criminal liability, even for conduct that is seriously wrongful and even if the actor believed it was a crime, if the conduct had not in fact previously been officially defined to be an offense. Thus, for example, a visiting Soviet who secretly takes photographs of military installations believing it to be a crime cannot be held criminally liable if such conduct has not in fact been clearly criminalized. Similarly, the crematorium operator who simply throws the dead bodies in the woods behind his crematorium rather than burning them cannot be held criminally liable even if there exists an abuse of corpse offense, if the offense definition does not unambiguously cover his specific kind of conduct.[2]

Although all American jurisdictions commit themselves to the legality principle, there is some variation among the states in how aggressively they adhere to the principle. Map 4 presents four different approaches found in American jurisdictions.

Offense Must Be Fully Codified

Thirty-three U.S. jurisdictions adhere strictly to the legality principle. In order to be criminally prosecuted for an offense in these jurisdictions, the offense must have been previously formally and fully codified by the legislature. This is the position taken by the states with the darkest shading on the map: Alabama, Alaska, Arizona, Arkansas, California, Colorado, Delaware, Georgia, Hawaii, Illinois, Iowa, Kansas, Kentucky, Louisiana, Maine, Minnesota, Missouri, Montana, Nebraska, Nevada, New Hampshire, New Jersey, North Dakota, Ohio, Oklahoma, Oregon, Pennsylvania, South Dakota, Tennessee, Texas, Utah, Wisconsin, and Wyoming.[3]

Offense Must Be Legislatively Recognized, but Not All of Its Elements Need Be Codified

In three jurisdictions—Indiana, Virginia, and West Virginia,[4] with medium shading on the map—a legislative codification of the offense is required but need not be full and complete. For example, the criminal code may formally recognize the offense and set a maximum punishment for it but leave the definition of one or more elements of the offense to the judicial case law.

Allow Uncodified Offenses but Limit Punishment for Them

In four jurisdictions—District of Columbia, Florida, Idaho, and Rhode Island,[5] designated with the lightest shading on the map—even common-law offenses may be prosecuted. These are offenses that have never been codified

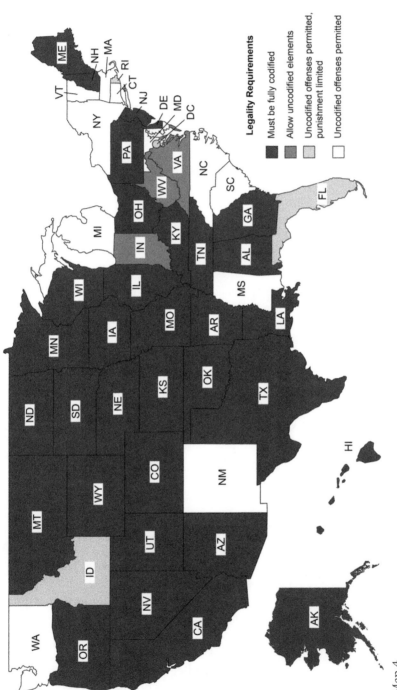

Legality Requirements

- Must be fully codified
- Allow uncodified elements
- Uncodified offenses permitted, punishment limited
- Uncodified offenses permitted

Map 4

by the legislature but exist by virtue of their judicial common-law creation. However, while the legislatures in these states authorize the prosecution of common-law offenses, they put a limit on the amount of punishment that can be imposed for such offenses, such as five years' imprisonment.

Allow Uncodified Offenses

The remaining 11 jurisdictions permit prosecution for uncodified or common-law offenses without any explicit ceiling in the penalty for such offenses. These states include Connecticut, Maryland, Massachusetts, Michigan, Mississippi, New Mexico, New York, North Carolina, South Carolina, Vermont, and Washington,[6] which have no shading on the map.

Majority View Formulation

If one were to construct a statutory formulation that reflected the majority view of all American jurisdictions on this issue, it might look something like the following:

Section 501. All Offenses Defined by Statute.

> No conduct constitutes an offense unless it is a crime or violation under this Code or other statute.[7]

Observations and Speculations

Given the important rationales behind the legality principle—fair notice, promoting uniformity in application, reserving the criminalization decision for the legislature[8]—one may wonder about the 18 jurisdictions in the last three groups, which allow some, or a lot, of corner-cutting of the legality principle. It is hard enough to expect citizens to consult the criminal code in order to know what the law demands of them, but it borders on ridiculous to think that fair notice has been given when citizens must go read a series of common-law judicial opinions to determine the criminal law's demands. To take this view is essentially to give up on the idea of criminal law providing fair notice. Such callousness makes criminal law somewhat hypocritical when it also enforces the traditional rule that "ignorance or mistake of law is no excuse."

One might seek to excuse these legality corner-cutters on the grounds that it is simply too difficult to draft a criminal code that is fully comprehensive. And this would have been a plausible argument until 1962, when the American Law Institute promulgated the Model Penal Code, which demonstrated that a jurisdiction really could quite easily codify all offenses and liability rules in a clear, concise, and coherent manner. What's more, the effectiveness of this modern codification form has now been proven many times over, as three-quarters of the states recodified their criminal laws during the 1960s and 1970s using to a greater or lesser extent the approach of the Model Penal Code. Further, the drafting advances of the Model Penal Code have over the past several decades been further improved,[9] to the point where it is now almost inexplicable, if not irresponsible, for jurisdictions to continue to tolerate the prosecution of uncodified common-law offenses.

What may help explain this continuing legality principle corner-cutting is the fact that a large number of the corner-cutting states are the one-quarter of the states that never enacted a modern criminal code during the Model Penal Code recodification wave in 1960s and 1970s. But if one cares about fairness and effectiveness in imposing criminal liability and punishment, these jurisdictions ought to join the 20th century by enacting a modern criminal code that will allow them to discontinue their tolerance of uncodified common-law offenses.

Notes

1. Paul H. Robinson and Michael T. Cahill, *Criminal Law*, 2nd ed., § 2.4.1 (Wolters Kluwer 2012).

2. This is similar to the facts in the case of Ray Brent Marsh. See Paul H. Robinson and Michael T. Cahill, *Law without Justice: Why Criminal Law Doesn't Give People What They Deserve,* Chapter 5 (Oxford 2006).

3. Ala. Code Ann. § 13A-1-4; Alaska Stat. Ann. § 11.81.220; Ariz. Rev. Stat. Ann. § 13-103; Ark. Code Ann. § 5-1-105; Cal. Penal Code § 6; Colo. Rev. Stat. Ann. § 18-1-104; Del. Code Ann. tit. 11, § 202; Ga. Code Ann. § 16-1-4; Haw. Rev. Stat. Ann. § 701-102; 720 Ill. Comp. Stat. Ann. 5/1-3; Iowa Code Ann. § 701.2; Kan. Stat. Ann. § 21-5103; Ky. Rev. Stat. Ann. § 500.020; La. Stat. Ann. § 14:7; Me. Rev. Stat. tit. 17-A, § 3; Minn. Stat. Ann. § 609.015; Mo. Ann. Stat. § 556.026; Mont. Code Ann. § 45-1-104; Neb. Rev. Stat. Ann. § 28-104; Nev. Rev. Stat. Ann. § 193.050; N.H. Rev. Stat. Ann. § 625:6; N.J. Stat. Ann. § 2C:1-5; N.D. Cent. Code Ann. § 12.1-02-01; Ohio Rev. Code Ann. § 2901.03; Okla. Stat. Ann. tit. 21, § 2; Or. Rev. Stat. Ann. § 161.505; 18 Pa. Stat. and Cons. Stat. Ann. § 107, S.D. Codified Laws § 22-1-8; Tenn. Code Ann. § 39-11-102; Tex. Penal Code Ann. § 1.03; Utah Code Ann. § 76-1-105; Wis. Stat. Ann. § 939.10; Wyo. Stat. Ann. § 6-1-102.

4. State v. Berdetta, 73 Ind. 185 (1880) (no common-law offenses, but if the statute does not provide a definition for a recognized offense, the common-law definition prevails); Va. Code Ann. § 18.2-16 (common-law offenses must be punished according to statute); W. Va. Code Ann. § 61-11-3 (common-law offenses must be punished according to statute).

5. D.C. Code Ann. § 22-1807 (common-law crimes cannot be punished by more than five years' imprisonment); Fla. Stat. Ann. § 775.02 (common-law crimes

cannot be punished by more than a $500 fine or 12-month imprisonment); Idaho Code Ann. § 18-112, Idaho Code Ann. § 18-113 (common-law felonies cannot be punished by more than five years' imprisonment, and common-law misdemeanors cannot be punished by more than six months' imprisonment); 11 R.I. Gen. Laws Ann. § 11-1-1 (common-law felonies cannot be punished by more than five years' imprisonment, and common-law misdemeanors cannot be punished by more than one year's imprisonment).

6. Conn. Gen. Stat. Ann. § 53a-4; Lutz v. State, 167 Md. 12 (1934); Mass. Const. Pt. 2, C. 6, art. VI; Gruskin v. Fisher, 405 Mich. 51 (1979) (courts may decide whether or not to retain a common-law offense); Hemingway v. Scales, 42 Miss. 1 (1868); N.M. Stat. Ann. § 30-1-3; N.Y. Stat. Law § 4; N.C. Gen. Stat. Ann. § 14-1; S.C. Code Ann. § 14-1-50; Vt. Stat. Ann. tit. 1, § 271; Wash. Rev. Code Ann. § 9A.04.060.

7. Paul H. Robinson et al., *The American Criminal Code: General Defenses,* 7 Journal of Legal Analysis 37, 61 (2015).

8. See Paul H. Robinson and Michael T. Cahill, *Criminal Law,* 2nd ed., § 2.4.2 (Wolters Kluwer 2012).

9. See, e.g., Paul H. Robinson et al., *Report of the Delaware Recodification Project* (April 2017) (two volumes); see also Paul H. Robinson et al., *Final Report of the Kentucky Penal Code Revision Project* (Commonwealth of Kentucky 2003) (two volumes); Paul H. Robinson et al., *Final Report of the Illinois Criminal Code Rewrite and Reform Commission* (State of Illinois 2003) (two volumes); Paul H. Robinson et al., *Final Report of the Maldives Penal Law & Sentencing Codification Project* (Republic of Maldives 2006) (two volumes).

PART 2

Homicide

CHAPTER FIVE

Provocation/Extreme Emotional Disturbance

When a person intentionally kills another, the person will satisfy the requirements for murder. Yet, one can imagine very different kinds of murders. If one person shoots another because he does not want a competitor in a business deal, or for a woman's affections, it would seem to be a classic case of the worst kind of wrongdoing, deserving the highest levels of punishment. The person is simply putting his or her interests above those of others and even above the value of other people's lives.

But imagine a different kind of intentional killing. While the defendant is helplessly drunk, another person sodomizes him. Then, over the next several weeks, he publicly brags about the victimization in the hopes of humiliating the defendant among their shared social circle. The defendant is angry and upset but holds himself in check. His appeal to the legal authorities goes nowhere because his victimizer has friends on the police force. As he is increasingly mocked and humiliated by his victimizer in public, his anger begins to rise to the point that it consumes him. After a round of public taunting by a friend of the victimizer, the defendant goes back to his apartment, gets his gun, goes to the house of his victimizer, and, in a fit of rage, shoots him dead.[1]

This is clearly an intentional killing, but it is generally agreed that it carries significantly less blameworthiness, because of the mitigating circumstances of the provocation, than the case of the unmitigated killing for advantage described above. The criminal law typically recognizes the difference between these two cases by recognizing that *provocation*, or it's more modern and broader form, *extreme emotional disturbance*, mitigates murder to a lesser form of homicide, such as manslaughter.

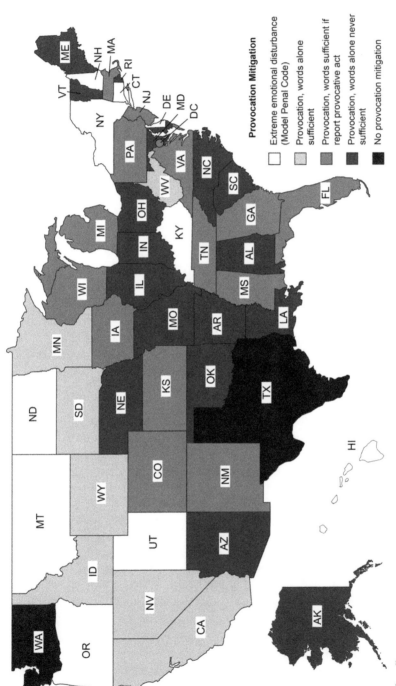

Provocation Mitigation

☐ Extreme emotional disturbance (Model Penal Code)

☐ Provocation, words alone sufficient

☐ Provocation, words sufficient if report provocative act

☐ Provocation, words alone never sufficient

■ No provocation mitigation

Map 5

Although almost all jurisdictions recognize such a mitigation, there are a number of important differences in their approach. Map 5 identifies five such different legal approaches to the subject.

Model Penal Code's Extreme Emotional Disturbance Mitigation

The broadest mitigation is provided by Connecticut, Delaware, Hawaii, Kentucky, Montana, New Hampshire, New York, North Dakota, Oregon, and Utah—the states with no shading on the map.[2] These jurisdictions follow the Model Penal Code in providing a mitigation from murder to a lower degree of homicide where the defendant acted under extreme mental or emotional disturbance for which there was a reasonable explanation or excuse. Typically, the explanation or excuse must be objectively reasonable. That is, it must be determined from the perspective of an objectively reasonable person in the actor's situation under circumstances as the actor believed them to be.

Note that some jurisdictions use only the language "extreme emotional disturbance," presumably leaving out cases of "extreme *mental* disturbance" (perhaps because they think these cases are better handled by a doctrine specifically addressing issues of mental illness).

Common-Law Provocation Generally

The alternative approach, taken by the next three groups of states discussed below, retain the common-law "provocation" rule, which permits a mitigation to a lower degree of homicide in a more narrow set of circumstances. For example, while the Model Penal Code's formulation allows a mitigation for any killing during extreme emotional disturbance for which there is a reasonable explanation or excuse, the more narrow common-law approach permits the mitigation only when the actor is responding immediately to the provocation. That is, the defendant must be adequately or sufficiently provoked such that he or she acted in the sudden "heat of passion."

Thus, under the common-law approach, the mitigation is available only if the killing immediately follows the provocation; "cooling time" vitiates the mitigation. In the hypothetical above, while the original sodomy might have qualified as a sufficiently provocative act, enough time had passed for him to cool off, so his subsequent killing would have been ineligible for the mitigation. The defendant would be barred from the common-law provocation mitigation on these grounds.[3]

For another example of the narrow nature of common-law provocation, the rule allows mitigation only if force is used against the person who provides the immediate provocation, such as the person who does the taunting that finally sets off the defendant in the hypothetical; the earlier sodomizer was not the provoker on the immediate occasion, and thus there could be no mitigation for killing him.

Still further, the common-law mitigation recognizes only certain events as adequate under the law to qualify as the basis for a provocation mitigation. The map presents the three approaches that common-law provocation jurisdictions commonly take on this matter: in the broadest formulation, words alone are allowed to be sufficient provocation; in the second group, the only time words alone are sufficient to provide a mitigation is if they report an act which itself is legally recognized as adequate provocation (such as a man having just been told that another man raped his wife); and in the third group words alone are never sufficient, i.e., only the provocative act itself is legally sufficient to trigger mitigation. Below is a bit more detail on each of these three groups.

Common-Law Provocation: Words Alone Are Sufficient

California, Idaho, Minnesota, Nevada, South Dakota, West Virginia, and Wyoming—the states with light shading on the map—take the view that mere words, such as insults or abusive language, can be sufficient for adequate provocation.[4] They do not require mitigation in such cases; they permit it only if it is found under all the circumstances that the words really were sufficient to provoke the defendant to kill in the heat of passion.

This is an expansion of the traditional common-law mitigation and is the broadest formulation short of the Model Penal Code's. It allows application of the mitigation in instances where the two groups of states below would not.

Common-Law Provocation: Words Alone Are Sufficient Only If They Report Provocative Act

Jurisdictions designated with medium shading on the map—Colorado, District of Columbia, Florida, Georgia, Iowa, Kansas, Massachusetts, Michigan, Mississippi, New Jersey, New Mexico, Pennsylvania, Tennessee, Virginia, and Wisconsin—do not normally allow words alone to be sufficient provocation.[5] In keeping with the strict common-law rule, adequate provocation is reserved for particularly shocking events, such as catching one's spouse in an act of infidelity. But these jurisdictions have carved out a narrow exception for verbal reports of such provocative acts, such as a spouse's confession of infidelity. In these jurisdictions, such "informational words" may suffice for adequate provocation.

Common-Law Provocation: Words Alone Are Never Sufficient

Finally, the states with darker shading on the map—Alabama, Alaska, Arizona, Arkansas, Illinois, Indiana, Louisiana, Maine, Maryland, Missouri, Nebraska, North Carolina, Ohio, Oklahoma, Rhode Island, South Carolina, and Vermont—retain the hard-line rule that mere words are never adequate provocation.[6] Even a spouse's confession of infidelity is held insufficient to provoke an ordinary person to lethal violence. (Some of these jurisdictions have not addressed the informational-words exception, while others have expressly addressed and rejected it.)

No Provocation Mitigation

Two states, Texas and Washington—shaded black on the map—do not offer a mitigation for extreme emotional disturbance or for provocation causing a killing in the heat of passion.[7] In these jurisdictions, provocation or emotional disturbance is relevant only if it negates an offense culpability requirement, which normally it would not. In Texas, adequate provocation may be raised as a substantial mitigating factor at sentencing.

Observations and Speculations

The wide diversity among the states on this issue may reflect the awkward nature of the mitigation. It is easy enough to see that many cases of provocation or extreme emotional disturbance are meaningfully different from the case of unprovoked clear-eyed killing for advantage. But the provocation/ extreme emotional disturbance mitigation must answer the perhaps unanswerable question: How much less blameworthy must the provocation/extreme emotional disturbance case be to be different enough to merit a mitigation from murder to a lesser form of homicide?

Ideally, we would want the extent of the offender's mitigation to match the extent of his reduced blameworthiness due to provocation. Adherence to such a proportionality principle might be easy to achieve in the context of sentencing, with its large number of incremental punishment options. But in the grading context, which is where provocation/extreme emotional disturbance operates, there is no such possibility. All that can be done is to sort all intentional killing cases into the two categories: the unmitigated and the mitigated. There is inevitably a certain arbitrariness in deciding exactly where the line between the two categories is to be drawn.

One might be tempted to discard the grading distinction altogether and to leave the matter to sentencing, as Texas does, but this would be bucking the trend. There is an increasing appreciation that juries ought to be involved more in assessing the grade of an offender's liability and that the punishment determination ought not to be left to the broad discretion of sentencing judges.[8]

Notes

1. For a case of similar facts, see State v. Gounagias, 153 P. 9 (Wash. 1915).

2. Conn. Gen. Stat. Ann. § 53a-54a; State v. Person, 60 Conn. App. 820, 828, 761 A.2d 269, 274–75 (2000); Del. Code Ann. tit. 11, § 641; State v. Magner, 732 A.2d 234, 241 (Del. Super. Ct. 1997); Haw. Rev. Stat. Ann. § 707-702; State v. Adviento, 132 Haw. 123, 137, 319 P.3d 1131, 1145 (2014); Ky. Rev. Stat. Ann. § 507.030; Ky. Rev. Stat. Ann. § 507.020; Spears v. Com., 30 S.W.3d 152, 155 (Ky. 2000), as amended (Jan. 24, 2001); Mont. Code Ann. § 45-5-103; N.H. Rev. Stat. Ann. § 630:2; State v. O'Leary, 153 N.H. 710, 716, 903 A.2d 997, 1002 (2006); State v. Little, 123 N.H. 433, 435, 462 A.2d 117, 118 (1983); N.Y. Penal Law § 125.25; People v. Drake, 216 A.D.2d 873, 873, 629 N.Y.S.2d 361, 362 (1995); People v. Harris, 95 N.Y.2d 316, 319, 740 N.E.2d 227, 229 (2000); N.D. Cent. Code Ann. § 12.1-16-01; Or. Rev. Stat. Ann. § 163.118; Or. Rev. Stat. Ann. § 163.135; State v. Carson, 292 Or. 451, 458, 640 P.2d 586, 590 (1982); Utah Code Ann. § 76-5-205.5; State v. White, 2011 UT 21, ¶ 25, 251 P.3d 820, 826.

3. Indeed, in the *Gounagias* case on which the hypothetical is based, the defendant was denied a provocation mitigation.

4. Cal. Penal Code § 192; People v. Millbrook, 222 Cal. App. 4th 1122, 1147 (2014); Idaho Code Ann. § 18-4006; Carsner v. State, 132 Idaho 235, 241, 970 P.2d 28, 34 (Ct. App. 1998); Minn. Stat. Ann. § 609.20; Nev. Rev. Stat. Ann. § 200.040; Nev. Rev. Stat. Ann. § 200.050; Schoels v. State, 114 Nev. 981, 986, 966 P.2d 735, 738 (1998); S.D. Codified Laws § 22-16-15; S.D. Codified Laws § 22-16-31; State v. Nelson, 272 N.W.2d 817, 820 (S.D. 1978); State v. Hart, 1998 S.D. 93, ¶ 15, 584 N.W.2d 863, 865–66; State v. Edmunds, 20 S.D. 135, 104 N.W. 1115, 1117 (1905), aff'd, 21 S.D. 5, 108 N.W. 556 (1906); State v. McGuire, 200 W. Va. 823, 835, 490 S.E.2d 912, 924 (1997); State ex rel. Combs v. Boles, 151 W. Va. 194, 199, 151 S.E.2d 115, 118–19 (1966); Wyo. Stat. Ann. § 6-2-105; State v. Flory, 40 Wyo. 184, 276 P. 458 (1929); State v. Helton, 73 Wyo. 92, 115, 276 P.2d 434, 442 (1954).

5. Colo. Rev. Stat. § 18-3-104(1); Cassels v. People, 92 P.3d 951, 960 (Colo. 2004); Lee v. United States, 959 A.2d 1141, 1142 (D.C. 2008); High v. United States, 972 A.2d 829, 839 (D.C. 2009); Fla. Stat. Ann. § 782.03; Whidden v. State, 64 Fla. 165, 167, 59 So. 561, 561 (1912); Rountree v. State, 113 Fla. 443, 445, 152 So. 20, 21 (1934); Fowler v. Sec'y, Florida Dep't of Corr., No. 5:13-CV-514-JSM-PRL, 2014 WL 3809126, at *4 (M.D. Fla. Aug. 1, 2014); Ga. Code Ann. § 16-5-2; Mack v. State, 272 Ga. 415, 417, 529 S.E.2d 132, 134 (2000); Strickland v. State, 257 Ga. 230, 231, 357 S.E.2d 85, 86–87 (1987); Raines v. State, 247 Ga. 504, 277 S.E.2d 47 (1981); State v. Thompson, 836 N.W.2d 470 (Iowa 2013); Kan. Stat. Ann. § 21-5404; State v. Bernhardt, 372 P.3d 1161 (Kan. 2016); State v. Paulson, 358 P.3d 877 (Kan. Ct. App. 2015), review denied (Apr. 21, 2016); Com. v. Mercado, 452 Mass. 662, 671, 896 N.E.2d 1262, 1270 (2008); Com. v. Groome, 435 Mass. 201, 220, 755 N.E.2d 1224, 1240 (2001); Maher v. People, 10 Mich. 212, 224 (1862); People v. Young, No. 239997, 2003 WL 22064247, at *3 (Mich. Ct. App. Sept. 4, 2003); Miss. Code.

Ann. § 97-3-35; Haley v. State, 123 Miss. 87, 85 So. 129 (1920); Turner v. State, 773 So. 2d 952, 953 (Miss. Ct. App. 2000); N.J. Stat. Ann. § 2C:11-4; State v. Crisantos, 102 N.J. 265, 274, 508 A.2d 167, 171–72 (1986); State v. Coyle, 119 N.J. 194, 226, 574 A.2d 951, 967 (1990); N.M. Stat. Ann. § 30-2-3; Sells v. State, 1982-NMSC-125, 98 N.M. 786, 788, 653 P.2d 162, 164; 18 Pa. Stat. and Cons. Stat. Ann. § 2503; Commonwealth v. Berry, 461 Pa. 233, 238, 336 A.2d 262, 264 (1975); Tenn. Code Ann. § 39-13-211; Whitsett v. State, 201 Tenn. 317, 323, 299 S.W.2d 2, 5 (1957); Freddo v. State, 127 Tenn. 376, 155 S.W. 170, 172 (1913); Rhodes v. Com., 41 Va. App. 195, 201, 583 S.E.2d 773, 776 (2003); Hannah v. Com., 153 Va. 863, 868, 149 S.E. 419, 421 (1929); Wis. Stat. Ann. § 939.44; State v. Thomas, 2000 WI App 143, ¶ 14, 237 Wis. 2d 694, 616 N.W.2d 922.

6. Knight v. State, 907 So. 2d 470, 478 (Ala. Crim. App. 2004); Speake v. State, 610 So. 2d 1238 (Ala. Crim. App. 1992); Alaska Stat. Ann. § 11.41.115; Ariz. Rev. Stat. Ann. § 13-1103; Ariz. Rev. Stat. Ann. § 13-1101; State v. Love, No. 1 CA-CR 09-0329, 2010 WL 5050551, at *2 (Ariz. Ct. App. Nov. 9, 2010); Bankston v. State, 361 Ark. 123, 129 (2005); 720 Ill. Comp. Stat. Ann. 5/9-2; People v. Blackwell, 171 Ill. 2d 338, 358, 665 N.E.2d 782, 791 (1996); People v. Sutton, 353 Ill. App.3d 487, 288 Ill. Dec. 858, 818 N.E.2d 793 (2004); People v. Schorle, 206 Ill. App. 3d 748, 151 Ill. Dec. 813, 565 N.E.2d 84 (1st Dist. 1990); Ind. Code Ann. § 35-42-1-3; Gibson v. State, 43 N.E.3d 231, 240 (Ind. 2015); Perigo v. State, 541 N.E.2d 936, 938 (Ind. 1989); La. Stat. Ann. § 14:31; State v. Cumbrera, 2014-372 (La. App. 3 Cir. 10/1/14), 149 So. 3d 869, 873; Me. Rev. Stat. tit. 17-A, § 203; Me. Rev. Stat. tit. 17-A, § 201; State v. Michaud, 611 A.2d 61, 63 (Me. 1992); Md. Code Ann., Crim. Law § 2-207; Christian v. State, 405 Md. 306, 323, 951 A.2d 832, 842 (2008); Wood v. State, 209 Md. App. 246, 312, 58 A.3d 556, 595 (2012); Mo. Ann. Stat. § 565.002; Mo. Ann. Stat. § 565.023; State v. Avery, 120 S.W.3d 196, 206 (Mo. 2003); Neb. Rev. Stat. Ann. § 28-305; State v. Pettit, 233 Neb. 436, 454, 445 N.W.2d 890, 901 (1989); Wright v. State, 169 Neb. 497, 503, 100 N.W.2d 51, 56 (1959); Lowe v. State, 110 Neb. 325, 193 N.W. 707, 708 (1923); State v. Simonovich, 688 S.E.2d 67 (N.C. Ct. App. 2010); State v. Durham, 625 S.E.2d 831 (N.C. Ct. App. 2006); Ohio Rev. Code Ann. § 2903.03; State v. Shane, 63 Ohio St. 3d 630, 637, 590 N.E.2d 272, 278 (1992); State v. Mack, 1998-Ohio-375, 82 Ohio St. 3d 198, 201, 694 N.E.2d 1328, 1331; State v. Shane, 63 Ohio St. 3d 630, 637, 590 N.E.2d 272, 278 (1992); Okla. Stat. Ann. tit. 21, § 711; Marquez-Burrola v. State, 2007 OK CR 14, ¶ 22, 157 P.3d 749, 758; Washington v. State, 1999 OK CR 22, 989 P.2d 960, 969; State v. Ruffner, 911 A.2d 680, 686 (R.I. 2006); State v. McGuy, 841 A.2d 1109, 1112 (R.I. 2003); State v. Cooley, 342 S.C. 63, 68, 536 S.E.2d 666, 669 (2000); State v. Hernandez, 386 S.C. 655, 661, 690 S.E.2d 582, 585 (Ct. App. 2010); State v. Holland, 385 S.C. 159, 165, 682 S.E.2d 898, 901 (Ct. App. 2009); Vt. Stat. Ann. tit. 13, § 2303; State v. Kulzer, 2009 VT 79, ¶ 26, 186 Vt. 264, 275, 979 A.2d 1031, 1039 (2009); State v. Perez, 180 Vt. 388, 912 A.2d 944 (2006).

7. Packer v. State, 106 Wash. App. 1049 (2001); State v. Van Zante, 26 Wash. App. 739, 741, 614 P.2d 217, 219 (1980); Tex. Penal Code Ann. § 19.02.

8. Note, for example, the dramatic increase in the use of sentencing guidelines, together with the recently clarified constitutional requirement that the jury rather than the judge must determine any facts that increase a penalty beyond the maximum permitted by the facts established by a guilty plea or jury verdict. See United States v. Booker, 543 U.S. 220, 244 (2005). For another example, note the dramatic increase in the grading nuance that legislatures now routinely add to existing offenses. See, e.g., *Report of the Delaware Criminal Law Recodification Project* (2017), https://ssrn.com/abstract=2950728.

CHAPTER SIX

Felony Murder

The defendant plans to rob a liquor store by brandishing a pen knife to the clerk. If the sight of the knife does not induce the clerk to cooperate, the defendant plans to immediately flee, on assumption that the clerk probably has a gun. When he enters the store, the clerk is in fact not intimidated, and the defendant turns to leave. But the clerk quickly grabs his gun and leaps over the counter, causing the gun to discharge in the process. The bullet strikes the clerk's leg, and because it hits an artery, he bleeds to death before surgeons can repair the injury.

Under the standard scheme for graded homicide, the defendant's liability will mirror his level of culpability as to causing the death. On these facts, when he robbed the liquor store brandishing his pen knife, he might have been only negligent or at most reckless as to causing the death. That is, a jury might conclude that he was aware of a substantial risk that his conduct in entering the store with the pen knife created a substantial risk of causing death or, if he was not aware of this, that a reasonable person would have been aware. Or they might even conclude that he was not even negligent as to causing the death; that is, that even a reasonable person would not have thought that such conduct created a substantial risk of causing death. Depending on the conclusion the jury reaches, the defendant would be held liable for manslaughter, negligent homicide, or no homicide, respectively.[1] (He obviously will remain liable for his attempted robbery.)

Under the felony-murder rule, however, the defendant will be liable for murder on these facts, because he caused the death of another person in the course of committing a felony. His culpability level as to causing the death becomes irrelevant. In its strictest form, the rule essentially imputes to the defendant the standard culpability required for murder—typically intentionally or knowingly causing the death—based on his commission of the underlying felony.

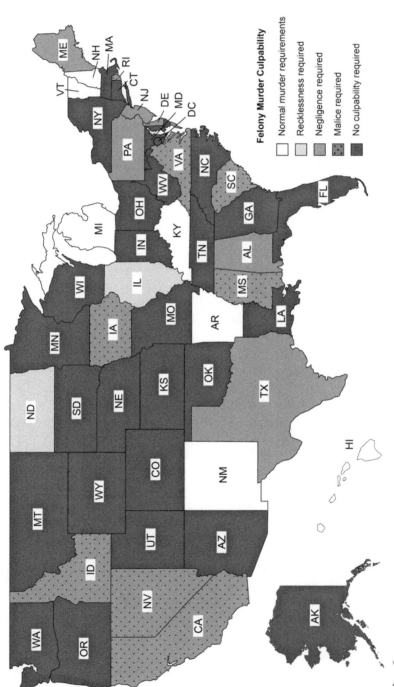

Felony Murder Culpability

- ☐ Normal murder requirements
- Recklessness required
- Negligence required
- Malice required
- No culpability required

Map 6

The states may be divided into five categories for the approach they take in felony-murder cases, as presented in Map 6.[2]

Normal Murder Requirements

The first group, represented on the map without shading, has effectively rejected the felony-murder rule. These seven jurisdictions either do not have a felony-murder rule or, if they do have one, the culpability required for it is the same as that required for murder. In other words, their felony-murder rule does not expand murder liability to actors other than those normally liable for murder. The states of Arkansas, Hawaii, Kentucky, Michigan, New Hampshire, New Mexico, and Vermont take this view.[3] Each of the states takes a somewhat different approach from the others in exactly how they formulate their murder offense.[4]

The effect of this approach is consistent with that recommended by the Model Penal Code, which defines murder as follows:

Section 210.2. Murder.

1. Except as provided in Section 210.3(1)(b), criminal homicide constitutes murder when:

    a. it is committed purposely or knowingly; or

    b. it is committed recklessly under circumstances manifesting extreme indifference to the value of human life. *Such recklessness and indifference are presumed if the actor is engaged or is an accomplice in the commission of, or an attempt to commit, or flight after committing or attempting to commit robbery, rape or deviate sexual intercourse by force or threat of force, arson, burglary, kidnapping or felonious escape.* . . .

Notice that the last sentence of subsection (1)(b) seems to provide something like a felony-murder rule: it allows the recklessness and indifference that would constitute murder under subsection (1)(b) to be presumed under felony-murder-like conditions. As a technical matter, however, the effect of this apparent presumption is essentially vitiated by Model Penal Code section 1.12(5)(b), which defines the effect of presumptions in such a way as to render them of little practical effect. The jury is still instructed that they must find the recklessness and extreme indifference required for murder beyond a reasonable doubt.

Recklessness Required for Felony-Murder Liability

Two other jurisdictions, represented on the map with light shading—Illinois and North Dakota[5]—do have true felony-murder rules, but their rules are formulated in such a way as to require proof of at least recklessness in causing the death of another human being in the course of committing a felony. Without the felony-murder rule, such actors would commonly be liable for a lesser offense of reckless homicide or manslaughter. Again, the two jurisdictions take different approaches in reaching a similar result.[6]

Negligence Required for Felony-Murder Liability

Six jurisdictions, with medium shading on the table—Alabama, Delaware, Maine, New Jersey, Pennsylvania, and Texas[7]—impose felony-murder liability, but only on actors who are at least negligent as to causing the death of another human being in the course of a felony. Without a felony-murder rule, an actor in these jurisdictions might otherwise be liable for negligent homicide or involuntary manslaughter. The jurisdictions reach this result through a number of different formulations.[8]

Malice Required for Felony-Murder Liability

The eight jurisdictions shown on the map with medium shading plus dots impose felony-murder liability but nonetheless require that the government prove malice: California, Idaho, Iowa, Mississippi, Nevada, Rhode Island, South Carolina, and Virginia.[9] Malice is generally presumed when the actor should have foreseen the danger in his or her conduct—that is, when the actor was *negligent* in causing the death, perhaps by engaging in inherently dangerous conduct or conduct dangerous under the circumstances. Possibly, in some jurisdictions, malice may be imputed to the actor even when the actor could not have foreseen the danger. In such cases, felony murder per se is a strict-liability offense.[10] In other words, these "malice" jurisdictions end up requiring something in the nature of negligence or less, although without the clear and specific definitions typically found in modern American criminal codes using the Model Penal Code's culpability definitions. Again, the actual formulations within this group of jurisdictions vary considerably.[11]

No Culpability Required for Felony-Murder Liability

A final group of 28 jurisdictions appear in black on the map: Alaska, Arizona, Colorado, Connecticut, District of Columbia, Florida, Georgia, Indiana, Kansas, Louisiana, Maryland, Massachusetts, Minnesota, Missouri, Montana, Nebraska, New York, North Carolina, Ohio, Oklahoma, Oregon, South Dakota, Tennessee, Utah, Washington, West Virginia, Wisconsin, and Wyoming.[12] These jurisdictions impose felony-murder liability on actors who unlawfully cause the death of a human being in the course of committing felonies even if the actor was not negligent in causing the death, including actors who reasonably believe that their participation in the felony does not create a risk of death. These jurisdictions take a variety of different approaches in reaching this result.[13]

Observations and Speculations

What accounts for the relatively broad level of disagreement among the states regarding the felony-murder rule? Each of the many sides in the debate has some plausible argument to offer. On the one hand, the rule has a certain appeal: people who commit felonies have already demonstrated their willingness to disregard societal norms and to put their interests ahead of others. Why shouldn't they be criminally liable for everything that follows?

On the other hand, criminal law has increasingly tried to capture the blameworthiness nuance of each offense situation. That is, the liquor store robber who goes in to the store with the intention of stabbing the clerk to death and the robber in our hypothetical at the start of the chapter, who goes in with his pen knife and ready to run away, are people of two very different degrees of moral blameworthiness. A just criminal law is one that will distinguish the two cases and give greater punishment, as deserved, to the robber who plans the death. The jurisdictions that reject the felony-murder rule may do so on this reasoning.

Notice that the Model Penal Code formulation recognizes that one can have the blameworthiness of an intentional murderer if one creates a substantial risk of causing death "under circumstances manifesting an extreme indifference the value of human life" and that such recklessness and indifference might exist in some felony-murder cases. In other words, there is a kernel of truth to the fact that the felony-murder situation can, under some circumstances, raise a reckless killing to the same level of blameworthiness as an intentional or knowing killing. This kernel may have helped sustain the felony-murder rule even in those jurisdictions committed to following a principle of strict proportionality between the blameworthiness of the offender and the extent of his or her punishment.

The moral complexity in these kinds of cases may help explain the many jurisdictions that seek some middle ground between the abolitionists and those who strictly adhere to the classic felony-murder rule. That is, many jurisdictions keep the rule but limit it by requiring some minimum culpability as to causing the death—recklessness, malice, or at least negligence. Perhaps these jurisdictions see the limitation that they have added as excluding from the operation of the rule at least the most egregious instances of disproportionality between blameworthiness and punishment.

The analysis above has been one that focuses exclusively on desert as a distributive principle, but it seems likely that many, if not most, of the jurisdictions have been influenced by alternative distributive principles, especially general deterrence.[14] A felony-murder rule may be attractive under a general

deterrence program because the threat of greater punishment may be thought
to induce felons to be more careful, and indeed may provide some additional
disincentive for the commission of the underlying felony itself. On the other
hand, as has been detailed elsewhere, it may be unrealistic to think that such
nuanced calculations by lawmakers can have any real-world effect. For example,
given the diversity among the states, how likely is it that the potential liquor
store robbers out there will even know what the felony-murder rule is in their
jurisdiction?[15]

The trend appears to be to move away from distributive principles that conflict with just deserts, as reflected, for example, in the 2007 amendment to the
Model Penal Code's "purposes" section—the only amendment to the Model
Penal Code since its promulgation by the American Law Institute in 1962.[16]
If this is the trend, then one might expect the number of abolition states to
grow, or at least the strict application states to migrate to groups of states that
have adopted greater limitations on the rule. Of course, this assumes that
legislatures actively reexamine the appropriateness of their criminal law rules,
when the truth may be that the force of inertia is greater than the force of
being just.[17]

Notes

1. See Paul H. Robinson and Michael T. Cahill, *Criminal Law*, 2nd ed. § 15.1,
§ 15.2 (Wolters Kluwer 2012).

2. What is described here might be called the "aggravation of culpability"
aspect of felony-murder rule. The traditional role also has a "complicity aspect,"
which applies the same imputation of murder culpability to all accomplices in
the underlying felony. There exists significant diversity among the states on how
they deal with this aspect of the felony-murder rule as well. See Paul H. Robinson and Michael T. Cahill, *Criminal Law*, 2nd ed. § 15.3 (Wolters Kluwer 2012).

3. Ark. Code Ann. § 5-10-102 (2006); Ark. Code Ann. § 5-10-103 (2006); Haw.
Rev. Stat. § 707–701 (2006) (no felony murder rule); Ky. Rev. Stat. Ann. § 507.020
(1984) (no felony murder rule); People v. Aaron, 409 Mich. 672, 708–709,
299 N.W.2d 304 (1980); N.H. Rev. Stat. Ann. § 630:1-b (1974); N.H. Rev. Stat. Ann.
§ 626:7 (2) (1971); N.M. Stat. § 30-2-1 (1978); State v. Ortega, 112 N.M. 554, 563,
817 P.2d 1196, 1205 (1991); State v. Doucette, 143 Vt. 573, 579, 470 A.2d 676, 680
(1983), from Guyora Binder, *Felony Murder*, 183–89 (Stanford 2012).

4. "A person commits the offense of murder in the first degree if the person
intentionally or knowingly causes the death of: (a) More than one person in the
same or separate incident; (b) A law enforcement officer, judge, or prosecutor arising
out of the performance of official duties; (c) A person known by the defendant to
be a witness in a criminal prosecution and the killing is related to the person's
status as a witness; (d) A person by a hired killer, in which event both the person
hired and the person responsible for hiring the killer shall be punished under

this section; (e) A person while the defendant was imprisoned. . . ." Haw. Rev. Stat. Ann. § 707-701. "Except as provided in section 707-701, a person commits the offense of murder in the second degree if the person intentionally or knowingly causes the death of another person." Haw. Rev. Stat. Ann. § 707-701.5.

"A person commits murder in the first degree if [a]cting alone or with one . . . or more other persons. . . . [t]he person commits or attempts to commit a felony . . . and . . . [i]n the course of and in the furtherance of the felony or in immediate flight from the felony, the person or an accomplice causes the death of any person under circumstances manifesting extreme indifference to the value of human life. . . ." Ark. Code Ann. § 5-10-102.

"Murder in the first degree is the killing of one human being by another without lawful justification or excuse, by any of the means with which death may be caused . . . in the commission of or attempt to commit any felony. . . ." N.M. Stat. Ann. § 30-2-1.

"[P]roof that a killing occurred during the commission or attempted commission of a felony will no longer suffice to establish murder in the first degree. In addition to proof that the defendant caused (or aided and abetted) the killing, . . . there must be proof that the defendant intended to kill (or was knowingly heedless that death might result from his conduct). An unintentional or accidental killing will not suffice [for felony murder liability]." State v. Ortega, 1991-NMSC-084, 112 N.M. 554, 563, 817 P.2d 1196, 1205.

"[T]he prosecution [must] prove the defendant acted with the mens rea commensurate with second-degree murder to secure a felony-murder conviction. . . ." State v. Marquez, 2016-NMSC-025, 376 P.3d 815, 833.

5. See 720 Ill. Comp. Stat. 5/9-1 (a) (3) (2010); 720 Ill. Comp. Stat. 5/2-8 (1996); 720 Ill. Comp. Stat. 5/9-1 (a) (2) (2010); 720 Ill. Comp. Stat. 5/9-1 (1961), Illinois Laws 1961, 1983, § 9-1 (Criminal Code of 1961 committee comment at 15); People v. McEwen 157, 510 N.E.2d 74,79 Ill. App. 3d 222, 228–29 (Ill. App. Ct. 1987); People v. Guest, 115 Ill.2d 72, 503 N.E.2d 255 (1986); N.D. Cent. Code § 12.1-02-02.3 (1973); N.D. Cent. Code § 12.1-02-02.1, 2.2 (1973); N.D. Cent. Code § 12.1-16-01 (1993).

6. "A person is guilty of murder . . . if the person . . . [a]cting either alone or with one or more other persons, commits or attempts to commit treason, robbery, burglary, kidnapping, felonious restraint, arson, gross sexual imposition, a felony offense against a child . . . , or escape and, in the course of and in furtherance of such crime or of immediate flight therefrom, the person or any other participant in the crime causes the death of any person." N.D. Cent. Code Ann. § 12.1-16-01.

"For the purposes of this title, a person engages in conduct . . . 'Willfully' if he engages in the conduct intentionally, knowingly, or recklessly. . . . If a statute or regulation thereunder defining a crime does not specify any culpability and does not provide explicitly that a person may be guilty without culpability, the culpability that is required is willfully." N.D. Cent. Code Ann. § 12.1-02-02.

7. Ala. Code § 13A-6-1 (2006); Ala. Code § 13A-6-2 (2006); Ala. Code § 13A-6-2 (2006) (Official Commentary, 256); Ex parte Mitchell, 936 So. 2d 1094 (Ala.

Crim. App. 2006); Witherspoon v. State, 2009 WL 1164989 (Ala. Crim. App. 2009); Lewis v. State, 474 So. 2d 766 (Ala. Crim. App. 1985); Ala. Code § 13A-2-4 (b) (1977); Del. Code Ann. tit. 11 § 636 (2009); Del. Code Ann. tit. 11 § 635 (2004); Me. Rev. Stat. Ann. tit. 17-A § 202 (1991); N.J. Stat. Ann. § 2C:2-2 (1981); N.J. Stat. Ann. § 2C:2-3 (1978); State v. Martin, 119 N.J. 2, 31, 32, 573 A.2d 1359 (1990); 18 Pa. Cons. Stat. § 302 (A) (1973); 18 Pa. Cons. Stat. § 2501 (1973); 18 Pa. Cons. Stat. § 2502 (1978); Commonwealth v. Hassein, 490 A.2d 438, 454, 340 Pa. Super. 318, 348 (Pa. Super. Ct. 1985); Tex. Penal Code Ann. § 19.01 (1993); Tex. Penal Code Ann. § 6.02 (2005); State v. Kuykendall, 609 S.W.2d 791 (Tex. Crim. App. 1980); State v. Rodriguez, 953 S.W.2d 342 (Tex. App. 1997).

8. "A person is guilty of felony murder if acting alone or with one or more other persons in the commission of, or an attempt to commit, or immediate flight after committing or attempting to commit, murder, robbery, burglary, kidnapping, arson, gross sexual assault, or escape, the person or another participant in fact causes the death of a human being, and the death is a reasonably foreseeable consequence of such commission, attempt or flight. . . . It is an affirmative defense to prosecution under this section that the defendant . . . [d]id not commit the homicidal act or in any way solicit, command, induce, procure or aid the commission thereof[, w]as not armed with a dangerous weapon, or other weapon which under circumstances indicated a readiness to inflict serious bodily injury[, r]easonably believed that no other participant was armed with such a weapon[, and r]easonably believed that no other participant intended to engage in conduct likely to result in death or serious bodily injury." Me. Rev. Stat. tit. 17-A, § 202.

"A person is guilty of criminal homicide if he intentionally, knowingly, recklessly or negligently causes the death of another human being. . . . Criminal homicide shall be classified as murder, voluntary manslaughter, or involuntary manslaughter." 18 Pa. Stat. and Cons. Stat. Ann. § 2501.

"A criminal homicide constitutes murder of the second degree when it is committed while defendant was engaged as a principal or an accomplice in the perpetration of a felony[, defined as] engaging in or being an accomplice in the commission of, or an attempt to commit, or flight after committing, or attempting to commit robbery, rape, or deviate sexual intercourse by force or threat of force, arson, burglary or kidnapping." 18 Pa. Stat. and Cons. Stat. Ann. § 2502.

9. Cal. Penal Code § 189 (2002); People v. Washington, 62 Cal. 2d 777 (1965); People v. Chun, 203 P.3d. 425 (Cal. 2009); Idaho Code Ann. § 18-4001, 4003 (2002); State v. Lankford, 781 P.2d 197, 116 Idaho 860, 866 (1989); Iowa Code Ann. § 707.1; State v. Taylor, 287 N.W.2d 576, 577 (Iowa 1980); State v. Ragland, 420 N.W.2d 791 (Iowa 1988) (overruled on other grounds); State v. Bennet, 503 N.W.2d 42, 45 (Iowa Ct. App. 1993); State v. Heemstra, 721 N.W.2d 554 (Iowa 2006); Miss. Code Ann. § 97–3–19(c) (2004); Boyd v. State, 2006–KAA-00562–SCT, 977 S. 2d 329 (Miss. 2008); Lee v. State, 98–CA-00015–SCT, 759 S. 2d 390 (Miss. 2000); Nev. Rev. Stat. § 200.010 (2005); Nay v. State, 123 Nev. 326, 332, 167 P.3d 430, 434 (2007); Labastida v. State, 986 P.2d 443, 115 Nev. 298 (1999); R.I. Gen. Laws § 11–23–1 (2008); In re Leon, 122 R.I. 548, 553, 410 A.2d 121, 124,

quoting Perkins, *Criminal Law* 44 (2d ed. 1969); S.C. Code Ann. § 16-3-10 (1962); State v. Norris, 328 S.E.2d 339, 285 S.C. 86, 91 (1985) (overruled on other grounds); Gore v. Leeke, 199 S.E.2d 755, 261 S.C. 308 (1973); Lowry v. State, 657 S.E.2d 760, 376 S.C. 499 (2008); S.C. Jury Instr.–Crim. § 2–1, SC JI CRIMI-NAL § 2–1 (Lexis 2007) (jury instructions on murder); S.C. Jury Instr.–Crim. § 2–3, SC JI CRIMINAL § 2–3 (Lexis 2007) (jury instructions on felony murder); Va. Code Ann. § 18.2–33 (1999); Wooden v. Commonwealth, 284 S.E.2d 811, 814, 222 Va. 758, 762 (1981); Cotton v. Commonwealth, 35 Va. App. 511, 515, 546 S.E.2d 241, 243 (Va. Ct. App. 2001) (quoting John L. Costello, *Virginia Criminal Law and Procedure* § 3.4–3, 33 (2d ed. 1995)); accord Kennemore v. Commonwealth, 653 S.E.2d 606, 50 Va. App. 703 (Va. Ct. App. 2007); see also Guyora Binder, *Felony Murder* 186 (Stanford 2012) (describing these jurisdictions as conditioning felony murder on malice, which is characterized by "the imposition of danger").

10. See Guyora Binder, *Felony Murder,* 186–89 (Stanford 2012) (describing the various constructions of malice in these jurisdictions).

11. "Murder is the unlawful killing of a human being . . . with malice aforethought. . . ." Idaho Code Ann. § 18-4001. "Any murder committed in the perpetration of, or attempt to perpetrate, aggravated battery on a child under twelve (12) years of age, arson, rape, robbery, burglary, kidnapping or mayhem, or an act of terrorism, . . . or the use of a weapon of mass destruction, biological weapon or chemical weapon, is murder of the first degree." Idaho Code Ann. § 18-4003. "The term malice does not necessarily import ill will toward the individual injured, but signifies rather a general malignant recklessness toward the lives and safety of others. Malice may be shown from the fact that an unlawful killing took place during the perpetration or attempted perpetration of the crime of robbery." State v. Lankford, 116 Idaho 860, 866, 781 P.2d 197, 203 (1989) (quoting jury instructions in approval).

"The unlawful killing of a human being with malice aforethought is murder. Every murder perpetrated by poison, lying in wait, or any other kind of willful, deliberate, malicious, and premeditated killing, or committed in the perpetration of, or attempt to perpetrate, any arson . . . , rape, any degree of sexual assault or child molestation, burglary or breaking and entering, robbery, kidnapping, or committed during the course of the perpetration, or attempted perpetration, of felony manufacture, sale, delivery, or other distribution of a controlled substance otherwise prohibited by [state law], . . . is murder in the first degree." 11 R.I. Gen. Laws Ann. § 11-23-1. "Homicide is murder if the death results from the perpetration or attempted perpetration of an inherently dangerous felony." In re Leon, 122 R.I. 548, 553, 410 A.2d 121, 124 (1980) (quoting Perkins, Criminal Law 44 (2d ed. 1969)).

12. See, e.g., Conn. Gen. Stat. Ann. § 53a-54c; D.C. Code Ann. § 22-2101; Fla. Stat. Ann. § 782.04; Md. Code Ann., Crim. Law § 2-201; Mo. Ann. Stat. § 565.021; Okla. Stat. Ann. tit. 21, § 701.7; see also Guyora Binder, *Felony Murder,* 183–89 (Stanford 2012) (sorting the nation's jurisdictions by what culpability requirement is required for felony murder liability).

13. "A person is guilty of murder when, acting either alone or with one or more persons, such person commits or attempts to commit robbery, home invasion, burglary, kidnapping, sexual assault in the first degree, aggravated sexual assault in the first degree, sexual assault in the third degree, sexual assault in the third degree with a firearm, escape in the first degree, or escape in the second degree and, in the course of and in furtherance of such crime or of flight therefrom, such person, or another participant, if any, causes the death of a person other than one of the participants, except that in any prosecution under this section, in which the defendant was not the only participant in the underlying crime, it shall be an affirmative defense that the defendant: (1) Did not commit the homicidal act or in any way solicit, request, command, importune, cause or aid the commission thereof; and (2) was not armed with a deadly weapon, or any dangerous instrument; and (3) had no reasonable ground to believe that any other participant was armed with such a weapon or instrument; and (4) had no reasonable ground to believe that any other participant intended to engage in conduct likely to result in death or serious physical injury." Conn. Gen. Stat. Ann. § 53a-54c.

"A person commits the crime of murder in the second degree if he [k]nowingly causes the death of another person or, with the purpose of causing serious physical injury to another person, causes the death of another person; . . . or [c]ommits or attempts to commit any felony, and, in the perpetration or the attempted perpetration of such felony or in the flight from the perpetration or attempted perpetration of such felony, another person is killed as a result of the perpetration or attempted perpetration of such felony or immediate flight from the perpetration of such felony or attempted perpetration of such felony." Mo. Ann. Stat. § 565.021.

"A person . . . commits the crime of murder in the first degree, regardless of malice, when that person or any other person takes the life of a human being during, or if the death of a human being results from, the commission or attempted commission of murder of another person, shooting or discharge of a firearm or crossbow with intent to kill, intentional discharge of a firearm or other deadly weapon into any dwelling or building . . . , forcible rape, robbery with a dangerous weapon, kidnapping, escape from lawful custody, eluding an officer, first degree burglary, first degree arson, unlawful distributing or dispensing of controlled dangerous substances or synthetic controlled substances, trafficking in illegal drugs, or manufacturing or attempting to manufacture a controlled dangerous substance." Okla. Stat. Ann. tit. 21, § 701.7.

14. See, e.g., Model Penal Code §1.02 (2007) (defining the general purposes of the Model Code's provisions governing the sentencing and correction of individual offenders to include goals of rehabilitation, general deterrence, incapacitation, and restorative justice, "provided that these goals are pursued within the boundaries" of what is required by desert).

15. See generally Paul H. Robinson, *Distributive Principles of Criminal Law: Who Should Be Punished How Much?* 21–98 (Oxford 2008) (discussing general deterrence).

16. See id. at 240–246; see generally Paul H. Robinson, *The A.L.I.'s Proposed Distributive Principle of "Limiting Retributivism": Does It Mean in Practice Anything Other Than Pure Desert?* 7 Buff. Crim. L. Rev. 3 (2003).

17. Paul H. Robinson, *The Rise and Fall and Resurrection of American Criminal Codes,* Conference Keynote Address, 53 U. Louisville Law Review 173–191 (2015); Paul H. Robinson and Michael T. Cahill, *The Accelerating Degradation of American Criminal Codes,* 56 Hastings Law Journal 633–655 (2005).

CHAPTER SEVEN

Causation

To secure a murder conviction, the prosecution must prove that at the time of the killing the defendant had the offense culpability required, typically that the person intended or knew that his conduct would cause the death. But that is not enough. Liability for murder also requires proof beyond a reasonable doubt that the person's conduct did *actually cause* the death—that there was a legally sufficient causal connection between the defendant's conduct and the death. This causation requirement exists even in cases of felony-murder, where often no culpability as to causing death need be shown. The prosecution still must prove that the causal connection between the actor's conduct and the death meets the legal requirements.[1]

Indeed, the legal requirements for causation must be shown not only for murder and other homicide offenses but also for every offense for which there is a result element of any kind. Assault offenses commonly require a result of bodily injury of a particular sort. Property damage offenses require proof of physical damage or destruction of property. Even minor offenses such as "obstructing a public highway" require proof of an adequate causal connection between the defendant's conduct and the prohibited obstruction. (Not every offense has a result element, however; in fact, most offenses do not.[2]) Empirical studies confirm that people share a strong intuition that, in the absence of an adequate causal connection, an offender's liability should be markedly reduced.[3] Where causation fails, the offense is at most an attempt to commit the offense, typically punished at one offense grade less than the substantive offense, which typically means half the maximum punishment.

The legal requirements for causation are of two sorts: the factual cause requirement (sometimes called the "but-for cause" requirement), and the proximate cause requirement (sometimes called the "legal cause" requirement). There is almost universal agreement on some aspects of these requirements but some noticeable differences regarding other aspects.

Regarding the factual cause requirement, it is almost universally agreed that an actor's conduct cannot be a factual cause of a result unless the result would not have occurred "but for" the actor's conduct.[4] That is, the actor's conduct must have been *necessary* for the result to occur when it did. If the same result would have occurred when it did even without the defendant's conduct, then the defendant's conduct cannot be a factual cause of that result.

The rule seems pretty simple, and it is. Things only get a bit complicated, and a bit messy, in situations where there are multiple causes by different actors contributing to a particular result. Even these situations can be simplified into a clear rule if the different actors are accomplices of one another, which is commonly the case. Each accomplice is accountable for the conduct of all other accomplices,[5] so, for the purposes of the factual causation analysis, all of the acts and all of the causal contributions by all of the accomplices can be lumped together as if they were performed by a single entity. The question then becomes: Was the combined effect of the conduct of all of these accomplices together a *but for* cause—a necessary cause—of the result?

The remaining issue is how to handle cases of multiple causes from independent actors who are *not* accomplices of one another. When Actor A attacks the victim and later Actor B attacks the same victim, is the first attacker, the second attacker, or both causally accountable for the resulting death? In most instances, the standard but-for test gives a clear answer: if an actor's conduct was *necessary* for the death—if the actor would not have died *but for* the actor's conduct—then the actor is a factual cause of the death.

There is, however, a quirk in the operation of the but-for test. If two independent actors each *simultaneously* inflict a lethal wound, each actor can accurately say that the victim would have died when he or she did even without that actor's lethal wounding. Two people acting independently shoot the victim at the same time, each inflicting a lethal wound. Neither actor's conduct was *necessary* for the death, given the other concurrent lethal wound. But clearly this seems an intuitively absurd result. Everyone seems to agree that both of these actors ought to be held causally accountable for the death. But to reach that proper result, a jurisdiction must adopt some kind of special rule that compensates for this quirk in the but-for test in cases of concurrent sufficient causes. As will become apparent from Map 7 and the analysis below, there is no universal agreement among the jurisdictions on how to best to fix the flaw.

The second causation requirement—the proximate cause requirement—is conceptually quite distinct from the factual cause requirement. The latter (factual cause requirement) asks a hypothetical scientific question: Would the prohibited result have occurred without the defendant's conduct? In contrast, the proximate cause requirement asks a more judgmental, normative question—a

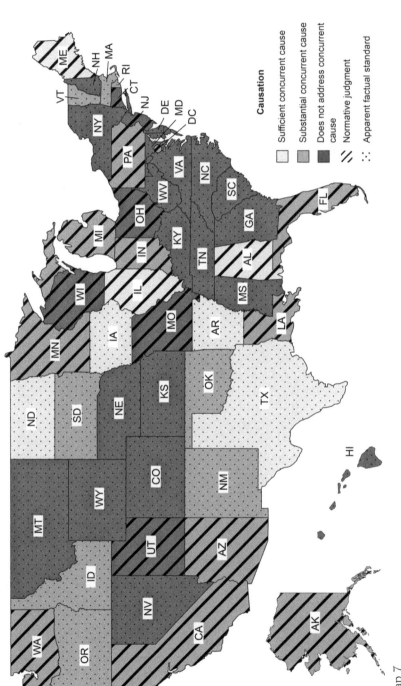

Causation

Sufficient concurrent cause

Substantial concurrent cause

Does not address concurrent cause

/// Normative judgment

∴∴ Apparent factual standard

Map 7

question that may not be answered strictly according to scientific calculation (depending on the jurisdiction's particular formulation of the proximate cause requirement). Specifically, even if an actor's conduct is necessary to bring about the prohibited result, is the nature of the causal connection between the actor's conduct and the result so remote or bizarre or accidental in its occurrence that the actor should not properly be held accountable for the result?

For example, assume the defendant shoots at the victim, intending to kill him, but misses. The victim runs away and 20 blocks later just happens to be under a piano that is being hauled up to the fourth floor when the rope breaks. The piano falls and kills the victim. The victim would not have died when he did *but for* the actor's conduct in shooting at him earlier, so the factual cause (but-for) requirement is satisfied. However, there is general agreement that this ought not be adequate for proximate cause; it ought not be a case of murder but rather a case of attempted murder, because the death by falling piano is simply too remote from the defendant's original conduct to have that original conduct count as the cause of the death.

To give another example, imagine the defendant intentionally inflicts a minor cut on the victim who is taken to the hospital. The cut is not serious but the doctor on duty is both incompetent and drunk and his treatment of the wound is so bad that the victim in fact dies. Again, while the defendant's original conduct of attacking the victim is a necessary factual cause for the death—the death would not have occurred *but for* the initial cutting that sent the victim to the hospital—most people would think that the defendant ought not be causally accountable for the death; the defendant's liability ought to be something less than murder, perhaps assault or aggravated assault.

As Map 7 and the analysis below suggest, however, jurisdictions take somewhat different views about how to formulate the proximate cause requirement.

Factual Causal Accountability If Sufficient Concurrent Cause

Recall from the discussion above the quirk in the but-for factual cause test that would seem to allow two independent actors simultaneously inflicting a lethal wound to escape causal accountability for the resulting death because each can accurately claim that their lethal wound was not necessary for the death—each can correctly claim that the victim would have died when he did even without their conduct.

A common way of fixing this flaw in the but-for test is to simply adopt a special rule. If each of two independent concurrent causes are sufficient to cause the result, then they will be deemed legally adequate to be a factual cause. This is the approach taken in seven jurisdictions: Alabama, Arkansas, Illinois, Iowa, Maine, North Dakota, and Texas.[6] They are shown with light shading on the map.

Factual Causal Accountability If Substantial Concurrent Cause

Other jurisdictions adopt a different rule: instead of requiring that each actor's conduct itself be sufficient to cause the result—for example, is lethal—they require only that each actor's conduct made a "substantial" contribution to the result. This is the approach taken in 19 jurisdictions: Alaska, Arizona, California, District of Columbia, Florida, Idaho, Indiana, Louisiana, Massachusetts, Michigan, Minnesota, New Mexico, Oklahoma, Oregon, Pennsylvania, Rhode Island, South Dakota, Vermont, and Washington.[7] They are shown with medium shading on the map.

Have Adopted No Solution to the Factual Cause But-For Test Problem in Concurrent-Cause Cases

Twenty-five jurisdictions, shown with darkest shading on the map, have simply failed to address the problem: Colorado, Connecticut, Delaware, Georgia, Hawaii, Kansas, Kentucky, Maryland, Mississippi, Missouri, Montana, Nebraska, Nevada, New Hampshire, New Jersey, New York, North Carolina, Ohio, South Carolina, Tennessee, Utah, Virginia, West Virginia, Wisconsin, and Wyoming. In these states, either the independent concurrent cause actors will get off from murder because their conduct does not satisfy the but-for test, or the state court will recognize the problem and on their own adopt one of the solutions used by the states in the two groups above.

One might normally criticize these states for failing to adopt any codified rule governing the factual cause requirement. Why should this criminalization authority be left to the determination of the courts? Like all other aspects of criminal law, why isn't the definition of causation requirements appropriately determined by the legislature? In this instance, however, some of these states may be forgiven their lapse. The American Law Institute's Model Penal Code, which served as the model for three-quarters of the criminal codes in the United States, failed miserably in its attempt to draft a model causation provision.[8] Faced with a model provision that made little sense to them, many states apparently chose not to codify any causation provision at all.

Proximate Cause as a Normative Judgment

Regarding the second causation requirement, the proximate cause requirement, 20 jurisdictions shown with diagonal lines on the map—Alabama, Alaska, Arizona, California, Connecticut, District of Columbia, Florida, Illinois, Indiana, Louisiana, Maine, Michigan, Minnesota, Missouri, New Jersey, Ohio, Pennsylvania, Utah, Washington, and Wisconsin[9]—adopt a proximate cause requirement that asks for an essentially normative judgment. For example, many jurisdictions follow the Model Penal Code and prescribe that proximate cause is established only if the actual result is "not too remote or accidental to have a *just* bearing on the actor's liability."[10] In the same vein, a jurisdiction may conclude that proximate cause is not established if it would be "*unfair* to hold him responsible" for the result, or may require that "the defendant may *fairly* be held responsible for the actual result."

The common denominator of these formulations is that they understand the proximate cause judgment to be a jury's intuitive judgment of what is fair and just to the defendant. The issue is not a factual one but a normative one.

Proximate Cause as an Apparent Factual Standard

A different approach, taken by 31 jurisdictions designated with dots on the map—Arkansas, Colorado, Delaware, Georgia, Hawaii, Idaho, Iowa, Kansas, Kentucky, Maryland, Massachusetts, Mississippi, Montana, Nebraska, Nevada, New Hampshire, New Mexico, New York, North Carolina, North Dakota, Oklahoma, Oregon, Rhode Island, South Carolina, South Dakota, Tennessee, Texas, Vermont, Virginia, West Virginia, and Wyoming[11]—presents the proximate cause issue as if it were a factual one of some sort. The defendant's conduct is the proximate cause of a result if the result was a "natural and probable consequence" or the result was "reasonably foreseeable" or the result was "a substantial and currently operative factor in bringing about the result" or the result "falls within the scope of the risk" or the conduct "directly" caused the result.

In reality, these standards are so broad as to ultimately require the same kind of normative judgment of a jury that one sees in the category above. That is, how is a jury to decide whether the defendant's conduct was a "substantial" factor? How is a jury to decide whether the result was "reasonably" foreseeable? Ultimately, despite the attempt to clothe the standard in apparent factual terms, the jury will have to make some kind of normative judgment in deciding the issue.

Nonetheless, the approach is noticeably different from that of the group above because these jurisdictions wish to hide or at least downplay the normative nature of the judgment.

Observations and Speculations

Causation is an area that nicely illustrates the criminal law's strong commitment to tracking people's shared intuitions of justice. For example, one can identify all sorts of technical criticisms of the factual cause but-for test.

The test has an actor's causal accountability depend on the lethality *of the other actor's conduct*, for example, not on the lethality of his own conduct. (If the other person's conduct is nonlethal, then the actor's conduct was necessary to cause the death and therefore is a factual cause of the death. If the other person's conduct is lethal, then the actor's conduct was not necessary for the death and is not a factual cause of the death.) Another example of the technical peculiarity of the but-for test is its apparently erroneous results in the case of the concurrent lethal wounds from independent actors, discussed above.

Yet, despite these problems, the test is almost universally relied on in determining factual causation. Why? Because its operation in the typical case best reflects people's shared intuitions of justice.

The issue of proximate cause teaches the same lesson. Whether the legal formulation openly admits its reliance on people's intuitions of justice—"not too remote or accidental to have a just bearing on the actor's liability"—or whether the legal formulation relies on such intuitions of justice in a less open way—by asking a jury if a result was "reasonably" foreseeable or was a "substantial" factor—in the end, it is clear that proximate cause judgments necessarily depend on people's intuitive judgments of justice.

If the legal doctrine could bring itself to admit this reality—that the law necessarily depends on people's shared intuitions of justice—it might be in a better position to more accurately capture those shared justice judgments. To give one example, the empirical studies make it clear that people's judgments of justice on causation matters would have an actor's extent of criminal liability reflect *the strength* of the actor's causal contribution to the prohibited result. That is, people don't think of causation in purely binary terms: causation, and thus liability for the full substantive offense, versus no causation, thus liability only for an attempt (at typically half the punishment). Instead, people see a continuum of causal accountability and believe that an offender's liability ought to shift incrementally depending on the strength of the causal connection.

In a study of proximate cause cases, for example, the study's subjects assigned varying degrees of liability to different proximate cause cases involving a variety of situations that tend to weaken the original attacker's causal accountability (the victim's unexpected allergy to a medication at the hospital, an incompetent nurse, unexpected causal paths such as the "falling piano," etc.).[12] The legal doctrine asks in each case whether the causation requirements are satisfied and, if they are, imposes full liability for the substantive offense. If the requirements are not satisfied, the law imposes liability only for an attempt. The test subjects, in contrast, impose liability along a continuous curve that runs between attempt liability and full substantive liability, depending on the strength of the causal connection.

If the law were to acknowledge its role as capturing people's shared intuitions of justice, it would forgo the binary approach that it currently uses in favor of a mechanism that allows judgments on the strength of the causal connection, whereby the extent of liability varies with the strength of that connection.

Notes

1. Paul H. Robinson and Michael T. Cahill, *Criminal Law,* 2nd ed. §3.2 (Wolters Kluwer 2012).

2. Robinson and Cahill, *Criminal Law,* 2nd ed. §3.1 (Wolters Kluwer 2012).

3. See Paul H. Robinson, *Intuitions of Justice and the Utility of Desert,* 385–93 (Oxford 2013).

4. The but-for requirement is part of common understanding of factual cause in the criminal law context. See Burrage v. United States, 134 S. Ct. 881, 887–92 (2014) (rejecting the government's argument that, under the Controlled Substances Act, a victim's death "results from" illegal drugs when the drug merely "contributes to an aggregate force" that leads to death). Some courts have suggested that a "contribution" test has replaced the traditional but-for test of factual causation. See, e.g., Com. v. McLeod, 394 Mass. 727, 735, 477 N.E.2d 972, 979 (1985); People v. Bailey, 451 Mich. 657, 676, 549 N.W.2d 325, 334, amended on denial of reh'g, 453 Mich. 1204, 551 N.W.2d 163 (1996); State v. Dorn, 875 N.W.2d 357, 362 (Minn. Ct. App.), review granted (Apr. 19, 2016), aff'd, 887 N.W.2d 826 (Minn. 2016).

5. Robinson and Cahill, *Criminal Law,* 2nd ed. §6.1 (Wolters Kluwer 2012).

6. Ala. Code § 13A-2-5; Ark. Code Ann. § 5-2-205; People v. Nere, 2017 IL App (2d) 141143, ¶ 103; State v. Tribble, 790 N.W.2d 121, 127 (Iowa 2010); Me. Rev. Stat. Ann. tit. 17-A, § 33; N.D. Cent. Code § 12.1-02-05; Tex. Penal Code Ann. § 6.04.

7. Adams v. State, 359 P.3d 990 (Alaska App. 2015); Ariz. Rev. Stat. Ann. § 13-203; State v. Marty, 166 Ariz. 233, 236, 801 P.2d 468, 471 (Ct. App. 1990); People v. Jennings, 50 Cal. 4th 616, 643, 237 P.3d 474, 496 (2010); Roy v. United States, 871 A.2d 498, 506 (D.C. 2005); Blaize v. United States, 21 A.3d 78, 82 (D.C. 2011); Eversley v. State, 748 So. 2d 963, 967 (Fla. 1999); State v. Wisdom, 161 Idaho 916, 921, 393 P.3d 576, 581 (2017); Bowman v. State, 564 N.E.2d 309, 313 (Ind. Ct. App. 1990), aff'd in part, vacated in part, 577 N.E.2d 569 (Ind. 1991); State v. Matthews, 450 So. 2d 644, 646 (La. 1984); State v. Small, 2011–2796 (La. 10/16/12), 100 So. 3d 797, 812; Com. v. Osachuk, 43 Mass. App. Ct. 71, 73, 681 N.E.2d 292, 294 (1997); Com. v. McLeod, 394 Mass. 727, 735, 477 N.E.2d 972, 979 (1985); Com. v. Osachuk, 43 Mass. App. Ct. 71, 73, 681 N.E.2d 292, 294 (1997); People v. Bailey, 451 Mich. 657, 676, 549 N.W.2d 325, 334, amended on denial of reh'g, 453 Mich. 1204, 551 N.W.2d 163 (1996); People v. Tims, 449 Mich. 83, 95, 534 N.W.2d 675, 680 (1995); State v. Dorn, 875 N.W.2d 357, 362 (Minn. Ct. App.), review granted (Apr. 19, 2016), aff'd, 887 N.W.2d 826 (Minn. 2016); State v. Southern, 304 N.W.2d 329, 330 (Minn. 1981); State v. Montoya, 2003-NMSC-004, ¶ 21, 133 N.M. 84, 90, 61 P.3d 793, 799; Ochoa v. State, 1998 OK CR 41, ¶ 50, 963 P.2d 583, 600; State v. Turnidge, 359 Or. 364, 471, 374 P.3d

853, 918 (2016), cert. denied, 137 S. Ct. 665, 196 L. Ed. 2d 554 (2017); State v. Petersen, 17 Or. App. 478, 489, 522 P.2d 912, 918, aff'd in part, rev'd in part, 270 Or. 166, 526 P.2d 1008 (1974); Pa. Cons. Stat. Ann. tit. 18, § 303; Com. v. Buterbaugh, 2014 PA Super 102, 91 A.3d 1247, 1258 (2014); State v. Texieira, 944 A.2d 132, 141 (R.I. 2008); State v. Watkins, 448 A.2d 1260, 1265 (R.I. 1982); State v. Two Bulls, 1996 S.D. 53, 10, ¶ 10, 547 N.W.2d 764, 765–66; State v. Sexton, 2006 VT 55, ¶ 96, 180 Vt. 34, 78, 904 A.2d 1092, 1124–25 (2006); State v. Christman, 160 Wash. App. 741, 755, 249 P.3d 680, 687 (2011); State v. McDonald, 953 P.2d 470, 474 (Wash. Ct. App. 1998). Note that Oregon courts have held that causation, for purposes of criminal liability, is purely a matter of factual causation. See State v. Petersen, 17 Or. App. 478, 489, 522 P.2d 912, 918, aff'd in part, rev'd in part, 270 Or. 166, 526 P.2d 1008 (1974).

8. See Paul H. Robinson, *The Model Penal Code's Conceptual Error on the Nature of Proximate Cause, and How to Fix It,* 51 Criminal Law Bulletin 1311 (2015).

9. Witherspoon v. State, 33 So. 3d 625, 630 (Ala. Crim. App. 2009); Johnson v. State, 224 P.3d 105, 111 (Alaska 2010); State v. Sommerfield, 2017 WL 3597411, at *3 (Ariz. Ct. App. Aug. 22, 2017); State v. Marty, 166 Ariz. 233, 237, 801 P.2d 468, 472 (Ct. App. 1990); Ariz. Rev. Stat. Ann. § 13-203; People v. Acosta, 232 Cal. App. 3d 1375, 284 Cal. Rptr. 117, 121 (Ct. App. 1991); State v. Leroy, 232 Conn. 1, 6, 653 A.2d 161, 163 (1995); McKinnon v. United States, 550 A.2d 915, 917 (D.C. 1988); Roy v. United States, 871 A.2d 498, 507 (D.C. 2005); Eversley v. State, 748 So. 2d 963, 967 (Fla. 1999); Santarelli v. State, 62 So. 3d 1211, 1214–15 (Fla. Dist. Ct. App. 2011); People v. Hudson, 222 Ill. 2d 392, 401, 856 N.E.2d 1078, 1083 (2006); Duncan v. State, 857 N.E.2d 955, 958 (Ind. 2006); Bowman v. State, 564 N.E.2d 309, 313 (Ind. Ct. App. 1990), aff'd in part, vacated in part, 577 N.E.2d 569 (Ind. 1991); State v. Phillips, 514 So. 2d 743, 745–46 (La. Ct. App. 1987); State v. Kalathakis, 563 So. 2d 228, 231 (La. 1990); State v. Peaslee, 571 A.2d 825, 827 (Me. 1990); State v. Snow, 464 A.2d 958, 962 (Me. 1983); People v. Tims, 449 Mich. 83, 122, 534 N.W.2d 675, 692 (1995); State v. Meeks, No. A10-767, 2011 WL 1743748, at *8 (Minn. Ct. App. May 9, 2011); State v. Burton, 370 S.W.3d 926, 931 (Mo. Ct. App. 2012); State v. Huff, 789 S.W.2d 71, 77 (Mo. Ct. App. 1990); N.J. Stat. Ann. § 2C:2-3; State v. Pelham, 176 N.J. 448, 475, 824 A.2d 1082, 1098 (2003); State v. Maldonado, 137 N.J. 536, 566, 645 A.2d 1165, 1179–80 (1994); State v. Lovelace, 137 Ohio App. 3d 206, 216, 738 N.E.2d 418, 425 (1999); State v. Buck, No. C-000425, 2001 WL 557875, at *3 (Ohio Ct. App. May 25, 2001); State v. Dykas, 2010-Ohio-359, ¶ 25, 185 Ohio App. 3d 763, 770, 925 N.E.2d 685, 691; State v. Mills, 2011-Ohio-5793, ¶ 34; State v. Winbush, 2017-Ohio-696, ¶ 62; Com. v. Rementer, 410 Pa. Super. 9, 18–19, 598 A.2d 1300, 1304–05 (1991); 18 Pa. Stat. and Cons. Stat. Ann. § 303; State v. Dunn, 850 P.2d 1201, 1215 (Utah 1993); State v. Christman, 160 Wash. App. 741, 753, 249 P.3d 680, 686 (2011); State v. Bauer, 174 Wash. App. 59, 72, 295 P.3d 1227, 1233–34 (2013), rev'd, 180 Wash. 2d 929, 329 P.3d 67 (2014); State v. Brouillette, 179 Wis. 2d 504, 508 N.W.2d 75 (Ct. App. 1993).

10. Model Penal Code §2.03(2)(b), (3)(b) (emphasis added).

11. Jefferson v. State, 372 Ark. 307, 314, 276 S.W.3d 214, 220–21 (2008); People v. Saavedra-Rodriguez, 971 P.2d 223, 225–26 (Colo. 1998), as modified (Feb. 11, 1999); Del. Code Ann. tit. 11, § 263; Rivers v. State, 296 Ga. 396, 404, 768 S.E.2d 486, 493 (2015); Haw. Rev. Stat. Ann. § 702-215; State v. Grant, 125 Haw. 381, 262 P.3d 670 (Ct. App. 2011); State v. Corbus, 150 Idaho 599, 603, 249 P.3d 398, 402 (2011); State v. McFadden, 320 N.W.2d 608, 613 (Iowa 1982); State v. Hensley, 672 N.W.2d 333 (Iowa Ct. App. 2003); State v. Mays, 277 Kan. 359, 379, 85 P.3d 1208, 1222 (2004); Ky. Rev. Stat. Ann. § 501.060; Robertson v. Com., 82 S.W.3d 832, 836 (Ky. 2002); Castle v. Commonwealth, No. 2014-CA-000970-MR, 2016 WL 4410098, at *4 (Ky. Ct. App. Aug. 19, 2016); Palmer v. State, 223 Md. 341, 353, 164 A.2d 467, 474 (1960); Com. v. McLeod, 394 Mass. 727, 735–36, 477 N.E.2d 972, 979–80 (1985); Williams v. State, 154 So. 3d 64, 69 (Miss. Ct. App. 2014); Goudy v. State, 203 Miss. 366, 370–71, 35 So. 2d 308, 309 (1948); Mont. Code Ann. § 45-2-201; State v. Sherer, 2002 MT 337, ¶ 19, 313 Mont. 299, 304, 60 P.3d 1010, 1013; State v. William, 231 Neb. 84, 88, 435 N.W.2d 174, 177 (1989); State v. Irish, 292 Neb. 513, 520–21, 873 N.W.2d 161, 168 (2016); McClain v. State, 127 Nev. 1158, 373 P.3d 940 (2011); Garrett v. State, No. 62191, 2014 WL 590479, at *1 (Nev. Feb. 12, 2014); State v. Seymour, 140 N.H. 736, 745–46, 673 A.2d 786, 794 (1996); State v. Lamprey, 149 N.H. 364, 367, 821 A.2d 1080, 1083–84 (2003); State v. Elliott, 133 N.H. 759, 763, 585 A.2d 304, 306 (1990); State v. Seymour, 140 N.H. 736, 745–46, 673 A.2d 786, 794 (1996); State v. Lamprey, 149 N.H. 364, 367, 821 A.2d 1080, 1083–84 (2003); State v. Elliott, 133 N.H. 759, 763, 585 A.2d 304, 306 (1990); State v. Hernandez, 1994-NMSC-045, ¶ 6, 117 N.M. 497, 499, 873 P.2d 243, 245; State v. Munoz, 1998-NMSC-041, ¶ 22, 126 N.M. 371, 376, 970 P.2d 143, 148; People v. DaCosta, 6 N.Y.3d 181, 184, 844 N.E.2d 762, 764 (2006); People v. Sadacca, 128 Misc. 2d 494, 499, 489 N.Y.S.2d 824, 828 (Sup. Ct. 1985); People v. Kibbe, 35 N.Y.2d 407, 412, 321 N.E.2d 773, 776 (1974); State v. Cummings, 46 N.C. App. 680, 683, 265 S.E.2d 923, 925–26, aff'd, 301 N.C. 374, 271 S.E.2d 277 (1980); State v. Williams, 203 N.C. App. 150, 692 S.E.2d 195 (2010); State v. Broom, 225 N.C. App. 137, 143, 736 S.E.2d 802, 808 (2013); N.D. Cent. Code Ann. § 12.1-02-05; State v. Ceasar, 2010 OK CR 15, ¶ 11, 237 P.3d 792, 794–95; State v. Turnidge, 359 Or. 364, 374 P.3d 853 (2016), cert. denied, 137 S. Ct. 665, 196 L. Ed. 2d 554 (2017); State v. Biechele, No. K1-03-653A, 2005 WL 3338331, at *8 (R.I. Super. Dec. 5, 2005); State v. Watkins, 448 A.2d 1260, 1265 (R.I. 1982); State v. Dantonio, 376 S.C. 594, 608–09, 658 S.E.2d 337, 345 (Ct. App. 2008); State v. Two Bulls, 1996 S.D. 53, 10, ¶ 10, 547 N.W.2d 764, 765; State v. Pack, 421 S.W.3d 629, 640 (Tenn. Crim. App. 2013); State v. Richardson, 995 S.W.2d 119, 125 (Tenn. Crim. App. 1998); State v. Farner, 66 S.W.3d 188, 203 (Tenn. 2001); Thompson v. State, 236 S.W.3d 787, 798 (Tex. Crim. App. 2007); State v. Sullivan, 2017 VT 24, ¶ 17 (Vt. Apr. 14, 2017); Rivers v. State, 133 Vt. 11, 14, 328 A.2d 398, 400 (1974); State v. Dodge, 152 Vt. 503, 505, 567 A.2d 1143, 1144 (1989); Coyle v. Com., 50 Va. App. 656, 666, 653 S.E.2d 291, 296 (2007); Wagoner v. Com., 289 Va. 476, 485, 770 S.E.2d 479, 484 (2015); Brown v. Com., 278 Va. 523, 529, 685 S.E.2d 43, 46 (2009); State v.

Surbaugh, 237 W. Va. 242, 255, 786 S.E.2d 601, 614, cert. denied sub nom. Surbaugh v. W. Virginia, 137 S. Ct. 448, 196 L. Ed. 2d 331 (2016); Grimes v. State, 2013 WY 84, ¶ 10, 304 P.3d 972, 975 (Wyo. 2013); Edwards v. State, 2007 WY 146, ¶ 10, 167 P.3d 636, 639 (Wyo. 2007).

12. See Paul H. Robinson, *Intuitions of Justice and the Utility of Desert*, 385–93 (Oxford 2013).

PART 3

Liability Doctrines

CHAPTER EIGHT

Transferred Intent

Culpability requirements play a central role in criminal law. Unlike civil liability for some civil wrongs, a criminal offender does not deserve punishment or the condemnation of criminal conviction simply because he caused a harm. Criminal liability depends on his having some personal culpability as to causing the harm, such as intending to cause the harm. Even if he does not intend the harm but only knows that it will occur because of his conduct, his culpability is typically enough to support criminal liability. Indeed, it is commonly enough that his awareness of a substantial risk that his conduct would cause the harm—he was reckless as to causing the harm—is enough for criminal liability, albeit at a reduced level. Finally, while it is controversial in some quarters, the majority rule would allow criminal liability for serious wrongdoing, such as homicide, based on negligence—that is, although unaware of a substantial risk that his conduct would cause the death, the offender should have been aware of such a risk; a reasonable person in his situation would have been aware of such a risk. Again, when criminal liability is based on only negligence, the corresponding punishment is typically reduced accordingly.

But what is one to do in a situation like the following? The offender, intending to kill X, shoots at X, misses, and completely accidentally kills Y. He may have had not the slightest inkling that Y was even in the area and may consider the death of Y a serious tragedy. Should he be held liable for causing Y's death and, if so, for what offense? Murder? Reckless homicide (manslaughter)? Negligent homicide? (Though he did not cause the death of X, at whom he was shooting, he might nonetheless be liable for the attempted murder of X.)

The offender was at most negligent, and perhaps not even that, as to causing the death of Y. A reasonable person in his situation might well have had no reason to think that Y was even in the area. Should we say, then, that the

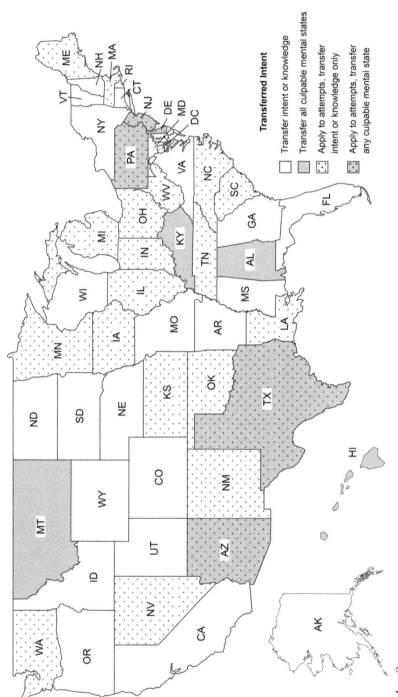

Transferred Intent

☐ Transfer intent or knowledge

▨ Transfer all culpable mental states

⊡ Apply to attempts, transfer intent or knowledge only

⊡ Apply to attempts, transfer any culpable mental state

Map 8

killing of Y was completely accidental, an unfortunate tragedy for which he has no criminal responsibility, and that he should be held liable only for the attempted murder of X? (Typically, attempted murder is punished an offense grade lower than murder, which typically is about half the penalty.)

The approach that criminal law traditionally takes in such cases is to take the offender's intention to kill X and to "transfer" it to Y, thereby allowing the offender to be held liable for the murder of Y even though Y's death was entirely unforeseen and unforeseeable. That is, the doctrine of *transferred intent* allows the person's culpable mental state as to causing a particular result, such as intending the death of X, to be used as the basis for justifying the imputation to the person on a culpable state of mind that he does not actually have, such as the intention to kill Y.

Should the same "transfer" of culpability be applied in cases where the offender is reckless as to causing the death of X—he consciously disregards a substantial risk that his conduct will cause X's death—and ends up unforeseeably causing Y's death? In other words, should the criminal law "transfer" not only intention but also the lesser culpability of recklessness or negligence?

One final, related question asks whether the criminal law should transfer culpability not only in cases of completed offenses, such as homicide, but also in cases of failed attempts. For example, if the offender shoots at what he thinks is X intending to kill him (in fact X is nowhere around) but misses and instead injures a bystander Y, who he has no intention or desire to hurt. Should he be liable for the attempted murder of Y even though he lacked any intention to kill Y?

Map 8 shows each state's position on each of these issues.

Transfer Only Intent or Knowledge, Not in Attempt Cases

Every jurisdiction permits liability by imputing a culpable mental state on a theory of transferred intent, but jurisdictions vary according to which mental states may be imputed in this way, and whether transferred intent may give rise to liability for attempts (or for substantive offenses whose elements include an attempt, such as certain assault with intent to kill statutes). In the "transfer intent or knowledge" jurisdictions, the law permits intent, purpose, or knowledge to be imputed on a theory of transferred intent, but not lesser culpability levels of recklessness or negligence. Further, these jurisdictions do not permit transferred intent to give rise to liability for attempts.

This most narrow version of the transferred intent doctrine is adopted in the 23 jurisdictions with no shading on the map: Alaska, Arkansas, California, Colorado, Connecticut, Florida, Georgia, Idaho, Maryland, Mississippi, Missouri, Nebraska, New Hampshire, New York, North Dakota, Oregon, Rhode Island, South Dakota, Utah, Vermont, Virginia, Wisconsin, and Wyoming.[1]

Transfer All Culpability Levels, Not in Attempt Cases

Four other states, shown with shading on the map—Alabama, Hawaii, Kentucky, and Montana—permit all mental states to be imputed on a theory of transferred intent, including wantonness, recklessness, or negligence. For instance, where the defendant threw a poker at her child for correction under circumstances which, if it had killed the child, would have made her guilty of manslaughter, a court held that she would be equally guilty where the poker accidentally hits and kills another child.[2]

Together with the first group above, then, 27 jurisdictions permit transferred culpability but do not permit the doctrine to be applied in prosecutions for attempt. Twelve of these 27 jurisdictions have expressly rejected attempt liability on a theory of transferred intent: Alabama, Alaska, Arkansas, California, Connecticut, Florida, Maryland, Mississippi, Missouri, New York, South Dakota, and Virginia.[3] The remaining 15 states have simply never extended the doctrine of transferred intent to attempts, yet have not conclusively rejected the theory: Colorado, Georgia, Hawaii, Idaho, Kentucky, Montana, Nebraska, New Hampshire, North Dakota, Oregon, Rhode Island, Utah, Vermont, Wisconsin, and Wyoming.

Transfer Intent or Knowledge Even in Cases of Attempt

Some jurisdictions permit transferred intent to give rise to liability for attempts or for certain substantive offenses that include an attempt element, such as certain assault with intent to kill statutes. For instance, a person who intends to kill one party but instead accidentally injures another party, may be liable for attempted murder of that other party. Nineteen jurisdictions, shown with no shading but with dots, take this approach: District of Columbia, Illinois, Indiana, Iowa, Kansas, Louisiana, Maine, Massachusetts, Michigan, Minnesota, Nevada, New Mexico, North Carolina, Ohio, Oklahoma, South Carolina, Tennessee, Washington, and West Virginia.[4]

Transfer All Levels Even in Cases of Attempt

Five jurisdictions, designated with shading and dots on the map—Arizona, Delaware, New Jersey, Pennsylvania, and Texas—permit transferred intent to give rise to liability for attempts and permit all mental states to be imputed, including wantonness, recklessness, or negligence. (Of course, because attempt commonly requires intent or purpose, transferred recklessness may not be sufficient to give rise to attempt liability.)

The 5 jurisdictions in this group and the 19 jurisdictions in the group above mean that 24 states have expressly permitted liability for an attempt on a theory of transferred intent. They are the jurisdictions with an overlay of dots on the map: Arizona, Delaware, District of Columbia, Illinois, Indiana, Iowa, Kansas, Louisiana, Maine, Massachusetts, Michigan, Minnesota, Nevada, New Jersey, New Mexico, North Carolina, Ohio, Oklahoma, Pennsylvania, South Carolina, Tennessee, Texas, Washington, and West Virginia.[5]

The five states in this group and the four states in the second group above mean that a total of nine states permit the transfer of recklessness or negligence. They are the jurisdictions with dark shading on the map: Alabama, Arizona, Delaware, Hawaii, Kentucky, Montana, New Jersey, Pennsylvania, and Texas.[6]

Observations and Speculations

Some courts and scholars have been critical of the entire notion of "imputing" a required offense element that does not in fact exist, as the doctrine of transferred intent does, but the fact is that such imputation is not only quite principled but also quite common in criminal law.[7] The doctrine of voluntary intoxication, for example, regularly imputes culpability to an actor—treats him as if he had a required offense culpability element that he did not in fact have—when he would have had such element had he been sober. Similarly, the doctrine of complicity imputes to an actor another person's conduct—treats her as if she had engaged in such conduct—whenever the persons satisfies the special requirements for accomplice liability.

There is nothing unusual or unprincipled about imputation itself. The critical question in each instance is, rather, whether the basis for the imputation— the conditions required before imputation is allowed—in fact provides an adequate basis to fairly treat the defendant as if he had the offense element that is being imputed to him. A person who voluntarily intoxicates himself and thereby is unaware of a risk that he would have been aware of had he remained sober, can at least arguably be held as having created the unawareness by his own conduct, and therefore should be legally responsible for it.[8]

There are some doctrines of imputation, however, where the imputation goes beyond what may be fairly justified by the circumstances that trigger the imputation. For example, it is unclear what the principled basis is for treating a defendant as if he had a culpable state of mind that he does not in fact have because of his mental illness, yet many jurisdictions adopt rules that provide for just such imputation.[9]

In contrast, the doctrine of transferred intent under discussion here is one of the doctrines of imputation that would seem to be defensible under the conditions that it requires in order to be applied. Where the offender shoots at X intending to kill him and instead unforeseeably kills Y, it is no great leap to see the offender's intention to kill X as morally equivalent to an intention to kill Y, and thus appropriate to impute that intention to him and hold him liable for the murder of Y.

The same can be said for any culpability level, including recklessness, for example: consciously disregarding a substantial risk that his conduct will cause X's death is the moral equivalent of consciously disregarding a substantial risk that his conduct will cause Y's death. Thus, those jurisdictions that go beyond transferred intent to allow the transfer of recklessness also seem to be on sound moral ground.

This is also true of the application of transferred culpability doctrines in instances of a different victim than intended. For example, where the offender thought he was raping an unconscious woman but she had in fact just died from a heart attack, the doctrine of transferred culpability can properly hold the person liable for the offense of abusing a dead body even though he did not have the culpability normally required for the offense (he reasonably believed the woman was alive). Although he did not have the required offense culpability, he did have the considerably more serious intention to rape, and that provides a strong moral justification to impute to him the required culpability of abusing a dead body.

There is a potential for unfairness where the seriousness of the offenses is reversed: for example, where the peculiar morgue attendant believes he is having intercourse with a dead body when in fact the woman is still alive and has been erroneously declared to be dead by the doctors. The morgue attendant's intention to commit the less serious offense of abusing a dead body may serve as the basis for convicting him of rape, even though he did not have the culpability required for rape (believing that his victim was alive). Here, justice would seem to require that his rape conviction carry an offense grade no higher than that for the mistreatment of a dead body that he thought he was committing. And, indeed, this is exactly the rule that the Model Penal Code follows in its formulation of its general doctrine for imputing culpability elements under Model Penal Code section 2.04(2).[10]

Notes

1. See notes 3, 5–6 infra.

2. Rex v. Conner (1836) 7 Car. & P. (Eng.) 438.

3. See Cockrell v. State, 890 So. 2d 174, 177 (Ala. 2004); Ramsey v. State, 56 P.3d 675 (Alaska App.2002); Jones v. State, 159 Ark. 215, 251 S.W. 690 (1923); People v. Chinchilla, 52 Cal. App.4th 683, 60 Cal. Rptr.2d 761, 765 (1997); People v. Calderon, 232 Cal. App.3d 930, 283 Cal. Rptr. 833 (1991); People v. Bland, 28 Cal.4th 313, 121 Cal. Rptr.2d 546, 48 P.3d 1107 (2002); People v. Czahara, 203 Cal. App.3d 1468 (1st App. Dist. 1988); State v. Hinton, 630 A.2d 593 (Conn.1993); State v. Brady, 745 So. 2d 954, 958 (Fla. 1999); State v. Brady, 393 Md. 502, 521–22, 903 A.2d 870, 881–82 (2006); Harrison v. State, 382 Md. 477, 855 A.2d 1220 (2004); Harvey v. State, 111 Md. App. 401, 681 A.2d 628 (1996); Craig v. State, 201 So. 3d 1108, 1113 (Miss. Ct. App. 2016); State v. Williamson, 203 Mo. 591,

102 S.W. 519 (1907); State v. Mulhall, 199 Mo. 202, 97 S.W. 583 (1906); State v. Martin, 119 S.W.2d 298, 302 (Mo. 1938); People v. Fernandez, 88 N.Y.2d 777, 650 N.Y.S.2d 625, 673 N.E.2d 910, 914 (1996); State v. Shanley, 20 S.D. 18, 104 N.W. 522 (1905); State v. Herbert, 234 W. Va. 576, 590, 767 S.E.2d 471, 485 (2014).

    4. See notes 3, 5–6.

    5. See State v. Rodriguez-Gonzales, 164 Ariz. 1, 790 P.2d 287, 288 (Ct. App. 1990); Robinson v. State, 620 A.2d 859 (Del. 1992); Lloyd v. United States, 806 A.2d 1243, 1250 (D.C. 2002); West v. United States, 866 A.2d 74, 80 (D.C. 2005); Brooks v. United States, 655 A.2d 844, 848 (D.C. 1995); People v. Dorn, 378 Ill. App. 3d 693, 700, 883 N.E.2d 584, 589 (2008); Blanche v. State, 690 N.E.2d 709, 712 (Ind.1998); State v. Alford, 151 N.W.2d 573, 575 (Iowa 1967); State v. Kelley, 339 P.3d 412 (Kan. Ct. App. 2014); State v. Daniels, 326 P.3d 1089 (Kan. Ct. App. 2014); State v. Carrasco, 380 P.3d 721 (Kan. Ct. App. 2016); State v. Thomas, 127 La. 576, 53 So. 868, 869 (1910); State v. Gilman, 69 Me. 163 (1879); Com. v. Melton, 436 Mass. 291, 292, 763 N.E.2d 1092, 1094 (2002); Com. v. Thomas, 469 Mass. 531, 552b, 21 N.E.3d 901, 921 (2014); People v. Tolbert, No. 298159, 2011 WL 6186840, at *1 (Mich. Ct. App. Dec. 13, 2011); People v. Lovett, 90 Mich. App. 169, 175, 283 N.W.2d 357, 360 (1979); People v. Ollie, No. 272247, 2008 WL 108952, at *3 (Mich. Ct. App. Jan. 10, 2008); State v. Livingston, 420 N.W.2d 223, 229 (Minn. Ct. App. 1988); Ochoa v. State, 115 Nev. 194, 981 P.2d 1201, 1204–1205 (1999); State v. Worlock, 569 A.2d 1314, 1325 (N.J. 1990); State v. Lockett, No. A-4607-11T4, 2014 WL 2807521; State v. Gillette, 102 N.M. 695, 699 P.2d 626, 635–636 (Ct. App. 1985); State v. Andrews, 572 S.E.2d 798, 802 (N.C. Ct. App. 2002); State v. Morston, 336 N.C. 381, 445 S.E.2d 1 (1994); State v. Dean, 2015-Ohio-4347, ¶ 147, 146 Ohio St. 3d 106, 134, 54 N.E.3d 80, 116; Short v. State, 980 P.2d 1081, 1098 (Okla. Crim. App. 1999); Com. v. Leach, No. 2618 EDA 2013, 2014 WL 10803154, at *5 (Pa. Super. Ct. Aug. 15, 2014); Com. v. Thompson, 559 Pa. 229, 739 A.2d 1023 (1999); Com. v. Jackson, 955 A.2d 441, 444 (Pa. Super. 2008); State v. Fennell, 531 S.E.2d 512, 517 (S.C. 2000); State v. Claxton, No. W2009-01679-CCA-R3CD, 2011 WL 807459, at *6 (Tenn. Crim. App. Mar. 7, 2011); Jackson v. State, No. W2006-00606-CCA-R3HC, 2007 WL 273649, at *1 (Tenn. Crim. App. Jan. 31, 2007); State v. Pulliam, No. M2001-00417-CCA-R3CD, 2002 WL 122928, at *5 (Tenn. Crim. App. Jan. 23, 2002); Millen v. State, 988 S.W.2d 164, 168 (Tenn.1999); Jones v. State, 89 Tex. Crim. 355, 357, 231 S.W. 122, 123 (1921); Johnson v. State, 151 Tex. Crim. 405, 408, 208 S.W.2d 94, 96 (1948); Martinez v. State, 844 S.W.2d 279 (Tex. App. 1992); State v. Elmi, 166 Wash. 2d 209, 207 P.3d 439 (2009); State v. Herbert, 234 W. Va. 576, 590, 767 S.E.2d 471, 485 (2014).

    6. Ala. Code § 13A-2-5; Ariz. Rev. Stat. Ann. § 13-203; Del. Code Ann. tit. 11, § 262; Haw. Rev. Stat. Ann. § 702-215; Haw. Rev. Stat. Ann. § 702-216; Ky. Rev. Stat. Ann. § 501.060; Phillips v. Com., 17 S.W.3d 870 (Ky. 2000); Mont. Code Ann. § 45-2-201; N.J. Stat. Ann. § 2C:2-3; 18 Pa. Stat. and Cons. Stat. Ann. § 303; Tex. Penal Code Ann. § 6.04. The following cases state or imply that recklessness may be transferred: Hill v. State (1914) 74 Tex. Crim. Rep. 481, 168 S.W.

864; Whiten v. State (1913) 71 Tex. Crim. Rep. 555, 160 S.W. 462; Clark v. State (1885) 19 Tex. App. 495; Rex v. Conner (1836) 7 Car. & P. (Eng.) 438; Shelton v. Com. (1911) 145 Ky. 543, 140 S.W. 670; Trabue v. Com. (1902) 23 Ky. L. Rep. 2135, 66 S.W. 718; Com. v. Flanigan (1869) 8 Phila. (Pa.) 430; Sims v. Com. (1890) 12 Ky. L. Rep. 215, 13 S.W. 1079.

7. See Paul H. Robinson and Michael T. Cahill, *Criminal Law,* 2nd ed. §5.0, §5.1 (Wolters Kluwer 2012).

8. Id. at §5.3.

9. See Chapter 10.

10. The Model Penal Code section provides:

Although ignorance or mistake would otherwise afford a defense to the offense charged, the defense is not available if the defendant would be guilty of another offense had the situation been as he supposed. In such case, however, the ignorance or mistake of the defendant shall reduce the grade and degree of the offense of which he may be convicted to those of the offense of which he would be guilty had the situation been as he supposed.

CHAPTER NINE

Consent to Injury

In the context of civil liability, it makes sense that the valid consent of the "victim" should be a defense to liability. It would seem odd for a fully consenting adult to clearly permit or even request that another person injure him or her in some way, then turn around and sue that person for doing as requested.

But civil liability is about fair compensation for harm done, while criminal liability serves a very different purpose: the enforcement of societal norms against conduct seen as seriously condemnable. The rationale for criminal punishment is not fair compensation of victims, who generally receive no financial benefit from an offender's punishment, but rather the reinforcement of those societal norms against wrongdoing—wrongdoing that is so serious as to deserve the condemnation of criminal conviction. In the criminal context, then, the consent of the victim to injury is of little relevance unless that consent brings the conduct within societal norms.

An examination of the criminal laws in the American jurisdictions suggests that there is some disagreement about whether a victim's consent vitiates what is normally the criminal harm of bodily injury, as Map 9 illustrates.

Consent as a Defense to Even Serious Bodily Injury

Four states, designated with darker shading—Alaska, Kansas, Louisiana, and Maryland[1]—permit a defense to assault or battery where the victim consented to the conduct, even where the resulting injury is serious. Typically, serious injury includes protracted or extreme pain, permanent disfigurement, loss or impaired functions of bodily organs or members, reduced mental capacity, or injury creating substantial risk of death.

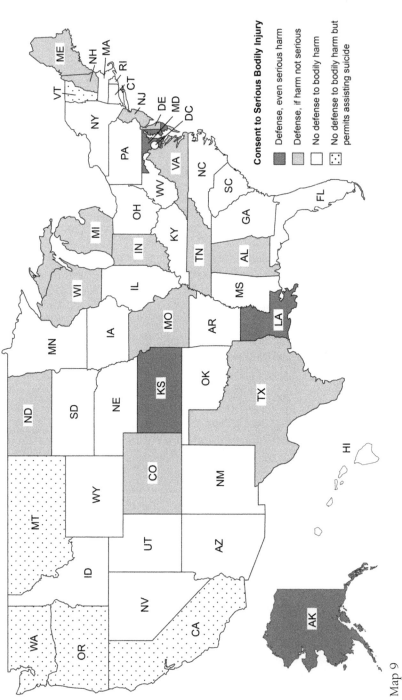

Consent to Serious Bodily Injury

Defense, even serious harm

Defense, if harm not serious

No defense to bodily harm

No defense to bodily harm but permits assisting suicide

Map 9

Consent as a Defense to Nonserious Injury

Fourteen states, shown with light shading—Alabama, Colorado, Delaware, Indiana, Maine, Michigan, Missouri, New Hampshire, New Jersey, North Dakota, Tennessee, Texas, Virginia, and Wisconsin[2]—permit a defense to assault or battery where the victim consented to the conduct and the harm or threatened harm is not serious. Typically, such conduct includes consensual choking, whipping, or slapping, as might occur in hazing or the context of a BDSM relationship (bondage, discipline, dominance and submission, sado-masochism, and other related activity).[3] Where the harm is serious, the consent defense is not generally available in the states, though other defenses may be available, such as for a physician's lawful practice of medicine or for participation in a lawful athletic competition.

Consent Not a Defense to Bodily Injury

However, a strong majority of jurisdictions (33), shown with no shading on the map—Arizona, Arkansas, California, Connecticut, District of Columbia, Florida, Georgia, Hawaii, Idaho, Illinois, Iowa, Kentucky, Massachusetts, Minnesota, Mississippi, Montana, Nebraska, Nevada, New Mexico, New York, North Carolina, Ohio, Oklahoma, Oregon, Pennsylvania, Rhode Island, South Carolina, South Dakota, Utah, Vermont, Washington, West Virginia, and Wyoming[4]—do not permit a defense to assault or battery where the conduct threatens or causes bodily harm. For instance, people who agree to participate in a "choking game," even where no serious harm is threatened, may be liable for battery notwithstanding the consent of all parties. (As above, although consent is not a defense, other defenses are available, such as for a physician's lawful practice of medicine or for participants in a lawful athletic competition.)

Permitting Assistance of Suicide

Five of the jurisdictions in the group above, marked with dots on the map, deny a consent defense for any bodily injury but nonetheless permit assisting a suicide: California, Montana, Oregon, Vermont, and Washington.[5] Four jurisdictions have created a statutory exception to permit assisted suicide, while Montana's highest court has interpreted its general consent-defense statute to permit assisted suicide.[6]

One might expect that the jurisdictions that permit consent to serious bodily injury are the jurisdictions most likely to permit assisting suicide. But in fact the reverse relationship seems to be the case: all the jurisdictions that allow assisting suicide are jurisdictions that purport to forbid the infliction of bodily injury, even that which is not serious. To the extent that the suicide assistance is limited to physicians, the legal rule may be simply a move to protect doctors from criminal liability rather than any indication of a weakening of the norm against consent to injury.

Observations and Speculations

A strong majority, two-thirds of the states, purport to allow no consent defense to any bodily injury even if it is not serious, unless it is a medical treatment or an authorized sport. What may seem puzzling about this is that such a rule seems to bear little resemblance to how the criminal law is actually applied in practice. People get their ears pierced and their bodies tattooed at a prodigious rate.[7] Perhaps even more striking is the rise and increasing tolerance if not acceptance of sadomasochism (S&M) as a lifestyle choice.[8]

It may well be that criminal law here is being offered to express a societal preference rather than to announce a real criminal prohibition. That is, it might be like the adultery or seduction offenses that continue to linger in some jurisdictions.[9] But this use of criminal law is both dangerous and damaging.

It is dangerous because it leaves the application of the offense to the unfettered discretion of the local prosecutor. One person holding that office might choose to enforce the rule as enacted, while another might choose to treat it as a symbolic preference rather than a true criminal prohibition. Yet, clearly it would be more appropriate for the legislature to decide the criminal law of the land, rather than the local prosecutor. And one must worry about what sort of fair notice citizens are given when the meaning and effect of the criminal prohibitions can change overnight when the prosecutor changes.

But even if the rule applied in practice is publicly announced and consistently applied, if it conflicts with the legislature's announced legal rule, it would produce immediate damage: to the criminal law's reputation as a reliable moral authority. The existence of the gap between the law and the practice invites people to speculate whether other gaps exist with regard to other rules. Thus, citizens no longer have reason to take seriously the criminal law as written. What is written may or may not be the "real" law.

This, of course, was part of the social-legal disaster that occurred with American Prohibition in the 1920s. The law prohibited the consumption of alcohol, but it was obvious that many if not most people, including political leaders, were simply ignoring the legal prohibition. The effect was not only rampant violation of the statutes criminalizing alcohol consumption but also an increase in non-alcohol-related offenses generally. Once the criminal law's reputation as a reliable legal and moral authority has been undermined, it loses some of its ability to gain deference from the community.[10]

Jurisdictions would be better off setting their criminal law rules to accurately reflect the conduct that their society is prepared to enforce as sufficiently condemnable to merit criminal conviction and punishment. Criminal law practices that deviate from the legal rules undermine their credibility; practices that track the rules reinforce their authority and increase the likelihood that the community will defer to them.

Notes

1. Dawson v. State, 264 P.3d 851, 858–59 (Alaska Ct. App. 2011); Prince v. State, No. A-11497, 2016 WL 3369193, at *1 (Alaska Ct. App. June 15, 2016); In re C.T., 286 P.3d 1160 (Kan. Ct. App. 2012); Kan. Stat. Ann. § 21-6314; State v. Hager, 13-546 (La. App. 5 Cir. 12/27/13), 131 So. 3d 1090, 1092–93; State v. Mullins, 537 So. 2d 386, 390 (La. Ct. App. 1988); State v. Helou, 2002–2302 (La. 10/23/03), 857 So. 2d 1024, 1027; Hickman v. State, 193 Md. App. 238, 257, 996 A.2d 974, 985 (2010); Pryor v. State, 195 Md. App. 311, 339, 6 A.3d 343, 359 (2010); King v. State, 36 Md. App. 124, 134, 373 A.2d 292, 298 (1977).

2. Ala. Code § 13A-2-7; Colo. Rev. Stat. Ann. § 18-1-505; Del. Code Ann. tit. 11, § 452; Helton v. State, 624 N.E.2d 499, 514 (Ind. Ct. App. 1993); Govan v. State, 913 N.E.2d 237, 242 (Ind. Ct. App. 2009); Me. Rev. Stat. tit. 17-A, § 109; Jarvis v. Palmer, No. CIV.A.06-CV-12829, 2008 WL 3285767, at *6 (E.D. Mich. Aug. 7, 2008); Mo. Ann. Stat. § 565.080; N.H. Rev. Stat. Ann. § 626:6; N.J. Stat. Ann. § 2C:2-10; N.D. Cent. Code Ann. § 12.1-17-08; Tenn. Code Ann. § 39-13-104; Tex. Penal Code Ann. § 22.06; Banovitch v. Com., 196 Va. 210, 219, 83 S.E.2d 369, 375 (1954); Wis. Stat. Ann. § 940.19; State v. Richards, 365 N.W.2d 7 (Wis. 1985).

3. See, e.g., People v. Ford, 2015 IL App (3d) 130810, ¶ 30, 43 N.E.3d 193, 201 (Oct. 28, 2015) (involving a "choking game" among friends); Com. v. Appleby, 380 Mass. 296, 298, 402 N.E.2d 1051, 1054 (1980) (involving whipping, where no serious injury resulted, in the context of a BDSM relationship); State v. Aguilar, No. 2 CA-CR 2006-0365, 2007 WL 5578377, at *2 (Ariz. Ct. App. Aug. 7, 2007) (involving slapping, where the court rejected the defendant's legal argument that consent is an affirmative defense to battery).

4. Ariz. Rev. Stat. Ann. § 13-1203; State v. Mace, 86 Ariz. 85, 88, 340 P.2d 994, 996 (1959); State v. Holle, 240 Ariz. 301, 379 P.3d 197, 206 (2016); Ark. Code Ann. § 5-13-203; Ark. Code Ann. § 5-13-206; Childs v. State, 15 Ark. 204, 205 (1854); State v. Brewer, 33 Ark. 176, 180 (1878); State v. Lonon, 19 Ark. 577, 577 (1858); People v. Samuels, 250 Cal. App. 2d 501, 513, 58 Cal. Rptr. 439, 447 (Ct. App. 1967); Conn. Gen. Stat. Ann. § 53a-61; Woods v. United States, 65 A.3d 667, 672 (D.C. 2013); Fla. Stat. Ann. § 784.03; Lyons v. State, 437 So. 2d 711, 712 (Fla. Dist. Ct. App. 1983); State v. Conley, 799 So. 2d 400, 402 (Fla. Dist. Ct. App. 2001) (Warner, J., concurring); Ramey v. State, 203 Ga. App. 650, 417 S.E.2d 699 (1992); Ogletree v. State, 211 Ga. App. 845, 440 S.E.2d 732 (1994); Haw. Rev. Stat. Ann. § 702-234; Idaho Code Ann. § 18-903; Idaho Code Ann. § 18-901; People v. Reckers, 251 Ill. App. 3d 790, 793, 623 N.E.2d 811, 814 (1993); People v. Ford, 2015 IL App (3d) 130810, ¶ 30, 43 N.E.3d 193, 201; State v. Roby, 194 Iowa 1032, 188 N.W. 709, 711 (1922); State v. Spargo, 364 N.W.2d 203, 211 (Iowa 1985); Iowa Code Ann. § 708.1; Ky. Rev. Stat. Ann. § 508.030; Ky. Rev. Stat. Ann. § 503.110; Com. v. Carey, 463 Mass. 378, 385, 974 N.E.2d 624, 630–31 (2012);

Com. v. Appleby, 380 Mass. 296, 402 N.E.2d 1051 (1980); Minn. Stat. Ann. §
609.224; State v. Peek, No. A04-1535, 2005 WL 2495773, at *5 (Minn. Ct. App.
Oct. 11, 2005); State v. Jones, No. A04-1131, 2005 WL 1545298, at *4 (Minn. Ct.
App. July 5, 2005); Durr v. State, 722 So. 2d 134, 135 (Miss. 1998); State v. Mack-
rill, 345 Mont. 469 (2008); Mont. Code Ann. § 45-2-211; Mont. Code Ann.
§ 45-5-201; State v. Hatfield, 218 Neb. 470, 474, 356 N.W.2d 872, 876 (1984); State
v. Van, 268 Neb. 814, 824, 688 N.W.2d 600, 614 (2004); Wright v. Starr, 42 Nev.
441, 179 P. 877, 878 (1919); Nev. Rev. Stat. Ann. § 200.400; Nev. Rev. Stat. Ann.
§ 200.471; State v. Fransua, 85 N.M. 173, 174, 510 P.2d 106, 107; Morris v. Bran-
denburg, 2016-NMSC-027, 376 P.3d 836, 844; N.M. Stat. Ann. § 30-3-1; N.M.
Stat. Ann. § 30-3-4; N.M. Stat. Ann. § 30-3-5; People, on Complaint of Burke, v.
Steinberg, 190 Misc. 413, 417, 73 N.Y.S.2d 475, 479 (N.Y. Magis. Ct. 1947); People v.
Jovanovic, 263 A.D.2d 182, 198, 700 N.Y.S.2d 156, 169 (1999); N.C. Gen. Stat.
Ann. § 14-33; State v. Bass, 255 N.C. 42, 44, 120 S.E.2d 580, 582 (1961); State v.
Britt, 270 N.C. 416, 418–19, 154 S.E.2d 519, 521 (1967); State v. Guidugli, 2004-
Ohio-2871, ¶ 35, 157 Ohio App. 3d 383, 394, 811 N.E.2d 567, 576; Johnson v.
Hardnett, 62 Ohio App. 2d 165, 167, 405 N.E.2d 324, 326 (Ohio Ct. App. 1978);
State v. Dunham, 118 Ohio App. 3d 724, 730, 693 N.E.2d 1175, 1179 (1997); Okla.
Stat. Ann. tit. 21, § 641; Okla. Stat. Ann. tit. 21, § 642; Whitaker v. State, 2015
OK CR 1, ¶ 4, 341 P.3d 87, 89; Or. Rev. Stat. Ann. § 163.160; Or. Rev. Stat. Ann.
§ 163.165; 18 Pa. Stat. and Cons. Stat. Ann. § 311; 11 R.I. Gen. Laws Ann. § 11-5-
2; 11 R.I. Gen. Laws Ann. § 11-5-3; S.C. Code Ann. § 16-3-600; S.D. Codified
Laws § 22-18-1; Utah Code Ann. § 76-5-102; Utah Code Ann. § 76-5-105; Willey v.
Carpenter, 64 Vt. 212, 23 A. 630, 631 (1892); State v. Roby, 83 Vt. 121, 74 A. 638,
641 (1909); White v. Levarn, 93 Vt. 218, 108 A. 564, 565 (1918); Vt. Stat. Ann. tit.
13, § 1023; Vt. Stat. Ann. tit. 13, § 1024; State v. Baxter, 134 Wash. App. 587, 599,
141 P.3d 92, 98 (2006); State v. Hiott, 97 Wash. App. 825, 828, 987 P.2d 135,
136–37 (1999); W. Va. Code Ann. § 61-2-9; W. Va. Code Ann. § 61-2-9d; Wyo.
Stat. Ann. § 6-2-501; Wyo. Stat. Ann. § 6-2-502; Ross v. State, 16 Wyo. 285, 93
P. 299, 302 (1908).

5. Cal. Health & Safety Code § 443 et seq.; Baxter v. State, 2009 MT 449,
¶ 13, 354 Mont. 234, 240, 224 P.3d 1211, 1215; Or. Rev. Stat. Ann. § 127.800 et seq.;
Vt. Stat. Ann. tit. 18, § 5281 et seq.; Wash. Rev. Code Ann. § 70.245.901 et seq.

6. Baxter v. State, 2009 MT 449, ¶ 13, 354 Mont. 234, 240, 224 P.3d 1211,
1215 ("[W]e find no indication in Montana law that physician aid in dying provided to terminally ill, mentally competent adult patients is against public policy
[for purposes of Montana's statutory consent defense under 2-111]").

7. Given the prevalence of body tattooing and body piercing, one wonders
how so many state courts purport to reject consent as a defense to bodily injury.
The question has not escaped notice of the courts. For instance, in State v. Van,
268 Neb. 814 (2004), a case involving BDSM activity, the Supreme Court of
Nebraska heard a defendant's constitutional challenge that "assault statutes are
arbitrarily applied, [because] their literal application would criminalize such
things as . . . [tattoos] and body piercing." State v. Van, 268 Neb. at 826. Unfortunately, the court never reached the question. But cf. In re Joshua W., No.

F042629, 2003 WL 22940757, at *2 (Cal. Ct. App. Dec. 15, 2003) (rejecting appellant's analogy to consensual body piercing and tattooing, where appellant 'consensually' scraped the word 'zero' into his nine-year-old sister's arm).

Though the answer may vary by state, in general the states apparently rely on prosecutors to bring charges only against actors whose conduct is not in the public interest. For example, where prosecutors choose to bring charges in the BDSM context, the consent defense has often been rejected by courts. See, e.g., Commonwealth v. Appleby, 380 Mass. 296, 402 N.E.2d 1051 (1980); People v. Samuels, 250 Cal. App.2d 501, 58 Cal. Rptr. 439 (1967).

One wonders whether prosecutors and judges will gradually phase such conduct into legality as community attitudes change. For instance, during a wave of assisted-suicide legalization efforts, Montana's Supreme Court held that its statutory consent-defense, which excludes the defense where the actor's conduct is outside the public interest, is available to physicians against a charge of homicide. See Baxter v. State, 2009 MT 449, ¶ 13, 354 Mont. 234, 240, 224 P.3d 1211, 1215.

8. Indeed, some courts have specifically carved out an exception for consensual bodily injury where there are "sexual overtones." See, e.g., Govan v. State, 913 N.E.2d 237, 242 (Ind. Ct. App. 2009) ("We [note] the general rule, however, that consent is ordinarily a defense to the charge of battery in cases involving sexual overtones."); State v. George, 937 S.W.2d 251, 254 (Mo. Ct. App. 1996) (citing a treatise, in dicta, that consent is no defense to battery or assault cases "without sexual overtones"); Ramey v. State, 203 Ga. App. 650, 654, 417 S.E.2d 699, 702 (1992) (same).

9. See Chapter 29.

10. See Paul H. Robinson and Sarah M. Robinson, *Pirates, Prisoners, and Lepers: Lessons from Life Outside the Law,* Chapter 8, "Credibility: America's Prohibition" (Potomac 2015).

CHAPTER TEN

Mental Illness and Culpability

Mental illness can provide a complete defense to an offense in either of two ways. The best known is the insanity defense, which serves as a "general defense" to exculpate an actor from any offense if, because of his mental illness at the time the offense, the actor lacked the capacity to appreciate the criminality of his conduct or, in some jurisdictions, to control his conduct.[1] Acquittal under an insanity defense often carries with it automatic civil commitment for a short period during which the acquitted defendant is psychologically evaluated to determine if he remains sufficiently dangerous to himself or others so as to qualify for longer-term civil commitment.

An insanity defense logically operates only after it is shown that the defendant satisfies all the requirements of the offense definition. There is no need for any general defense if the defendant is not liable for an offense—that is, if he or she does not satisfy all of the elements of some offense definition.

In fact, it can commonly occur that a defendant will lack a required offense culpability element because of his mental illness. For example, consider a defendant whose mental illness leaves him generally well-functioning with no general cognitive or control dysfunction but whose mental illness does have one specific effect in distorting his reaction to a surprise situation. (Perhaps he has a form of post-traumatic stress syndrome.) When an emergency situation is forced on him, he reacts in a way that seems unreasonable because his mental illness causes him to be blind to the risk that his conduct will endanger others. Another person in the same emergency situation would see this risk and avoid it, but because of his mental illness, the defendant simply does not see the risk.

He is charged with the offense of reckless endangerment, which requires the prosecution to prove beyond a reasonable doubt that he was *aware of a substantial risk* that his conduct creates a danger to others. But under the normal operation of the usual evidentiary rules, the defendant cannot be shown to have disregarded the risk to others because, as a result of his mental illness, he was never aware of such a risk and thus is not liable for the offense. He gets off because his mental illness negates an offense element (MINOE).

In a situation like this, the prosecution never really gets off the ground: because of mental illness, the person simply doesn't satisfy the culpability requirements of the offense definition. The defendant never has a need for an insanity defense because he does not satisfy the requirements of the offense.

Interestingly, not all jurisdictions actually allow MINOE. Some jurisdictions allow a defendant's mental illness to negate the higher level culpability elements, such as the premeditation requirement or the malice requirement for murder ("specific intent" requirements, in the language of the common law), but do not allow it to be introduced to negate any lower culpability element, such as the culpability required for manslaughter. In other words, they allow the defendant who, because of his mental illness, does not have the recklessness required for manslaughter (aware of a substantial risk that his conduct will cause death) *to be treated as if he did have* this required culpable state of mind. That is, they "impute" the required recklessness to the mentally ill actor even though he does not in fact satisfy the required element. In jurisdictions that take this approach, a jury in a trial may never learn that the defendant has a mental illness or of its effects on him. That fact may be hidden from the jury, even though the mental illness negates a required offense element.

Other jurisdictions go even further to impute to the mentally ill defendant all levels of culpability. That is, they forbid the introduction of evidence of mental illness to negate any culpability of any level required for any offense.

Map 10 shows which states take which position with regard to MINOE. It also shows which states have also abolished their general defense of insanity.

Mental Illness Can Negate Any Offense Element

Twenty-two states, shown with light shading on the map—Alaska, Arkansas, Colorado, Connecticut, Hawaii, Idaho, Indiana, Kansas, Maine, Maryland, Missouri, Montana, Nevada, New Hampshire, New Jersey, Ohio, Oregon, Tennessee, Utah, Vermont, Washington, and West Virginia[2]—follow the Model Penal Code in permitting mental illness evidence to negate any element.

Mental Illness Can Negate Only Specific Intent

Twelve states, designated with medium shading on the map—California, Iowa, Kentucky, Massachusetts, Nebraska, New Mexico, New York, North Carolina, North Dakota, Pennsylvania, Rhode Island, and South Dakota[3]—permit mental illness to negate only "specific intent." Occasionally courts speak in the "specific intent" context of "intent" or "knowledge."[4]

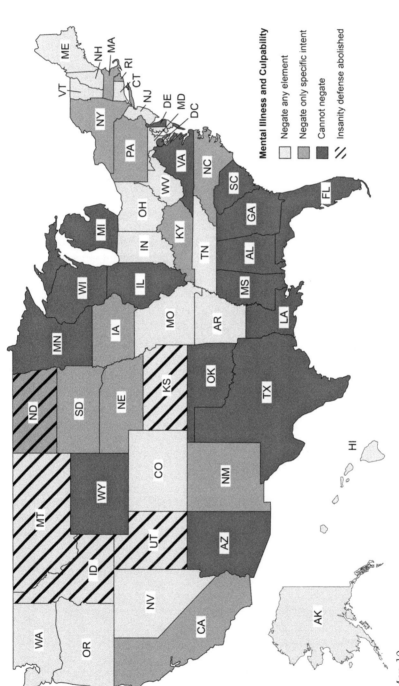

Mental Illness and Culpability

- Negate any element
- Negate only specific intent
- Cannot negate
- Insanity defense abolished

Map 10

The effect of this approach is that mentally ill defendants may get a defense to a specific intent offense, such as murder, but nonetheless be held liable for a lesser included offense with less demanding ("general intent") culpability requirements, such as manslaughter. Thus, the ultimate effect of the imputation of culpability by this group of states is to provide a mitigation perhaps but to still impose criminal liability, even though the defendant's mental illness means that the defendant did not have the culpability required for the offense of which he or she is being convicted.

Mental Illness Cannot Negate Any Offense Element

Seventeen jurisdictions, designated with dark shading on the map—Alabama, Arizona, Delaware, District of Columbia, Florida, Georgia, Illinois, Louisiana, Minnesota, Michigan, Mississippi, Oklahoma, South Carolina, Texas, Virginia, Wisconsin, and Wyoming[5]—do not permit mental illness to negate any culpability element. Under this approach, the state simply ignores the defendant's mental illness when evaluating whether he or she satisfies the elements of the offense charged, and allows the missing culpability to be imputed to the defendant for all culpability levels for all offenses.

Abolish Insanity Defense

Five of the states listed in the categories above—Idaho, Kansas, Montana, North Dakota, and Utah[6]—have abolished the general excuse of insanity. These states are shown with an overlay of diagonal lines on the map. Four of these six states—all but North Dakota—are in the first group, which allows mental illness to negate any offense element. North Dakota, however, is in the second group above. In other words, not only does it abolish its insanity defense, but it also bars the use of mental illness to negate a required offense culpability element other than "specific intent."

Observations and Speculations

The notion of "imputing" a required offense element that a defendant does not in fact satisfy may seem like an odd thing for the criminal law to do. The general rule is that the prosecution must prove all elements of the offense beyond a reasonable doubt. But there are any number of instances where criminal law doctrine regularly, and appropriately, imputes to a defendant a required offense element.

The doctrine of complicity, for example, operates for the sole purpose of imputing to a defendant the required conduct element of an offense that that defendant accomplice does not in fact satisfy.[7] The imputation of the perpetrator's conduct to the accomplice is generally agreed to be appropriate, however, because the special conditions that must be proven to establish complicity liability are enough to justify *treating the accomplice as if* he or she had performed the offense conduct: if he or she satisfies the requirements for complicity, his or her conduct in assisting is thought to be the moral equivalent of the conduct imputed—he or she assisted the perpetrator and did so for the purpose of promoting commission of the offense.

Similarly, the doctrine of voluntary intoxication imputes to the defendant the awareness of a risk required by an offense that the defendant in fact did not have; it does so in instances where the voluntarily-intoxicated defendant would have been aware of the risk had he or she been sober. Again, the defendant's voluntarily intoxication, which blinds him or her to the risk, is offered as a basis for treating the defendant as the moral equivalent to somebody who was aware of the risk and disregarded it.[8]

The lesson here is that there is nothing inherently improper with the process of "imputing" an offense element. The question is whether the special conditions that trigger the imputation are good enough to fully justify what is being done: Do the prerequisites for the imputation in fact establish the defendant as being morally equivalent to a person who in fact satisfies the element?[9]

From this perspective, the common rejection of MINOE, by the second and third groups above, seems to look wholly unjustifiable. Where actors voluntarily intoxicate themselves, we may have some justification for imputing to them an awareness of risk that they would have had had they remained sober. But people who are mentally ill are not suffering their cognitive dysfunction because of their free choices. There is rarely any moral blameworthiness in a defendant becoming mentally ill. Thus, on what grounds can we justify pretending that these actors have a required culpable state of mind that they do not in fact have? If they lack the culpability required for the offense definition, and have no blameworthiness whatever for lacking the culpability, there are no grounds for treating them as if they did have the culpability.

From this perspective, the 29 jurisdictions in the second and third groups—a majority of American jurisdictions—reflect a shocking indifference to the injustice of imposing criminal liability on a person who lacks the culpability required by law. The 12 jurisdictions in the second group, which only reject MINOE for specific intent, might claim that the injustice that they do is only moderate, but the 17 jurisdictions that ignore MINOE for all culpability for all offenses have a lot of explaining to do. Having defined the minimum requirements for offense liability, how can they think it just to impose liability in the absence of those culpability requirements when the defendant has no blameworthiness for causing their absence?

It is hardly a justification for these jurisdictions to claim that they have retained an insanity defense, which can exculpate the mentally ill who are blameless. The general insanity defense focuses not on whether the defendant satisfies the offense culpability requirements but instead on his or her general capacities to appreciate the wrongfulness or criminality of his conduct or, in some jurisdictions, upon his general capacity to control his conduct.[10] Yet many mentally ill defendants have their general capacities intact and live perfectly normal lives, with only fleeting instances of dangerous incapacity that could lead to arrest or prosecution.

For example, imagine a defendant charged with reckless endangerment who, because of his mental illness, was not aware of the substantial risk that his conduct created, as in the hypothetical above. Such a person does not satisfy the culpability requirement for reckless endangerment; he is not aware of a substantial risk that his conduct endangers others. He ought not be liable for the offense, because he does not satisfy its minimum requirements; yet the rejection of MINOE means that he can nonetheless be held liable for the offense, because the awareness is imputed to him. Will the recognition of a general insanity defense save him? No.

The effect of his mental illness is not so broad as to cause him to generally "lack substantial capacity to appreciate the criminality or wrongfulness of his conduct." He generally has such "capacity"; his mental illness is much more narrow in its effect. It is only in the particular situation at hand, where things were a bit chaotic and a bit overwhelming, that his mental illness showed itself in his bad response to a difficult situation. A person without his mental illness would not have made his mistake, but his mental illness, for which he is not morally responsible, fully explains why he handled the situation so badly. To deny him an acquittal under MINOE is to impose undeserved criminal liability, for he will not qualify for an insanity defense.

The better course for states is to follow the Model Penal Code in recognizing a MINOE defense and a general insanity defense.

Notes

1. See Model Penal Code § 4.01; Paul H. Robinson and Michael T. Cahill, *Criminal Law,* 2nd ed. §9.3 (Wolters Kluwer 2012).

2. Alaska Stat. § 12.47.020; Ark. Code Ann. § 5-2-303; Colo. Rev. Stat. Ann. § 18-1-803; State v. Burge, 487 A.2d 532 (Conn. 1985); Haw. Rev. Stat. § 704-401; Idaho Code Ann. § 18-207; Sanchez v. State, 749 N.E.2d 509 (Ind. 2001); Kan. Stat. Ann. § 21-5209; Me. Rev. Stat. tit. 17-A, § 38; Hoey v. State, 536 A.2d 622 (Md. 1988); Mo. Ann. Stat. §§ 552.020, 552,030; State v. Strubberg, 616 S.W.2d 809 (Mo. 1981); Mont. Code Ann. § 46-14-102; Finger v. State, 27 P.3d 66 (Nev. 2001); State v. Gourlay, 802 A.2d 1203 (N.H. 2002); N.J. Stat. Ann. § 2C:4-2; State v. Curry, 543 N.E.2d 1228 (Ohio 1989); Or. Rev. Stat. § 161.300; State v. Nebert, 260 P.3d 559 (Or. Ct. App. 2011); State v. Ferrell, 277 S.W.3d 372 (Tenn. 2009); Utah Code Ann. § 76-2-305; State v. Messier, 497 A.2d 740 (Vt. 1985);

State v. Lewis, 159 Wash. App. 1042 (2011); State v. Joseph, 590 S.E.2d 718 (W. Va. 2003).

3. Cal. Penal Code § 28; People v. Saille, 820 P.2d 588 (Cal. 1991); Anfinson v. State, 758 N.W.2d 496 (Iowa 2008); McGuire v. Commonwealth, 885 S.W.2d 931 (Ky. 1994); Commonwealth v. Johnston, 828 N.E.2d 568 (Mass. App. Ct. 2005); State v. Vosler, 345 N.W.2d 806 (Neb. 1984); State v. Balderama, 2004-NMSC-008, 135 N.M. 329; People v. Segal, 429 N.E.2d 107 (N.Y. 1981); State v. Staten, 616 S.E.2d 650 (N.C. 2005); N.D. Cent. Code Ann. § 12.1-04.1-01; Commonwealth v. Spotz, 47 A.2d 63 (Pa. 2012); State v. Amazeen, 526 A.2d 1268 (R.I. 1987); State v. Schouten, 2005 SD 122, 707 N.W.2d 820.

4. See Com. v. Johnston, 63 Mass. App. Ct. 680, 688, 828 N.E.2d 568, 575 (2005), aff'd, 446 Mass. 555, 845 N.E.2d 350 (2006) (holding that evidence of mental illness that negates defendant's "intent" or "knowledge" is relevant to showing defendant's incapacity to form "specific intent"); see also State v. Schmidkunz, 2006 ND 192, ¶ 16, 721 N.W.2d 387, 393 (permitting a psychiatrist to testify about defendant's inability to form the required criminal intent for murder, where psychiatrist apparently testified about the defendant's ability to act "intentionally" or "knowingly").

5. Ala. Code § 13A-3-1; State v. Mott, 931 P.2d 1046 (Ariz. 1997); Bethea v. United States, 365 A.2d 64 (D.C. 1976); Bates v. State, 386 A.2d 1139 (Del. 1978); Chestnut v. State, 538 So. 2d 820 (Fla. 1989); Hudson v. State, 319 S.E.2d 28 (Ga. Ct. App. 1984); People v. Hulitt, 838 N.E.2d 148 (Ill. App. Ct. 2005); State v. Jones, 359 So. 2d 95 (La. 1978); People v. Pahoski, 2012 WL 4900467 (Mich. Ct. App. Oct. 16, 2012) (unpublished); State v. Bouwman, 328 N.W.2d 703 (Minn. 1982); Stevens v. State, No. 2000-DP-00507-SCT (Miss. 2001); Jones v. State, 648 P.2d 1251 (Okla. Crim. App. 1982); Gill v. State, 552 S.E.2d 26 (S.C. 2001); Ruffin v. State, 270 S.W.3d 586 (Tex. Crim. App. 2008); Bowling v. Commonwealth, 403 S.E.2d 375 (Va. Ct. App. 1991); State v. Vega, 206 Wis. 2d 676 (Wis. Ct. App. 1996).

6. Idaho Code Ann. § 18-207; Kan. Stat. Ann. § 21-5209; State v. Korell, 690 P.2d 992 (Mont. 1984); N.D. Cent. Code Ann. § 12.1-04.1-01; Utah Code Ann. § 76-2-305; Dean v. State, 668 P.2d 639 (Wyo. 1983).

7. See Model Penal Code § 2.06; Robinson and Cahill, *Criminal Law,* 2nd ed. §6.1 (Wolters Kluwer 2012).

8. See Model Penal Code § 2.08(2); Robinson and Cahill, *Criminal Law,* 2nd ed. §5.3 (Wolters Kluwer 2012).

9. Robinson and Cahill, *Criminal Law,* 2nd ed. §5.0 (Wolters Kluwer 2012).

10. See Model Penal Code § 4.01; Robinson and Cahill, *Criminal Law,* 2nd ed. §9.3 (Wolters Kluwer 2012).

CHAPTER ELEVEN

Attempt

Criminal law typically prohibits harmful or evil conduct, but it also punishes attempts to engage in such conduct. Attempts to commit crimes can themselves be destabilizing and damaging to a society but, perhaps more importantly, they demonstrate the personal blameworthiness of the actor—a demonstrated willingness to commit the crime—which deserves the imposition of criminal liability and punishment.

Not every form of attempt to commit an offense is typically criminalized. Some jurisdictions require that the person actually came close to committing the offense, using one of what are called "proximity" tests for how close the person must come to qualify for attempt liability.[1] Thus, a person who decides to rob a bank but as yet has only collected the required equipment in the trunk of his car and backed out of his driveway may not yet have come close enough to be held liable for attempted bank robbery.

Other jurisdictions, typically those with more modern criminal codes based on the American Law Institute's Model Penal Code, commonly require something less to satisfy the objective conduct element for criminal attempt. Indeed, they shift the focus of the inquiry: Instead of asking whether the person *has come close enough* to commission of the offense, they ask whether the person *has gone far enough* from the starting point—the original idea to commit the offense.[2] Thus, the bank robbery suspect described above might well satisfy the conduct requirement for attempt, if it is judged that he has taken a "substantial step" toward its commission.[3]

Because the conduct requirement for attempt liability can be a bit thin, especially under the "substantial step" formulations as compared to the "proximity" formulations, the culpability requirement for attempt becomes that much more important. Attempt liability is in essence punishing a person's demonstrated willingness to commit an offense. Because of the great weight that the culpability requirement carries in assessing liability for attempt, the culpability

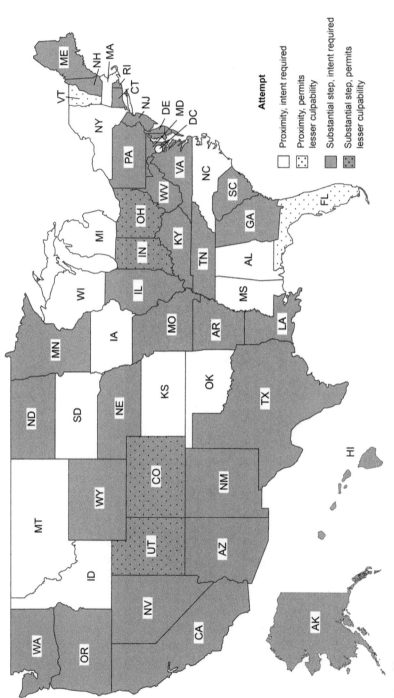

Attempt

☐ Proximity, intent required

⦂ Proximity, permits
   lesser culpability

▨ Substantial step, intent required

▨ Substantial step, permits
   lesser culpability

Map 11

requirement has traditionally been set quite high: many jurisdictions require proof of purpose or intention to commit the offense[4]—that is, proof that it was the person's "conscious object" or his or her "hope" or desire to commit the offense.[5]

Consider the case of the antiwar activist who plants a bomb to blow up the local military recruiting office after business hours when there are not likely to be people present. But when he triggers his bomb it malfunctions and never explodes. Although he cannot be liable for the offense of destroying the building by explosive, he can be liable for an attempt to commit that offense. His conduct has come close to committing the offense—satisfies the "proximity" test (as well as the "substantial step" test)—and it was his purpose to destroy the building.

Now assume that just before he triggers his bomb he sees that there is a night watchman in the building, which he was not expecting. He would prefer not to kill the watchman, but he also believes that his antiwar protest is more important. He decides to trigger the bomb anyway, aware that the explosion creates a substantial risk of killing the watchman but with no intention or hope or desire that the watchman will be killed. If his bomb had exploded and killed the watchman, he would be liable for the homicide—reckless homicide, manslaughter, if he was aware of a substantial risk that his conduct would cause the death, or knowing homicide, murder, if he was practically certain that his conduct would cause the death. But because his bomb does not go off, he cannot be held liable for attempted homicide because he does not satisfy the elevated purpose requirement demanded for attempt liability. The vast majority of jurisdictions—45 total—take this elevate-to-purpose approach, either by statute or case law.

There are some jurisdictions, however, that do not set the attempt culpability requirement at purpose, and instead allow attempt liability for some lesser culpability level, such as knowing or reckless.[6] In these jurisdictions, the antiwar activist could be held liable for attempted homicide.[7]

Map 11 indicates the position of each state with regard to each one of these central issues in defining the requirements for attempt liability.

Proximity and Intent Required

Fourteen jurisdictions, designated with no shading on the map—Alabama, District of Columbia, Idaho, Iowa, Kansas, Massachusetts, Michigan, Mississippi, Montana, New York, North Carolina, Oklahoma, South Dakota, and Wisconsin—are "proximity" jurisdictions, meaning that to be convicted of an attempt, the actor must have come close to committing the substantive offense.[8] For instance, the law may require that the actor "carr[y] the project forward within dangerous proximity to the criminal end to be attained."[9] Or it may require that the actor "comes very near to the accomplishment" of the offense such that "the intent to complete it renders the crime . . . probable."[10] Or the law may require that the attempter's act "demonstrate[s] that a crime is about to be committed unless frustrated by intervening circumstances."[11] These states are not likely to impose liability for attempted bank robbery in the hypothetical above, because the person has not come close enough to committing the offense.

These jurisdictions are also "purpose or intent required" jurisdictions, meaning that the actor must be purposeful or intentional as to commission of the substantive offense.[12] In these 14 states, the antiwar activist in the hypothetical above could not be held liable for attempted murder or attempted manslaughter of the watchman.

Proximity Required but Permits Lesser Culpability

Two states, those with no shading and dots on the map—Florida and Vermont—are proximity jurisdictions that would not impose liability for attempted bank robbery in the hypothetical above, but they do allow liability for an attempt if the person possesses whatever culpability is required by the target offense; he need not be purposeful as to the substantive offense.[13] Thus, these two states would hold the antiwar activist liable for attempted murder or attempted manslaughter in the hypothetical above.

Substantial Step Sufficient and Intent Required

Thirty-one states, shown with medium shading and no dots—Alaska, Arizona, Arkansas, California, Connecticut, Delaware, Georgia, Hawaii, Illinois, Kentucky, Louisiana, Maine, Maryland, Minnesota, Missouri, Nebraska, Nevada, New Hampshire, New Jersey, New Mexico, North Dakota, Oregon, Pennsylvania, Rhode Island, South Carolina, Tennessee, Texas, Virginia, Washington, West Virginia, and Wyoming—reject the proximity approach and require only that the person take a substantial step toward commission of the offense.[14] They typically require as well that the substantial-step conduct be "corroborative" or "strongly corroborative" of the actor's criminal purpose. However, some jurisdictions, such as Arizona, Nevada, and Virginia, have permitted "any" step, or even a "slight" step, to satisfy the conduct requirement for attempt. These 31 states would likely impose liability for attempted bank robbery in the hypothetical above (assuming, of course, that the person's intention to rob the bank could be proven beyond a reasonable doubt).

These jurisdictions also require that the actor be purposeful or intentional as to the target offense.[15] Thus, they would not impose liability on the antiwar activist for attempted murder or attempted manslaughter.

Substantial Step Sufficient and Permits Lesser Culpability

Four states, designated with medium shading and dots on the map—Colorado, Indiana, Ohio, and Utah—are "substantial step" jurisdictions that also permit lesser mental states than purpose to satisfy the culpability required for attempt liability.[16] In two of these substantial step jurisdictions, Colorado and Indiana, an actor may be liable for an attempt if the actor possesses whatever culpability is required by the target offense. In Ohio and Utah, an actor may be liable for an attempt when he or she acts knowingly as to the offense.[17]

Thus, it is only these jurisdictions that would allow liability for attempt in both of the hypotheticals above. Their adoption of the substantial-step test means that liability for attempted bank robbery can be imposed. And their adoption of a culpability requirement of less than purpose means that there can be attempted homicide liability for the antiwar activist. Ohio and Utah would allow liability for attempted murder (but not attempted manslaughter) assuming the activist was knowing as to causing death of the watchman. Colorado and Indiana would allow liability for attempted manslaughter, assuming the activist was reckless as to causing the death of the watchman.

Observations and Speculations

In drafting the requirements for attempt liability, it is appropriate to take into account the fact that something less than the full offense conduct is required. One can see why drafters might well want to increase the culpability requirements for attempt over that of the substantive offense, as a way of using increased culpability to compensate for decreased objective requirements.

But the 14 states in the first group seem to go too far. Their adoption of the proximity test, rather than the substantial step test, suggests that they hardly need the dramatic elevation to intent that they have adopted.

One could argue that the two states in the second group have struck an appropriate compromise. They do allow lesser culpability levels than intention or purpose but only because they keep the objective conduct requirement relatively high by using the proximity test.

One might be tempted to say the same thing about the third group: they have struck an appropriate balance, albeit a different one than that of the second group. Because they have adopted the less demanding substantial-step test, they keep the demanding elevation-to-intent requirement. But one can wonder whether this elevation requirement is really necessary. The antiwar activist knowingly killing the night watchman makes the point. Engaging in conduct by which a person believes he will cause the death of another human being is classic murder. But for the bomb malfunction, the antiwar activist would be liable for murder of the watchman. On what moral basis would we say that he should not be liable for attempted murder when, against all his hopes and desires, his bomb does not explode?

For those jurisdictions adopting a lower objective requirement such as the substantial step test, a better approach might be to impose a purpose requirement but one that makes more sense in judging the moral blameworthiness of the attempter. For example, it indeed ought to be required that it was the attempter's purpose to engage in the conduct that would constitute the substantive offense. In other words, it needs to be shown that the actor took the "substantial step" intentionally, not accidentally.

Further, it ought to be shown that it was the actor's true and committed purpose to complete the conduct constituting the substantive offense. In other words, it ought to be shown that his intention to engage in the offense conduct was indeed resolute, rather than just being a daydream or a fantasy. In the bank robbery case above, then, it would need to be proven beyond a reasonable doubt that the person really did intend to drive to the bank and rob it—that this was his resolute purpose—and not that he was just some Walter Mitty engaged in acting out, to a point, his latest fantasy.

These are both appropriate interpretations of the special "purpose" requirement for attempt liability. There is little reason to go further to apply the purpose requirement in a way that also elevates to purpose the reckless or knowing requirement of the substantive offense. With these two special purpose demands in place—assuring that the attempter's conduct toward the offense was not accidental and that his intention to complete that conduct was resolute—a jurisdiction can fairly impose attempt liability on a person who satisfies the normal culpability requirements for the substantive offense. In other words, the jurisdiction can impose attempted murder liability on the antiwar activist who attempts to knowingly kill the night watchman.

This is essentially the position taken by the four states in the last group, and it seems a morally justifiable position that probably better accords with the community's judgments of justice.

Notes

1. Ala. Code § 13A-4-2; Ex parte A.T.M., 804 So. 2d 171, 174 (Ala. 2000); Ex parte W.F., 214 So. 3d 1153, 1162 (Ala. 2015); D.C. Code Ann. § 22-1803; Frye v. United States, 926 A.2d 1085, 1095–96 (D.C. 2005); Davis v. United States, 873 A.2d 1101, 1107 (D.C. 2005); Evans v. United States, 779 A.2d 891, 894 (D.C. 2001); Fla. Stat. Ann. § 777.04 (West); Hudson v. State, 745 So. 2d 997, 1000 n.4 (Fla. Dist. Ct. App. 1999); Wiggins v. State, 816 So. 2d 745, 747 (Fla. Dist. Ct. App. 2002); Idaho Code Ann. § 18-305 (West); Idaho Code Ann. § 18-306 (West); State v. Allen, 149 Idaho 545, 547, 237 P.3d 14, 16 (Ct. App. 2010); State v. Glass, 139 Idaho 815, 818, 87 P.3d 302, 305 (Ct. App. 2003); State v. Spies, 672 N.W.2d 792, 797–98 (Iowa 2003); Kan. Stat. Ann. § 21-5301 (West); State v. Peterman,

280 Kan. 56, 60–61, 118 P.3d 1267, 1271 (2005); Com. v. Bell, 455 Mass. 408, 413, 917 N.E.2d 740, 747 (2009); Mich. Comp. Laws Ann. § 750.92 (West); People v. Burton, 252 Mich. App. 130, 141, 651 N.W.2d 143, 150 (2002); People v. Jones, 443 Mich. 88, 100, 504 N.W.2d 158, 164 (1993); Miss. Code. Ann. § 97-1-7 (West); Ishee v. State, 799 So. 2d 70, 73 (Miss. 2001); West v. State, 437 So. 2d 1212, 1214 (Miss. 1983); Mont. Code Ann. § 45-4-103 (West); State v. Gunderson, 2010 MT 166, ¶ 59, 357 Mont. 142, 155–56, 237 P.3d 74, 85; People v. Omwathath, 964 N.Y.S.2d 687, 689 (N.Y. App. Term 2013); N.C. Gen. Stat. Ann. § 15-170; State v. Miller, 344 N.C. 658, 668, 477 S.E.2d 915, 921 (1996); Okla. Stat. Ann. tit. 21, § 42 (West); Taylor v. State, 96 Okla. Crim. 188, 190, 251 P.2d 523, 526 (1952); Anderson v. State, 1976 OK CR 149, 551 P.2d 1155, 1161; State v. Disanto, 688 N.W.2d 201 (S.D. 2004); Vt. Stat. Ann. tit. 13, § 9 (West); State v. Devoid, 2010 VT 86, ¶ 11, 188 Vt. 445, 449, 8 A.3d 1076, 1079–80 (2010); Wis. Stat. Ann. § 939.32 (West); State v. Stewart, 143 Wis. 2d 28, 42, 420 N.W.2d 44, 50 (1988).

Note that Michigan authorities have occasionally suggested that a substantial step is enough. See People v. Thousand, 465 Mich. 149, 164, 631 N.W.2d 694, 701 (2001) (suggesting that "any act towards the commission of the intended offense" is enough).

Note that Wisconsin courts occasionally use what has been called a res ipsa loquitur test instead of proximity. See, e.g., State v. Stewart, 143 Wis. 2d 28, 42, 420 N.W.2d 44, 50 (1988). ("The aim of this 'stop the film' test is to determine whether the accused's acts unequivocally demonstrate an intent to commit the crime rendering voluntary desistance from the crime improbable.")

2. See Model Penal Code §5.01(1)(c); see generally Paul H. Robinson and Michael T. Cahill, *Criminal Law,* 2nd ed. §11.1 (Wolters Kluwer 2012).

3. Alaska Stat. Ann. § 11.31.100 (West); Ariz. Rev. Stat. Ann. § 13-1001; Mejak v. Granville, 212 Ariz. 555, 559, 136 P.3d 874, 878 (2006); Ark. Code Ann. § 5-3-201 (West); People v. Hajek, 58 Cal. 4th 1144, 1192, 324 P.3d 88, 134 (2014), as modified on denial of reh'g (July 23, 2014); People v. Watkins, 55 Cal. 4th 999, 1021, 290 P.3d 364, 382 (2012), as modified on denial of reh'g (Feb. 13, 2013); People v. Weddington, 246 Cal. App. 4th 468, 478, 200 Cal. Rptr. 3d 799, 808 (2016), review denied (July 27, 2016); Colo. Rev. Stat. Ann. § 18-2-101 (West); Conn. Gen. Stat. Ann. § 53a-49 (West); Del. Code Ann. tit. 11, § 531 (West); Del. Code Ann. tit. 11, § 532 (West); Ga. Code Ann. § 16-4-1 (West); Haw. Rev. Stat. Ann. § 705-500 (West); 720 Ill. Comp. Stat. Ann. 5/8-4; Ind. Code Ann. § 35-41-5-1 (West); Ky. Rev. Stat. Ann. § 506.010 (West); La. Stat. Ann. § 14:27; State v. Smith, 2007-1443 (La. App. 3 Cir. 1/21/09), 2 So. 3d 1187, 1198, writ denied, 2009-0407 (La. 11/6/09), 21 So. 3d 300; State v. Preston, 12-798 (La. App. 5 Cir. 5/16/13), 118 So. 3d 1129, 1135, writ denied, 2013-1431 (La. 1/10/14), 130 So. 3d 318; State v. Porter, 249 La. 784, 788, 191 So. 2d 498, 500 (1966); Me. Rev. Stat. tit. 17-A, § 152; Young v. State, 303 Md. 298, 311, 493 A.2d 352, 358 (1985); Minn. Stat. Ann. § 609.17 (West); Mo. Ann. Stat. § 562.012 (West); Neb. Rev. Stat. Ann. § 28-201 (West); Van Bell v. State, 105 Nev. 352, 354, 775 P.2d 1273, 1275 (1989); Stephens v. Sheriff, Clark Cty., 93 Nev. 338, 339, 565 P.2d 1007, 1008

(1977); Larsen v. State, 86 Nev. 451, 453, 470 P.2d 417, 418 (1970); United States v. Sarbia, 367 F.3d 1079, 1081 (9th Cir. 2004) (applying Nevada law); N.H. Rev. Stat. Ann. § 629:1; N.J. Stat. Ann. § 2C:5-1 (West); N.M. Stat. Ann. § 30-28-1 (West); State v. Brenn, 2005-NMCA-121, 138 N.M. 451, 455, 121 P.3d 1050, 1054; State v. Trejo, 1972-NMCA-019, 83 N.M. 511, 512, 494 P.2d 173, 174; N.D. Cent. Code Ann. § 12.1-06-01 (West); Ohio Rev. Code Ann. § 2923.02 (West); State v. Woods, 48 Ohio St. 2d 127, 131–32, 357 N.E.2d 1059, 1063 (1976); State v. Carson, 2013-Ohio-5785, ¶ 26, 6 N.E.3d 649, 655; Or. Rev. Stat. Ann. § 161.405 (West); 18 Pa. Stat. and Cons. Stat. Ann. § 901 (West); State v. Latraverse, 443 A.2d 890, 893–95 (R.I. 1982); State v. Reid, 383 S.C. 285, 299–300, 679 S.E.2d 194, 201 (Ct. App. 2009), aff'd, 393 S.C. 325, 713 S.E.2d 274 (2011); State v. Green, 397 S.C. 268, 284, 724 S.E.2d 664, 672 (2012); Tenn. Code Ann. § 39-12-101 (West); Tex. Penal Code Ann. § 15.01 (West); Gibbons v. State, 634 S.W.2d 700, 706 (Tex. Crim. App. 1982); Utah Code Ann. § 76-4-101 (West); Reaux-King v. Com., No. 0734-14-2, 2015 WL 1912642, at *3 (Va. Ct. App. Apr. 28, 2015); Fortune v. Com., 14 Va. App. 225, 229, 416 S.E.2d 25, 28 (1992); Wash. Rev. Code Ann. § 9A.28.020 (West); W. Va. Code Ann. § 61-11-8 (West); State v. Burd, 187 W. Va. 415, 419, 419 S.E.2d 676, 680 (1991); State v. Minigh, 224 W. Va. 112, 121, 680 S.E.2d 127, 136 (2009); Wyo. Stat. Ann. § 6-1-301 (West).

Note that some state courts have suggested that even "any" step, or a "slight" step, may suffice. See, e.g., Mejak v. Granville, 212 Ariz. 555, 559, 136 P.3d 874, 878 (2006) (requiring "a step to further that [illegal] contact"); Van Bell v. State, 105 Nev. 352, 354, 775 P.2d 1273, 1275 (1989) (permitting "slight acts done in furtherance" to constitute an attempt); Fortune v. Com., 14 Va. App. 225, 229, 416 S.E.2d 25, 28 (1992) (permitting "any slight act done in furtherance of [the actor's unlawful] intent").

4. Ala. Code § 13A-4-2; Alaska Stat. § 11.31.100; Ariz. Rev. Stat. Ann. § 13-1001; Ark. Code Ann. § 5-3-201; Cal. Penal Code § 21a; People v. Hanna, 218 Cal. App. 4th 455, 461, 160 Cal. Rptr. 3d 210, 214 (2013), as modified on denial of reh'g (Aug. 26, 2013); People v. Hanold, No. B149939, 2003 WL 21995447, at *4 (Cal. Ct. App. Aug. 22, 2003); Conn. Gen. Stat. Ann. § 53a-49; Del. Code Ann. tit. 11, § 531; Brawner v. United States, 979 A.2d 1191, 1194 (D.C. 2009); Ga. Code Ann. § 16-4-1; Haw. Rev. Stat. § 705-500; Fenstermaker v. State, 128 Idaho 285, 290, 912 P.2d 653, 658 (Ct. App. 1995); Ill. Comp. Stat. Ann. ch. 720, § 5/8-4; State v. Walker, 856 N.W.2d 179, 187 (Iowa 2014), as amended (Jan. 29, 2015) ("When our criminal law penalizes an 'attempt,' without a statutory definition, we have previously required . . . an intent to do an act or bring about certain consequences which would in law amount to a crime; and . . . an act in furtherance of that intent which . . . goes beyond mere preparation."); Kan. Stat. Ann. § 21-5301; Ky. Rev. Stat. Ann. § 506.010; La. Rev. Stat. Ann. § 14:27; Me. Rev. Stat. Ann. tit. 17-A, § 152; Maxwell v. State, 168 Md. App. 1, 6, 895 A.2d 327, 330 (2006); Com. v. McWilliams, 473 Mass. 606, 610, 45 N.E.3d 94, 101 (2016); Com. v. Ware, 375 Mass. 118, 118–20, 375 N.E.2d 1183, 1184 (1978); People v. Cervi, 270 Mich. App. 603, 618, 717 N.W.2d 356, 365 (2006); People v. Burton, 252 Mich. App. 130, 141, 651 N.W.2d 143, 149–50 (2002); Minn. Stat.

Ann. § 609.17; Miss. Code. Ann. § 97-1-7; Craig v. State, 201 So. 3d 1108, 1111 (Miss. Ct. App. 2016); Nichols v. State, 822 So. 2d 984, 989 (Miss. Ct. App. 2002); Mo. Ann. Stat. § 562.012; Mont. Code Ann. § 45-4-103; Neb. Rev. Stat. § 28-201; N.H. Rev. Stat. Ann. § 629:1; N.J. Stat. Ann. § 2C:5-1; N.M. Stat. Ann. § 30-28-1 (felony only); N.Y. Penal Law § 110.00; State v. Coble, 351 N.C. 448, 449, 527 S.E.2d 45, 46 (2000); N.D. Cent. Code § 12.1-06-01; Or. Rev. Stat. § 161.405; Pa. Cons. Stat. Ann. tit. 18, § 901; State v. Latraverse, 443 A.2d 890, 893-95 (R.I. 1982); State v. Sutton, 340 S.C. 393, 397, 532 S.E.2d 283, 285 (2000); State v. Lyerla, 424 N.W.2d 908, 912 (S.D. 1988); Tex. Penal Code Ann. § 15.01; Thacker v. Com., 134 Va. 767, 114 S.E. 504, 506 (1922); Wash. Rev. Code § 9A.28.020; State v. Minigh, 224 W. Va. 112, 121, 680 S.E.2d 127, 136 (2009); Wis. Stat. Ann. § 939.32; Wyo. Stat. § 6-1-301.

5. Model Penal Code § 2.02(2)(a).

6. In four states, Colorado, Florida, Indiana, and Vermont, an actor is liable for an attempt when he acts with the culpability required for commission of the target offense. See Colo. Rev. Stat. Ann. § 18-2-101 ("A person commits criminal attempt if, acting with the kind of culpability otherwise required for commission of an offense, he engages in conduct constituting a substantial step toward the commission of the offense."); Fla. Stat. Ann. § 777.04; State v. Overfelt, 457 So. 2d 1385, 1386 (Fla. 1984) ("[T]here are offenses that may be successfully prosecuted as an attempt without proof of a specific intent to commit the relevant completed offense. The key to recognizing these crimes is to first determine whether the completed offense is a crime requiring specific intent or general intent. If the state is not required to show specific intent to successfully prosecute the completed crime, it will not be required to show specific intent to successfully prosecute an attempt to commit that crime."); Williamson v. State, 510 So. 2d 335, 337 (Fla. Dist. Ct. App. 1987) (same); Ind. Code Ann. § 35-41-5-1 ("A person attempts to commit a crime when, acting with the culpability required for commission of the crime, the person engages in conduct that constitutes a substantial step toward commission of the crime."); State v. Dennis, 151 Vt. 223, 224, 559 A.2d 670, 671 (1989) ("The attempted commission of a criminal offense 'involves the same mental intent as would be required in the actual commission of that offense.'"); State v. D'Amico, 136 Vt. 153, 156, 385 A.2d 1082, 1084 (1978); State v. Petruccelli, 170 Vt. 51, 63, 743 A.2d 1062, 1071 (1999).

In two states, Ohio and Utah, an actor may be liable for an attempt when he acts knowingly as to the conduct constituting the offense. See Ohio Rev. Code Ann. § 2923.02 (purpose or knowledge permitted); Utah Code Ann. § 76-4-101 (knowledge permitted, but only where the target offense contains a result element).

7. See generally Robinson and Cahill, *Criminal Law,* 2nd ed. §11.2 (Wolters Kluwer 2012).

8. See supra note 1.

9. People v. Omwathath, 964 N.Y.S.2d 687, 689 (N.Y. App. Term 2013).

10. Com. v. Bell, 455 Mass. 408, 413 (2009).

11. State v. Disanto, 688 N.W.2d 201 (S.D. 2004).

12. See supra note 4.

13. See supra notes 1 and 6.

14. See supra note 3.

15. See supra note 4.

16. See supra notes 3 and 6.

17. See Ohio Rev. Code Ann. § 2923.02 (purpose or knowledge permitted); Utah Code Ann. § 76-4-101 (knowledge permitted, but only where the target offense contains a result element).

CHAPTER TWELVE

Complicity

If a person does not commit an offense but helps another to do so, he may be held liable for that offense under the doctrine of complicity. Though he does not satisfy the offense conduct element that is required by the offense definition, the conduct of the perpetrator will be imputed to him if he satisfies the requirements of the complicity doctrine (also referred to as "aiding and abetting").

To be held liable for an offense as an accomplice—to have the perpetrator's offense conduct imputed—the person must aid or encourage the perpetrator in the commission of the offense or, in modern codes, must at least attempt or agree to aid.[1] Further, at the time of aiding the perpetrator, the accomplice must have some culpable state of mind as to his conduct aiding the commission of the offense. In other words, it is not enough that the accomplice accidentally aided.[2]

Some states require that the accomplice purposely aid[3]—that he wanted or hoped that his conduct would aid the perpetrator; it was his conscious object that his conduct would aid commission of the offense. Other states require only that the accomplice knowingly aid[4]—that he did not necessarily want or hope to aid the commission of the offense, but he knew that his conduct would have such an effect.

In addition to this special culpability requirement as to aiding commission of the offense, the accomplice must, of course, satisfy the culpability requirements included in the offense definition itself. The complicity doctrine imputes only the perpetrator's conduct constituting the offense, not his culpable mental state. Thus, for example, one cannot be an accomplice to manslaughter (reckless homicide) unless one is at least reckless as to causing the death. In other words, to be held liable as an accomplice, the person must purposely, or depending on the jurisdiction, knowingly aid the perpetrator. In addition, at the time he provides such aid, he must also be aware that such conduct creates a substantial risk of causing death. For instance, a person may

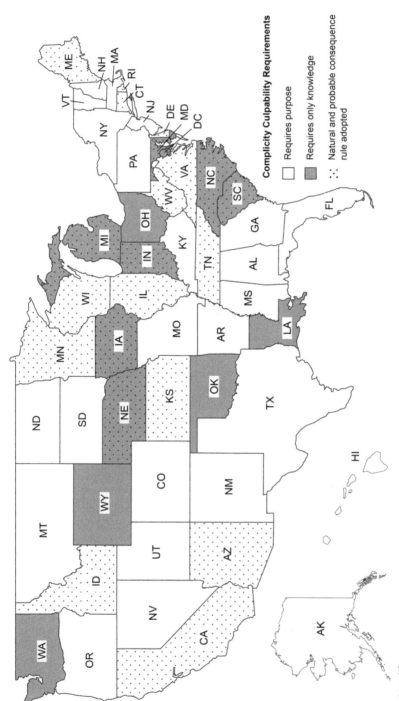

Complicity Culpability Requirements

☐ Requires purpose

▨ Requires only knowledge

∴ Natural and probable consequence rule adopted

Map 12

be held liable as an accomplice to manslaughter by intentionally giving his car keys to his drunk friend, wanting to aid him in the conduct of driving drunk and aware that he is intentionally aiding conduct that creates a substantial risk of causing death. When his drunk friend causes such a death, the person may be held liable for manslaughter as an accomplice to causing the death.[5]

Some states go beyond these standard requirements for complicity liability and significantly expand the potential liability of accomplices by adopting what is commonly called the "natural and probable consequence" rule. In these jurisdictions, once a person is held liable for an offense as an accomplice, the person is deemed to be also liable for any offense that is the "natural and probable consequence" of the offense for which the person is an accomplice. Thus, for example, an actor who is liable as an accomplice for a bank robbery may be held liable for a homicide committed by the perpetrator during the robbery if the perpetrator's killing is judged to be a natural and probable consequence of the robbery—even where the state cannot prove that the robbery accomplice had any culpable mental state as to the homicide.

As is apparent, the natural and probable consequence rule has a significant effect in essentially undercutting the traditional culpability requirements for complicity liability, at least with regard to any offense beyond the original offense for which the person is an accomplice. The standard requirements for complicity must be proven with regard to the bank robbery but not with regard to the subsequent killing by the perpetrator during the robbery.

While some states have adopted the "natural and probable consequence" rule,[6] others have rejected it.[7]

Map 12 shows the position of each state with regard to each of these two central issues on the requirements for being held legally accountable for another's crime.

Complicity Requires Purpose, Natural and Probable Consequence Rule Rejected

Twenty-four states, shown with no shading or dots on the map—Alabama, Alaska, Arkansas, Colorado, Florida, Georgia, Hawaii, Kentucky, Massachusetts, Mississippi, Missouri, Montana, Nevada, New Hampshire, New Jersey, New Mexico, New York, North Dakota, Oregon, Pennsylvania, South Dakota, Texas, Utah, and Vermont[8]—generally require that the actor have the purpose or intent to aid the offense commission. (Some jurisdictions use the term "purpose" while others use the term "intent" to mean the same thing, while others use the two terms interchangeably.) That purpose requirement is usually understood to mean that the actor is purposeful as to aiding the conduct constituting the offense.

These jurisdictions do not appear to permit liability under the natural and probable consequence rule. (However, some of the jurisdictions may impose liability under doctrines that operate in a similar way in other contexts, such as the Pinkerton rule or the felony-murder rule.[9])

Complicity Requires Purpose, Natural and Probable Consequence Rule Adopted

Fourteen jurisdictions, designated with no shading but with dots—Arizona, California, Connecticut, Delaware, Idaho, Illinois, Kansas, Maine, Minnesota, Rhode Island, Tennessee, Virginia, West Virginia, and Wisconsin[10]—generally require that the actor have the purpose or intent to aid the offense commission. Though there is some confusion and difference of opinion as to what this means, generally the actor must be purposeful as to aiding the conduct constituting the offense.

These jurisdictions have adopted the natural and probable consequence rule. As noted above, the rule imposes liability on an actor for offenses that occur as the "natural and probable consequence" of any offense for which the actor is liable as an accomplice.

Complicity Requires Only Knowledge, Natural Probable Consequence Rule Rejected

Six jurisdictions shown with shading but without dots—District of Columbia, Louisiana, Ohio, Oklahoma, Washington, and Wyoming[11]—generally require that the actor merely have knowledge that his conduct will aid the offense commission. That is usually understood to mean that the actor knows that his conduct aids in the commission of the offense. For instance, a person could be held liable as an accomplice to unlawful maiming where the person, a physician acting at the direction of the perpetrator, anesthetizes the fingers of the victim with the knowledge that the perpetrator intends to cut them off.[12]

These jurisdictions have not adopted the natural and probable consequence rule.

Complicity Requires Only Knowledge, Natural Probable Consequence Rule Adopted

Seven states shown on the map with shading and dots—Indiana, Iowa, Maryland, Michigan, Nebraska, North Carolina, and South Carolina[13]—generally require that the actor merely have knowledge as to aiding the offense commission. That is usually understood to mean that the actor knows that his conduct will aid the conduct constituting the offense, as with the group above.

These jurisdictions have adopted the natural and probable consequence rule.

Observations and Speculations

The culpability requirements for complicity liability have created enormous confusion and disagreement. Even the American Law Institute (ALI), which drafted the Model Penal Code on which three-quarters of the state codes are based, hotly debated the issue. The drafting committee after many years of work recommended to the members of the Institute that the Model Code require only knowing as to aiding the offense, but in the floor debates the Institute ended up adopting a purpose requirement.

But the greater source of disagreement, to some extent still unresolved today, is the question of what that purpose, or knowing, requirement means; what it applies to. Does it require the actor to be purposeful, or knowing, as to his conduct aiding the perpetrator's offense conduct? There seems to be a general agreement that it does. Does it also require that the actor be purposeful, or knowing, as to the commission of the offense—that is, as to the conduct, circumstance, and result elements of the offense? On this issue people disagree or are unsure.

The Model Penal Code drafters provided one bit of clarity in section 2.06(4) by explicitly providing that the actor need not be purposeful as to a result element of the substantive offense, but the commentary openly concedes that it is unsure whether the Model Code's "purpose" requirement in complicity should be interpreted to apply to other kinds of offense elements, such as circumstance elements. The confusion is the product of an essential weakness of the common-law rules in this area: those who shaped the common-law doctrine made the false assumption that every offense or liability doctrine had a single culpable state of mind attached to it, when in fact modern "element analysis" has made clear that all offenses and liability doctrines can have a wide variety of culpability requirements as to different elements, and the culpability level required as to one element may be different from that required as to another element within the same offense or liability doctrine.[14]

On policy grounds, the ALI was probably wrong to have adopted the more demanding purpose requirement,[15] but at least they, and the 24 states that followed them in the first group above, were being internally consistent when they adopted the purpose requirement and rejected the natural and probable consequence rule. Both positions serve to make more demanding the requirements for being accountable for another person's crime.

One might think that a better balance is struck by the six states in the third group above, which rejected the natural probable consequence rule but required only knowing as to aiding, as recommended by the original Model Penal Code drafting group.

The seven states in the fourth group above can also claim at least a rational and internally consistent position when they adopted the lower knowing requirement and also adopted the natural and probable consequence rule. Just as the first group above is trying to maximize the requirements for complicity liability, this group of states is consistent in trying to minimize those requirements.

What seems genuinely odd, however, is the position taken by the 14 states in the second group above. They reject the knowing requirement in favor of the more demanding purpose requirement but then dramatically subvert the culpability requirements for complicity liability altogether by adopting the natural probable consequence rule. It is hard to imagine a rational explanation for these two seemingly contradictory positions. One can only assume that this is an unfortunate leftover from the confusion that reigned at common law.

First, common law was generally ignorant of the modern nuance that distinguishes between purposeful and knowing culpability levels. Second, common law operated under the misapprehension of "offense analysis," as noted above. Before the shift to modern "element analysis," common-law judges simply didn't appreciate that the purpose requirement that they adopted for complicity—to make sure that one could not accidentally become an accomplice—could have the effect of requiring proof of an actor's purpose as to a number of different offense and doctrinal elements.

But with the shift from "offense analysis" to "element analysis," it should have been clear to modern code drafters that their adopting a purpose requirement for accomplice liability is doing much more than excluding the possibility of accidental accomplices. The purpose requirement we now see has the perhaps unfortunate effect of shielding from any criminal liability people who knowingly assist another in his criminal conduct. A jurisdiction that wants to exclude such knowing assistance cases from liability can hardly rationally also want to adopt a natural and probable consequence rule that short-circuits all complicity requirements as to the subsequent offense.

Notes

1. See Paul H. Robinson and Michael T. Cahill, *Criminal Law,* 2nd ed. §6.1.1 (Wolters Kluwer 2012).

2. See Robinson and Cahill, *Criminal Law,* 2nd ed. §6.1.2 (Wolters Kluwer 2012).

3. Ala. Code § 13A-2-23; Alaska Stat. Ann. § 11.16.110; Ariz. Rev. Stat. Ann. § 13-301; Ark. Code Ann. § 5-2-403; People v. Beeman, 35 Cal. 3d 547, 560, 674 P.2d 1318, 1326 (1984); Colo. Rev. Stat. Ann. § 18-1-603; Conn. Gen. Stat. Ann. § 53a-8; State v. Fruean, 63 Conn. App. 466, 472–73, 776 A.2d 508, 512 (2001); Del. Code Ann. tit. 11, § 271; Fulford v. State, App. 3 Dist., 311 So.2d 203 (1975);

Ga. Code Ann. § 16-2-20; Haw. Rev. Stat. Ann. § 702-222; State v. Reid, 151 Idaho 80, 85, 253 P.3d 754, 759 (Ct. App. 2011); State v. Mitchell, 146 Idaho 378, 383, 195 P.3d 737, 742 (Ct. App. 2008); 720 Ill. Comp. Stat. Ann. 5/5-2; Kan. Stat. Ann. § 21-5210; Ky. Rev. Stat. Ann. § 502.020; Me. Rev. Stat. tit. 17-A, § 57; Com. v. Filos, 420 Mass. 348, 354, 649 N.E.2d 1085, 1089 (1995); Robinson v. Cook, 863 F. Supp. 2d 49, 67 (D. Mass. 2012), aff'd, 706 F.3d 25 (1st Cir. 2013) (applying Massachusetts law); Minn. Stat. Ann. § 609.05; Milano v. State, 790 So. 2d 179, 185 (Miss. 2001); Mo. Ann. Stat. § 562.041; Mont. Code Ann. § 45-2-302; Tanksley v. State, 113 Nev. 844, 849–50, 944 P.2d 240, 243 (1997); Bolden v. State, 121 Nev. 908, 914, 124 P.3d 191, 195 (2005); N.H. Rev. Stat. Ann. § 626:8; State v. Anthony, 151 N.H. 492, 495, 861 A.2d 773, 776 (2004); N.J. Stat. Ann. § 2C:2-6; State v. Torres, 183 N.J. 554, 566, 874 A.2d 1084, 1092 (2005); State v. Vigil, 2010-NMSC-003, 147 N.M. 537, 540, 226 P.3d 636, 639; State v. Bankert, 1994-NMSC-052, 117 N.M. 614, 618, 875 P.2d 370, 374; State v. Carrasco, 1997-NMSC-047, 124 N.M. 64, 68, 946 P.2d 1075, 1079; N.Y. Penal Law § 20.00 ("intentionally aids"); People v. Johnson, 238 A.D.2d 267, 267, 657 N.Y.S.2d 27, 28 (1997); N.D. Cent. Code Ann. § 12.1-03-01; Or. Rev. Stat. Ann. § 161.155; 18 Pa. Stat. and Cons. Stat. Ann. § 306; State v. Delestre, 35 A.3d 886, 895 (R.I. 2012); S.D. Codified Laws § 22-3-3; Tenn. Code Ann. § 39-11-402; Tex. Penal Code Ann. § 7.02; Utah Code Ann. § 76-2-202 ("intentionally aids"); McGill v. Com., 24 Va. App. 728, 733, 485 S.E.2d 173, 175 (1997); Taylor v. Com., 31 Va. App. 54, 60, 521 S.E.2d 293, 295 (1999); State v. Mullins, 193 W. Va. 315, 319, 456 S.E.2d 42, 46 (1995); State v. Hoselton, 179 W. Va. 645, 649, 371 S.E.2d 366, 370 (1988); State v. West, 153 W. Va. 325, 335, 168 S.E.2d 716, 722 (1969); Wis. Stat. Ann. § 939.05.

4. Byrd v. United States, 364 A.2d 1215, 1219 (D.C. 1976); Murchison v. United States, 486 A.2d 77, 81 (D.C. 1984); Johnson v. United States, 883 A.2d 135, 142 (D.C. 2005); Ind. Code Ann. § 35-41-2-4; Iowa Code Ann. § 703.2; State v. Lott, 255 N.W.2d 105, 109 (Iowa 1977); State v. Neal, 2000-0674 (La. 6/29/01), 796 So. 2d 649, 659; State v. Knowles, 392 So. 2d 651, 657 (La. 1980); State v. Wright, 2001-0322 (La. 12/4/02), 834 So. 2d 974, 983; State v. Fernandez, 2009-1727 (La. App. 4 Cir. 10/6/10), 50 So. 3d 219, 226; State v. Anderson, 96-1515 (La. App. 3 Cir. 4/2/97), 691 So. 2d 336, 339–40; State v. Carpenter, 2000-436 (La. App. 3 Cir. 10/18/00), 772 So. 2d 200, 207; Davis v. State, 207 Md. App. 298, 319, 52 A.3d 148, 160 (2012); State v. Williams, 397 Md. 172, 195, 916 A.2d 294, 308 (2007); People v. King, 210 Mich. App. 425, 431, 534 N.W.2d 534, 537 (1995); Monica Lyn Schroth, *Reckless Aiding and Abetting: Sealing the Cracks That Publishers of Instructional Materials Fall Through*, 29 Sw. U. L. Rev. 567 (2000) ("The state of Michigan dispensed with the intent requirement and sets the mens rea at mere knowledge of the perpetrator's criminal purpose. Michigan allows for . . . complicity liability . . . where the aider and abettor knows that the principal has the requisite intent."); State v. Barfield, 272 Neb. 502, 520, 723 N.W.2d 303, 317–18 (2006); State v. Mantich, 249 Neb. 311, 324, 543 N.W.2d 181, 191 (1996) (Accomplice liability attaches where defendant "either personally intended" the offense commission or "aided another person whom the [defendant] knew had

such an intent."); State v. Bass, 255 N.C. 42, 51, 120 S.E.2d 580, 587 (1961); State v. Sauls, 291 N.C. 253, 257, 230 S.E.2d 390, 393 (1976); State v. Williams, 28 N.C. App. 320, 322–23, 220 S.E.2d 856, 858 (1976); State v. Sutton, 41 N.C. App. 603, 605, 255 S.E.2d 331, 333 (1979); State v. Bond, 345 N.C. 1, 24, 478 S.E.2d 163, 175 (1996); State v. Allen, 127 N.C. App. 182, 185, 488 S.E.2d 294, 296 (1997); State v. Smith, 2006-Ohio-1661, ¶ 33 (stating that knowledge is required for complicity); Conover v. State, 1997 OK CR 6, 933 P.2d 904, 915; Yetter v. State, 1974 OK CR 193, 528 P.2d 345, 347; Bowie v. State, 1995 OK CR 4, 906 P.2d 759, 763; Postelle v. State, 2011 OK CR 30, ¶ 15, 267 P.3d 114, 126–27; Vernon's Okla. Forms 2d, OUJI-CR 2-6 (pattern jury instruction permitting liability where defendant "knowingly did what he/she did either with criminal intent or with knowledge of the [perpetrator's] intent"); State v. Reid, 408 S.C. 461, 473, 758 S.E.2d 904, 910 (2014); State v. Leonard, 292 S.C. 133, 137, 355 S.E.2d 270, 272 (1987); Wash. Rev. Code Ann. § 9A.08.020; Wyo. Stat. Ann. § 6-1-201.

5. These are similar to the facts in State v. Etzweiler, 480 A.2d 870 (N.H. 1984).

6. Ariz. Rev. Stat. Ann. § 13-301; People v. Durham, 70 Cal.2d 171, 181, 74 Cal. Rptr. 262, 449 P.2d 198, 204 (1969); People v. Prettyman, 14 Cal.4th 248, 58 Cal. Rptr.2d 827, 926 P.2d 1013 (1996); State v. Henry, 253 Conn. 354, 362, 752 A.2d 40, 45 (2000); Chance v. State, 685 A.2d 351, 358 (Del. 1996); State v. Ehrmantrout, 100 Idaho 202, 202, 595 P.2d 1097, 1097 (1979); People v. Kessler, 57 Ill. 2d 493, 497, 315 N.E.2d 29, 32 (1974); Richardson v. State, 697 N.E.2d 462, 465 (Ind. 1998); Iowa Code Ann. § 703.2; Kan. Stat. Ann. § 21-5210; Me. Rev. Stat. tit. 17-A, § 57; State v. Linscott, 520 A.2d 1067, 1070 (Me. 1987); Sheppard v. State, 312 Md. 118, 123, 538 A.2d 773, 775 (1988); Watkins v. State, 357 Md. 258, 265, 744 A.2d 1, 4 (2000); People v. Robinson, 475 Mich. 1, 8–9, 715 N.W.2d 44, 49 (2006); Minn. Stat. Ann. § 609.05; State v. Leonor, 263 Neb. 86, 97, 638 N.W.2d 798, 807 (2002); State v. Gorham, 212 N.C. App. 236, 713 S.E.2d 252 (2011); State v. Delestre, 35 A.3d 886, 892 (R.I. 2012); State v. Williams, 189 S.C. 19, 199 S.E. 906, 908 (1938); State v. Richmond, 90 S.W.3d 648, 656 (Tenn. 2002); Charlton v. Com., 32 Va. App. 47, 52, 526 S.E.2d 289, 291 (2000); State v. Rodoussakis, 204 W. Va. 58, 77, 511 S.E.2d 469, 488 (1998); Wis. Stat. Ann. § 939.05.

7. Among these jurisdictions, many state courts have expressly or impliedly rejected the rule. See, e.g., Riley v. State, 60 P.3d 204, 214 (Alaska Ct. App. 2002); Bogdanov v. People, 941 P.2d 247, 251 (Colo. 1997); Wilson-Bey v. United States, 903 A.2d 818, 830 (D.C. 2006); Com. v. Richards, 363 Mass. 299, 307–08, 293 N.E.2d 854, 860 (1973); State v. Ferguson, 20 S.W.3d 485, 497 (Mo. 2000); State ex rel. Keyes v. Montana Thirteenth Judicial Dist. Court, Yellowstone Cty., 1998 MT 34, ¶ 22, 288 Mont. 27, 34, 955 P.2d 639, 643; Sharma v. State, 118 Nev. 648, 654, 56 P.3d 868, 872 (2002); State v. Carrasco, 1997-NMSC-047, 124 N.M. 64, 68, 946 P.2d 1075, 1079; State v. Lopez-Minjarez, 350 Or. 576, 583, 260 P.3d 439, 443 (2011); Com. v. Knox, 629 Pa. 467, 471, 105 A.3d 1194, 1197 (2014); State v. Bacon, 163 Vt. 279, 289, 658 A.2d 54, 62 (1995); State v. Stein, 144 Wash. 2d 236, 246, 27 P.3d 184, 189 (2001).

8. See supra notes 3 and 7.

9. Many jurisdictions that have rejected the natural and probable consequence rule nevertheless permit liability on the closely related but conceptually distinct Pinkerton rule. See Pinkerton v. United States, 328 U.S. 640, 647–48, 66 S. Ct. 1180, 1184 (1946) (adopting the rule that a conspirator, by virtue of his participation in a criminal agreement, is liable for all substantive offenses committed by his co-conspirators in furtherance of that agreement). Often courts use the language of Pinkerton interchangeably with the language of "natural and probable consequences," leading to confusion as to which theory of liability applies.

10. See supra notes 3 and 6.

11. See supra notes 4 and 7.

12. State v. Bass, 255 N.C. 42, 51, 120 S.E.2d 580, 587 (1961).

13. See supra notes 4 and 6.

14. See Robinson and Cahill, *Criminal Law,* 2nd ed. §4.1 (Wolters Kluwer 2012).

15. See Robinson and Cahill, *Criminal Law,* 2nd ed. §6.1.2 (Wolters Kluwer 2012).

CHAPTER THIRTEEN

Complicity Liability of Coconspirators

If two or more people agree that one of them will commit an offense and one of them then performs an overt act toward the offense, they can both be held liable for conspiracy to commit the offense, even if the offense is never consummated.[1] If the offense is in fact committed, the perpetrator can obviously be held liable for it, but a coconspirator can also be held liable for the substantive offense if he or she satisfies the requirements of complicity liability, discussed in the previous chapter, typically requiring that the person actually encourage, assist, or attempt to assist the perpetrator; the earlier agreement—the conspiracy—is not necessarily sufficient in itself.

The requirements for complicity are typically more demanding than the requirements for conspiracy. Conspiracy requires only the agreement, while complicity requires actual assistance or, in modern codes, an attempt to assist.[2] Thus, one might be held liable for conspiracy to commit an offense based on the agreement alone but not be an accomplice to the commission of the substantive offense, because the person did nothing to assist.

However, many jurisdictions have adopted what is called the Pinkerton rule,[3] which sets conspiracy to commit an offense as an adequate basis to treat the person as if he or she were an accomplice, and thus fully liable for the substantive offense. Under the Pinkerton rule, a conspirator can be held liable for all of the substantive offenses of coconspirators committed in furtherance of the agreement, even if the conspirator did not assist in any of the offenses.

Even where a jurisdiction adopts the Pinkerton rule, however, a conspirator can avoid the rule's imposition of liability for a subsequent offense if the conspirator withdraws from the conspiracy before the offense. But different jurisdictions adopt different requirements as to what a conspirator must do to withdraw in a way that cuts off Pinkerton liability for subsequent offenses.

This expansion of liability for the crimes of a coconspirator is controversial, and many jurisdictions reject the Pinkerton rule. Where that occurs, a conspirator can only be held liable for the substantive offense of a coconspirator if he or she satisfies the standard complicity requirements for that offense. Even there, however, an accomplice may escape liability for the substantive offense if he or she terminates his or her complicity before the offense and takes certain steps toward preventing the offense.

The position of each state with regard to these issues is indicated on Map 13. The first three groups of states described below adopt the Pinkerton rule, but disagree as to whether withdrawal from the conspiracy cuts off Pinkerton liability for subsequent offenses by coconspirators. The final two groups of states described below reject the Pinkerton rule—they allow complicity liability for an offense only if the special requirements for complicity liability are met—but disagree about whether an accomplice can avoid such standard complicity liability by withdrawing his aid and support before the offense is committed.

Adopts Pinkerton Rule, Rejects Withdrawal Defense

Six states, shown with dark shading on the map—Florida, Georgia, Indiana, Kansas, New Jersey, and Texas[4]—have adopted the Pinkerton rule that, as discussed above, makes a conspirator liable for all substantive offenses committed by his coconspirators in furtherance of that agreement.

These jurisdictions also do not permit a defendant to escape liability under the Pinkerton rule by showing that he or she withdrew from the conspiracy before the coconspirators' offenses. In some cases, the jurisdiction has a nominal withdrawal defense, but it is ineffective in practice—either because any withdrawal must take place before the defendant was legally a party to a conspiracy with an overt act requirement, or because an effective withdrawal must prevent the substantive offense itself. In other cases, the state simply has not recognized a withdrawal defense.

Adopts Pinkerton, Adopts Withdrawal Defense If Positive Steps

Nine states, designated on the map by medium shading—Alabama, Connecticut, Illinois, Kentucky, Louisiana, Maryland, Michigan, Minnesota, and Oklahoma[5]—have adopted the Pinkerton rule but permit a withdrawal defense that will cut off Pinkerton liability.

The withdrawal defense allows a defendant to escape Pinkerton liability by showing that the defendant took certain positive steps against the agreement. The requirements for an effective withdrawal vary by jurisdiction with some requiring a specific positive step and others requiring any one of several

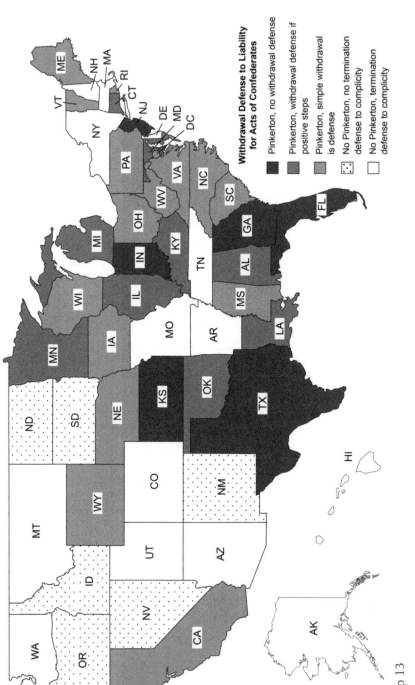

Withdrawal Defense to Liability for Acts of Confederates

- ■ Pinkerton, no withdrawal defense
- ▨ Pinkerton, withdrawal defense if positive steps
- ▨ Pinkerton, simple withdrawal is defense
- ⠿ No Pinkerton, no termination defense to complicity
- ☐ No Pinkerton, termination defense to complicity

Map 13

alternative steps. Positive steps include timely notifying law enforcement, timely notifying a targeted victim, successful efforts to deprive the actor's own involvement of its effectiveness, or efforts of varying degrees to prevent the offense itself.

Adopts Pinkerton, Adopts Simple Withdrawal Defense

Sixteen jurisdictions, identified with light shading on the map—California, District of Columbia, Iowa, Maine, Mississippi, Nebraska, North Carolina, Ohio, Pennsylvania, Rhode Island, South Carolina, Vermont, Virginia, West Virginia, Wisconsin, and Wyoming[6]—have adopted the Pinkerton rule but allow Pinkerton liability for subsequent offenses to cut off by a simple withdrawal from the conspiracy.

In a simple withdrawal jurisdiction, it is sufficient that the actor timely notified his coconspirators of his intention to withdraw from the agreement. This is still a demanding standard: mere fleeing, leaving the scene, or otherwise withdrawing in silence generally does not suffice. For instance, the law may require an "affirmative act" (California), or "unequivocal affirmative conduct" (Mississippi), or "outward displays" (North Carolina) that communicate the withdrawal to coconspirators. (Some of these jurisdictions also permit more than one method of withdrawal.) However, notice that this category of states does not even require notification of law enforcement authorities.

Rejects Pinkerton, Rejects Termination Defense to Complicity

Six states, shown with no shading and dots on the map—Idaho, Nevada, New Mexico, North Dakota, Oregon, and South Dakota[7]—have rejected the Pinkerton rule. In order to hold an actor liable for an offense committed by a coconspirator, the state must proceed on a different theory of liability, such as complicity. For instance, jurisdictions that take the approach of the Model Penal Code permit complicity liability for another substantive offense if the actor "with the purpose of promoting or facilitating the offense, . . . aids or agrees or attempts to aid such other person in planning or committing it."[8]

Where an actor may be found liable under a complicity theory, some jurisdictions permit a defense where the accomplice terminates his complicity before commission of the offense by the perpetrator, as is the case with the group of states below. However, the six states in this group provide no such termination defense for accomplice liability; once an accomplice to an offense, always an accomplice.

Rejects Pinkerton, Adopts Termination Defense to Complicity

Fourteen states, designated with no shading on the map—Alaska, Arizona, Arkansas, Colorado, Delaware, Hawaii, Massachusetts, Missouri, Montana, New Hampshire, New York, Tennessee, Utah, and Washington[9]—have rejected the Pinkerton rule and follow the Model Penal Code in permitting a defense to complicity liability where the person timely terminates his involvement.[10] Nearly all jurisdictions that permit a termination defense to complicity require that the actor take positive steps against the offense commission, such as timely notifying law enforcement, timely notifying the victim, effectively depriving his prior aid of its effectiveness, or taking reasonable or extreme steps to prevent the offense commission.

Observations and Speculations

As Chapter 12 on complicity has made clear, most jurisdictions take great care in defining the requirements that will allow one person to be held liable for the criminal conduct of another. Having worked out these requirements, why should a jurisdiction ever provide an exception to them? Yet, as this chapter makes clear, a great number of jurisdictions short-circuit the standard requirements for complicity liability by adopting the Pinkerton rule, which essentially substitutes the lesser requirements for conspiracy—an offense that is typically punished at a reduced level—and holds those conspiracy requirements as sufficient to support complicity liability for the full substantive offense.

The fact that there is some substantial diversity among the states in the formulation and application of the Pinkerton rule suggests some lack of clarity in its underlying rationale. It is probably fair to say that the rule is based less on some principled argument of equivalent blameworthiness and more on a wish to lighten and simplify the prosecutor's burden.

It is probably true that as a practical matter a coconspirator in a conspiracy that leads to commission of the substantive offense will in many cases satisfy the requirements of an accomplice in that substantive offense, because he will have aided its commission—thus no harm done. But this will not always be the case. There will be instances where the conspirator will not satisfy the requirements of complicity in the substantive offense and does not deserve liability for the full substantive offense, yet it will be imposed on him under the Pinkerton rule.

The situation here is much like the use of strict liability in place of a negligence standard. While it is true that many cases in which strict liability is imposed are cases where negligence in fact exists, that will not always be the case. If negligence does exist, then presumably liability could be imposed if the law set a negligence standard. So the practical effect of adopting strict liability rather than a negligence requirement is to allow the imposition of liability in cases where there is in fact no negligence.

Similarly, if there really is a basis for complicity liability in the full substantive offense, then such liability can be imposed under the traditional complicity requirements. The real effect of substituting the lesser requirements of conspiracy is to extend liability to the cases where the complicity require-ments are not satisfied. In other words, the Pinkerton rule, like the use of strict liability, is a device that will regularly generate liability beyond that which is deserved, at least according to the jurisdiction's complicity definition.

If one is concerned about avoiding injustice, then the use of the Pinkerton rule is objectionable. The excesses of that rule can be reduced (but not elimi-nated) by providing as broad a withdrawal defense as possible that will cut off Pinkerton liability. Preferable are those jurisdictions that reject the Pinker-ton rule, although even these jurisdictions risk injustice if they deny a termi-nation defense to complicity. In other words, for those who care about matching liability and punishment with the defendant's true desert, the five groups of states above are listed in rank order, from the most unjust to the least.

Notes

1. See Paul H. Robinson and Michael T. Cahill, *Criminal Law,* 2nd ed. §12.1 (Wolters Kluwer 2012).

2. See Robinson and Cahill, *Criminal Law,* 2nd ed. §6.1 (Wolters Kluwer 2012).

3. Pinkerton v. United States, 328 U.S. 640, 647–48, 66 S. Ct. 1180, 1184 (1946).

4. Florida is a Pinkerton jurisdiction that apparently permits a withdrawal defense only where the actor prevents the offense commission—effectively deny-ing the defense for crimes of coconspirators. Martinez v. State, 413 So.2d 429 (Fla. Dist. Ct. App. 1982) (upholding Pinkerton rule); Williams v. State, 383 So. 2d 722, 724 (Fla. Dist. Ct. App. 1980) ("[O]nce part of the conspiracy, he was liable for all subsequent criminal acts unless he withdrew from it."); Fla. Stat. Ann. § 777.04 (To withdraw from conspiracy, the actor must "persuade" his con-federates not to commit the offense or "otherwise prevent[its] commission."). Georgia is a Pinkerton jurisdiction. Everritt v. State, 277 Ga. 457, 588 S.E.2d 691, 693 (2003) (upholding Pinkerton rule); Crosby v. State, 232 Ga. 599, 601, 207 S.E.2d 515, 518 (1974) (stating and applying Pinkerton rule). In Georgia, courts and state statutes suggest that withdrawal is a defense for acts of cocon-spirators only in theory, because the withdrawal must take place before any overt act. Bailey v. State, 291 Ga. 144, 146, 728 S.E.2d 214, 216 (2012); Ga. Code Ann. § 16-4-9 ("A coconspirator may be relieved from the effects of [the statute pro-hibiting criminal conspiracy] if he can show that before the overt act occurred he withdrew his agreement to commit a crime."). See, e.g., Mikell v. State, 286 Ga. 434, 436, 689 S.E.2d 286, 288 (2010) (withdrawal defense for acts of coconspira-tors would have been available had defendant shown that he withdrew before any overt act to effect the object of the conspiracy). But see Caldwell v. State, 142 Ga. App. 831, 831, 237 S.E.2d 452, 454 (1977) (withdrawal defense may have been available to defendant who claimed that "when he saw his [coconspirators] pro-duce the guns[,] he refused to enter [the premises unlawfully] and elected to

wait in the car, and . . . told [his coconspirators] he would have nothing to do with any such plan [involving guns]"). Indiana is a Pinkerton jurisdiction. Wright v. State, 690 N.E.2d 1098, 1110 (Ind. 1997); Montgomery v. State, 439 N.E.2d 646, 647–48 (Ind. Ct. App. 1982). Indiana has codified a single abandonment defense to cover all attempt, complicity, and conspiracy liability, but because the defense is available only where the actor prevents the offense, in effect there is no withdrawal defense to Pinkerton liability. Ind. Code Ann. § 35-41-3-10. Despite the legislature's adoption of relevant sections of the Model Penal Code in 1969 and again recently, Kansas has retained the Pinkerton rule. State v. Tyler, 251 Kan. 616, 628, 840 P.2d 413, 424 (1992). However, because Kansas did not adopt the Model Penal Code's termination defense for accomplice liability, the state's highest court has held that the defense is not available. State v. Kaiser, 260 Kan. 235, 249, 918 P.2d 629, 639 (1996); see also State v. Jackson, 280 Kan. 16, 118 P.3d 1238 (2005); 2 Subst. Crim. L. § 13.3 (2d ed.). New Jersey is a Model Penal Code jurisdiction that incorporated Pinkerton liability in its complicity statute. N.J. Stat. Ann. § 2C:2-6; see also State v. Stein, 70 N.J. 369, 360 A.2d 347 (1976) (adopting Pinkerton rule). In New Jersey, a withdrawal or termination defense to accomplice, attempt, or conspiracy liability requires that the defendant success-fully prevent the offense commission. N.J. Stat. Ann. § 2C:5-2; N.J. Stat. Ann. § 2C:2-6; N.J. Stat. Ann. § 2C:5-1. Texas has adopted the Pinkerton rule by statute. Tex. Penal Code Ann. § 7.02; Anderson v. State, 416 S.W.3d 884, 889 (Tex. Crim. App. 2013); Williams v. State, 473 S.W.3d 319, 326 (Tex. App. 2014). Withdrawal or termination is no defense to Pinkerton liability in Texas. Love v. State, 199 S.W.3d 447, 456 (Tex. App. 2006); see also Rose v. State, No. 01-96-01448-CR, 1998 WL 751946, at *1 (Tex. App. Oct. 29, 1998); see generally Tex. Penal Code Ann. § 15.04.

5. Alabama, Connecticut, Illinois, Kentucky, Maryland, Michigan, Minnesota, and Oklahoma are Pinkerton jurisdictions. Pendleton v. State, 57 Ala. App. 454, 329 So.2d 145 (1976); Buford v. State, 891 So. 2d 423, 428 (Ala. Crim. App. 2004); State v. Walton, 227 Conn. 32, 44, 630 A.2d 990, 998 (1993); 720 Ill. Comp. Stat. Ann. 5/5-2; Ky. Rev. Stat. Ann. § 502.020; Commonwealth v. Wolford, 4 S.W.3d 534, 540 (Ky. 1999); Grandison v. State, 305 Md. 685, 696, 506 A.2d 580, 585 (1986); Sheppard v. State, 312 Md. 118, 121, 538 A.2d 773, 774 (1988); People v. Houseman, 128 Mich. App. 17, 24, 339 N.W.2d 666, 669 (1983); People v. Rob-inson, 475 Mich. 1, 12, 715 N.W.2d 44, 51 (2006); Minn. Stat. Ann. § 609.05; Fetter v. State, 1979 OK CR 77, 598 P.2d 262, 265; Johnson v. State, 1986 OK CR 134, 725 P.2d 1270, 1273; Matthews v. State, 2002 OK CR 16, ¶ 43, 45 P.3d 907, 921, as corrected (Apr. 23, 2002). Louisiana law is less clear, though it appears most courts have followed the rule. See State v. Bennett, 454 So. 2d 1165, 1187 (La. Ct. App.), writ denied, 460 So. 2d 604 (La. 1984); State v. Banford, 94-883 (La. App. 5 Cir. 3/15/95), 653 So. 2d 671, 676; State v. Welch, 2009-1609 (La. App. 1 Cir. 2/12/10); cf. La. Stat. Ann. § 15:455. But see State v. West, 568 So. 2d 1019, 1022 (La. 1990); Dale E. Bennett Cheney C., *The Louisiana Criminal Code of 1942—Doctrinal Provisions, Defenses, and Theories of Culpability*, 52 La. L. Rev. 1083 (1992). Alabama, Connecticut, Illinois, Kentucky, Louisiana, Maryland, Michigan, Minnesota, and

Oklahoma permit withdrawal as a defense to Pinkerton liability, but only where the defendant has taken positive steps against the purposes of the conspiracy, such as notifying authorities or the victim, depriving their own support of its effectiveness, or making some reasonable effort to prevent the offense. Ala. Code § 13A-2-24; Conn. Gen. Stat. Ann. § 53a-10; 720 Ill. Comp. Stat. Ann. 5/5-2; 2 Subst. Crim. L. § 13.3; Ky. Rev. Stat. Ann. § 502.040; State v. Taylor, 173 La. 1010, 139 So. 463 (1931); State v. Ellis, App. 5 Cir.1995, 657 So.2d 341, 94-599 (La. App. 5 Cir. 5/30/95); State v. Lobato, 603 So. 2d 739, 746 (La. 1992); State v. Interest of W.T.B., 34,269 (La. App. 2 Cir. 10/20/00), 771 So. 2d 807, 812; State v. Lobato, 603 So. 2d 739, 747 (La. 1992); Cantine v. State, 160 Md. App. 391, 411, 864 A.2d 226, 237–38 (2004); Sheppard v. State, 312 Md. 118, 121, 538 A.2d 773, 774 (1988); McMillan v. State, 181 Md. App. 298, 341, 956 A.2d 716, 741 (2008), rev'd, 428 Md. 333, 51 A.3d 623 (2012); People v. Garel, No. 258962, 2006 WL 1628221, at *1 (Mich. Ct. App. June 13, 2006); People v. Cunningham, No. 270990, 2007 WL 3408098, at *2 (Mich. Ct. App. Nov. 15, 2007); People v. Horn, No. 316757, 2014 WL 6804518, at *8 (Mich. Ct. App. Dec. 2, 2014); People v. Cherry, No. 232027, 2003 WL 1950242, at *14 (Mich. Ct. App. Apr. 24, 2003); Minn. Stat. Ann. § 609.05; 10 Minn. Prac., Jury Instr. Guides—Criminal CRIMJIG 5.15 (6th ed.); Collins v. State, 1977 OK CR 112, 561 P.2d 1373, 1382; Daniels v. State, 1976 OK CR 326, 558 P.2d 405, 411; Vernon's Okla. Forms 2d, OUJI-CR 2-20; Vernon's Okla. Forms 2d, OUJI-CR 2-7.

6. California, District of Columbia, Iowa, Maine, Mississippi, Nebraska, North Carolina, Ohio, Rhode Island, South Carolina, Vermont, Virginia, West Virginia, and Wisconsin are Pinkerton jurisdictions. People v. Zielesch, 179 Cal. App. 4th 731, 739, 101 Cal. Rptr. 3d 628, 633 (2009), as modified (Dec. 3, 2009); People v. Garewal, 173 Cal. App. 3d 285, 300, 218 Cal. Rptr. 690, 698 (Ct. App. 1985); People v. Carmichel, 106 Cal. App.3d 124, 164 Cal. Rptr. 872 (1980) (unpublished); Richardson v. United States, 116 A.3d 434, 442 (D.C. 2015); Iowa Code Ann. § 703.2; State v. Kneedy, 232 Iowa 21, 30, 3 N.W.2d 611, 616 (1942); Me. Rev. Stat. tit. 17-A, § 151; Me. Rev. Stat. tit. 17-A, § 57; Adams v. State, 726 So. 2d 1275, 1278 (Miss. Ct. App. 1998); Williams v. State, 984 So. 2d 989, 993 (Miss. Ct. App. 2007); Shedd v. State, 228 Miss. 381, 386, 87 So. 2d 898, 899 (1956); State v. Cortis, 237 Neb. 97, 113, 465 N.W.2d 132, 144 (1991); State v. Thomas, 210 Neb. 298, 302, 314 N.W.2d 15, 18 (1981); State v. Hairston, 280 N.C. 220, 237, 185 S.E.2d 633, 644 (1972); State v. Barnes, 345 N.C. 184, 228, 481 S.E.2d 44, 68 (1997); State v. Facyson, 367 N.C. 454, 460, 758 S.E.2d 359, 363 (2014); Ohio Rev. Code Ann. § 2923.03; State v. Barton, 424 A.2d 1033 (R.I. 1981); State v. Harnois, 853 A.2d 1249 (R.I. 2004); State v. Tully, 110 A.3d 1181, 1194 (R.I. 2015); State v. Miller, 52 R.I. 440, 445, 161 A. 222, 225 (1932); State v. Woods, 189 S.C. 281, 1 S.E.2d 190, 193 (1939); State v. Adams, 319 S.C. 509, 511, 462 S.E.2d 308, 309 (Ct. App. 1995); State v. Tyler, No. 2005-UP-274, 2005 WL 7083650, at *5 (S.C. Ct. App. Apr. 19, 2005); State v. Larmand, 780 S.E.2d 892, 896 n.6 (S.C. 2015); State v. Orlandi, 106 Vt. 165, 170 A. 908, 910 (1934); State v. Barr, 126 Vt. 112, 122, 223 A.2d 462, 469–70 (1966); State v. Brown, 147 Vt. 324, 326, 515 A.2d 1059, 1061 (1986); Carter v. Com., 232 Va. 122, 126, 348 S.E.2d

265, 267–68 (1986); Owens v. Com., 54 Va. App. 99, 104, 675 S.E.2d 879, 881 (2009); State v. Wisman, 93 W. Va. 183, 116 S.E. 698, 699 (1923), approved, 98 W. Va. 250, 126 S.E. 701 (1925); State v. Ray, 171 W. Va. 383, 389, 298 S.E.2d 921, 926 (1982); Wis. Stat. Ann. § 939.05. But see State v. Small, 301 N.C. 407, 272 S.E.2d 128 (1980); State v. Blankenship, 337 N.C. 543, 447 S.E.2d 727 (1994) (overruled by State v. Barnes, 345 N.C. 184, 481 S.E.2d 44 (1997)). Despite its adoption of relevant sections of the Model Penal Code, Pennsylvania permits Pinkerton liability for all crimes except first-degree murder. Com. v. Jackson, 506 Pa. 469, 474–75, 485 A.2d 1102, 1104 (1984); Com. v. Wayne, 553 Pa. 614, 630, 720 A.2d 456, 464 (1998); Commonwealth v. Roux, 465 Pa. 482, 350 A.2d 867 (1976); 5B Summ. Pa. Jur. 2d Criminal Law § 32:45. In Wyoming, it is not clear whether anyone has been convicted on a Pinkerton theory of liability, though courts have stated the rule with approval in a variety of contexts. See, e.g., Marquez v. State, 12 P.3d 711, 715 (Wyo. 2000) ("It is well established that each member of a conspiracy is criminally accountable for the acts of every other member."); Ekholm v. State, 2004 WY 159, ¶ 24, 102 P.3d 201, 209 (Wyo. 2004) ("[S]o long as the partnership in crime continues, the partners act for each other in carrying it forward"); Black v. State, 2002 WY 72, ¶ 31, 46 P.3d 298, 304 (Wyo. 2002).

A simple withdrawal is a defense to Pinkerton liability in California, District of Columbia, Iowa, Maine, Mississippi, Nebraska, North Carolina, Ohio, Pennsylvania, Rhode Island, South Carolina, Vermont, Virginia, West Virginia, Wisconsin, and Wyoming. In seven of these jurisdictions, it is necessary and sufficient that the actor notifies co-conspirators early enough that they might follow her example. Loser v. Superior Court in & for Alameda Cty., 78 Cal. App. 2d 30, 32, 177 P.2d 320, 321 (1947); People v. Battle, 198 Cal. App. 4th 50, 67, 129 Cal. Rptr. 3d 828, 842 (2011); Cal. Jury Instr.—Crim. 6.20, Cal. Jury Instr.—Crim. 6.20; Me. Rev. Stat. tit. 17-A, § 57; State v. Wilson, 192 Neb. 435, 436–37, 222 N.W.2d 128, 129 (1974); State v. Henry, 292 Neb. 834, 876, 875 N.W.2d 374, 404 (2016); State v. Wilson, 354 N.C. 493, 508, 556 S.E.2d 272, 282 (2001); State v. Graves, 208 N.C. App. 283, 702 S.E.2d 553 (2010); State v. Banner, 233 N.C. App. 599, 758 S.E.2d 902 (2014); Com. v. Laurin, 269 Pa. Super. 368, 372, 409 A.2d 1367, 1369 (1979); Com. v. Lee, 484 Pa. 335, 347, 399 A.2d 104, 110 (1979); Com. v. Spriggs, 463 Pa. 375, 380–81, 344 A.2d 880, 883 (1975); 5B Summ. Pa. Jur. 2d Criminal Law § 32:48; State v. Vang, 353 S.C. 78, 86, 577 S.E.2d 225, 229 (Ct. App. 2003); State v. Woods, 189 S.C. 281, 1 S.E.2d 190, 193–94 (1939); State v. Harris, 351 S.C. 643, 654, 572 S.E.2d 267, 273–74 (2002); State v. Crocker, 366 S.C. 394, 407, 621 S.E.2d 890, 897 (Ct. App. 2005); Wis. Stat. Ann. § 939.05. But see People v. Shelmire, 130 Cal. App. 4th 1044, 1055, 30 Cal. Rptr. 3d 696, 704 (2005). The same rule likely applies in Virginia and West Virginia, though the law is less clear. Virginia commentators suggest that timely notification of co-conspirators is necessary and sufficient to avoid Pinkerton liability. See, e.g., Va. Prac. Criminal Offenses & Defenses P31. But see Blevins v. Com., 209 Va. 622, 626, 166 S.E.2d 325, 328–29 (1969). One West Virginia court suggested the same. State v. Miller, 204 W. Va. 374, 513 S.E.2d 147 (1998). In three jurisdictions, District of Columbia, Mississippi, and Wyoming, the withdrawing co-conspirator may either timely notify coconspirators or timely notify law enforcement. Akins v. United States, 679 A.2d 1017, 1031 (D.C. 1996); United States v. Mardian, 546 F.2d 973, 983 (D.C. Cir. 1976); Norman v. State, 381 So. 2d 1024, 1029 (Miss. 1980); James v. State, 481 So. 2d 805, 809 (Miss. 1985); Marquez v. State, 12 P.3d 711, 715 (Wyo. 2000). In Vermont, the law is less clear, but it seems that the withdrawing coconspirator may timely notify law enforcement or coconspirators, or else make some reasonable effort to prevent the offense. Compare Vt. Stat. Ann. tit. 13, § 1406, with State v. Ballou, 127 Vt. 1, 7, 238 A.2d 658, 662 (1968). Two jurisdictions, Iowa and Ohio, have adopted vague standards for withdrawal that would nevertheless likely permit a simple withdrawal as a defense. State v. McCahill, 72 Iowa 111, 33 N.W. 599 (1887); Ohio Rev. Code Ann. § 2923.03; State v. Hernandez-Martinez, 2012-Ohio-3754, ¶ 40; State v. Rollins, 2008-Ohio-6116, ¶ 50; State v. Davis, 2007-Ohio-5843, ¶ 32, appeal allowed, judgment rev'd, 2008-Ohio-3879, ¶ 32, 119 Ohio St. 3d 113, 892 N.E.2d 446; State v. McMillan., No. 36348, 1977 WL 201507, at *3 (Ohio Ct. App. June 23, 1977). Rhode Island apparently yields to federal common law and thus would likely permit a simple withdrawal. State v. Ros, 973 A.2d 1148, 1164 (R.I. 2009); State v. Brown, 486 A.2d 595, 601 (R.I. 1985); State v. Brown, 486 A.2d 595, 601 (R.I. 1985); Smith v. United States, 133 S. Ct. 714, 719, 184 L. Ed. 2d 570 (2013); United States v. Ngige, 780 F.3d 497, 504 (1st Cir. 2015); United States v. Ciresi, 697 F.3d 19, 27 (1st Cir. 2012).

7. The Pinkerton rule has been rejected in Idaho, New Mexico, North Dakota, Oregon, and South Dakota, though Nevada allows Pinkerton liability for offenses of "general intent." State v. Nevarez, 142 Idaho 616, 621, 130 P.3d 1154, 1159 (Ct. App. 2005); Bolden v. State, 121 Nev. 908, 922, 124 P.3d 191, 200–01 (2005); Simpson v. State, 126 Nev. 756, 367 P.3d 819 (2010); State v. Carrasco, 1997-NMSC-047, 124 N.M. 64, 68, 946 P.2d 1075, 1079; N.D. Cent. Code Ann. § 12.1-03-01; Or. Rev. Stat. Ann. § 161.155; State v. Lopez-Minjarez, 350 Or. 576, 583, 260 P.3d 439, 443 (2011); S.D. Codified Laws § 22-3-3. In Idaho, there is no termination defense for complicity liability. State v. Nevarez, 142 Idaho 616, 621, 130 P.3d 1154, 1159 (Ct. App. 2005); Idaho Code Ann. § 18-204. In Nevada, there is no statutory termination defense, and courts have generally not permitted common-law defenses. Nev. Rev. Stat. Ann. § 195.020; cf. Moran v. Schwarz, 108 Nev. 200, 203, 826 P.2d 952, 954 (1992). There is probably no termination defense in New Mexico. N.M. Stat. Ann. § 30-1-13; State v. Flores, 2005-NMCA-092, 138 N.M. 61, 62, 116 P.3d 852, 853. In North Dakota, the legislature adopted a withdrawal or abandonment defense for conspiracy, solicitation, and attempt liability, but not for complicity liability. N.D. Cent. Code Ann. § 12.1-06-05. Similarly, Oregon's and South Dakota's statutes are silent as to the defense to complicity, suggesting legislative intent not to permit the defense. Or. Rev. Stat. Ann. § 161.155; S.D. Codified Laws § 22-3-3; cf. S.D. Codified Laws § 22-4A-4.

Note that under Nevada law, an actor may be convicted on a Pinkerton theory of liability where the required culpability of the substantive offense is one of general intent. See Simpson v. State, 126 Nev. 756, 367 P.3d 819 (2010). To avoid liability where the Pinkerton rule applies, a defendant may show that he withdrew from the conspiracy. See Barren v. State, 99 Nev. 661, 663, 669 P.2d 725, 726 (1983).

8. Model Penal Code § 2.06.

9. Alaska Stat. Ann. § 11.16.110; Ariz. Rev. Stat. Ann. § 13-303; State ex rel. Woods v. Cohen, 173 Ariz. 497, 501, 844 P.2d 1147, 1151 (1992); Ark. Code Ann. § 5-2-402; Ark. Code Ann. § 5-2-403; Colo. § 18-1-603; Del. Code Ann. tit. 11, § 271; Haw. Rev. Stat. Ann. § 702-222; Commonwealth v. Stasiun, 349 Mass. 38, 206 N.E.2d 672 (1965); Mo. Ann. Stat. § 562.041; Mo. Ann. Stat. § 562.014; Mont. Code Ann. § 45-2-302; Peter Buscemi, *Conspiracy: Statutory Reform Since the Model Penal Code,* 75 Colum. L. Rev. 1122 (1975); N.H. Rev. Stat. Ann. § 626:8; N.Y. Penal Law § 20.00; People v. McGee, 49 N.Y.2d 48, 399 N.E.2d 1177, 424 N.Y.S.2d 157 (1979) cert. denied sub nom. Quamina v. New York, 446 U.S. 942, 100 S. Ct. 2167, 64 L.Ed.2d 797 (1980); Tenn. Code Ann. § 39-11-402; State v. Howard, 30 S.W.3d 271, 276 (Tenn. 2000); 7 Tenn. Prac. Pattern Jury Instr. T.P.I.-Crim. 3.01; Utah Code Ann. § 76-2-202; Wash. Rev. Code Ann. § 9A.08.020; State v. Stein, 144 Wash.2d 236, 241, 27 P.3d 184 (2001).

All these jurisdictions permit a termination defense to complicity liability. Generally the jurisdictions permit the termination defense where the actor takes some positive steps against the offense commission, such as timely notifying law enforcement or the victim, depriving his complicity of its effectiveness, or making some reasonable effort to prevent the offense commission. Alaska Stat. Ann. § 11.16.120; Ariz. Rev. Stat. Ann. § 13-1005; Ark. Code Ann. § 5-2-404; Colo. Rev. Stat. Ann. § 18-1-604; Del. Code Ann. tit. 11, § 273; Haw. Rev. Stat. Ann. § 702-224; Mo. Ann. Stat. § 562.041; Mont. Code Ann. § 45-2-302; N.H. Rev. Stat. Ann. § 626:8; N.Y. Penal Law § 40.10; Utah Code Ann. § 76-2-307; Wash. Rev. Code Ann. § 9A.08.020. Among the jurisdictions that reject Pinkerton but permit a termination defense to complicity liability, only Massachusetts and Tennessee require that the actor timely notify his coconspirators of his withdrawal or termination. Com. v. Hogan, 426 Mass. 424, 435, 688 N.E.2d 977, 985 (1998); State v. Fowler, 23 S.W.3d 285, 288 (Tenn. 2000); State v. Hammonds, 616 S.W.2d 890, 894 (Tenn. Crim. App. 1981); State v. Kaylor, No. C.C.A. 85-258-III, 1986 WL 8507, at *1 (Tenn. Crim. App. Aug. 1, 1986) (unpublished opinion).

10. Model Penal Code § 2.06(6)(c).

PART 4

Justification Defenses

CHAPTER FOURTEEN

Lesser Evils/ Necessity Defense

The criminal law defines the conduct that a society prohibits on pain of criminal sanction, but it also acknowledges that there are some occasions when it may wish to tolerate and even encourage conduct that is normally prohibited. A forest fire is burning toward an unsuspecting town. While destroying another's property is normally a crime, society would very much prefer that a person take the initiative to create a firebreak to save the town, even if that means burning another's field. From a societal perspective, the destruction of the field is trivial in comparison to the destruction of the town and the risk to the lives of its residents.

The balance of interests is not always so clear, however. In one famous case, for example, four people adrift at sea on a raft after their ship sank were on the brink of death from dehydration and starvation. One more day without food or drink would leave them all too weak to survive. One of the four, a cabin boy who had been drinking seawater against the pleas of his mates, was now dying and was past the point of possible recovery. To save the remaining three, two of the men hastened the boy's death in order to drink his blood and survive. After the killing, the third man joined in. As a result, all three survived long enough to be rescued by a passing ship several days later. In reviewing the facts of the case, a court later determined that the men would not have survived if they had not killed and fed on the boy when they did. But the interests in balance involve more than just the tangible interests of losing all four lives versus losing one and saving three. The required balancing also takes account of the critical, intangible interest of having the law seem to approve the taking of the life of an innocent nonaggressor.[1] (The defendants, Dudley

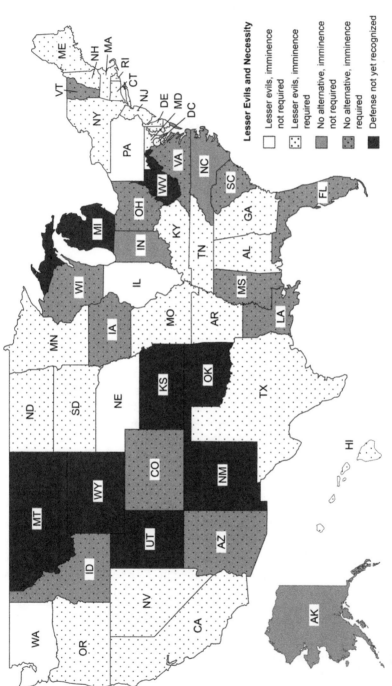

Lesser Evils and Necessity

☐	Lesser evils, imminence not required
⠿	Lesser evils, imminence required
▨	No alternative, imminence not required
▨	No alternative, imminence required
■	Defense not yet recognized

Map 14

and Stephens, were convicted at trial of murder and sentenced to death, but were later released with a minor penalty at the discretion of the Crown.)

In most instances, the law gives detailed rules beforehand about what prohibited conduct is legally justified under what circumstances. Modern American codes usually contain a range of specific justification defenses, including, for example, those concerning the use of force in self-defense or defense of others or defense of property, the use of force for law enforcement purposes, or by persons with special responsibility for the care, discipline, or safety of others, and for the performance of what would otherwise be criminal conduct when done in the execution of public duty.[2]

Occasionally, however, a case may arise in which the person's otherwise prohibited conduct is desirable or at least tolerable and is not covered by one of these specific justification defenses. This is the situation with the firebreak case and the cannibalism case noted above. Neither of these situations is addressed by one of the specific justification defenses. To fill this gap, the law typically recognizes what might be called a general justification defense— one that a person can look to for a defense if, but only if, their situation is not already addressed in one of the specific justification defenses.[3] (In other words, one cannot rely on the general justification defense in a case of self-defense, for example. Instead, one is bound by the specific rules governing self-defense laid down by the legislature in its definition of the self-defense justification.)

As Map 14 illustrates, jurisdictions take several different approaches to defining this catchall general justification defense. (The discussion in this chapter concerns only the objective requirements of the justification defense, not the subjective belief requirements. The issue of mistake as to a justification is dealt with in other chapters.[4])

Lesser Evils Formulation, Imminence Not Required

In the broadest formulation of the defense, modeled after Model Penal Code section 3.02, four states provide the lesser evils justification if the person's conduct avoids a greater harm or evil than that threatened. These states are shown with no shading on the map: Illinois, Nebraska, Pennsylvania, and Washington.[5]

Under this formulation, the person may not engage in the conduct that would otherwise be criminal until it becomes necessary; he or she must wait to see if some noncriminal option becomes available to avoid the threat. However, he or she need not wait until the threatened harm is imminent. Waiting until the harm or evil is imminent may be waiting until it is too late to avoid it. For example, waiting until the forest fire is literally bearing down on the town may leave no time to burn an effective firebreak. If the town is to be saved, the firebreak must be burned well ahead of time, before the destruction of the town is actually imminent.

Lesser Evils Formulation, Imminence Required

In 24 other jurisdictions, identified by no shading and dots on the map—Alabama, Arkansas, California, Connecticut, Delaware, District of Columbia, Georgia, Hawaii, Kentucky, Maine, Maryland, Massachusetts, Minnesota, Missouri, Nevada, New Hampshire, New Jersey, New York, North Dakota, Oregon, Rhode Island, South Dakota, Tennessee, and Texas[6]—the same lesser evils formulation is provided: the person is justified if his conduct avoids a greater harm or evil than it causes.

In these jurisdictions, however, an imminence requirement is added: the defendant cannot get a lesser evils defense unless the threatened harm or evil was imminent. For reasons noted above, this is probably a bad policy judgment; however, the potential breadth of the lesser evils defense worries some jurisdictions, and this limitation is one of the ways that they often narrow it.

"No Alternative" Formulation, Imminence Not Required

A minority of jurisdictions adopt a narrower form of the general justification defense. They typically require, like the two groups above, that the harm caused must be less than the harm threatened, although they commonly express it as requiring a "proportionality of the harm done compared to the harm avoided"[7] or at least not a disproportionality.[8] However, they go further and also require that the person had "no alternative" or "no reasonable alternative" means of avoiding the threatened harm or evil. In these jurisdictions, in light shading on the map—Alaska, Indiana, and North Carolina[9]—the person's course of conduct must be the only course open to him that would avoid the threatened harm or evil.

It is not entirely clear that the additional "no alternative" requirement will in practice narrow the defense in the way that these jurisdictions might expect it. If there are two different courses of conduct by which a threatened harm or evil can be avoided and both are less harmful than what is threatened, the lesser evils formulation described in first two groups would allow the person a lesser evils defense for either course of conduct. In contrast, the "no alternative" formulation would seem to deny a defense because, whichever course of conduct the person took, there was *an alternative* course that the person could have taken.

It is possible that a jury's intuitions of justice would reject this technical application of the "no alternative" formulation and would absolve a defendant even where the defendant did have an alternative course of conduct. In other words, in practice, the addition of the "no alternative" requirement might be taken more as a point of emphasis that the conduct must be necessary to avoid the greater harm than as a limitation to be applied literally as written. On the other hand, jurors might well follow their instructions as given. Part of the problem here is that different juries may respond differently to the limitation and thereby introduce a certain degree of unpredictability in the process.

"No Alternative" Formulation, Imminence Required

Twelve other jurisdictions, designated with light shading and dots on the map—Arizona, Colorado, Florida, Idaho, Iowa, Louisiana, Mississippi, Ohio, South Carolina, Vermont, Virginia, and Wisconsin[10]—adopt the "no alternative" formulation and narrow it further by imposing an imminence requirement. Thus, under this formulation, even if the person had no alternative to avoid the threatened harm or evil, the person will get no defense if he or she does not wait until the threat is imminent. For the reasons noted above, this imminence requirement may be a bad policy. It should be enough to require, as the imminence-not-required formulations do, that it was necessary for the person to act when he or she did in order to avoid the threat, even if that means acting before the threat is fully imminent.

Lesser Evils/Necessity Defense Not Yet Recognized

Eight other states, those shaded black on the map—Kansas, Michigan, Montana, New Mexico, Oklahoma, Utah, West Virginia, and Wyoming[11]—have not yet recognized a general justification defense. This is sometimes because they simply have not yet had a case that requires recognizing such a defense in order to do justice.[12] But this simply points to a legislative failure. The criminal law ought to be predictable, and ought to be determined by the legislature rather than the judicial branch. Leaving the issue unresolved until some court decides whether and what lesser evils defense to recognize is hardly consistent with the principle of legality (discussed in Chapter 4).

In other jurisdictions, a lesser evils/necessity defense is not yet recognized because the lawmaker, frequently courts, confuse the issue of a lesser evils/necessity justification with the issue of a compulsion/duress excuse.[13] They mistakenly believe that the justification cases can be fully and adequately dealt with by a coercion defense. In the examples above, one can see that the sailors adrift at sea might well be able to make a duress of circumstances claim, but that clearly is not true for the good Samaritan passerby who sees the forest fire headed for the unsuspecting town. It is not his interest that is at stake; he is under no duress of circumstances. Yet we very much hope he will burn the firebreak, even at some risk to himself, because it will save the town. If only a duress of circumstances excuse is available, he will get no defense and would be criminally liable if he did act to save the town. (It should also be noted that many if not most jurisdictions may recognize a duress excuse when the source of the duress is another person but may not recognize a duress excuse when the coercion is applied by natural circumstances.)

Perhaps more importantly, these states create significant problems by confusing justification and excuse.[14] Burning the firebreak is not conduct to be excused, as we would excuse somebody who commits an offense because he is insane, under duress, involuntarily intoxicated, or immature. The firebreak burner is blameless *not despite the harmfulness* of his conduct but rather *because his conduct causes no net harm* but rather a net benefit for society. Justified conduct is conduct that we want to signal to others that they too can and perhaps should do under similar circumstances in the future. Excused conduct, in contrast, is conduct that we would prefer was never performed, but we are willing to exculpate the excused actor because, despite the harmfulness of his conduct, we find him to be blameless for doing it.

Majority View Formulation

If one were to construct a general justification defense formulation that reflected the majority view on all points, it would look most like the formulations of the second group above and might look something like the following:

Section 301. Lesser Evils.

1. An actor is justified in engaging in otherwise criminal conduct if [he reasonably believes] his conduct is necessary to avoid an imminent harm or evil to himself or to another, and:

    a.   the harm or evil [sought to be] avoided is greater than that sought to be prevented by the law prohibiting the actor's conduct,

    b.   neither the Code nor other law defining the offense provides exceptions or defenses dealing with the specific situation involved, and

    c.   a contrary legislative balance does not otherwise plainly appear.

2. The defense is not available when the actor was culpable in creating the harm or evil to be avoided.[15]

Observations and Speculations

One might conclude that, because few cases arise under the lesser evils justification, perhaps the absence or misformulation of such a defense ought not be a matter of concern. But the fact is that the defense plays a critical role in a just society committed to the rule of law. First, there inevitably will be cases that raise issues of justification where the situation is not addressed by one of the more specialized justification defenses such as self-defense or law enforcement authority. If the society cares about justice, the defendants in these cases ought to have the benefit of a defense where their conduct avoids the greater harm or evil.

Second, the cases in which the lesser evils defense arise tend to be important cases with a high profile. The criminal law must be seen as having a clear and just answer in such cases. Sometimes, it may be just as important that the criminal law publicly rejects a lesser evils defense as it is in other cases that the law grants the defense. For example, protesters seek a lesser evils defense for damaging an oil pipeline or a nuclear reactor or the Pentagon or an abortion clinic, on the view that their actions are justified in the name of preventing a greater evil. In each instance, the law's resolution of the case can have far-reaching implications.

Finally, the lesser evils defense is unique among justification defenses because it is the one instance in which the criminal law must speak to a justification claim when the legislature has not previously set out a specific rule. The legislature has provided special rules for self-defense and law enforcement authority, for example, but has not set a governing rule in the cases that fall under the lesser evils defense. What is special about the lesser evils justification, then, is that in the absence of such legislative determination the law turns to the jury to do the balancing of interests for the community, rather than leaving it to individual judges. To the extent that one believes in democratic values and the importance of criminal law reflecting community judgments in balancing competing interests, it is the lesser evils defense that assures this deference to community views.

Notes

1. Regina v. Dudley and Stephens, 14 Q.B.D. 273 (1884); see Paul H. Robinson, *Criminal Law Case Studies,* 5th ed., 29–37 (West 2010).

2. See, e.g., Model Penal Code article 3, General Principles of Justification; Paul H. Robinson and Michael T. Cahill, *Criminal Law,* 2nd ed. §8.1 (Wolters Kluwer 2012).

3. See Robinson and Cahill, *Criminal Law,* 2nd ed. 8.2 (Wolters Kluwer 2012).

4. See Chapters 15 and 16.

5. 720 Ill. Comp. Stat. Ann. 5/7-13; Neb. Rev. Stat. Ann. § 28-1407; 18 Pa. Stat. and Cons. Stat. Ann. § 503; State v. Gallegos, 73 Wash. App. 644 (1994); State v. Diana, 24 Wash. App. 908 (1979).

6. Allison v. City of Birmingham, 580 So. 2d 1377, 1379–80 (Ala. Crim. App. 1991); Kauffman v. State, 620 So. 2d 90, 91 (Ala. Crim. App. 1992); Ark. Code Ann. § 5-2-604; People v. Heath, 207 Cal. App. 3d 892, 900-01, 255 Cal. Rptr. 120, 124-25 (Ct. App. 1989); People v. Galambos, 104 Cal. App. 4th 1147, 1160, 128 Cal. Rptr. 2d 844 (2002); Conn. Gen. Stat. Ann. § 53a-4 (West); State v. Drummy, 18 Conn. App. 303, 309, 557 A.2d 574, 578 (1989); Del. Code Ann. tit. 11, § 463; State v. Ramos, No. NONE SUPPLIED, 2013 WL 4718104, at *2 (Del. Super. Ct. Aug. 22, 2013); Griffin v. United States, 447 A.2d 776, 777–78 (D.C. 1982); Emry v. United States, 829 A.2d 970, 972–73 (D.C. 2003); Ga. Code Ann. § 16-3-20;

Tarvestad v. State, 261 Ga. 605, 606, 409 S.E.2d 513, 514 (1991); Isenhower v. State, 324 Ga. App. 380, 384–85, 750 S.E.2d 703, 707 (2013); Jones v. State, 315 Ga. App. 688, 691, 727 S.E.2d 512, 514–15 (2012); Haw. Rev. Stat. Ann. § 703-302; Ky. Rev. Stat. Ann. § 503.030; Me. Rev. Stat. tit. 17-A, § 103; State v. Crawford, 308 Md. 683, 698–99, 521 A.2d 1193, 1200–01 (1987); Johnson v. State, No. 0404 SEPT. TERM 2015, 2016 WL 3569935, at *3; Sigma Reprod. Health Ctr. v. State, 297 Md. 660, 680, 467 A.2d 483, 493 (1983); Frasher v. State, 8 Md. App. 439, 448, 260 A.2d 656, 661–62 (1970); Robinson v. State, 42 Md. App. 617, 621, 402 A.2d 115, 117 (1979); Marquardt v. State, 164 Md. App. 95, 137, 882 A.2d 900, 925 (2005); Com. v. Pike, 428 Mass. 393, 400, 701 N.E.2d 951, 957–58 (1998); Com. v. Kendall, 451 Mass. 10, 13–14, 883 N.E.2d 269, 272–73 (2008); State v. Johnson, 289 Minn. 196, 199, 183 N.W.2d 541, 543 (1971); State v. Hanson, 468 N.W.2d 77, 78 (Minn. Ct. App. 1991); Axelberg v. Comm'r of Pub. Safety, 831 N.W.2d 682, 685 (Minn. Ct. App. 2013), aff'd, 848 N.W.2d 206 (Minn. 2014); State v. Rein, 477 N.W.2d 716, 717 (Minn. Ct. App. 1991); State v. Shief, No. A09-1676, 2010 WL 3395710, at *2 (Minn. Ct. App. Aug. 31, 2010); State v. Davis, No. A07-0331, 2008 WL 2020402, at *5 (Minn. Ct. App. May 13, 2008); State v. Martinelli, No. A06-564, 2007 WL 1191573, at *3 (Minn. Ct. App. Apr. 24, 2007); Mo. Ann. Stat. § 563.026; Hoagland v. State, 126 Nev. 381, 385-886, 240 P.3d 1043, 1045-46 (2010); Jorgensen v. State, 100 Nev. 541, 543-44, 688 P.2d 308, 309-10 (1984); N.H. Rev. Stat. Ann. § 627:3; State v. Stevens, No. 2009-0503, 2010 WL 11437228, at *1 (N.H. June 7, 2010); State v. Tate, 102 N.J. 64, 75, 505 A.2d 941, 946–47 (1986); State v. Lovett, No. A-3211-05T1, 2006 WL 3716432, at *2 (N.J. Super. Ct. App. Div. Dec. 19, 2006); N.Y. Penal Law § 35.05; People v. Bucci, 54 Misc. 3d 1211(A) (N.Y. Just. Ct. 2016); People v. Craig, 78 N.Y.2d 616, 621, 585 N.E.2d 783, 785–86 (1991); N.D. Cent. Code Ann. § 12.1-05-10; State v. Rasmussen, 524 N.W.2d 843, 845-46 (N.D. 1994); Or. Rev. Stat. Ann. § 161.200; State v. Dewhitt, 276 Or. App. 373, 390, 368 P.3d 27, 36–37, review denied, 359 Or. 667, 379 P.3d 526 (2016); State v. Champa, 494 A.2d 102, 105 (R.I. 1985); State v. Ducheneaux, 2003 S.D. 131, ¶ 11, 671 N.W.2d 841, 844; State v. Bowers, 498 N.W.2d 202, 206 (S.D. 1993); State v. Rome, 452 N.W.2d 790, 792 (S.D. 1990); Tenn. Code Ann. § 39-11-609; State v. Boles, No. M201401030CCA-R3CD, 2015 WL 3814061, at *5 (Tenn. Crim. App. June 19, 2015); Texas Penal Code § 9.22. Notwithstanding the apparent availability of the defense in certain cases, the Supreme Court of North Dakota recently suggested that there may not be a general defense of necessity under state law. See State v. Manning, 2006 ND 125, ¶ 10, 716 N.W.2d 466, 468.

  7. Allen v. State, 123 P.3d 1106, 1108 (Alaska Ct. App. 2005).

  8. For example: "the act must not have been disproportionate to the harm avoided." Patton v. State, 760 N.E.2d 672, 676 (Ind. Ct. App. 2002).

  9. Alaska Stat. Ann. § 11.81.320 (West); Allen v. State, 123 P.3d 1106, 1108 (Alaska Ct. App. 2005); Seibold v. State, 959 P.2d 780, 782 (Alaska Ct. App. 1998); Cleveland v. Municipality of Anchorage, 631 P.2d 1073, 1078 (Alaska 1981); Patton v. State, 760 N.E.2d 672, 676 (Ind. Ct. App. 2002); Hernandez v. State, 35 N.E.3d 675 (Ind. Ct. App.), vacated, 45 N.E.3d 373 (Ind. 2015); State v. Thomas,

103 N.C. App. 264, 265, 405 S.E.2d 214, 215 (1991); State v. Hudgins, 167 N.C. App. 705, 710, 606 S.E.2d 443, 447 (2005); City of Kettering v. Berry, 57 Ohio App. 3d 66, 68, 567 N.E.2d 316, 319 (1990); State v. Solivan, 2007-Ohio-5957, ¶ 28

10. Ariz. Rev. Stat. Ann. § 13-417; Colo. Rev. Stat. Ann. § 18-1-702 (West); Andrews v. People, 800 P.2d 607, 609–10 (Colo. 1990); Jenks v. State, 582 So. 2d 676, 679 (Fla. Dist. Ct. App. 1991); Bozeman v. State, 714 So. 2d 570, 572 (Fla. Dist. Ct. App. 1998); Knight v. State, 187 So. 3d 307, 309 (Fla. Dist. Ct. App. 2016); State v. Kopsa, 126 Idaho 512, 520 (Ct. App. 1994); State v. Bonjour, 694 N.W.2d 511, 512 (Iowa 2005); State v. Walton, 311 N.W.2d 113, 115 (Iowa 1981); State v. Moment, 782 N.W.2d 169 (Iowa Ct. App. 2010); State v. Jackson, 452 So. 2d 776, 779 (La. Ct. App. 1984); State v. Perkins, 2012-0662 (La. App. 4 Cir. 7/31/13), 120 So. 3d 912, 918–19; Davis v. State, 18 So. 3d 842, 849 (Miss. 2009); Stodghill v. State, 892 So. 2d 236, 238 (Miss. 2005); Smith v. State, 208 So. 3d 1, 3 (Miss. Ct. App. 2016), reh'g denied (Jan. 17, 2017); Anderson v. State, 185 So. 3d 1015, 1024 (Miss. Ct. App. 2014), aff'd, 185 So. 3d 966 (Miss. 2015); State v. Cole, 304 S.C. 47, 49–50, 403 S.E.2d 117, 118–19 (1991); State v. Myers, 2011 VT 43, ¶ 38, 190 Vt. 29, 50–51, 26 A.3d 9, 24–25 (2011); Buckley v. City of Falls Church, 7 Va. App. 32, 33, 371 S.E.2d 827, 827–28 (1988); Humphrey v. Com., 37 Va. App. 36, 45, 553 S.E.2d 546, 550 (2001); Small v. Commonwealth, 292 Va. 292, 299, 788 S.E.2d 702, 705 (2016); Wis. Stat. Ann. § 939.47; State v. Dix, 2013 WI App 30, ¶ 13, 346 Wis. 2d 280, 827 N.W.2d 929.

11. City of Wichita v. Tilson, 253 Kan. 285, 291, 855 P.2d 911, 915 (1993); City of Wichita v. Holick, 151 P.3d 864 (Kan. Ct. App. 2007); State v. Roeder, 300 Kan. 901, 919, 336 P.3d 831, 846 (2014); People v. Lemons, 454 Mich. 234, 245–47, 562 N.W.2d 447, 453–54 (1997); People v. Penrose, No. 214588, 2000 WL 33538534, at *1–2 (Mich. Ct. App. Jan. 21, 2000); Mont. Code Ann. § 45-2-212; City of Helena v. Lewis, 260 Mont. 421, 426, 860 P.2d 698, 701 (1993); State v. Nelson, 2001 MT 236, ¶¶ 12-13, 307 Mont. 34, 36–37, 36 P.3d 405, 406; State v. Leprowse, 2009 MT 387, ¶ 12, 353 Mont. 312, 315, 221 P.3d 648, 650; State v. Rios, 1999-NMCA-069, 127 N.M. 334, 335–36, 980 P.2d 1068, 1069–70; State v. Gurule, 2011-NMCA-042, 149 N.M. 599, 605, 252 P.3d 823, 829; State v. Tom, 2010-NMCA-062, 148 N.M. 348, 356, 236 P.3d 660, 668 overruled on other grounds by State v. Tollardo, 2012-NMSC-008, 275 P.3d 110; Long v. State, 2003 OK CR 14, ¶¶ 11-13, 74 P.3d 105, 108; Spunaugle v. State, 1997 OK CR 47, 946 P.2d 246, 249 overruled by Long v. State, 2003 OK CR 14, 74 P.3d 105 overruled by Golden v. State, 2006 OK CR 2, 127 P.3d 1150; State v. Ott, 763 P.2d 810, 812 (Utah Ct. App. 1988); State v. Magee, 837 P.2d 993, 995 (Utah Ct. App. 1992); Amin v. State, 811 P.2d 255, 260 (Wyo. 1991); Forbes v. State, 2009 WY 146, ¶ 16, 220 P.3d 510, 512, 515 (Wyo. 2009); Huber v. City of Casper, 727 P.2d 1002, 1005 (Wyo. 1986).

12. As one court concluded, for example, "Whether the necessity defense should be adopted or recognized in Kansas may best be left for another day." City of Wichita v. Tilson, 253 Kan. 285, 291, 855 P.2d 911, 915 (1993).

13. For example: "This Court recently clarified the applicability of the 'necessity' defense in Montana and concluded that the defense has been codified in

§ 45–2–212, MCA. State v. Ottwell (1989), 240 Mont. 376, 379, 784 P.2d 402, 404. In Ottwell, we explained that the defenses of necessity, justification, compulsion, duress, and the 'choice of two evils' have been merged statutorily and labeled 'compulsion' under § 45–2–212, MCA." City of Helena v. Lewis, 260 Mont. 421, 427, 860 P.2d 698, 701 (1993).

14. See Paul H. Robinson, *Structure and Function in Criminal Law*, Chapter 5 (Oxford 1997).

15. From Paul H. Robinson et al., *The American Criminal Code: General Defenses*, 7 Journal of Legal Analysis 37, 21 (2015).

CHAPTER FIFTEEN

Self-Defense

The criminal law normally prohibits the use of force against another person, but such use of force is sometimes authorized. The justification defenses of defensive force define a variety of such situations, one of the most common being the justification of self-defense.[1] A person may use whatever force is necessary to defend himself or herself against the threat of unlawful force by an aggressor. But in addition to this "necessary" requirement, the self-defense justification has a proportionality requirement of sorts: a person may use deadly force in self-defense—that is, force that risks causing death or, in some jurisdictions, serious bodily injury[2]—only when the person is threatened with serious bodily injury or, in some jurisdictions, with other felonies. Map 15 shows the different threat requirements that will trigger the right to use of deadly defensive force in the different jurisdictions.

In the kind of chaotic situations in which self-defense typically arises, it is not uncommon for offenders to make a mistake—for example, in perceiving the exact nature of the threat, in judging what kind of force is necessary to effectively defend against it, or with regard to a wide variety of other legally relevant factors (such as whether a safe retreat is possible).

Every state will excuse a defender for making a reasonable mistake—that is, a mistake that a reasonable person would have made under the same circumstances.[3] However, jurisdictions disagree about what to do if a defender makes an unreasonable mistake—that is, a reckless or negligent mistake. For example, if the defender mistakenly believes that she is threatened with serious bodily injury—it never occurs to her that the threat only involves mere bodily injury—then she has made a negligent mistake if a reasonable person in her situation would realize that the threat involves mere bodily injury.

Most states would deny any excuse defense to such a defender, so she would be fully liable for the offense—such as murder, if she killed her attacker mistakenly believing he was threatening serious bodily injury when in fact he was threatening only bodily injury. These jurisdictions take what is

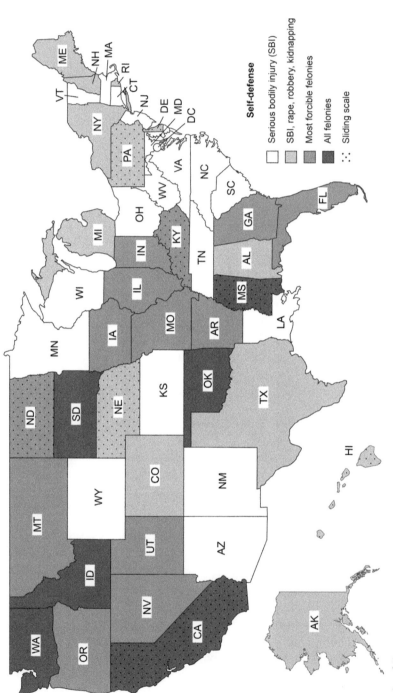

Self-defense

☐	Serious bodily injury (SBI)
	SBI, rape, robbery, kidnapping
	Most forcible felonies
■	All felonies
⋰	Sliding scale

Map 15

commonly called the "all-or-nothing" approach, which means that an actor's reckless or negligent belief that she was justified will not provide a defense or mitigation—she instead incurs full liability. Only a fully reasonable mistake—a non-negligent mistake—provides an excuse and thus avoids criminal liability.[4]

Eight states take instead a "sliding-scale" approach. Under this approach, a defender's reasonable mistake will provide a complete defense, but an actor's honest but negligent mistake is treated differently than under the all-or-nothing approach. Under the sliding-scale approach, the mistaken defender will incur criminal liability, but her level of liability will be tied to her level of culpability in making the mistake. If she makes a negligent mistake in using defensive force, she can be held liable only for an offense of negligence; if she makes a reckless mistake, she can be held liable for an offense of recklessness. Under the sliding-scale approach, the extent of her liability shifts according to the extent of her culpability in making the mistake.[5] This approach was pioneered under Model Penal Code section 3.09(2). Map 15 identifies with an overlay of dots the eight states that adopt the sliding-scale approach.

Authorizes Deadly Force Only against Threat of Serious Bodily Injury

Nineteen jurisdictions, identified on the map with no shading—Arizona, Connecticut, District of Columbia, Kansas, Louisiana, Maryland, Massachusetts, Minnesota, New Jersey, New Mexico, North Carolina, Ohio, South Carolina, Tennessee, Vermont, Virginia, West Virginia, Wisconsin, and Wyoming[6]—limit the use of deadly force to defend against a threat of serious bodily injury or death.

All of these states take the all-or-nothing approach to mistake as to justification.[7]

Authorizes Deadly Force against Threat of Serious Bodily Injury or Enumerated Serious Felonies

Thirteen jurisdictions, shown with light shading on the map—Alabama, Alaska, Colorado, Delaware, Hawaii, Maine, Michigan, Nebraska, New Hampshire, New York, Pennsylvania, Rhode Island, and Texas—permit deadly force against threats of death or serious bodily injury, as well as against certain other serious forcible felonies. Michigan specifies death, serious bodily injury, and rape.[8] Delaware, Hawaii, Nebraska, and Pennsylvania permit deadly force specifically against death, serious bodily injury, rape, and kidnapping.[9] Seven states—Alabama, Alaska, Colorado, Maine, New Hampshire, New York, and Texas—permit deadly force against threat of death, serious bodily injury, rape, kidnapping, or robbery.[10] Rhode Island, rather than enumerating cases where deadly force may be used, embraces a "totality of the circumstances" test,[11] which presumably would at least permit deadly force in cases of very serious felonies like rape, kidnapping, and robbery.

Nine of these 13 states take the all-or-nothing approach to mistake as to justification. Four of the states—Delaware, Hawaii, Nebraska, and Pennsylvania—take the sliding-scale approach.[12]

Authorizes Deadly Force against Threat of Most Forcible Felonies

Thirteen jurisdictions, those with medium shading on the map—Arkansas, Florida, Georgia, Illinois, Indiana, Iowa, Kentucky, Missouri, Montana, Nevada, North Dakota, Oregon, and Utah[13]—specifically permit deadly force against threats of death or serious bodily injury, as well as an extensive list of enumerated, forcible felonies, including, for example, burglary, aggravated battery, and arson.

Eleven of these 13 states take the all-or-nothing approach to mistake as to justification. Only two—Kentucky and North Dakota—take the sliding-scale approach.[14]

Authorizes Deadly Force against Threat of Any Felony

Six jurisdictions, those with darker shading on the map—California, Idaho, Mississippi, Oklahoma, South Dakota, and Washington[15]—permit deadly force against threats of "any felony." For instance, Mississippi law states that deadly force may be used "in resisting any attempt unlawfully to kill such person or to commit any felony upon him."[16]

Four of the six jurisdictions take the all-or-nothing approach to mistake of justice justification. Only two of the six—California and Mississippi—take the sliding-scale approach.[17]

Majority View Formulations

The self-defense justification is commonly combined with a justification defense for defense of others, under a general "defense of person" justification. If one were to formulate such a defense in a way that reflected the majority American rule in all respects, it might look something like this:

Section 303. Defense of Persons

1. An actor is justified in using force that [he reasonably believes] is necessary to defend himself or a third person against imminent unlawful force by an aggressor.

2. The use of deadly force in self-defense is justified if [the actor reasonably believes that] such force is necessary to protect himself or a third person

against death, serious bodily injury, sexual intercourse compelled by force, or kidnapping.

3. An actor is not justified in using force against another person:

    a. if he intentionally provoked unlawful action by the other person in order to cause bodily injury to the person;

    b. if he is the initial aggressor, unless he has withdrawn from the encounter and effectively communicated his withdrawal to the other person, but the other person persists in continuing the conflict by force;

    c. if the force was the product of mutual combat by agreement not specifically authorized by law; or

    d. to resist an arrest that the actor knows is being made by a peace officer, even if the arrest is unlawful, except force may be used to resist an arrest that is unlawful because the officer is using excessive force.

4. An actor has no duty to retreat from a place he has a right to be before using deadly or non-deadly force that is necessary to defend himself or a third person.[18]

Most jurisdictions provide an excuse for a reasonable mistake as to justification simply by including in the defensive force provision a requirement that the defendant "reasonably believes" that the justifying circumstances exist. See the bracketed language in the majority formulation above. If one were to formulate a separate mistake as to a justification excuse, as North Dakota does,[19] such a formulation that reflected the majority American view on all issues might look something like the following:

Section 307. Mistake as to a Justification Excuse

1. Mistake. A person's conduct is excused if he reasonably believes that the factual situation is such that his conduct is necessary and appropriate for any of the purposes that would establish a justification defense under this Chapter.

2. The excuse defense provided in Subsection (1) is unavailable if:

    a. the actor's belief in the unlawfulness of the force or conduct against which he employs protective force or his belief in the lawfulness of an arrest which he endeavors to effect by force is erroneous; and

    b. his error is due to ignorance or mistake as to the provisions of the Code, any other provision of the criminal law or the law governing the legality of an arrest or search.[20]

Observations and Speculations

There seems to be some considerable disagreement among the jurisdictions about what kind of threats should give rise to the right to use deadly force in self-defense. As noted above, 19 states limit deadly force to defending against a threat of death or serious bodily injury; 1 state adds to that list the threat of rape; 4 others add the crime of kidnapping; 8 more add the offense of robbery; 13 states add miscellaneous other serious felonies, such as arson, aggravated battery, and burglary—in other words, most forcible felonies—while 16 states drop the list approach altogether and authorize the use of deadly force to defend against any felony.[21]

One can imagine criticisms that could be made against each of these approaches, especially those at the extremes of the continuum. Why should the use of deadly force be limited to threats of death or serious bodily injury and not other serious offenses, such as rape? Or, is it clear that deadly force should be authorized to defend against all felonies, including nonforcible felonies? But, to some extent, both of these kinds of objections may miss the point.

As to the latter objection—that authorizing deadly force against all felonies is too broad—the legislative proportionality judgments reflected in this statutory rule is only one aspect of the requirements for the use of deadly defensive force. To get a defense, the defender must also show that her use of deadly force was in fact *necessary* to protect herself. That is, she must show that no lesser amount of force, such as nondeadly force, would have been adequate to protect herself and, further, she must show that she had to use the deadly force when she did and could not have waited until some later time. From this perspective, the danger of justifying too much seems significantly reduced. If a defender has no other means to successfully defend herself against a felony other than by the use deadly force, do we really want to insist that she must simply suffer the victimization? If the unlawfully threatened victimization is a felony, many people will feel uncomfortable demanding such sacrifice by the victim in order to minimize risk to the unlawful, felonious aggressor.

As to the former objection—that authorizing deadly force only against the threat of serious bodily injury is too narrow—it is worth noting that the concept of "serious bodily injury" can well be interpreted to include all sorts of conduct, including, for example, rape. Similarly, if one examines the various felonies that other jurisdictions add, such as kidnapping, robbery, and arson, it would not be too difficult to see each one of them as containing a threat of "serious bodily injury." On the other hand, it may well be a clearer and more reliable approach to explicitly list the offenses for which deadly force is authorized rather than depend on judges to interpret the "serious bodily injury" requirement broadly enough to include threats of such injury that arise in the context of these other offenses.

Perhaps a greater problem with limiting the use of deadly force to threats of "serious bodily injury," rather than giving a full list of forcible felonies, is that it creates an additional hurdle for defenders. In the chaotic situation of self-defense, defenders could well make mistakes about this triggering condition. A defender may use deadly force that is absolutely necessary to defend herself against an unlawful threat but may make an honest but negligent mistake about whether the threat is on the official list of triggering offenses. Such an actor will get no mistake defense whatever under the more common all-or-nothing approach, and thus will be held liable for murder, as if she killed in the absence of any aggression at all. The sliding-scale approach would give her a mitigation to negligent homicide, but this approach is taken by only eight jurisdictions.

The broader the list of triggering offenses for deadly force, such as "all forcible felonies" or "all felonies," the less the all-or-nothing approach can do its damage. (The problem of the all-or-nothing approach and the advantages of the sliding-scale approach are explored in greater detail in Chapter 16, concerning the law enforcement justification, and those same points apply here to the use of defensive force as well.)

Notes

1. See Paul H. Robinson and Michael T. Cahill, *Criminal Law,* 2nd ed. §8.4 (Wolters Kluwer 2012).

2. See, e.g., State v. Jackson, 384 S.C. 29, 35–36, 681 S.E.2d 17, 20 (Ct. App. 2009) (stating that, to justify the use of deadly force, a defendant must have been in "actual imminent danger of losing his life or sustaining serious bodily injury, or he must have actually [reasonably] believed he was in imminent danger of losing his life or sustaining serious bodily injury"); Tex. Penal Code Ann. § 9.31 ("[A] person is justified in using force against another when and to the degree the actor reasonably believes the force is immediately necessary to protect the actor against the other's use or attempted use of unlawful force. [Such force] is presumed to be reasonable if the actor . . . had reason to believe that the person . . . was committing . . . aggravated kidnapping, murder, sexual assault, aggravated sexual assault, robbery, or aggravated robbery.").

3. See Robinson and Cahill, *Criminal Law,* 2nd ed. §8.5 (Wolters Kluwer 2012).

4. Quates v. State, 439 So.2d 199 (1983); Lacy v. State, 629 So.2d 688 (1993); Weston v. State, 682 P.2d 1119 (Alaska 1984); Ariz. Rev. Stat. Ann. § 13-401; Ariz. Rev. Stat. Ann. § 13-404; Ariz. Rev. Stat. Ann. § 13-405; Ariz. Rev. Stat. Ann. § 13-406; Ariz. Rev. Stat. Ann. § 13-407; Ariz. Rev. Stat. Ann. § 13-415; Ark. Code Ann. § 5-2-614; Kendrick v. State, 644 S.W.2d 297 (1982); People v. Gross, 287 P.3d 105 (Colo. 2012); Daniel v. Commissioner of Correction, 57 Conn. App. 651 (2000); Swann v. U.S., 648 A.2d 928 (1994); Fla. Stat. Ann. § 776.012; Fla. Stat. Ann. § 776.013; Fla. Stat. Ann. § 776.031; Fla. Stat. Ann. § 776.032; Fla. Stat. Ann. § 776.04; Fla. Stat. Ann. § 776.041; Reese v. State, 289 Ga. 446 (2011); Paz v. State, 123 Idaho 758 (1993); People v. Brown, 19 Ill. App.3d 757 (1974); Littler v. State, 871 N.E.2d 276 (Ind. 2007); State v. Gomez-Rodriguez, 736 N.W.2d 267 (Iowa 2007); State v. Pennington, 43 Kan. App.2d 446 (2010); State v. Morris, 22 So.3d 1002 (La. 2009); Me. Rev. Stat. Ann. tit 17-A, § 101; State v. Grant, 418 A.2d 154 (Me. 1980); State v. Martin, 329 Md. 351 (1993); Com. v. Robinson, 382 Mass.

189 (1981); People v. Reese, 491 Mich. 127 (2012); State v. Thompson, 544 N.W.2d 8 (Minn. 1996); State v. Sanders, 556 S.W.2d 75 (Mo. 1977); Mont. Code Ann. § 45-3-102; Mont. Code Ann. § 45-3-105; Hill v. State, 98 Nev. 295 (1982); N.H. Rev. Stat. Ann. § 627:4; State v. Finley, 714 A.2d 918 (N.J. 1998); State v. Abeyta, 120 N.M. 233 (1995); People v. Goetz, 68 N.Y.2d 96 (1986); State v. Ramseur, 739 S.E.2d 599 (N.C. 2013); State v. Goff, WL 139545 (Ohio 2013); Davis v. State, 268 P.3d 86 (Okla. Ct. Crim. App. 2011); Or. Rev. Stat. Ann. § 161.209; Or. Rev. Stat. Ann. § 161.215; Or. Rev. Stat. Ann. § 161.219; Or. Rev. Stat. Ann. § 161.225; State v. Garcia, 883 A.2d 1131 (R.I. 2005); S.C. Code Ann. § 16-11-410; S.C. Code Ann. § 16-11-420; S.C. Code Ann. § 16-11-430; S.C. Code Ann. § 16-11-440; S.C. Code Ann. § 16-11-450; S.D. Codified Laws § 22-5-9; State v. Boyland, WL 2464211 (Tenn. 2011); Alonzo v. State, 353 S.W.3d 778 (Tex. Ct. Crim. App. 2011); State v. Coonce, 36 P.3d 533 (Utah 2001); State v. Shaw, 168 Vt. 412 (1998); Couture v. Com., 51 Va. App. 239 (2008); State v. Hughes, 106 Wash.2d 176 (1986); State v. Miller, 178 W. Va. 618 (1987); State v. Camacho, 176 Wis.2d 860 (1993); Wyo. Stat. Ann. § 7-11-304.

5. In re Christian S., 7 Cal.4th 768 (1994); Del. Code Ann. tit. 11, § 470; State v. Mathis, WL 3271148 (Del. 2008); Haw. Rev. Stat. § 703-310; Com. v. Hager, 41 S.W.3d 828 (Ky. 2001); Lanier v. State, 684 So.2d 93 (Miss. 1996); Neb. Rev. Stat. Ann. § 1412; Neb. Rev. Stat. Ann. § 1414; State v. Leidholm, 334 N.W.2d 811 (N.D. 1983); 18 Pa. Cons. Stat. Ann. § 2503.

6. Ariz. Rev. Stat. Ann. § 13-405; Conn. Gen. Stat. Ann. § 53a-19; Muschette v. U.S., 936 A.2d 791 (2007); Kan. Stat. Ann. § 21-5222; La. Rev. Stat. Ann. § 14:20; Sydnor v. State, 365 Md. 205 (2001); Com. v. Toon, 55 Mass. App. Ct. 642 (2002); Minn. Stat. Ann. § 609.065; N.J. Stat. Ann. § 2C:3-4; State v. Gallegos, 130 N.M. 221 (2001); State v. Ramseur, 739 S.E.2d 599 (N.C. 2013); Goldfuss v. Davidson, 79 Ohio St.3d 116 (1997); State v. Jackson, 384 S.C. 29 (2009); Tenn. Code Ann. § 39-11-611; State v. Wheelock, 158 Vt. 302 (1992); Lynn v. Com., 27 Va. App. 336 (1998); Bailey v. Com., 200 Va. 92 (1958); Feliciano v. 7-Eleven, 210 W. Va. 740 (2001); Wis. Stat. Ann. § 939.48; Wyo. Stat. Ann. § 6-2-602.

7. See supra note 4.

8. Mich. Comp. Laws Ann. § 780.972.

9. Del. Code Ann. tit. 11, § 464; Haw. Rev. Stat. § 703-304; Neb. Rev. Stat. Ann. § 28-1409; 18 Pa. Cons. Stat. Ann. § 505.

10. Ala. Code § 13A-3-23; Alaska Stat. Ann. § 11.81.335; Colo. Rev. Stat. Ann. § 18-1-704; Del. Code Ann. tit 11, § 464; Me. Rev. Stat. Ann. tit. 17-A, § 108; N.H. Rev. Stat. Ann. § 627:4; N.Y. Penal Law § 35:15; Tex. Penal Code Ann. § 9.31.

11. Rather than stating specifically which kind of unlawful force triggers a person's right to use deadly force, Rhode Island courts have held that the permissible degree of force is "that which is necessary under all the circumstances to prevent any injury to the person." State v. Ventre, 811 A.2d 1178, 1183 (R.I. 2002). Thus, a jury "may consider the size of the parties, the circumstances of the assault, as well as the relative strength, weaknesses of the parties, and the like . . . in light of the time, place and surrounding circumstances." State v. Marquis, 588 A.2d 1053, 1055 (R.I. 1991).

12. See supra notes 4 and 5.

13. Ark. Code Ann. § 5-2-607; Fla. Stat. Ann. § 776.012; Fla. Stat. Ann. § 776.013; Ga. Code Ann. § 16-3-21720 Ill. Comp. Stat. Ann. 5/7-1; Ind. Code § 35-41-3-2; Iowa Code § 704.1; Ky. Rev. Stat. Ann. § 503.050; Mo. Ann. Stat. § 563.031; Mont. Code Ann. § 45-3-102; Nev. Rev. Stat. Ann. § 200.120; N.D. Cent. Code § 12.1-05-07; Or. Rev. Stat. Ann. § 161.219; Utah Code Ann. § 76-2-402.

14. See supra notes 4 and 5.

15. Cal. Penal Code § 197; People v. Zuckerman, 56 Cal. App. 2d 366 (1942); Idaho Code Ann. § 18-4009; Miss. Code Ann. § 97-3-15; Okla. Stat. tit. 21, § 733; S.D. Codified Laws § 22-16-34; Wash. Rev. Code Ann. § 9A.16.050.

16. Miss. Code. Ann. § 97-3-15.

17. See supra notes 4 and 5.

18. From Paul H. Robinson et al., *The American Criminal Code: General Defenses,* 7 Journal of Legal Analysis 37, 13 (2015).

19. See N.D. Cent. Code Ann. § 12.1-05-08, which provides:

> A person's conduct is excused if he believes that the facts are such that his conduct is necessary and appropriate for any of the purposes which would establish a justification or excuse under this chapter, even though his belief is mistaken. However, if his belief is negligently or recklessly held, it is not an excuse in a prosecution for an offense for which negligence or recklessness, as the case may be, suffices to establish culpability. Excuse under this section is a defense or affirmative defense according to which type of defense would be established had the facts been as the person believed them to be.

20. From Paul H. Robinson et al., *The American Criminal Code: General Defenses,* 7 Journal of Legal Analysis 37, 39 (2015).

21. See supra notes 4 through 7.

CHAPTER SIXTEEN

Law Enforcement Authority

When police officers use force to make an arrest, their conduct may satisfy the requirements of an assault offense, but they typically will have a justification defense that protects them from criminal liability.[1] Every state provides such a justification defense but with limits on how much force an officer may use in what situations. For example, an officer is not justified in using deadly force to catch an offender fleeing from an unarmed burglary even if the officer has no other way of apprehending the offender.[2]

If one were to draft a law enforcement justification defense that reflects the majority view of American jurisdictions on the justified use of force by police officers, it might look something like this:

Law Enforcement Authority.

1. *Use of Force Justifiable to Effectuate an Arrest.* The use of force upon or toward the person of another is justifiable when a peace officer, or private actor under the direction of a peace officer, is making or assisting in making an arrest and [reasonably believes that] such force is necessary to effectuate the arrest.

2. *Limitations on the Use of Deadly Force.* The use of deadly force is not justifiable under this Section unless:

   a. the actor, where feasible, warns the suspect that he or she intends to effectuate an arrest; and

   b. the actor has probable cause to believe:

      i. the suspect poses a threat of serious physical harm to any individual, be it the officer or another; or

      ii. the suspect committed a crime that involved the infliction or threatened infliction of serious physical harm; or

      iii. the suspect is threatening the actor with a weapon.

3. *Use of Force to Prevent Escape from Custody.* The use of force authorized in Subsections 1 and 2 can be used to prevent an escape from custody either during or after an arrest.

4. *Use of Force to Prevent Escape from Detention Facility.* A peace officer is justified in using force that [he or she reasonably believes] is necessary to prevent the escape of a charged or convicted detainee from a jail, prison, or other such institution. However, a peace officer may not use deadly force unless [he or she reasonably believes] the escapee is in custody for committing a felony.[3]

A sometimes more difficult issue is that of mistake as to a law enforcement justification. Suspect-police confrontations are commonly chaotic, requiring split-second decision making. Is the object that the suspect is pulling from his jacket a gun or a cell phone? The officer's duty is to arrest the subject, not run away from the situation, so the officer must confront the uncertainty, despite the risks to officers and to suspects.

In other words, jurisdictions must not only set out the ex ante rules defining when an officer may use force in making an arrest but also must specify the rules by which an officer is to be judged ex post if he or she turns out to be wrong in the use of force—if, for example, the suspect's weapon turns out to be a realistic toy gun. How is a court and jury to determine whether the officer should be criminally liable for shooting a suspect who turns out to be unarmed?

Every American jurisdiction has adopted some rules governing the treatment of mistakes as to justification.[4] Map 16 indicates the three different approaches the jurisdictions take in formulating this aspect of the law enforcement justification.

Defense Only Requires Defendant Believed Force Was Necessary, but Separate Provision Imposes Sliding-Scale Liability for Mistake

Five states, identified with no shading on the map—Delaware, Hawaii, Kentucky, Nebraska, and Pennsylvania[5]—provide a justification defense if the officer "believes" that the conditions exist that would justify the use of force. If the officer's belief is mistaken, he or she may not get a complete defense.

If the officer has made an honest but a reckless mistake as to the necessity for the use of force, then he or she may have a defense to offenses requiring intentional or knowing, such as murder, but would have no defense to an offense that requires only recklessness, such as manslaughter. Similarly, if the officer is negligent in mistakenly believing that the use of force is necessary, then he or she can be held liable for an offense requiring negligence, such as negligent homicide, but would get a defense to offenses requiring recklessness, knowledge, or intention, such as manslaughter or murder.

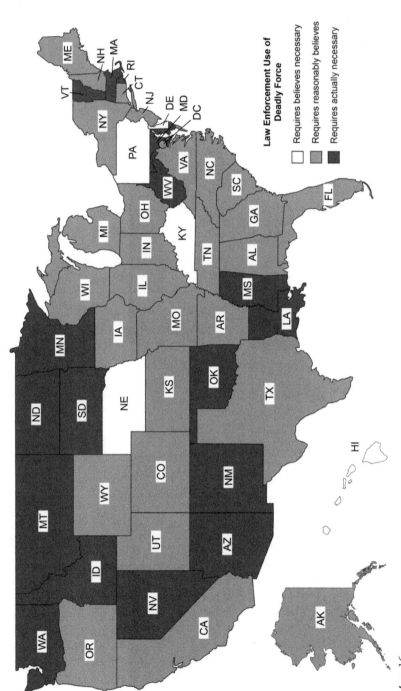

Law Enforcement Use of
Deadly Force

☐ Requires believes necessary

▨ Requires reasonably believes

■ Requires actually necessary

Map 16

In other words under this approach—what has been called the "sliding-scale approach"—the extent of the officer's criminal liability will depend on the level of culpability in the mistake he or she has made. Pioneered by the American Law Institute's Model Penal Code,[6] the approach adheres nicely to the principle of blameworthiness proportionality: it sets the extent of the officer's liability and punishment to be proportionate to the extent of the officer's blameworthiness for his or her mistake in the use of force.

Defense Requires Defendant Reasonably Believed Force Was Necessary (Imposing All-or-Nothing Liability)

A more common approach, however, is what has been termed the "all-or-nothing" approach. It gives a complete defense to an officer who mistakenly but reasonably believed his conduct was justified, that is, a reasonable mistake, but it gives no defense or mitigation whatever to an officer whose mistake was unreasonable in any way, that is, if it is either reckless or negligent. Twenty-nine jurisdictions, those with medium shading, take this approach: Alabama, Alaska, Arkansas, California, Colorado, Connecticut, District of Columbia, Florida, Georgia, Illinois, Indiana, Iowa, Kansas, Maine, Michigan, Missouri, New Hampshire, New Jersey, New York, North Carolina, Ohio, Oregon, South Carolina, Tennessee, Texas, Utah, Virginia, Wisconsin, and Wyoming.[7]

This approach is thought to cause officers to be more careful in their use of force, for only a completely reasonable mistake will give them a defense; an honest but unreasonable mistake will leave them fully liable for the offense without even a mitigation. On the other hand, this approach has been criticized as violating the blameworthiness proportionality principle. Consider the officer who honestly believes that force is necessary but turns out to be negligent in that belief—that is, it never occurred to him or her that force might not be necessary, but a reasonable person in the situation would have been aware of at least a risk that it was unnecessary. Clearly such a person does not have the same degree of blameworthiness of the classic murderer who has no claim of being justified, yet the all-or-nothing approach equates the two by convicting the negligent officer of murder.

Defense Requires Force Was Actually Necessary, but Provides a Separate Mistake Excuse

Seventeen jurisdictions, marked with dark shading on the map—Arizona, Idaho, Louisiana, Maryland, Massachusetts, Minnesota, Mississippi, Montana, Nevada, New Mexico, North Dakota, Oklahoma, Rhode Island, South Dakota, Vermont, Washington, and West Virginia[8]—have neither "reasonably believes" or "believes" language in their statutory formulations of the defense. Instead, their justification defense is written in purely objective terms: "An actor is justified if his use of force is necessary to . . . ."

One might initially think that these jurisdictions are denying a mistake defense to an officer who gets it wrong, even one who "reasonably believes" his or her conduct is necessary, but this is not the case. These jurisdictions simply take a different approach to the drafting of their justification defense by segregating from it the rules governing the defense of mistake as to justification. That is, they provide a mistake as to justification defense or mitigation but do so in a separate mistake excuse provision apart from their objective justification defense.

There is good reason for this segregation, and some writers have argued that it is to be much preferred over the more common mixing of justification and mistake as to justification seen in the two groups above.[9] There is an important conceptual difference between objective justification and mistake as to justification. The former are ex ante rules of conduct by which the criminal law describes how officers should behave—the circumstances under which we are happy to have, or at least willing to tolerate, the officers' use of force. The latter—mistakes as to justification—are instances where we disapprove of the conduct and want to signal to others that they should not engage in such conduct under such circumstances in the future. We are giving a defense to the actor despite our condemning the conduct, because we hold the actor blameless (or, in the sliding-scale approach, less blameworthy). That is, true objective justification and mistake as to justification send exactly opposite signals about the propriety of the officer's conduct.

Observations and Speculations

It is easy enough to understand why jurisdictions may be tempted by the all-or-nothing approach. After all, the officer has turned out to be not only wrong—his conduct is not actually objectively justified—but also has turned out to be unreasonable in his mistaken belief that it was right. It is also understandable that we would want officers to be particularly careful in their use of force; if they make a mistake, they ought to have entirely reasonable explanations for it or they should be criminally liable.

On the other hand, the all-or-nothing approach has some serious problems. One of them has already been noted above: it may well be that the actor who makes an honest but unreasonable mistake is blameworthy and deserves some criminal liability, but it is also clear that the extent of the person's blameworthiness is importantly different from that of the person who acts without any claim of justification whatever. The officer who kills in a mistaken belief that it is necessary and whose mistake is reckless or negligent ought to have some criminal liability, such as liability for manslaughter or negligent homicide, but not liability for murder, for that would equate his blameworthiness with that of the person who kills as an aggressor, without even any claim of acting defensively.

Another serious problem with the all-or-nothing approach is less obvious. The problem is that, while the all-or-nothing approach ignores the blame-worthiness proportionality principle, ordinary people, including jurors, do not. The empirical research makes it clear that the proportionality of punishment and blameworthiness is fundamental to ordinary people's judgments of justice.[10]

Consider, then, what happens in all-or-nothing jurisdictions when juries are given their legal instructions in a case where an officer has made an honest but unreasonable mistake in the use of force. The jurisdiction's all-or-nothing approach means that the jury will be given only two options: to convict the officer of murder if his mistake is unreasonable in any way, or to acquit the officer if his mistake is entirely reasonable. But in such cases, the jury will find neither option attractive. If they believe his mistake is honest but negligent, they will be reluctant to pretend that it is fully reasonable and thus reluctant to give the officer a complete defense that he does not deserve. On the other hand, they will be reluctant to give the officer no defense or mitigation of any kind, because that would mean holding the officer liable as a standard murderer. Faced with these two bad options, it is common for juries to give the officer a complete defense that he does not deserve, as their only means of avoiding treating the officer as a murderer, which they do not believe he is.

Thus, in practice, the all-or-nothing approach has the opposite effect from what is intended. Instead of being an approach that takes a hard line on police use of force, supposedly forcing officers to be more careful and punishing them severely whenever they are not reasonable, it turns out that the all-or-nothing approach in practice gives blameworthy officers a complete defense even though they deserve some punishment.

Notes

1. For discussion of public authority justifications generally, see Paul H. Robinson and Michael T. Cahill, *Criminal Law*, 2nd ed. §8.3 (Wolters Kluwer 2012).

2. See Tennessee v. Garner, 471 U.S. 1 (1985).

3. From Paul H. Robinson et al., *The American Criminal Code: General Defenses,* 7 Journal of Legal Analysis 37, 25–26 (2015).

4. For discussion of mistake as to a justification generally, see Robinson and Cahill, *Criminal Law*, 2nd ed. §8.4 (Wolters Kluwer 2012).

5. Del. Code Ann. tit. 11, § 467; Haw. Rev. Stat. § 703-307; Ky. Rev. Stat. Ann. § 503.090; Neb. Rev. Stat. Ann. § 28-1412; 18 Pa. Cons. Stat. Ann. § 508.

6. See Model Penal Code article 3, especially § 3.09(2).

7. Ala. Code § 13A-3-27; Alaska Stat. Ann. § 11.81.370; Alaska Stat. Ann. § 11.81.410; Ark. Code Ann. § 5-2-610; Ark. Code Ann. § 5-2-613; Cal. Penal

Code § 835a; Colo. Rev. Stat. Ann. § 18-1-707; Conn. Gen. Stat. Ann. § 53a-22; Smith v. District of Columbia, 882 A.2d 778 (D.C. Cir. 2005); Fla. Stat. Ann. § 776.05; Fla. Stat. Ann. § 776.07; Ga. Code Ann. § 17-4-20; 720 Ill. Comp. Stat. Ann. 5/7-5; 720 Ill. Comp. Stat. Ann. 5/7-9; Ind. Code § 35-41-3-3; Iowa Code § 804.8; Iowa Code § 804.10; State v. Lawler, 571 N.W.2d 486 (Iowa 1997); Kan. Stat. Ann. § 21-5227; Me. Rev. Stat. Ann. tit. 17-A, § 107; People v. Couch, 176 Mich. App. 254 (1989); Mo. Ann. Stat. § 563.046; Mo. Ann. Stat. § 563.056; N.H. Rev. Stat. Ann. § 627:5; N.J. Stat. Ann. § 2C:3-7; N.Y. Penal Law § 35.30; N.C. Gen. Stat. § 15A-401; State v. White, 29 N.E.3d 939 (Ohio 2015); Or. Rev. Stat. Ann. § 161.235; Or. Rev. Stat. Ann. § 161.239; Or. Rev. Stat. Ann. § 161.267; S.C. Code Ann. § 24-13-30; Tenn. Code Ann. § 39-11-620; Tex. Penal Code Ann. § 9.51; Tex. Penal Code Ann. § 9.52; Utah Code Ann. § 64-13-32; Utah Code Ann. § 74-2-403; Utah Code Ann. § 74-2-404; Hendricks v. Com., 44 S.E.2d 419 (Va. 1947); Smith v. Norfolk City Sch. Bd., 46 Va. Cir. 238 (Va. Cir. Ct. 1998); State v. Mendoza, 258 N.W.2d 260 (Wis. 1977); Wilson v. City of Kenosha, 2016 WI App 16, ¶¶ 10-12, 366 Wis. 2d 810, 874 N.W.2d 347; Keser v. State, 706 P.2d 263 (Wyo. 1985); Wyo. Stat. Ann. § 6-1-102.

8. Ariz. Rev. Stat. Ann. § 13-409; Ariz. Rev. Stat. Ann. § 13-410; Ariz. Rev. Stat. Ann. § 13-416; Idaho Code Ann. § 18-4011; Idaho Code Ann. § 19-610; La. Rev. Stat. Ann. C. Cr. P. Art. 220; La. Rev. Stat. Ann. C. Cr. P. Art. 227.1; Tavakoli-Nouri v. State, 779 A.2d 992 (Md. Ct. Spec. App. 2001); Julian v. Randazzo, 403 N.E.2d 931 (Mass. 1980); Minn. Stat. Ann. § 609.06; Minn. Stat. Ann. § 609.066; Miss. Code Ann. § 97-3-15; Miss. Code Ann. § 47-5-1215; Mont. Code Ann. § 45-3-106; Nev. Rev. Stat. Ann. § 200.140; N.M. Stat. Ann. § 30-2-6; State v. Ellis, 186 P.3d 245 (N.M. 2008); N.D. Cent. Code § 12.1-05-07; N.D. Cent. Code § 29-06-13; Okla. Stat. tit. 21, § 643; Okla. Stat. tit. 21, § 732; R.I. Gen. Laws Ann. § 12-7-8; R.I. Gen. Laws Ann. § 12-7-9; S.D. Codified Laws § 22-16-32; S.D. Codified Laws § 22-18-2; S.D. Codified Laws § 24-2-6; Coll v. Johnson, 636 A.2d 336 (Vt. 1993); Wash. Rev. Code Ann. § 9A.16.020; Wash. Rev. Code Ann. § 9A. 16.040; State ex rel. Mullins v. McClung, 17 S.E.2d 621 (W. Va. 1941).

9. Paul H. Robinson et al., *Criminal Law Conversations*, Chapter 16, "Objective Versus Subjective Justification: A Case Study in Function and Form in Constructing a System of Criminal Law Theory" (Oxford 2009).

10. See, e.g., Paul H. Robinson, *Intuitions of Justice and Utility of Desert*, Chapters 16 and 20 (Oxford 2013).

PART 5

Excuse Defenses

CHAPTER SEVENTEEN

Insanity Defense

A 30-year-old man waits on the subway train platform. He was only recently deinstitutionalized to live with his parents with the aid of medication that controls his apparently overwhelming impulses to engage in random conduct that he neither wants nor understands. Normally passive and retiring, when he is not fully medicated he sometimes feels compelled to do things that injure himself—he once put his hand into a spinning machine, permanently losing the ends of his fingers—or that injure others—he once strangled to death for no apparent reason a neighborhood dog that he liked. Within the last year, however, doctors have found a combination of drugs that seem to effectively control his random impulses.

Now he is waiting for the subway train that will take him to the rehabilitation center where he works each day at a menial job. Unfortunately, his parents have forgotten to give him his medication this morning. There are several dozen people on the platform, including a uniformed police officer standing several yards away from him. As the train pulls into the station, he deliberately pushes a person standing next to him in front of the oncoming train. As the police officer rushes forward to grab him, he says, "I pushed that man in front of the train. I think I might have hurt him badly." The seriously injured man is pulled from beneath the train and carried away. The policeman asks him why he did it. He replies, "I don't know. Whosh, whosh. I just got the idea and I had to do it. I'm so sorry."[1]

The criminal law generally commits itself to impose criminal liability and punishment only on offenders who are morally blameworthy for their conduct. If the offender's conduct is the result of serious mental illness, it may undermine that required blameworthiness. A person who strangles another to death in a hallucination, believing he is squeezing an orange, simply does not have the kind of moral responsibility for his conduct that would give rise to sufficient blameworthiness to punish.

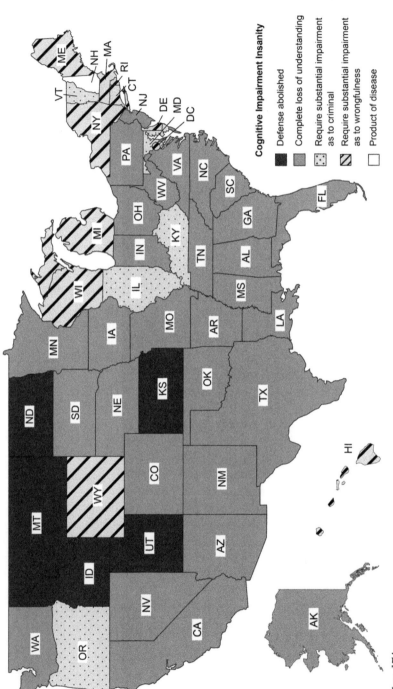

Cognitive Impairment Insanity

- ■ Defense abolished
- Complete loss of understanding
- ⊡ Require substantial impairment as to criminal
- ⧄ Require substantial impairment as to wrongfulness
- ☐ Product of disease

Map 17A

But how is the criminal law to define the conditions under which mental disease or defect can exculpate an offender? Certainly, there is a significant portion of the population, some would say a majority, who have some kind of mental dysfunction, and some kinds of dysfunctions may make it more difficult for a person to remain law abiding. Yet we expect people to remain law abiding even if it is sometimes difficult for them. How does the criminal law draw the line that distinguishes the small group of people who are so dysfunctional, and dysfunctional in such a way, so as to fully exculpate them from criminal liability for an offense?

The criminal law has come to distinguish two kinds of mental dysfunction. *Cognitive dysfunction* occurs when an offender's mental disease or defect distorts his cognitive ability to understand his surroundings, the consequences of his conduct, or the criminal or wrongful nature of his conduct. *Control dysfunction* occurs when an offender's mental disease or defect impairs his ability to control his conduct, which he may very well know to be criminal and wrongful. (Mental illness can also provide a defense by negating an offense element, the doctrine that we examine in Chapter 10).

The states may be divided into five categories for the approach they take in recognizing an offender's cognitive dysfunction as the basis for an insanity defense, as presented in Map 17A.

Insanity Defense Abolished

Five states abolish the insanity defense: Idaho, Kansas, Montana, North Dakota, and Utah.[2] They are shown in black on the map.

Insanity Defense Requires Complete Loss of Understanding

Twenty-nine states, identified with medium shading on the map, follow the traditional common-law rule in providing an insanity defense where defendant has lost his or her ability to understand the nature of his or her conduct in some very fundamental way. This common position is taken in Alabama, Alaska, Arizona, Arkansas, California, Colorado, Florida, Georgia, Indiana, Iowa, Louisiana, Minnesota, Mississippi, Missouri, Nebraska, Nevada, New Jersey, New Mexico, North Carolina, Ohio, Oklahoma, Pennsylvania, South Carolina, South Dakota, Tennessee, Texas, Virginia, Washington, and West Virginia.[3] This position is commonly referred to as the "M'Naghten test," from the old English case that required that the offender "was laboring under such a defect of reason, from disease of the mind, as not to know the nature and quality of the act he was doing; or, if he did know it, that he did not know he was doing what was wrong."[4]

As this language suggests, the insanity defenses in these jurisdictions require a *complete loss* of understanding—in contrast to the next two groups of states, which allow the defense even if the dysfunction at the time of the offense is not a complete loss but rather a *substantial impairment* of cognitive capacity. Note, however, some of the 29 jurisdictions in the complete-loss group leave some wiggle room by allowing a defense when the defendant, as a result of mental disease or defect, was "unable to appreciate" the nature and quality of his or her conduct or its wrongfulness.[5] The word "appreciate" here might give a court or jury some ability to move off the demand that the defendant have a total loss of capacity to "know" or "distinguish"[6] the nature of his or her conduct.[7]

Insanity Defense Requires Substantial Impairment of Capacity to Appreciate Criminality of Conduct

The light shade on Map 17A indicates those states that allow a somewhat broader insanity defense, making it available, as noted above, to defendants who have only a substantial impairment of their cognitive functioning rather than a complete loss. This is the approach recommended by the Model Penal Code:

Section 4.01. Mental Disease or Defect Excluding Responsibility.

1.   A person is not responsible for criminal conduct if at the time of such con-
     duct as a result of mental disease or defect he *lacks substantial capacity* either
     to appreciate the criminality [wrongfulness] of his conduct or to conform
     his conduct to the requirements of law. . . .

Five states, identified with light shading and dots—Illinois, Kentucky, Maryland, Oregon, and Vermont—adopt this substantial-impairment approach.[8] More specifically, these five states require that the defendant at the time of the offense lacks substantial capacity to appreciate "the criminality" of his or her conduct.[9]

Insanity Defense Requires Substantial Impairment of Capacity to Appreciate Wrongfulness of Conduct

Another 11 jurisdictions, identified with light shading and diagonal lines— Connecticut, Delaware, District of Columbia, Hawaii, Maine, Massachusetts, Michigan, New York, Rhode Island, Wisconsin, and Wyoming[10]—bring the substantial-impairment total to 16. These jurisdictions adopt the Model Penal Code's "lacks substantial capacity" formulation but adopt the Model Code's bracketed alternative formulation (quoted above): the defendant must lack the substantial capacity to appreciate the "wrongfulness" of his or her conduct rather than the "criminality" of the conduct.[11]

To see how these alternative formulations might have a different effect in practice, imagine a situation in which the mentally ill defendant believes that

God has directed him to commit the offense. He would continue to fully appreciate that his conduct was "criminal" although his mental illness would also lead him to conclude that it was not "wrongful" in some larger moral sense. Thus, he would get a defense under the wrongfulness formulation of this group but not under the criminality formulation of the previous group.

In our hypothetical at the beginning of this chapter, the mentally ill man who pushes another in front of the subway train is suffering from a purely control dysfunction. He fully understands the criminality and wrongfulness of his conduct. Thus, he would be ineligible for a defense under the purely cognitive-dysfunction formulations of this group or of the two groups immediately above.

Insanity Defense If Offense Is Product of Disease

One jurisdiction, New Hampshire,[12] rejects even the Model Penal Code's "substantial impairment" limitation on the insanity defense. It requires nothing more than the fact that the defendant would not have committed the offense but for his or her mental disease or defect. That is, it is enough that the offense was "the product of" mental disease.[13] The mentally ill man in the hypothetical at the beginning of the chapter probably would get a defense under New Hampshire's "product test."

If he is to get defense in other jurisdictions, it can only be in jurisdiction whose insanity defense includes a "control prong"—that is, an insanity defense formulation that accounts for a control dysfunction. Yet, as Map 17B indicates, 32 states—the majority of American jurisdictions—do not recognize control dysfunction as a basis for an insanity defense.

Insanity Defense Has No Control Prong

All of the black states on Map 17B have only the cognitive-impairment form of the insanity defense, discussed in the subsections above, or no insanity defense at all. Only the nonblack states allow an insanity defense where the offender's dysfunction is a control dysfunction rather than the cognitive dysfunction. These 32 states include Alabama, Alaska, Arizona, California, Colorado, Florida, Georgia, Idaho, Illinois, Indiana, Iowa, Kansas, Louisiana, Maine, Minnesota, Mississippi, Missouri, Montana, Nebraska, Nevada, New Jersey, New York, North Carolina, North Dakota, Oklahoma, Pennsylvania, South Carolina, South Dakota, Tennessee, Texas, Utah, and Washington.[14] (The five states that have abolished the insanity defense, noted in section "Insanity Defense Abolished" above, also obviously do not provide a defense in a control-dysfunction case.)

As the map illustrates, however, some states go beyond the loss or impairment of cognitive functioning as a basis for an insanity defense and

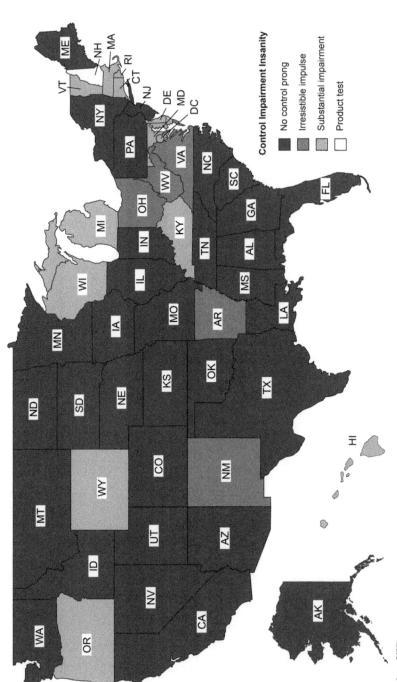

Control Impairment Insanity

- No control prong
- Irresistible impulse
- Substantial impairment
- Product test

Map 17B

recognize the loss or impairment of a person's ability to control his or her conduct as the potential basis for a defense.

Insanity Defense If Irresistible Impulse

Five jurisdictions, with medium shading on Map 17B, adopt what has been called an "irresistible impulse" formulation: Arkansas, New Mexico, Ohio, Virginia, and West Virginia.[15] This essentially requires that the defendants at the time of the offense no longer had any choice with regard to their engaging in the offense conduct. They had lost all ability to control it.

Insanity Defense If Substantial Impairment

Compare that formulation with the Model Penal Code's "lacks substantial capacity" formulation, which is adopted by the 13 jurisdictions in light shading on Map 17B: Connecticut, Delaware, District of Columbia, Hawaii, Kentucky, Maryland, Massachusetts, Michigan, Oregon, Rhode Island, Vermont, Wisconsin, and Wyoming.[16] Under this approach, the defendant may gain an insanity defense, as long as the jury concludes that the extent of his or her impairment of control is sufficient to render the defendant blameless. Under the language of the Model Penal Code quoted above, the defendant "lacks substantial capacity . . . to conform his conduct to the requirements of law."

Taken together, the five irresistible-impulse jurisdictions plus the 13 substantial-impairment jurisdictions plus New Hampshire's product test means that only 19 of the 51 American jurisdictions recognize an insanity defense in control-dysfunction cases. It is only in these jurisdictions that the mentally ill offender in our train station hypothetical would be eligible for the insanity defense.

Majority View Formulation

If one were to construct an insanity defense that in each respect reflected the majority view of American jurisdictions, the defense formulation would look something like this:

Section 401. Insanity.

1. An actor is not responsible for criminal conduct if at the time of such conduct as a result of mental disease or defect he did not know his conduct was wrong.

2. As used in Subsection 1, the phrase "mental disease or defect" does not include an abnormality manifested only by repeated criminal or otherwise anti-social conduct.[17]

Observations and Speculations

The disagreement that we see among the jurisdictions moves along two dimensions. On the one hand, jurisdictions disagree about how severe a dysfunction must be in affecting the offender's conduct in order to entitle the offender to an excuse. The M'Naghten test and the irresistible impulse test require complete loss of cognitive or control ability, respectively. In contrast, the Model Penal Code's insanity formulation requires only a "substantial impairment" of the offender's ability to appreciate the criminality or wrongfulness of his conduct or of the offender's ability to conform his conduct to the requirements of the law.

Why do we see the pattern that we see between the complete-loss states and the substantial-impairment states? It may well reflect some general reservation about how easy or hard it is for the insanity defense to be abused. Studies have shown that, although there is a common perception that the insanity defense is frequently given—too frequently given—the reality is that even the substantial-impairment form is a very difficult defense for a defendant to obtain.[18]

Perhaps even more interesting, the evidence suggests that the particular formulation of the defense given to a jury may make little difference—the academic and legislative skirmishing on the issue may be all for nothing. There is evidence that, no matter what instruction a jury is given, its members tend to look to their own shared intuitions of justice in deciding whether a particular defendant's mental illness in a given case renders him or her sufficiently blameless to deserve a defense.[19]

A second dimension of disagreement among the states is whether to recognize a control dysfunction (of any sort) as an adequate basis for an insanity defense. Recall that our hypothetical train-station offender at the beginning of the chapter could not obtain an insanity defense of any kind in those jurisdictions that have no control prong. It used to be the case that a majority of states had a control prong. The Model Penal Code formulation, which has a control prong, was influential in this regard in encouraging states to adopt it in their new codifications in the 1960s and 1970s. But the legal landscape changed after the successful insanity defense of John Hinckley for the attempted assassination of President Reagan. By September 1985, 36 states had reformed their insanity defense, and several states dropped the control prong or repealed the defense altogether.[20]

Again, the split among the states may reflect different degrees of skepticism about whether recognition of a control prong promotes abuse of the insanity defense, a concern highlighted by the Hinckley acquittal. Ironically, Hinckley obtained an insanity defense probably not because the District of Columbia formulation had a control prong but rather because the District had an unusual, and probably unwise, rule that put the burden on the prosecution to disprove the insanity defense rather than on the defense to prove it.[21] A more appropriate legislative reform response would have been to make clear that the burden of persuasion is on the defendant rather than the government, rather than in dropping the control prong altogether.

Unlike the disagreement among the states about whether to require a complete loss versus a substantial impairment—a difference that may in practice have little effect on juries—the removal of the control prong will have a dramatic practical effect. It means that in cases where the dysfunction affects control (rather than cognitive functioning), even a dramatic loss of control—an irresistible impulse—the jury may never hear about the offender's mental illness. In states that have only a cognitive prong, only mental illness producing cognitive dysfunction is relevant under the legal rules; evidence of control dysfunction, no matter how dramatic the dysfunction, may be simply irrelevant and therefore inadmissible at trial.

Notes

1. The facts of this hypothetical are similar in many respects to the case of Andrew Goldstein. See People v. Goldstein, 14 A.D.3d 32, 786 N.Y.S.2d 428 (2004), rev'd, 6 N.Y.3d 119, 843 N.E.2d 727 (2005). For a fuller case narrative, see Paul H. Robinson et al., *Criminal Law: Case Studies and Controversies,* 4th ed., 713–17 (Wolters Kluwer 2016).

2. Idaho Code Ann. § 18-207; Kan. Stat. Ann. § 21-5209; State v. Korell, 213 Mont. 316, 690 P.2d 992 (1984); N.D. Cent. Code Ann. § 12.1-04.1-01; Utah Code Ann. § 76-2-305. Note that North Dakota permits insanity defense where willfulness is an essential element of the offense and the person "lacks substantial capacity to comprehend the harmful nature or consequences" of his conduct or the conduct is the "result of a loss or serious distortion of the individual's capacity to recognize reality." N.D. Cent. Code Ann. § 12.1-04.1-01.

3. See Ala. Code § 13A-3-1; Alaska Stat. Ann. § 12.47.010; Ariz. Rev. Stat. Ann. § 13-502; Ark. Code Ann. § 5-2-301; Cal. Penal Code § 25; Colo. Rev. Stat. Ann. § 16-8-101; Fla. Stat. Ann. § 775.027; Ga. Code Ann. § 16-3-2; Ind. Code Ann. § 35-41-3-6; Iowa Code Ann. § 701.4; La. Stat. Ann. § 14:14; Minn. Stat. Ann. § 611.026; Nolan v. State, 61 So. 3d 887, 895 (Miss. 2011); Mo. Ann. Stat. § 562.086; State v. Hotz, 281 Neb. 260, 270, 795 N.W.2d 645, 653 (2011); Finger v. State, 117 Nev. 548, 576, 27 P.3d 66, 84–85 (2001) (holding that state legislature's abolition of the general defense of insanity is unconstitutional, and reinstating the M'Naghten test for insanity); N.J. Stat. Ann. § 2C:4-1; State v. Hartley, 1977-NMSC-043, ¶ 14, 90 N.M. 488, 490–91, 565 P.2d 658, 660–61; State v. Thompson, 328 N.C. 477, 485–86, 402 S.E.2d 386, 390 (1991); Ohio Rev. Code Ann. § 2901.01; State v. Staten, 18 Ohio St. 2d 13, 20–21, 247 N.E.2d 293, 299 (1969); Okla. Stat. Ann. tit. 21, § 152; 18 Pa. Stat. and Cons. Stat. Ann. § 315; S.C. Code Ann. § 17-24-10; S.D. Codified Laws § 22-1-2; Tenn. Code Ann. § 39-11-501; Tex. Penal Code Ann. § 8.01; Orndorff v. Com., 279 Va. 597, 601, 691 S.E.2d 177, 179

(2010); Wash. Rev. Code Ann. § 9A.12.010; State v. Grimm, 156 W. Va. 615, 629, 195 S.E.2d 637, 645 (1973); State v. Parsons, 181 W. Va. 131, 136, 381 S.E.2d 246, 251 (1989).

4. Daniel M'Naghten's Case, 8 Eng. Rep. 718, 722 (1843).

5. Alabama, Alaska, Arkansas, Indiana, Missouri, and Tennessee take the M'Naghten approach but use the softer language of "appreciate." See Ala. Code § 13A-3-1; Alaska Stat. Ann. § 12.47.010; Ark. Code Ann. § 5-2-301; Ind. Code Ann. § 35-41-3-6; Mo. Ann. Stat. § 562.086.

6. See S.C. Code Ann. § 17-24-10 (defense available where defendant "lacked the capacity to distinguish" right from wrong).

7. See, e.g, the Alabama formulation of the defense in Ala. Code § 13A-3-1. Mental disease or defect:

A. It is an affirmative defense to a prosecution for any crime that, at the time of the commission of the acts constituting the offense, the defendant, as a result of severe mental disease or defect, was unable to appreciate the nature and quality or wrongfulness of his acts. Mental disease or defect does not otherwise constitute a defense.

B. "Severe mental disease or defect" does not include an abnormality manifested only by repeated criminal or otherwise antisocial conduct.

C. The defendant has the burden of proving the defense of insanity by clear and convincing evidence.

8. See 720 Ill. Comp. Stat. Ann. 5/6-2; Ky. Rev. Stat. Ann. § 504.020; Md. Code Ann., Crim. Proc. § 3-109; Or. Rev. Stat. Ann. § 161.295; Vt. Stat. Ann. tit. 13, § 4801.

9. For example, Oregon section 161.295, Mental Disease or Defect, follows the Model Penal Code formulation:

1. A person is guilty except for insanity if, as a result of mental disease or defect at the time of engaging in criminal conduct, the person *lacks substantial capacity* either *to appreciate the criminality* of the conduct or to conform the conduct to the requirements of law.

2. As used in chapter 743, Oregon Laws 1971, the terms "mental disease or defect" do not include an abnormality manifested only by repeated criminal or otherwise antisocial conduct, nor do they include any abnormality constituting solely a personality disorder.

10. See Conn. Gen. Stat. Ann. § 53a-13; Del. Code Ann. tit. 11, § 401; Bethea v. United States, 365 A.2d 64, 79 (D.C. 1976); Haw. Rev. Stat. Ann. § 704-400; Me. Rev. Stat. tit. 17-A, § 39; Com. v. McHoul, 352 Mass. 544, 555, 226 N.E.2d 556, 563 (1967); Com. v. DiPadova, 460 Mass. 424, 428, 951 N.E.2d 891, 895 (2011); Mich. Comp. Laws Ann. § 768.21a; N.Y. Penal Law § 40.15; State v. Johnson, 121 R.I. 254, 267, 399 A.2d 469, 476 (1979); Wis. Stat. Ann. § 971.15; Wyo. Stat. Ann. § 7-11-304.

11. See, e.g., the formulation in Haw. Rev. Stat. Ann. § 704-400. Physical or mental disease, disorder, or defect excluding penal responsibility: "(1) A person

is not responsible, under this Code, for conduct if at the time of the conduct as a result of physical or mental disease, disorder, or defect the person lacks substantial capacity either to appreciate the wrongfulness of the person's conduct or to conform the person's conduct to the requirements of law."

12. State v. Fichera, 153 N.H. 588 (2006).

13. "A defendant asserting an insanity defense must prove two elements: first, that at the time he acted, he was suffering from a mental disease or defect; and, second, that a mental disease or defect caused his actions." State v. Fichera, 153 N.H. 588, 593, 903 A.2d 1030, 1034 (2006).

14. See Ala. Code § 13A-3-1; Alaska Stat. Ann. § 12.47.010; Ariz. Rev. Stat. Ann. § 13-502; Cal. Penal Code § 25; Colo. Rev. Stat. Ann. § 16-8-101; Fla. Stat. Ann. § 775.027; Ga. Code Ann. § 16-3-2; Idaho Code Ann. § 18-207; 720 Ill. Comp. Stat. Ann. 5/6-2; Ind. Code Ann. § 35-41-3-6; Iowa Code Ann. § 701.4; Kan. Stat. Ann. § 21-5209; La. Stat. Ann. § 14:14; Me. Rev. Stat. tit. 17-A, § 39; Minn. Stat. Ann. § 611.026; Nolan v. State, 61 So. 3d 887, 895 (Miss. 2011); Mo. Ann. Stat. § 562.086; State v. Korell, 213 Mont. 316, 690 P.2d 992 (1984); State v. Hotz, 281 Neb. 260, 270, 795 N.W.2d 645, 653 (2011); Finger v. State, 117 Nev. 548, 567, 27 P.3d 66, 79 (2001); N.J. Stat. Ann. § 2C:4-1; N.Y. Penal Law § 40.15; State v. Thompson, 328 N.C. 477, 485–86, 402 S.E.2d 386, 390 (1991); N.D. Cent. Code Ann. § 12.1-04.1-01; Okla. Stat. Ann. tit. 21, § 152; 18 Pa. Stat. and Cons. Stat. Ann. § 315; S.C. Code Ann. § 17-24-10; S.D. Codified Laws § 22-1-2; Tenn. Code Ann. § 39-11-501; Tex. Penal Code Ann. § 8.01; Utah Code Ann. § 76-2-305; Wash. Rev. Code Ann. § 9A.12.010; see also Paul H. Robinson et al., *The American Criminal Code: General Defenses*, 7 J. Legal Analysis 77–79 (2015) (cataloguing jurisdictions that expressly embrace M'Naghten language or are for other reasons de facto M'Naghten jurisdictions).

15. See Ark. Code Ann. § 5-2-301; State v. Hartley, 1977-NMSC-043, ¶ 14, 90 N.M. 488, 490–91, 565 P.2d 658, 660–61; Ohio Rev. Code Ann. § 2901.01; State v. Staten, 18 Ohio St. 2d 13, 20–21, 247 N.E.2d 293, 299 (1969); Orndorff v. Com., 279 Va. 597, 601, 691 S.E.2d 177, 179 (2010); State v. Grimm, 156 W. Va. 615, 629, 195 S.E.2d 637, 645 (1973); State v. Parsons, 181 W. Va. 131, 136, 381 S.E.2d 246, 251 (1989).

16. Model Penal Code § 4.01(1); Conn. Gen. Stat. Ann. § 53a-13; Del. Code Ann. tit. 11, § 401; Bethea v. United States, 365 A.2d 64, 79 (D.C. 1976); Haw. Rev. Stat. Ann. § 704-400; Ky. Rev. Stat. Ann. § 504.020; Md. Code Ann., Crim. Proc. § 3-109; Com. v. McHoul, 352 Mass. 544, 555, 226 N.E.2d 556, 563 (1967); Com. v. DiPadova, 460 Mass. 424, 428, 951 N.E.2d 891, 895 (2011); Mich. Comp. Laws Ann. § 768.21a; Or. Rev. Stat. Ann. § 161.295; State v. Johnson, 121 R.I. 254, 267, 399 A.2d 469, 476 (1979); Vt. Stat. Ann. tit. 13, § 4801; Wis. Stat. Ann. § 971.15; Wyo. Stat. Ann. § 7-11-304.

17. From Paul H. Robinson et al., *The American Criminal Code: General Defenses*, 7 Journal of Legal Analysis 37, 41 (2015).

18. See Lisa A. Callahan et al., *The Volume and Characteristics of Insanity Defense Pleas: An Eight-State Study*, 19 Bull. Am. Acad. Psychiatry & L. 331, 334 (1991).

19. See Jennifer L. Skeem and Stephen L. Golding, *Describing Jurors' Personal Conceptions of Insanity and Their Relationship to Case Judgments*, 7 Psychol. Pub. Pol'y & L. 561 (2001) (cataloguing empirical studies that suggest that jurors "do not apply judicial instruction on legal definitions of insanity," but instead "rely on their own conceptions of insanity to decide whether a defendant is insane").

20. See Lisa Callahan et al., *Insanity Defense Reform in the United States—Post Hinckley*, Mental & Phys. Disability L. Rep. 54–59 (1987).

21. See Henry J. Steadman et al., *Before and After Hinckley: Evaluating Insanity Defense Reform,* 63–64 (Guilford 1993).

CHAPTER EIGHTEEN

Immaturity Defense

Every American jurisdiction recognizes in statutes or court opinions a number of different excuse defenses. Unlike justification defenses, which exculpate the offender because what he or she did under the circumstances was something approved or at least tolerated by the criminal law as the right thing to do, excuse defenses condemn the conduct as something that should not be done by others in a similar situation in the future, but exculpate this offender on this occasion. They do so not because of the rightness of the defendant's conduct but rather despite its wrongfulness. Violators are excused because they are not blameworthy for what they have done, perhaps due to insanity, duress, involuntarily intoxication, or some physiological condition that causes involuntary action, such as a brain tumor, or a variety of other circumstances that undermine their accountability.

One of the excuse defenses that every jurisdiction recognizes is that of immaturity. It is hard to blame a seven-year-old for committing a crime when the child is just starting to learn the social rules, let alone the legal rules, and hardly has the kind of foresight of consequences or control of impulses that the normal adult would have.

Rather than having the prosecution and defense litigate the extent of a young defendant's immaturity, the criminal law typically adopts a rule that promotes efficiency by presuming that all defendants under a certain age—say, 14—are immature and thus exempts them from liability,[1] while all defendants over a certain age—say, 17—are presumed mature and thus ineligible for an immaturity defense.[2] These age cutoff provisions are often expressed not in the form of an "immaturity defense" available in criminal court, but rather expressed in terms of court jurisdiction, preventing the case from reaching either the juvenile court or the criminal court, as the case may be.[3]

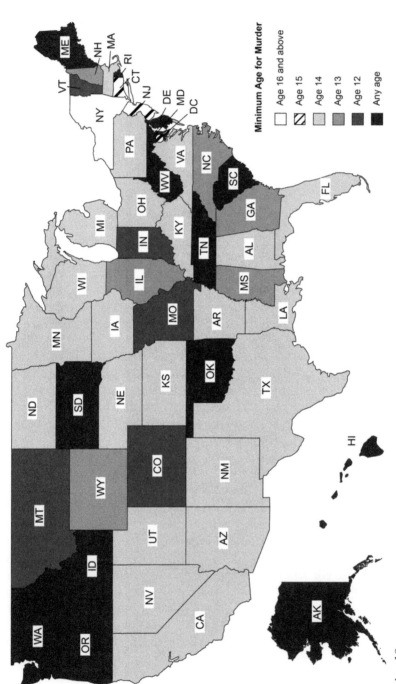

Minimum Age for Murder

- ☐ Age 16 and above
- ▨ Age 15
- ☐ Age 14
- ▨ Age 13
- ▨ Age 12
- ■ Any age

Map 18

Defendants who fall between the age cutoffs—say, between ages 14 and 17—may be tried in adult court depending on the seriousness of the offense and perhaps other factors, often subject to a hearing.[4] Those factors often include the seriousness of the offense, the defendant's personal history, and the defendant's actual physical or mental maturity.[5] Generally, the more serious the offense, the more likely a young offender will be tried in adult court.

For the most serious offense—murder—states generally adopt a special rule permitting criminal jurisdiction over young juveniles.[6] Map 18 displays the minimum age at the time of offense at which a juvenile may be transferred to criminal court over his or her objection.[7]

16 and Above as the Minimum Age

One jurisdiction—only New York—sets the minimum age for murder prosecution as an adult at 16 or more years old.

15 as the Minimum Age

Three jurisdictions, those with diagonal lines on the map—District of Columbia, Connecticut, and New Jersey—set the minimum age for murder prosecution as an adult at 15 years old.

14 as the Minimum Age

Twenty-two states, designated with the lightest shading on the map—Alabama, Arizona, Arkansas, California, Florida, Iowa, Kansas, Kentucky, Louisiana, Massachusetts, Michigan, Minnesota, Nebraska, Nevada, New Mexico, North Dakota, Ohio, Pennsylvania, Texas, Utah, Virginia, and Wisconsin—allow the prosecution for murder of 14-year-old defendants.

13 as the Minimum Age

Six states, those with medium shading on the map—Georgia, Illinois, Mississippi, New Hampshire, North Carolina, and Wyoming—allow 13-year-olds to be prosecuted for murder as an adult.

12 as the Minimum Age

Five states, identified with dark shading on the map—Colorado, Indiana, Missouri, Montana, and Vermont—allow the prosecution for murder as an adult when the defendant is 12 years old or older at the time of the offense.

No Minimum Age

Fourteen states shaded black on the map—Alaska, Delaware, Hawaii, Idaho, Maine, Maryland, Oklahoma, Oregon, Rhode Island, South Carolina, South Dakota, Tennessee, Washington, and West Virginia—allow juveniles of any age to be prosecuted for murder as an adult.

Majority View Formulation

Map 18 describes a situation with specific reference to prosecution for murder. If one were to formulate an immaturity defense that reflected the majority view of American jurisdictions on all issues, it might look something like this:

Section 403. Immaturity.

1. A person may be prosecuted as an adult if he is:
    a. 18 years old or older,
    b. 15 years old or older and is charged with [specified serious offenses], or
    c. 14 years old or older and the court determines after a hearing that he should be transferred to a criminal court for prosecution as an adult.

2. In determining whether a person should be transferred to a criminal court for prosecution as an adult under Subsection 1c, the court shall consider the following factors:
    a. the nature and seriousness of the alleged offense,
    b. whether there is probable cause to believe that the person in question committed the alleged offense,
    c. the person's prior history and record in the juvenile or criminal system,
    d. the person's age and physical and mental maturity,
    e. the facilities available to serve the person's needs, and
    f. his amenability to treatment and the prospect of rehabilitation in the juvenile system.[8]

Observations and Speculations

It is easy to understand why the immaturity defense has in most cases been converted into a presumption of jurisdiction in the juvenile court. Most 10-year-old defendants will lack the maturity needed to render them appropriate subjects for adult prosecution; that is, virtually all will lack the blameworthiness needed to deserve criminal liability.

But one of the side effects of converting an immaturity defense into a matter of juvenile court jurisdiction is that such an approach means that, at least in some cases, those defendants who ultimately end up in adult criminal court will have no immaturity defense available to them. They will be conclusively presumed to be sufficiently mature to warrant criminal conviction.[9]

One might think that they might have available to them an insanity defense: the immature offender might well "lack substantial capacity either to appreciate the criminality or wrongfulness of his conduct or to conform his conduct to the requirements of law."[10] It is well documented, for example, that juveniles frequently do not fully appreciate the nature or consequences of their conduct and commonly lack the impulse control that commonly comes with reaching adulthood.[11] Unfortunately, being a normal 10-year-old does not qualify as a "mental disease or defect," as required by the insanity defense.[12]

But if the 10-year-old has limitations on mental or emotional functioning that would fully excuse him or her if they were the result of mental disease or defect, then it follows that the immature defendant deserves an excuse defense just as the insane defendant does. To be rational and internally consistent—and, more importantly, to be just—adult criminal court ought to recognize an immaturity defense that applies whenever a defendant suffers the limitations on cognitive or control functioning that would provide an insanity defense when the excusing conditions required by those defenses result from immaturity.

The absence of such an immaturity defense in criminal court reveals a serious failure in all American jurisdictions. However, the failure is dramatically more damaging in those jurisdictions shown in Map 18 to authorize criminal court prosecution of even very young offenders. Indeed, given the demonstrated cognitive and control limitations of juveniles,[13] it seems hard to understand how so many jurisdictions can justify having such young offenders tried as adults in the first place. If there was ever a rational basis for a conclusive presumption of immaturity, it would certainly apply to offenders aged 13 or younger, for example—yet roughly half the jurisdictions, 25, permit such defendants to be transferred to criminal court for murder prosecution.

It seems particularly odd that many jurisdictions significantly lower their age for criminal court prosecution when the charge is murder. The difference between murder and other offenses against the person is in the extent of the harm caused. There is nothing about the offense of murder that makes the offender necessarily less susceptible to cognitive or control dysfunction. Yes, the community may be more upset by a killing than by other harms, but community upset is not a rational basis for altering the criminal law's blameworthiness rules. Perhaps the states' different treatment of murder suggests an assumption of policy makers—that only criminal prosecution can effectively incapacitate the most dangerous, incorrigible juveniles.

Justice has two essential components. It must take account of the seriousness of the harm or evil, and impose greater punishment for greater harm caused, all other things being equal. But to be morally credible it must also take account of the offender's circumstances and capabilities. Any offense, including murder, can be tragic yet not an appropriate basis for punishment if the violator is blameless for the offense.

This is the lesson of the insanity defense discussed in the previous chapter, for example, which is available as a defense to all offenses, including murder. The same principle applies to the immaturity defense: it ought to be available in any court and for any offense if the offender's immaturity is so great as to render him or her blameless for the offense charged.

Notes

1. As a matter of substantive criminal law, immaturity or infancy is an absolute defense where the individual is under a specified age. Many states have codified the defense in their criminal codes. See, e.g., Colo. Rev. Stat. Ann. § 18-1-801 ("No child under ten years of age shall be found guilty of any offense."); Ga. Code Ann. § 16-3-1 ("A person shall not be considered or found guilty of a crime unless he has attained the age of 13 years at the time of the act, omission, or negligence constituting the crime."); 720 Ill. Comp. Stat. Ann. 5/6-1 ("No person shall be convicted of any offense unless he had attained his 13th birthday at the time the offense was committed."); La. Stat. Ann. § 14:13 ("Those who have not reached the age of ten years are exempt from criminal responsibility."); Minn. Stat. Ann. § 609.055 ("Children under the age of 14 years are incapable of committing crime."). However, states generally express this cutoff by implication, through statutes permitting or denying jurisdiction over certain defendants. See infra note 3 and accompanying text.

2. The vast majority of jurisdictions permit anyone 18 years of age or older to be prosecuted as an adult for any offense. See Paul H. Robinson et al., *The American Criminal Code: General Defenses*, 7 J. Legal Analysis 37, 85 (2015) (finding that all but six states set the age of majority at 18).

3. See, e.g., Cal. Welf. & Inst. Code § 602 (stating that individuals under 18 years of age at the time of the offense are "within the jurisdiction of the juvenile court"); Cal. Welf. & Inst. Code § 707 (permitting the prosecutor to make a motion to transfer a minor to an adult court where the minor is at least 14 years old and is alleged to have committed enumerated serious felonies, including murder).

4. See, e.g., Ariz. Rev. Stat. Ann. § 13-501 (permitting certain juveniles over 14 to be tried in adult court, depending on the seriousness of the offense, the juvenile's criminal history, and subject to a hearing); Kan. Stat. Ann. § 38-2347 (permitting criminal jurisdiction over certain juveniles over 14, depending on the seriousness of the offense, the manner in which it was committed, the offender's criminal history, the offender's "sophistication or maturity," and other factors, subject to a hearing). The same holds true for those states that do not have an absolute minimum age cutoff for criminal court jurisdiction. See, e.g., Alaska Stat. Ann. § 47.12.100 (requiring a hearing to determine whether a minor

is "amenable to treatment" in a juvenile program, which is determined by a number of factors, including "the seriousness of the offense . . . , the minor's history of delinquency, [and] the probable cause of the minor's delinquent behavior").

5. See statutes cited supra note 4.

6. Note that though a statute may confer criminal jurisdiction over a young juvenile, there remains the separate issue of whether a court would find that a juvenile was simply too young to be criminally liable. The immaturity or infancy defense is sometimes treated differently. For instance, though Oregon permits a juvenile of any age to be transferred to adult court for murder prosecution, the criminal code's immaturity defense separately provides that "[a] person who is tried as an adult in a court of criminal jurisdiction is not criminally responsible for any conduct which occurred when the person was under 12 years of age." Or. Rev. Stat. Ann. § 161.290. Similarly, though Colorado does *not* allow jurisdiction over a juvenile under 12, even for murder, the criminal code's immaturity defense separately provides that "[n]o child under *ten* years of age [may] be found guilty of any offense." Colo. Rev. Code Ann. § 18-1-801 (emphasis added).

7. Research for Alabama, Arkansas, Colorado, District of Columbia, Georgia, Illinois, Iowa, Kentucky, Louisiana, Maine, Maryland, Michigan, Minnesota, Mississippi, Missouri, Nevada, New Hampshire, North Carolina, North Dakota, Ohio, Oklahoma, Oregon, Pennsylvania, Rhode Island, South Carolina, South Dakota, Tennessee, Texas, Utah, Vermont, Virginia, Washington, West Virginia, Wisconsin, and Wyoming is taken from Office of Justice Programs, U.S. Dep't of Justice, *Trying Juveniles as Adults: An Analysis of State Transfer Laws and Reporting* 4 (2011), https://www.ncjrs.gov/pdffiles1/ojjdp/232434.pdf.

Research for Alaska, Arizona, California, Connecticut, Delaware, Florida, Hawaii, Idaho, Indiana, Kansas, Massachusetts, Montana, Nebraska, New Jersey, New Mexico, and New York was collected separately and is current as of June 12, 2017. See Alaska Stat. Ann. § 47.12.100 (no minimum); Ariz. Rev. Stat. Ann. § 13-501 (minimum age of 14); Cal. Welf. & Inst. Code § 602; Cal. Welf. & Inst. Code § 707 (minimum age of 14); Conn. Gen. Stat. Ann. § 46b-127 (minimum age of 15); Del. Code Ann. tit. 10, § 1010 (no minimum); Fla. Stat. Ann. § 985.556 (minimum age of 14); Haw. Rev. Stat. Ann. § 571-22 (no minimum age); Idaho Code Ann. § 20-508; Idaho Code Ann. § 20-509; Ind. Code Ann. § 31-30-3-4 (minimum age of 12); Kan. Stat. Ann. § 38-2347 (minimum age of 14); Mass. Gen. Laws Ann. ch. 119, § 72B (minimum age of 14); Mont. Code Ann. § 41-5-206 (minimum age of 12); Neb. Rev. Stat. Ann. § 43-245 (minimum age of 14); Neb. Rev. Stat. Ann. § 29-1816; Neb. Rev. Stat. Ann. § 28-303; N.J. Stat. Ann. § 2C:4-11 (minimum age of 14); N.J. Stat. Ann. § 2A:4A-27; N.J. Stat. Ann. § 2A:4A-26.1; N.M. Stat. Ann. § 32A-2-3; N.M. Stat. Ann. § 32A-2-20 (minimum age of 14); N.Y. Penal Law § 30.00 (minimum age of 16, if the offense is committed between October 1, 2018, and September 30, 2019; minimum age of 17, if the offense is committed after October 1, 2019); N.Y. Crim. Proc. Law § 180.75.

8. From Paul H. Robinson et al., *The American Criminal Code: General Defenses*, 7 J. Legal Analysis 37, 48 (2015).

9. But see supra note 1.

10. Model Penal Code §4.01 (1), Insanity.

11. See Tracy Rightmer, *Arrested Development: Juveniles' Immature Brains Make Them Less Culpable Than Adults*, 9 Quinnippiac Health L.J. 1, 4–5 (2005) (reviewing behavior science research that suggests that juveniles "may not be able to fully understand the consequences of their actions or be able to resist their impulses as adults can," and therefore "may not be fully culpable for their crimes"); Andrew Walkover, *The Infancy Defense in the New Juvenile Court*, 31 UCLA L. Rev. 503, 543 (1984) (reviewing behavioral sciences research, which suggests that "children under seven generally lack the capacity to be culpable," and that "adolescent children may be generally regarded as possessing the capacity to be culpable, although quite often not at the level . . . of a mature adult").

12. Model Penal Code §4.01 (1), Insanity.

13. See supra note 11.

PART 6

Nonexculpatory Defenses

CHAPTER NINETEEN

Statute of Limitations

A young woman is kidnapped and brutally assaulted by a stranger. She escapes but is too traumatized to help police with their inquiries and thus unable to confirm the guilt of their prime suspect. Several years later, after a good deal of counseling and therapy, she realizes that her recovery will depend on coming to terms with this past brutality, and she works hard to deal with the painful events. After putting herself back together and regaining her footing, she goes to the police and describes her attacker—a description that just happens to match exactly the man who was their prime suspect at the time of the offense. They reopen the investigation and amass compelling evidence against the attacker. But the prosecution of the woman's tormentor is now barred because the statute of limitation has passed, putting him forever beyond the reach of justice.[1]

Every jurisdiction in the United States has a statute of limitation of one kind or another. In general, this means that if the prosecution of a crime has not begun within a certain period of time, it can no longer be prosecuted at all. (Each state also typically provides specific rules governing when the period-of-limitation clock starts, when it may be tolled—that is, paused, such as when an offender is out of the state—and when it is stopped—that is, what counts as starting a prosecution).[2]

Although statutes of limitation are common, they are also controversial, and there exists a trend toward lengthening the limitation periods and increasing the number of offenses that are altogether exempt. The controversial nature of the defense may help explain why there is a fair amount of diversity among the states. Map 19 illustrates four different approaches in the formulation of statutes of limitation for felonies.

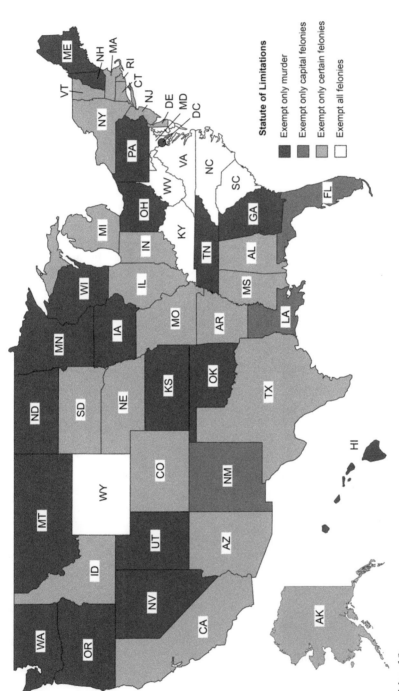

Statute of Limitations

- Exempt only murder
- Exempt only capital felonies
- Exempt only certain felonies
- Exempt all felonies

Map 19

Only Murder Is Exempt from the Statute of Limitation

Nineteen jurisdictions designated in dark shading on the map—District of Columbia, Georgia, Hawaii, Iowa, Kansas, Maine, Minnesota, Montana, Nevada, New Hampshire, North Dakota, Ohio, Oklahoma, Oregon, Pennsylvania, Tennessee, Utah, Washington, and Wisconsin[3]—exempt only cases of murder from the statute of limitation. In other words, every jurisdiction exempts murder, but some jurisdictions, such as those in the three groups below, go further to exempt some felonies other than murder.

Statute of Limitation Does Not Apply to Any Capital Offense

Three states, indicated with medium shading on the map—Florida, Louisiana, and New Mexico[4]—exempt any capital offense, not just murder. The exemption would apply, for example, in states that authorize the death penalty for rape where the victim is a young child.[5]

Statute of Limitation Does Not Apply to Certain Enumerated Felonies

Twenty-two states identified by light shading on the map—Alabama, Alaska, Arizona, Arkansas, California, Colorado, Connecticut, Delaware, Idaho, Illinois, Indiana, Massachusetts, Michigan, Mississippi, Missouri, Nebraska, New Jersey, New York, Rhode Island, South Dakota, Texas, and Vermont[6]—exempt an even broader group of felonies, with different states having somewhat different lists of the felonies exempted.

Missouri, for example, exempts "murder, rape in the first degree, forcible rape, attempted rape in the first degree, attempted forcible rape, sodomy in the first degree, forcible sodomy, attempted sodomy in the first degree, attempted forcible sodomy, or any class A felony,"[7] while Texas exempts murder and manslaughter, certain cases of sexual assault, continuous sexual abuse of a young child or children, indecency with a child, leaving the scene of an accident if the accident resulted in the death of a person, and trafficking of persons.[8]

Statute of Limitation Does Not Apply to Any Felonies

Finally, seven states designated on the map with no shading—Kentucky, Maryland, North Carolina, South Carolina, Virginia, West Virginia, and Wyoming[9]—exempt all felonies from any statute of limitation. More on the reason for this hostility to limitation periods can be found in the Observations and Speculations below.

Majority View Formulation

If one were to construct a statute of limitation that reflects the majority rule in the United States, it would look like this:

Section 502. Statute of Limitations.

1. The prosecution of murder [and other specified serious felonies] may be commenced at any time.
2. The prosecution of a felony is barred unless commenced within 6 years of the commission of the offense.
3. The prosecution of any other offense is barred unless commenced within 2 years of the commission of the offense.
4. The period of limitation is extended for any period during which the defendant is continuously absent from the State or has no reasonably ascertainable place of abode or work within the State.[10]

Observations and Speculations

What explains the significant diversity among the states? And what explains the continuing trend toward lengthening the statute of limitation or increasing the offenses that are altogether exempt from it? The answer may be that it was a defense originally formulated somewhat more broadly than its underlying rationales, and a defense that, with the changes in adjudication and evidence rules over the past century, has come to be somewhat less justifiable than it once was.

One of the arguments that can be made in support of having a statute of limitation is that with the passage of time it is quite possible that the offender is now a different person than he or she was and may no longer need restraint or control. But this rationale hardly supports the statutes of limitation as they are drafted, for the defense never inquires into the offender's criminal record since the original offense. The offender may have been committing offenses regularly—may have committed a new offense yesterday—yet is still protected by any applicable statute of limitation defense.

One also might argue that with the passage of time the retributive impulse may have passed, and that the community ought not be forever preoccupied with the past but rather should be forward-looking. But if the retributive impulse really has passed, then presumably prosecutors would be disinclined to spend their limited resources prosecuting an old case that nobody cares about any longer. The best test of whether the offense has become irrelevant may be whether the system is still driven to prosecute it. If the community does still care enough, why should prosecution be barred? Indeed, the justice system's failure to prosecute an identifiable past offender may continue as an open wound that distracts a society from focusing on the future. The only way to move ahead in some instances may be to deal with the past so it can be put to rest.

Finally, there was a time when one could plausibly argue that a long-delayed prosecution increases the chance of wrongful conviction, as evidence degrades and witnesses' memories fade. But the modern rules of criminal adjudication and evidence have just the opposite effect: delay that degrades evidence or witnesses' memories makes it increasingly less likely that a prosecution can succeed. The burdens of proof are on the prosecution, and the ability of defense counsel to fully cross-examine and challenge the evidence means that the passage of time that degrades evidence works to the *defendant's* benefit, not the prosecution's.

No doubt there remains some kernel of truth in the original arguments in support of the limitations. And perhaps that is why there is less pressure to extend or eliminate statutes of limitation for misdemeanors. It is primarily serious offenses—felonies—for which the bar to doing justice for a clearly guilty offender can undermine criminal law's moral credibility.

Notes

1. The facts are similar to those in the case of Herbert Howard. See Paul H. Robinson and Michael T. Cahill, *Law without Justice: Why Criminal Law Doesn't Give People What They Deserve,* Chapter 3 (Oxford 2006).

2. See Paul H. Robinson and Michael T. Cahill, *Criminal Law,* 2nd ed. §10.2.1 (Wolters Kluwer 2012).

3. D.C. Code § 23-113; Ga. Code Ann. § 17-3-1; Haw. Rev. Stat. § 701-108; Iowa Code § 802; Kan. Stat. Ann. § 21-3106; Me. Rev. Stat. Ann. tit. 17-A, § 8; Minn. Stat. Ann. § 628.26; Mont. Code Ann. § 45-1- 205; Nev. Rev. Stat. Ann. § 171.080; N.H. Rev. Stat. Ann. § 625:8; N.D. Cent. Code § 29-04; Ohio Rev. Code Ann. § 2901.13; Okla. Stat. tit. 21, § 152; Or. Rev. Stat. Ann. § 131.125; 42 Pa. Cons. Stat. Ann. § 5551; Tenn. Code Ann. § 40-2-101; Utah Code Ann. § 76-1-301.5; Wash. Rev. Code Ann. § 9A.04.080; Wis. Stat. Ann. § 939.74.

4. Fla. Stat. Ann. § 775.15; La. Rev. Stat. Ann. § 572; N.M. Stat. Ann. § 30-1-8.

5. See, e.g., La. Stat. Ann. § 14:42 (providing that the government may seek the death penalty where the defendant is guilty of first degree rape of a child under 13); Fla. Stat. Ann. § 794.011 (death penalty for rape of a child under 12). Note, however, that while Florida law permits the death penalty for child rape, the state supreme court has invalidated this provision. See Buford v. State, 403 So. 2d 943, 951 (Fla. 1981).

6. Ala. Code § 15-3-1; Alaska Stat. Ann. § 12.10.010; Ariz. Rev. Stat. Ann. § 13-107; Ark. Code Ann. § 5-1-109; Cal. Penal Code § 801; Colo. Rev. Stat. Ann. § 16-5-401; Conn. Gen. Stat. Ann § 54-193; Del. Code Ann. tit. 11, § 205; Idaho

Code Ann. § 19-402; 720 Ill. Comp. Stat. Ann. 5/3-5; Ind. Code § 35-41-4- 2; Mass. Gen. Laws Ann. ch. 277, § 63; Mich. Comp. Laws Ann. § 767.24; Miss. Code Ann. § 99-1- 5; Mo. Ann. Stat. § 556.036; Neb. Rev. Stat. Ann. § 29-110; N.J. Stat. Ann. § 2C:1-6; N.Y. Penal Law § 30.10; R.I. Gen. Laws Ann. § 12-12-17; S.D. Codified Laws § 23A-42; Tex. Penal Code Ann. § 12.01; Vt. Stat. Ann. tit. 13, § 4501.

7. Mo. Ann. Stat. § 556.036, Time limitations.

8. Tex. Penal Code Ann. § 12.01, Felonies.

9. Ky. Rev. Stat. Ann. § 500.050; Md. Code Ann., Crim. Law § 5-106 (and all misdemeanors punishable by imprisonment); N.C. Gen. Stat. § 15-1; South Carolina (no statute of limitations for any crime); Va. Code Ann. § 19.2-8; W. Va. Code § 61-11-9; Wyoming (no statute of limitations for any crime).

10. From Paul H. Robinson et al., *The American Criminal Code: General Defenses*, 7 Journal of Legal Analysis 37, 62 (2015).

CHAPTER TWENTY

Exclusionary Rule

A free society must put limits on governmental intrusion into people's lives, and thus the Fourth Amendment prohibits "unreasonable searches and sei- zures." It is not enough to announce this prohibition, of course; there must be some mechanism to enforce it, a mechanism that will restrain the powerful executive branch of government and specifically its police and prosecutors.

One might deal with governmental infringement of these rights in the same way that other civil rights violations are dealt with, by allowing citizens to sue the government and to gain financial compensation for the violations. But that remedy seems of limited effectiveness because such litigation and its costs are probably beyond the capacity of the kinds of people the police are most likely to improperly search or seize. A legislature might well be able to con- struct a special set of procedures that could make it easy for citizens to be compensated for improper police intrusions, but absent such legislative action, how is the Fourth Amendment right against unreasonable searches and sei- zures to be made real?

This was the problem that faced the courts for more than a century. They could create rules that gave more specific and detailed meaning to the Fourth Amendment prohibition but had little assurance that their rules would be fol- lowed by police. Some sanction for violating the rules was needed in order to induce compliance.

One proposed solution was to discourage police search and seizure viola- tion by barring the use at trial of any evidence that was obtained as a result of it. If police and prosecutors are in the business of convicting criminals, this penalty for violation would seem to provide a means of effectively dis- couraging such violations: it takes away the benefit presumably sought to be gained by the unreasonable search or seizure in the first place. This "exclu- sionary rule," as it is called, was expanded to apply not only to evidence seized during the unreasonable search but also to evidence obtained even pursuant to a judicial warrant, if part of the basis for obtaining the warrant was evidence obtained through an unreasonable search, on the grounds that such evidence is "fruit of the poisonous tree," as it is so colorfully explained.[1]

Selecting the exclusionary rule as the enforcement mechanism did have some disadvantages. First, by excluding even reliable and compelling evidence of guilt, it would turn the trial of the case into a fantasy of sorts: the evidence presented to the jury would be a false representation of what all the parties knew to be the true facts of the case. Further, this particular remedy only helped criminals. The rule had no effect on or benefit for innocent persons suffering unreasonable searches or seizures. Similarly, the exclusionary rule remedy would discourage police overreaching only in those instances where the police were seeking evidence for subsequent prosecution, not when they had other motivations.

Finally, and most importantly, the exclusion of reliable and compelling evidence of guilt, which could allow clearly blameworthy offenders to go free, tends to undermine the moral credibility of the criminal justice system, and that loss of moral credibility can undermine people's willingness to defer to the system and internalize its norms. Instead, such regular and institutionalized failures of justice can inspire vigilantism.[2] Imagine, for example, a case where a serial rapist, torturer, and murderer has been victimizing young gay men, then dismembering their bodies. An officer just happens to stumble on the man as he is isolating yet another victim for attack, and the officer's suspicions lead him to call headquarters to check out the man. He learns additional information that leads him to take the man to headquarters and to search his truck, where he finds the torture kit and other incriminating evidence, which police use to obtain a warrant to search the man's house. There they find overwhelming evidence of the entire series of brutal crimes.

However, a court later determines that the grounds for the officer's first suspicions were not strong enough to justify the length of the original detention, and the evidence seized at the police station is excluded from use in a prosecution by operation of the exclusionary rule. Similarly, the mountain of evidence obtained at the man's house under judicial warrant is similarly excluded as "fruit of the poisonous tree." The man is ordered released and all of his property returned to him. He subsequently attacks, tortures, murders, and dismembers another young man.[3] People are understandably outraged when the criminal justice system seems insensitive or even indifferent to the importance of doing justice.

Perhaps because of these disadvantages of the exclusionary rule approach, many jurisdictions considered but rejected the rule. However, in 1914, in the case of the *United States v. Weeks*, the U.S. Supreme Court adopted the remedy for the federal courts.[4] (The ruling does not bind the states and therefore had limited practical effect, because it is the states, not the federal government, that are given the police power under the federal constitution. Federal criminal jurisdiction is limited to special cases where there is some special federal interest at stake.) After *Weeks*, some states considered the exclusionary rule for their state but rejected it, while others chose to adopt it. Map 20 shows the approach taken by the different states.

Exclusionary Rule Rejected, before 1914

Sixteen states, designated on the map with no shading—Alabama, Arkansas, Connecticut, Georgia, Kansas, Maine, Maryland, Massachusetts, Minnesota, Nebraska, New Hampshire, New York, North Carolina, Oregon, South Carolina, and Vermont[5]—expressly addressed and rejected the exclusionary rule, before the Supreme Court's 1914 decision in *United States v. Weeks* adopting the rule for the federal courts.

Exclusionary Rule Rejected, after 1914

Another 15 states, identified with light shading on the map—Arizona, California, Colorado, Delaware, Louisiana, Nevada, New Jersey, New Mexico, North Dakota, Ohio, Pennsylvania, Rhode Island, Texas, Utah, and Virginia[6]—expressly addressed and rejected the exclusionary rule after the U.S. Supreme Court's 1914 decision in *Weeks*, for a total of 31 of the 48 states rejecting the exclusionary rule. (Alaska and Hawaii were not yet admitted to the Union.)

Exclusionary Rule Adopted, before 1961

In the years following *Weeks*, 17 states followed the Supreme Court in adopting an exclusionary rule: Florida, Idaho, Illinois, Indiana, Iowa, Kentucky, Michigan, Mississippi, Missouri, Montana, Oklahoma, South Dakota, Tennessee, Washington, West Virginia, Wisconsin, and Wyoming.[7] These are the states with dark shading on the map.

Yet, despite the fact that almost two-thirds of the states had considered and *rejected* the federal approach, in 1961, in the case of *Mapp v. Ohio*,[8] the U.S. Supreme Court forced its rule on all of the states. As a result, today there is necessarily perfect uniformity across all states on the issue.

Had Not Addressed Exclusionary Rule as of 1961

Two states—Alaska and Hawaii,[9] shown on the map with dots—did not address the issue before the Supreme Court's 1961 *Mapp v. Ohio* case forced the federal rule on them. (The two states were admitted to the Union in 1959.)

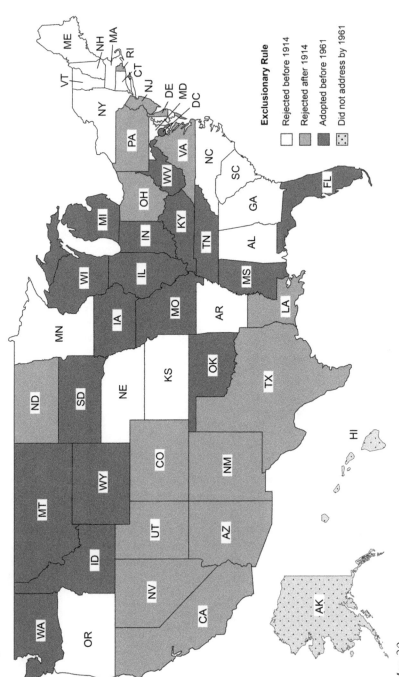

Exclusionary Rule

- ☐ Rejected before 1914
- ▨ Rejected after 1914
- ▧ Adopted before 1961
- ⠿ Did not address by 1961

Map 20

Observations and Speculations

One may wonder what would have happened in the 50 experimental laboratories of American states if the U.S. Supreme Court had not foreclosed the issue of how best to enforce the Fourth Amendment's prohibition against unreasonable searches and seizures. Might some states have enacted an alternative system that would have more effectively deterred unreasonable searches and seizures, yet in a way that did not let guilty offenders go free or otherwise undermine the moral credibility of the criminal law?

Technically, a state might still try to do this. The Supreme Court has repeatedly confirmed that nothing in the Fourth Amendment requires the exclusion of evidence. That is, the exclusionary rule is not constitutionally required but rather is the Supreme Court's attempt to provide some enforcement mechanism for Fourth Amendment rights in the absence of some other effective mechanism.[10] On the other hand, now that the Court's exclusionary rule is in place, what legislature would want to undertake such a project when their efforts might never see the light of day unless the Supreme Court subsequently approves them?

One can imagine a system that would be more effective than the exclusionary rule in deterring unreasonable searches and seizures and, at the same time, does not suffer the costs to crime control and moral credibility in letting guilty offenders go free. A citizen oversight board or a judicial panel that sanctions officers who undertake improper searches or seizures could provide more effective deterrence and provide it not only to criminals but also to innocent persons. In the more egregious and willful cases, one can imagine that such a panel could recommend criminal prosecution of offending officers. And this greater level of protection of Fourth Amendment rights could be done without perverting the truth-finding process in criminal adjudication and without undermining the justice system's moral credibility.

Notes

1. See, e.g., Wong Sun v. United States, 371 U.S. 471 (1963).

2. See Paul H. Robinson, *Intuitions of Justice and Utility of Desert,* Chapters 8 and 9 (Oxford 2013).

3. The facts are similar to the case of Larry Eyler. See Paul H. Robinson and Michael T. Cahill, *Law without Justice: Why Criminal Law Doesn't Give People What They Deserve,* 139–155 (Oxford 2006).

4. United States v. Weeks, 232 U.S. 383 (1914).

5. See Wolf v. Colorado, 338 U.S. 25, 33–39 (1949) (listing jurisdictions that expressly rejected the exclusionary rule before the Supreme Court's decision in United States v. Weeks in 1914, which adopted a federal exclusionary rule).

6. See Wolf, 338 U.S. at 33–39 (listing jurisdictions that expressly rejected the exclusionary rule before the Supreme Court's decision in United States v. Weeks in 1914); State v. Olynik, 113 A.2d 123 (R.I. 1955) (expressly rejecting the exclusionary rule in Rhode Island).

7. See Wolf, 338 U.S. at 33–39 (listing jurisdictions that expressly adopted the exclusionary rule as of the date of the Wolf decision in 1949). Note the District of Columbia follows the federal rule. See, e.g., Nueslein v. District of Columbia, 115 F.2d 690, 694–95 (D.C. Cir. 1940) ("Under the federal rule some illegally obtained evidence is inadmissible, inadmissible because of the IVth Amendment. Critics may assail this rule, but it is well established. The issue for us is not whether the rule should be voided, but whether this situation should be held to come within the rule.").

8. Mapp v. Ohio, 367 U.S. 643 (1961).

9. Alaska and Hawaii were admitted as states in 1959, two years before the Supreme Court's decision in *Mapp v. Ohio*. Before *Mapp*, the highest courts of Alaska and Hawaii had not expressly addressed the exclusionary rule.

10. See the authorities cited at Paul H. Robinson and Michael T. Cahill, *Law without Justice* at 282 n.18 and accompanying text on 151.

CHAPTER TWENTY-ONE

Entrapment Defense

As a society, we don't want our police and prosecutors or their agents creating crime by inducing citizens to commit it. On the other hand, in many situations the only effective means of stopping an ongoing pattern of criminal activity is for the police to go undercover to act as potential accomplices or as victims. For example, a city whose main industries are gambling and tourism experiences a flurry of robberies, and the targets are the city's cash-laden, intoxicated visitors. The local police run a "sting" operation in an area where such robberies are known to occur, in which an officer pretends to be a drunken visitor passed out on the sidewalk, cash slightly protruding from his pocket.[1] By arresting those who victimize the apparent drunk, the police are able to arrest the victimizers and deter future attacks.

Although the offense of entrapment may not be common in the rest of the world, all American jurisdictions offer it, albeit with some variation in formulation among the states.[2] Map 21 presents the state alignment for the two major approaches seen in the United States, together with the competing positions on an important variation.

Defense Available If Not Predisposed, but Not Offense of Violence

The narrowest form of the American entrapment defense is provided in the three states with light shading on the map: Delaware, Kentucky, and Missouri.[3] In Missouri, for example, the defense is available if a law enforcement officer or his agent "for the purpose of obtaining evidence of the commission of an offense, solicits, encourages or otherwise induces another person to engage in conduct when he was not ready and willing to engage in such conduct."[4]

The effect of the "not ready and willing to engage in such conduct" language is to exclude from the defense those persons, such as professional

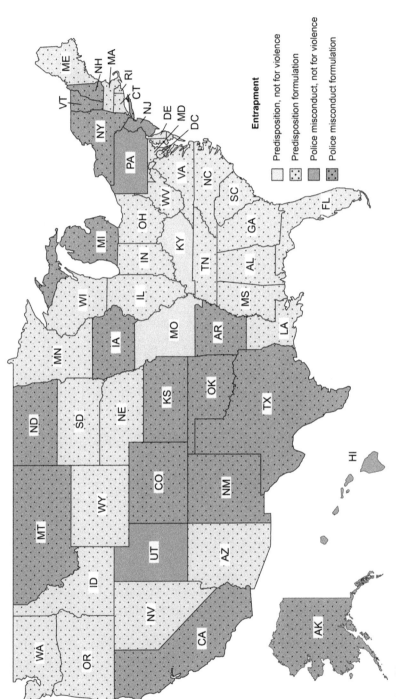

Map 21

criminals, who would have committed the offense anyway, and may well have been out looking for the opportunity to commit such an offense. That is, this formulation of the defense provides a defense only to people who are "not predisposed" to commit the offense.

All five of these states exclude the defense for a crime of violence.

Defense Available If Not Predisposed, Even If Crime of Violence

The most common approach to the defense is taken by 29 jurisdictions, identified with light shading and dots on the map: Alabama, Arizona, Connecticut, District of Columbia, Florida, Georgia, Idaho, Illinois, Indiana, Louisiana, Maine, Maryland, Massachusetts, Minnesota, Mississippi, Nebraska, Nevada, North Carolina, Ohio, Oregon, Rhode Island, South Carolina, South Dakota, Tennessee, Virginia, Washington, West Virginia, Wisconsin, and Wyoming.[5] They follow the same "not predisposed" formulation described above but do not explicitly exclude the defense for an offense of violence.

While the defense is not explicitly excluded for an offense of violence, as it is for the group above, as a practical matter the defense often may not be available in such cases. A judge or jury might conclude that a law enforcement agent "induced or persuaded an otherwise unwilling person to commit an unlawful act when the person was not predisposed to do so"[6] if that act is theft or the sale of drugs, for example. But the same judge or jury might find it more difficult to conclude that the offender's crime of violence was similarly "induced or persuaded" by a law enforcement agent and that the offender was an "unwilling person . . . not predisposed to [commit the offense]." In other words, one might speculate that persons "not predisposed" are more likely to be induced to commit crimes of theft or drugs than crimes of violence.

Defense Available If Police Misconduct Even If Offender Is Predisposed, but Not for Crime of Violence

The last two groups of states, with darker shading on the map, take an approach that is conceptually quite different from the "not predisposed" approach of the two groups above. In these two groups, the characteristics of the particular offender—even the offender's criminal history and criminal predisposition—are treated as essentially irrelevant. The only focus is on the police conduct. If the police conduct is improper, then the offender, even if a career criminal, is entitled to an entrapment defense.

Four states—Hawaii, New Jersey, Pennsylvania, and Utah,[7] with darker shading on the map (and no dots)—provide this broader defense triggered by "police misconduct," though they exclude its availability for offenses of violence.

Defense Available If Police Misconduct Even If Offender Is Predisposed, Even If Crime of Violence

Fifteen states—Alaska, Arkansas, California, Colorado, Iowa, Kansas, Michigan, Montana, New Hampshire, New Mexico, New York, North Dakota, Oklahoma, Texas, and Vermont,[8] shown with darker shading and dots on the map—provide the broadest defense: available for any instance of "police misconduct" and even if it is an offense of violence. Under this broadest formulation of the defense, if the police acted improperly, the entrapment defense is available even to those who are predisposed to commit the offense and even for an offense of violence. Thus, the career leg-breaker for an organized crime syndicate who was planning on committing the offense before any interaction with a police agent is entitled to the defense under this formulation if the police act improperly.[9]

Majority View Formulation

If one were to construct a formulation of the entrapment defense that reflected the majority view on each of the formulation issues, it might look something like this:

Section 503. Entrapment.

A person has a defense to an offense if:

1. he was induced to commit it by a public law enforcement official, or a person acting in cooperation with such an official, for the purpose of obtaining evidence of the commission of the offense; however,
2. the defense is unavailable if the person was predisposed to commit the offense and the public law enforcement official, or agent of such, merely afforded the person an opportunity to commit the offense.[10]

Observations and Speculations

Certainly the "police misconduct" formulation of the defense, in the last two groups above, is nothing like an excuse defense, such as duress, that is based on the offender's blamelessness. For under this formulation even a career criminal out looking for an opportunity to commit the offense may be entitled to an entrapment defense; the only focus of the inquiry is the *police* conduct, not the defendant's.

In contrast, one might initially be tempted to think of the "not predisposed" formulation of the defense, in the first two groups above, to be a form of excuse, like duress. One might say, for example, that it is the government's inducement rather than the offender's own selfishness or greed that caused the offense. But that conception is simply inconsistent with the defense requirements for entrapment. Under the exculpatory duress defense, for example, an offender is excused for his offense if he was coerced by another to commit the offense and a person of reasonable firmness in his situation would have been unable to resist the coercion.[11] But the "not predisposed" formulation of the entrapment defense fails to account for this latter element—the firmness of an actor in his situation.

Further, if an offender is "entrapped" by a nongovernment agent, then under the "not predisposed" formulation no defense is available at all. If the "not predisposed" formulation had something to do with accounting for the offender's blameworthiness, then it would continue to provide the defense no matter who does the entrapping. The fact that the entrapment defense entirely disappears when the entrapping is done by a nongovernment agent makes clear that the defense's focus—even under the "not predisposed" formulation— is the character of the *entrapper* as a government officer or agent. It is a non-exculpatory defense meant to control government officials, not an exculpating defense that excuses blameless offenders.

In this respect, the entrapment defense is much like the exclusionary rule: we use the threat of denying a conviction of the offender as a means of controlling the conduct of police and prosecutors. The formulations of the defense that limit its use to persons who are "not predisposed" are simply formulations that limit the price we are willing to pay in suffering failures of justice in order to control police and prosecutor misconduct.

The same is true of those entrapment formulations that bar the defense for crimes of violence. We are willing to pay some price in terms of suffering failures of justice in order to discourage police and prosecutors from running sting operations that we think are too intrusive, for example, but we are willing to pay only so much to provide this discouragement. We are not willing to let go blameworthy offenders who commit crimes of violence.

Those who see substantial costs in allowing blameworthy offenders to go free under the nonexculpatory defense of entrapment typically seek to narrow the defense as much as possible or, ideally, to abolish it in favor of some other mechanism for controlling police and prosecutor misconduct.[12] For example, they might prefer administrative sanctions of officers, rather than letting guilty offenders go free. If one were really serious about deterring police misconduct, one might consider abolishing the entrapment defense for the offender in favor of creating an entrapment *offense* for the entrapper. If the overreach of entrapment by officials is so intolerable that it should allow blameworthy offenders to go free, why should it not support at least the potential for criminal liability of those who engage in unlawful entrapment?

Notes

1. The facts are similar to those of the Reno, Nevada, case of David Kenny Hawkins discussed in Paul H. Robinson, *Would You Convict? 17 Cases That Challenged the Law*, 166–177 (NYU 1999).

2. See generally Paul H. Robinson and Michael T. Cahill, *Criminal Law*, 2nd ed. §10.3 (Oxford 2012).

3. Del. Code Ann. tit. 11, § 432; Ky. Rev. Stat. Ann. § 505.010; Mo. Ann. Stat. § 562.066.

4. Mo. Ann. Stat. § 562.066.

5. Johnson v. State, 285 So. 2d 723 (Ala. 1973); Ariz. Rev. Stat. Ann. § 13-206; Conn. Gen. Stat. Ann § 53a-15; Blyther v. United States, 577 A.2d 1154, 1158 (D.C. 1990); Wajer v. United States, 222 A.2d 68, 69–70 (D.C. 1966); Fla. Stat. Ann. § 777.201; Ga. Code Ann. § 16-3- 25; State v. Mata, 106 Idaho 184 (1984); 720 Ill. Comp. Stat. Ann. 5/7-12; Ind. Code § 35-41-3- 9; State v. Tate, 593 So. 2d 864 (La. Ct. App. 1992); State v. Farnsworth, 447 A.2d 1216 (Me. 1982); Moore v. State, 7 A.3d 617 (Md. 2010); Com. v. Madigan, 449 Mass. 702 (2007); State v. Grilli, 230 N.W.2d 445 (Minn. 1975); Walls v. State, 672 So. 2d 1227 (Miss. 1996); State v. Swenson, 352 N.W.2d 149 (Neb. 1984); Miller v. State, 121 Nev. Adv. Op. 10 (2005); State v. Branham, 569 S.E.2d 24 (N.C. 2002); State v. Doran, 449 N.E.2d 1295 (Ohio 1983); Or. Rev. Stat. Ann. § 161.275; State v. Jones, 416 A.2d 676 (R.I. 1980); State v. Johnson, 367 S.E.2d 700 (S.C. 1988); State v. Nelsen, 228 N.W.2d 143 (S.D. 1975); Tenn. Code Ann. § 39-11-505; McCoy v. Com., 385 S.E.2d 628 (Va. 1989); Wash. Rev. Code Ann. § 9A.16.070; State v. Miller, 475 S.E.2d 307 (W.V. 1996); State v. Hochman, 86 N.W.2d 446 (Wis. 1957); Swartz v. State, 971 P.2d 137 (Wyo.1998).

6. Tenn. Code Ann. § 39-11-505.

7. Haw. Rev. Stat. § 702-237; N.J. Stat. Ann. § 2C:2-12; 18 Pa. Cons. Stat. Ann. § 313; Utah Code Ann. § 76- 2-303.

8. Alaska Stat. Ann. § 11.81.450; Ark. Code Ann. § 5-2-209; People v. Watson, 22 Cal.4th 220 (2000); Colo. Rev. Stat. Ann. § 18-1-709; State v. Tomlinson, 243 N.W.2d 551 (Iowa 1976); Kan. Stat. Ann. § 21-5208; People v. Juillet, 475 N.W.2d 786 (Mich. 1991); Mont. Code Ann. § 45-2-213; N.H. Rev. Stat. Ann. § 626:5; State v. Vallejos, 123 N.M. 739 (1997); N.Y. Penal Law § 40.05; N.D. Cent. Code § 12.1-05-11; Raymer v. City of Tulsa, 595 P.2d 810 n.2 (Okla. 1979); Tex. Penal Code Ann. § 8.06; State v. George, 602 A.2d 953 (Vt. 1991).

9. Under a common formulation of this approach, the entrapment defense would be available to the professional leg-breaker even if the police conduct had no effect on him but "employed methods of persuasion or inducement which created a substantial risk that the offense would be committed by persons other than those who are ready to commit it." Haw. Rev. Stat. § 702-237.

10. From Paul H. Robinson et al., *The American Criminal Code: General Defenses*, 7 Journal of Legal Analysis 37, 66 (2015).

11. See, e.g., Model Penal Code § 2.09(1).

12. See, e.g., Paul H. Robinson and Michael T. Cahill, *Law without Justice: Why Criminal Law Doesn't Give People What They Deserve*, 180–83, 218–24 (Oxford 2006).

PART 7

Offenses against the Person and Property

CHAPTER TWENTY-TWO

Criminalizing Risk Creation

Many of the standard criminal offenses prohibit and punish causing harm to people, property, or even public institutions. Assaulting another person, taking another's property, or undermining the value of the official currency by counterfeiting it are all harms, tangible or intangible, that are serious enough to be criminalized.

But the criminal law does not limit itself to criminalizing conduct that causes tangible harm. It also criminalizes conduct that creates a risk of harm even if that risk never comes to fruition. Creating a risk of causing death or serious bodily injury to another person is frequently punished by the offense of endangerment. Creating a risk of damage to property is sometimes criminalized even if no such damage ever occurs.[1]

In some respects, the criminalization of risk creation is more challenging than that of causing a harm, tangible or intangible.[2] First, the ordinary person's daily life is full of risk creation. Even a drive to the local convenience store to get a newspaper creates some degree of risk to persons or property. This is simply the nature of our highly complex and interactive society, where nearly everything we do implicates another's interests. Obviously, all of these low-level risks are risks that we must accept as the price we pay for the benefits that flow from our modern lives. So part of the challenge in criminalizing risk creation is to be able to exclude from the offense all of those risks that are not serious enough to be criminal.

Further, some risks may be significant but also may be justified. For example, any large construction project is likely to create a substantial risk that someone in the course of the project will be injured or even killed. Nonetheless, even though the project organizers know this beforehand, we don't think them criminally condemnable for moving ahead with the project. Rather, we think that such risk-taking, within bounds, is an acceptable price to pay for the societal benefits that the project will bring.

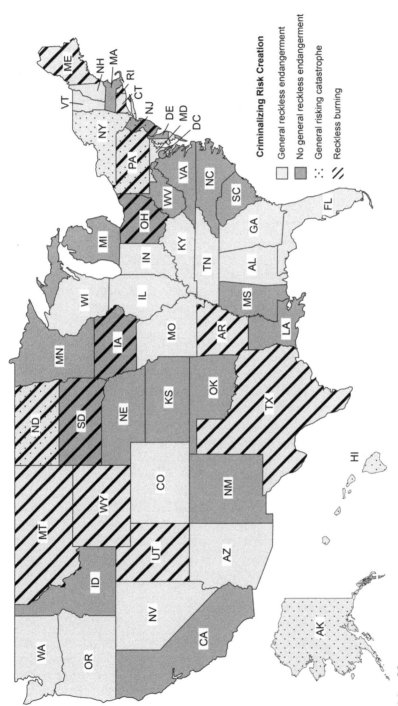

Criminalizing Risk Creation

General reckless endangerment

No general reckless endangerment

General risking catastrophe

Reckless burning

Map 22

Perhaps because of these complexities, a number of jurisdictions have been hesitant to adopt criminal offenses that punish the creation of risks, even substantial and unjustified risks. Some jurisdictions create an offense that punishes endangering the life or health of another person, but many other jurisdictions have no such offense. Some jurisdictions have adopted an offense that criminalizes the creation of a risk of widespread property damage, but many other jurisdictions do not.

Map 22 shows how each state stands on these issues.

General Reckless Endangerment Offense

Thirty states marked with lighter shading on the map—Alabama, Alaska, Arizona, Arkansas, Colorado, Connecticut, Delaware, Florida, Georgia, Hawaii, Illinois, Indiana, Kentucky, Maine, Maryland, Missouri, Montana, Nevada, New Hampshire, New York, North Dakota, Oregon, Pennsylvania, Tennessee, Texas, Utah, Vermont, Washington, Wisconsin, and Wyoming[3]—have adopted a general reckless endangerment offense.[4] The remaining 21 jurisdictions have no such general offense.

The offense criminalizes recklessly (in some states, wantonly or negligently) creating a risk of death or serious bodily injury (in some states, bodily injury) to another person, even if no harm occurs. These are not merely statutes of limited applicability, such as those that criminalize placing a child or vulnerable adult at risk of serious injury. These are statutes of general applicability: the risk may be created by any means, and the party at risk may be any other person.

Risking Catastrophe Offense

Six states follow the Model Penal Code in adopting a general offense for risking catastrophe. These states are shown with dots on the map: Alaska, Hawaii, New Jersey, New York, North Dakota, and Pennsylvania.[5] The statutes criminalize recklessly (in some states, wilfully or negligently) creating a risk of catastrophe, widespread damage to property (or in New York, simply damage to another's property exceeding $250), even if no damage occurs.[6] The statutes commonly specify that the risk be created by "widespread dangerous means"—that is, by any means that commonly risk widespread damage, such as fire, flood, or avalanche.

Reckless Burning Offense

Fourteen states, shown with diagonal lines on the map, have adopted reckless burning statutes: Arkansas, Connecticut, Iowa, Maine, Montana, New Jersey, North Dakota, Ohio, Pennsylvania, Rhode Island, South Dakota, Texas, Utah, and Wyoming.[7] These statutes criminalize recklessly (in some states, negligently) creating a risk (in some states, "substantial" risk) of injury to persons or property. The required risk varies by state, with some states requiring risk of bodily injury (or serious bodily injury) to persons, and one state requiring risk to buildings. These are statutes of *limited* applicability, in the sense that the risk must be created by fire.

Observations and Speculations

General offenses that criminalize endangering others or risking widespread property damage would seem to be fairly important for every jurisdiction, yet many have none—as with the darker shaded states in Map 22. Why should this be so?

It is true, as noted at the start of the chapter, that risk-creation offenses present challenges in their formulation that ordinary harm-causing offenses do not, but the Model Penal Code and the experience of the many states described above that have general risk-creation offenses make it clear that those challenges can be met. It is quite feasible to limit such criminal liability to cases of substantial risk of substantial harm and where no countervailing societal interest justifies the risk.[8]

The absence of general risk-creation offenses in many jurisdictions is probably less a principled concern for properly defining the prohibited risks, and more likely a result of the bad habit of state legislatures to respond to one lobbying group or one newspaper headline without thinking about the larger picture.

In every jurisdiction on the map that lacks a general reckless endangerment offense, one can probably find lots of very specific crimes of very specific endangering of another person. For instance, many jurisdictions specifically criminalize endangering the welfare of a child or certain vulnerable adults.[9] But if these specific instances of endangerment are to be criminalized, why not all instances of endangerment that create a risk just as high and just as likely?

Similarly, in every jurisdiction on the map that lacks an offense for creating a risk of widespread injury, one probably can find a host of very specialized offenses that prohibit very specific forms of such conduct. For instance, many jurisdictions criminalize risk-creating activities involving motor vehicles or firearms.[10] But if these forms of risk creation are to be punished, why not other forms of conduct that create risks that are just as serious and just as likely?

Indeed, for those jurisdictions that have a general reckless burning offense, shown on the map with horizontal lines, why should it not also be an offense to create an identical risk through some other means, as by explosion or flooding—or risk of similar scale through radiation exposure or biological or toxic contamination?

The problem exists in large part because of the nature of the American legislative process as it relates to criminal law. A specific interest group asks for a specific criminal offense to be created that addresses their specific problem. For example, the milk lobby wants the creation of a special offense that criminalizes the taking of the plastic crates that are used to deliver bottles of milk. Or a newspaper headline tells the story of a particular criminal episode that prompts legislators to want to show their constituents that they are responsive to an apparent issue. For example, car thieves pull a woman from her car and drive off with it. The legislature promptly creates a "carjacking" offense, as if the robbery, assault, and auto theft offenses didn't already criminalize and seriously punish such conduct.

This unfortunate legislative dynamic leads to piecemeal criminal code drafting with hundreds, if not thousands, of specialized offenses. But the approach simply makes the criminal code enormously long and complicated and at the same time incomplete, filled with lots of inexplicable holes in coverage. The better approach is, first, to resist creating new offenses if they are already covered by the existing criminal code and, second, when gaps in current coverage are discovered, to look beyond the special case at hand to define an offense that covers the general harm or evil and not just this special version of it.[11]

Notes

1. See generally Paul H. Robinson and Michael T. Cahill, *Criminal Law*, 2nd ed. §15.4, §16.1 (Wolters Kluwer 2012).

2. See Paul H. Robinson, *Prohibited Risks and Culpable Disregard or Inattentiveness: Challenge and Confusion in the Formulation of Risk-Creation Offenses*, 4 Theoretical Inquiries in Law 367 (2002).

3. Ala. Code § 13A-6-24; Alaska Stat. Ann. § 11.41.250; Ariz. Rev. Stat. Ann. § 13-1201; Ark. Code Ann. § 5-13-205; Ark. Code Ann. § 5-13-206; Colo. Rev. Stat. Ann. § 18-3-208; Conn. Gen. Stat. Ann. § 53a-63; Del. Code Ann. tit. 11, § 603; Fla. Stat. Ann. § 784.05; Ga. Code Ann. § 16-5-60; Haw. Rev. Stat. Ann. § 707-713; 720 Ill. Comp. Stat. Ann. 5/12-5; Ind. Code Ann. § 35-42-2-2; Ky. Rev. Stat. Ann. § 508.060; Me. Rev. Stat. tit. 17-A, § 211; Md. Code Ann., Crim. Law § 3-204; Mo. Ann. Stat. § 565.056; Mont. Code Ann. § 45-5-208; Nev. Rev. Stat. Ann. § 202.595; N.H. Rev. Stat. Ann. § 631:3; N.Y. Penal Law § 120.20; N.D. Cent. Code Ann. § 12.1-21-02; Or. Rev. Stat. Ann. § 163.195; 18 Pa. Stat. and Cons. Stat. Ann. § 2705; Tenn. Code Ann. § 39-13-103; Tex. Penal Code Ann. § 22.05; Utah Code Ann. § 76-5-112; Vt. Stat. Ann. tit. 13, § 1025; Wash. Rev. Code Ann. § 9A.36.050; Wis. Stat. Ann. § 941.30; Wyo. Stat. Ann. § 6-2-504.

4. Many of these statutes are based on Model Penal Code §211.2, Recklessly Endangering Another Person.

5. Alaska Stat. Ann. § 11.46.482; Alaska Stat. Ann. § 11.46.495; N.J. Stat. Ann. § 2C:17-2; N.D. Cent. Code Ann. § 12.1-21-04; 18 Pa. Stat. and Cons. Stat. Ann. § 3302.

Hawaii criminalizes a "failure to control widely dangerous means," such as flood or release of radioactive material, when the actor knows that the means "are endangering life or property," the actor "negligently fails to take measure to prevent or mitigate the danger," and the actor is either under a legal duty to control the danger or is in some way responsible for the means. See Haw. Rev. Stat. Ann. § 708-824; Haw. Rev. Stat. Ann. § 708-800.

New York criminalizes "reckless endangerment of property," where the actor recklessly creates a substantial risk of damage to another's property in an amount exceeding $250. See N.Y. Penal Law § 145.25.

6. Some of these offenses are based on Model Penal Code §220.2, Causing or Risking Catastrophe.

7. Ark. Code Ann. § 5-38-302; Conn. Gen. Stat. Ann. § 53a-114; Iowa Code Ann. § 712.5; Me. Rev. Stat. tit. 17-A, § 802; Mont. Code Ann. § 45-6-102; N.J. Stat. Ann. § 2C:17-1; N.D. Cent. Code Ann. § 12.1-21-02; Ohio Rev. Code Ann. § 2909.03; 18 Pa. Stat. and Cons. Stat. Ann. § 3301; 11 R.I. Gen. Laws Ann. § 11-4-2; S.D. Codified Laws § 22-33-9.3; Tex. Penal Code Ann. § 28.02; Utah Code Ann. § 76-6-104; Wyo. Stat. Ann. § 6-3-103.

Arkansas, New Mexico, and Utah criminalize creating fires without taking precautions. For instance, New Mexico does not have a general reckless burning statute, but the code criminalizes "improper handling of fire," which includes starting fires under certain conditions without taking proper precautions. See N.M. Stat. Ann. § 30-17-1; see also Ark. Code Ann. § 5-38-310; Utah Code Ann. § 76-6-104.

8. See Model Penal Code § 211.2 (Recklessly Endangering Another Person); Model Penal Code § 220.2 (Causing or Risking Catastrophe); Model Penal Code § 2.02(2)(c) (defining culpable mental state of recklessness).

9. See, e.g., Ala. Code § 13A-13-6 (child endangerment); Iowa Code Ann. § 726.6 (child endangerment); Alaska Stat. Ann. § 11.51.200 (endangerment of a vulnerable adult); Me. Rev. Stat. tit. 17-A, § 555 (endangerment of a dependent person).

10. See, e.g., Fla. Stat. Ann. § 316.192 (reckless driving); N.D. Cent. Code Ann. § 39-08-03 (reckless driving); Tex. Transp. Code Ann. § 545.401 (reckless driving); Cal. Penal Code § 25100 (storage of firearm in a location where a child is likely to gain unsupervised access); Okla. Stat. Ann. tit. 21, § 1289.11 (imposing criminal liability for "engaging in reckless conduct while having in . . . possession any [firearm] . . . creating a situation of unreasonable risk . . . of death or great bodily harm"); W. Va. Code Ann. § 61-7-12 (criminalizing "[wanton] perform[ance] [of] any act with a firearm which creates a substantial risk of death or serious bodily injury").

11. See Paul H. Robinson, *The Rise and Fall and Resurrection of American Criminal Codes*, 53 U. Louisville Law Review 173 (2015); Paul H. Robinson and Michael T. Cahill, *The Accelerating Degradation of American Criminal Codes*, 56 Hastings Law Journal 633–655 (2005).

CHAPTER TWENTY-THREE

Statutory Rape

Every state puts some limitation on how young a sexual partner can be, although there is disagreement as to what the "age of consent," as it is called, should be and as to whether special exemptions should be recognized, such as the youthfulness of the defendant. The limitations contained in the offense are based in part on the norms and customs of the community but also on a recognition that young persons below a certain age may not fully appreciate the implications and consequences of their sexual activity. Legislators have reasoned that without this full appreciation, the young person's consent may not be fully informed and therefore ought not to be seen as valid.

In the United States, the age below which sexual intercourse with an adult is considered statutory rape varies from 16 years to 18 years of age, as reflected in Map 23. (No state generally permits an adult to engage in intercourse with a partner under 16 years old, although in some states younger persons may have intercourse with a person under 16 without committing a crime.) The darker the shading on the map, the more restrictive the rules governing intercourse with a young person. Some states define their statutory rape offense to exempt defendants who are close in age to their underage partner, although even these close-in-age statutes set some limit on how young the partner can be.

Criminal for Adult to Have Intercourse with a Partner under 16

Thirty-three jurisdictions identified with light shading on the map—Alabama, Alaska, Arkansas, Connecticut, District of Columbia, Georgia, Hawaii, Indiana, Iowa, Kansas, Kentucky, Maine, Maryland, Massachusetts, Michigan, Minnesota, Mississippi, Montana, Nebraska, Nevada, New Hampshire, New Jersey, New Mexico, North Carolina, Ohio, Oklahoma, Pennsylvania, Rhode Island, South Carolina, South Dakota, Vermont, Washington, and West Virginia[1]—ordinarily permit an adult to engage in intercourse with a consenting

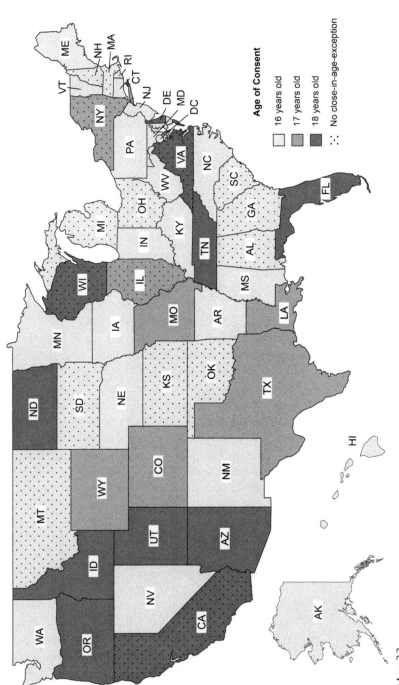

Age of Consent

- 16 years old
- 17 years old
- 18 years old
- No close-in-age-exception

Map 23

person who is 16 years old or older, provided that the actor does not stand in any relationship of authority to the partner, such as the relationship of guardian, teacher, or coach. (Most states have a special statute addressing age of consent where a relationship of authority exists.[2])

Criminal for Adult to Have Intercourse with a Partner under 17

Seven states shown with medium shading on the map—Colorado, Illinois, Louisiana, Missouri, New York, Texas, and Wyoming[3]—are somewhat more restrictive by prohibiting intercourse with a person under 17.

Criminal for Adult to Have Intercourse with a Partner under 18

Eleven states, those with dark shading on the map—Arizona, California, Delaware, Florida, Idaho, North Dakota, Oregon, Tennessee, Utah, Virginia, and Wisconsin[4]—are most restrictive by prohibiting intercourse with a person under 18.

Recognizing a Close-in-Age Exception

About two-thirds of the jurisdictions, identified without a dots overlay on the map—Alaska, Arizona, Arkansas, Colorado, Connecticut, Delaware, District of Columbia, Florida, Hawaii, Idaho, Indiana, Iowa, Kentucky, Louisiana, Maine, Maryland, Minnesota, Mississippi, Missouri, Nebraska, Nevada, New Jersey, New Mexico, North Carolina, North Dakota, Oregon, Pennsylvania, Tennessee, Texas, Utah, Vermont, Washington, West Virginia, and Wyoming[5]—recognize an exception to the statutory rape offense for persons who are close in age to the underage partner.

States with a "close-in-age exception" permit an adult actor to engage in intercourse with a party below the age of consent, where the adult actor is within a defined age range. This is expressed either as an absolute age, such as where the actor is less than 21 years old, or as a relative age, such as where the actor is no more than four years older than the consenting party.

Different states employ many different variations in defining the scope of the exception. Here are two examples. Colorado provides:

1. Any actor who knowingly inflicts sexual intrusion or sexual penetration on a victim commits sexual assault if: . . .

   (d) At the time of the commission of the act, the victim is less than fifteen years of age and the actor is at least four years older than the victim and is not the spouse of the victim; or

(e) At the time of the commission of the act, the victim is at least fifteen years of age but less than seventeen years of age and the actor is at least ten years older than the victim and is not the spouse of the victim; . . . [6]

Alaska provides:

A. An offender commits the crime of sexual abuse of a minor in the first degree if,

1. being 16 years of age or older, the offender engages in sexual penetration with a person who is under 13 years of age or aids, induces, causes, or encourages a person who is under 13 years of age to engage in sexual penetration with another person . . .

B. An offender commits the crime of sexual abuse of a minor in the second degree if,

1. being 17 years of age or older, the offender engages in sexual penetration with a person who is 13, 14, or 15 years of age and at least four years younger than the offender, or aids, induces, causes, or encourages a person who is 13, 14, or 15 years of age and at least four years younger than the offender to engage in sexual penetration with another person . . . [7]

No Close-in-Age Exception Recognized

The remaining third of the states, those with a dots overlay on the map—Alabama, California, Georgia, Illinois, Kansas, Massachusetts, Michigan, Montana, New Hampshire, New York, Ohio, Oklahoma, Rhode Island, South Carolina, South Dakota, Virginia, and Wisconsin[8]—provide no close-in-age exception to the statutory rape offense. Thus, even persons close in age to the underage partner can be liable for the crime of statutory rape.

For example, Virginia provides:

Any person 18 years of age or older . . . who . . . engages in consensual sexual intercourse or anal intercourse with or performs cunnilingus, fellatio, or anilingus upon or by a child 15 or older not his spouse, . . . is guilty of a Class 1 misdemeanor.[9]

For example, an 18-year-old boyfriend who wishes to engage in consensual intercourse with his 16-year-old girlfriend would escape liability in a state with a close-in-age exception, like Texas, but not in a state that lacks the exception, such as New York. In New York, a person less than 17 years old is "deemed incapable of consent" by statute.[10] In Texas, on the other hand, the 18-year-old boyfriend may assert an affirmative defense, that he "was not more than three years older than the victim."[11]

Observations and Speculations

As the analysis above indicates, different states take significantly different approaches in defining statutory rape. The existence of such diversity is consistent with the idea that the proper age below which sexual intercourse should be criminalized is in some part a function of existing community norms and customs. The collection of darker shaded states in the West, with a line of medium shaded states separating them from a somewhat lighter shaded Midwest and East suggest that some of the cultural differences may be regional.

However, it is also possible that a variety of other factors influence the cutoff age. Perhaps some state legislatures are inclined to be influenced by what their neighboring states do. Or perhaps news coverage of some particular case in the state has prompted the legislature to undertake a reform, where their neighboring states may or may not have had such news coverage or public upset.[12]

Interestingly, there seems to be no obvious connection between the baseline age of consent in a state and the recognition of a close-in-age exception; the exception is used across states with varying age cutoffs of 16, 17 and 18.

The diversity among the states does create some significant points of contrast, even for neighboring states. Consider two examples of pairs of neighboring states. Alabama provides a cutoff age of 16 years of age, while across the state line in Florida the cutoff age is 18. Even more striking, in Alabama, a 16-year-old could be convicted of statutory rape of his 15-year-old girlfriend, while in Florida, with its permissive close-in-age exception, a 23-year-old may engage in consensual intercourse with a 16-year-old. Similarly, Virginia sets the cutoff at 18 and does not provide a close-in-age exception, while neighboring North Carolina's cutoff is 16, with a close-in-age exception. An 18-year-old boyfriend is liable for statutory rape of his 17-year-old girlfriend in Virginia, while the same 18-year-old would be permitted to have sex with a consenting 15-year-old in North Carolina, provided their age difference is less than four years.

These kinds of criminal law differences among the states can have regular and important practical effects. To promote compliance and to provide fair notice, this might be the kind of criminal law information that should be made readily available to the general population, especially young people, which tends not to be the case today.

Notes

1. Ala. Code § 13A-6-62; Ala. Code § 13A-6-67; Alaska Stat. Ann. § 11.41.434; Alaska Stat. Ann. § 11.41.436; Alaska Stat. Ann. § 11.41.438; Alaska Stat. Ann. § 11.41.440; Ark. Code Ann. § 5-14-127; Conn. Gen. Stat. Ann. § 53a-71; D.C. Code Ann. § 22-3001; D.C. Code Ann. § 22-3008; Ga. Code Ann. § 16-6-3; Haw. Rev.

Stat. Ann. § 707-730; Ind. Code Ann. § 35-42-4-9; Iowa Code Ann. § 709.4; Kan. Stat. Ann. § 21-5506; Ky. Rev. Stat. Ann. § 510.050; Ky. Rev. Stat. Ann. § 510.020; Ky. Rev. Stat. Ann. § 510.060; Me. Rev. Stat. tit. 17-A, § 254; Md. Code Ann., Crim. Law § 3-308; Md. Code Ann., Crim. Law § 3-307; Mass. Gen. Laws Ann. ch. 265, § 23; Mich. Comp. Laws Ann. § 750.520d; Minn. Stat. Ann. § 609.344; Miss. Code. Ann. § 97-3-65; Mont. Code Ann. § 45-5-501; Mont. Code Ann. § 45-5-503; Neb. Rev. Stat. Ann. § 28-319; Neb. Rev. Stat. Ann. § 28-319.01; Nev. Rev. Stat. Ann. § 200.364; Nev. Rev. Stat. Ann. § 200.368; N.H. Rev. Stat. Ann. § 632-A:3; N.H. Rev. Stat. Ann. § 632-A:4; N.J. Stat. Ann. § 2C:14-2; N.M. Stat. Ann. § 30-9-11; N.C. Gen. Stat. Ann. § 14-27.25; Ohio Rev. Code Ann. § 2907.04; Ohio Rev. Code Ann. § 2907.06; Okla. Stat. Ann. tit. 21, § 1111; 18 Pa. Stat. and Cons. Stat. Ann. § 3122.1; 18 Pa. Stat. and Cons. Stat. Ann. § 3125; 18 Pa. Stat. and Cons. Stat. Ann. § 3126; 11 R.I. Gen. Laws Ann. § 11-37-6; S.C. Code Ann. § 16-3-655; S.D. Codified Laws § 22-22-1; S.D. Codified Laws § 22-22-7; S.D. Codified Laws § 22-22-7.3; Vt. Stat. Ann. tit. 13, § 2602; Vt. Stat. Ann. tit. 13, § 3252; Wash. Rev. Code Ann. § 9A.44.079; Wash. Rev. Code Ann. § 9A.44.089; W. Va. Code Ann. § 61-8B-2; W. Va. Code Ann. § 61-8B-5; W. Va. Code Ann. § 61-8B-9.

2. See, e.g., Ohio Rev. Code Ann. § 2907.03.

3. Colo. Rev. Stat. Ann. § 18-3-402; 720 Ill. Comp. Stat. Ann. 5/11-1.50; 720 Ill. Comp. Stat. Ann. 5/11-1.60; La. Stat. Ann. § 14:80; La. Stat. Ann. § 14:80.1; La. Stat. Ann. § 14:81; Mo. Ann. Stat. § 566.034; N.Y. Penal Law § 130.05; N.Y. Penal Law § 130.20; N.Y. Penal Law § 130.25; Tex. Penal Code Ann. § 21.11; Tex. Penal Code Ann. § 21.011; Wyo. Stat. Ann. § 6-2-315; Wyo. Stat. Ann. § 6-2-316; Rogers v. State, 2015 WY 48, ¶ 23, 346 P.3d 934, 941 (Wyo. 2015) (defining the term "immodest, immoral[,] or indecent liberties" for purposes of the child pornography possession statute).

4. Ariz. Rev. Stat. Ann. § 13-1405; Ariz. Rev. Stat. Ann. § 13-1407; Cal. Penal Code § 261.5; Cal. Penal Code § 261; Cal. Penal Code § 264; Del. Code Ann. tit. 11, § 770; Fla. Stat. Ann. § 794.05; Fla. Stat. Ann. § 800.04; Idaho Code Ann. § 18-6101; N.D. Cent. Code Ann. § 12.1-20-01; N.D. Cent. Code Ann. § 12.1-20-02; N.D. Cent. Code Ann. § 12.1-20-05; N.D. Cent. Code Ann. § 12.1-20-07; Or. Rev. Stat. Ann. § 163.315; Or. Rev. Stat. Ann. § 163.345; Or. Rev. Stat. Ann. § 163.415; Or. Rev. Stat. Ann. § 163.427; Or. Rev. Stat. Ann. § 163.435; Or. Rev. Stat. Ann. § 163.445; Tenn. Code Ann. § 39-13-506; Utah Code Ann. § 76-5-401.2; Va. Code Ann. § 18.2-371; Va. Code Ann. § 1-207; Wis. Stat. Ann. § 948.09; Wis. Stat. Ann. § 948.02.

5. For each state listed in the text, see that state's citation in supra notes 1, 3, and 4.

6. Colo. Rev. Stat. Ann. § 18-3-402.

7. Alaska Stat. Ann. §§ 11.41.434, 11.41.436.

8. For each state listed in the text, see sources cited supra notes 1, 3, and 4.

9. Va. Code Ann. § 18.2-371. Note, many statutes, such as Virginia's, do not define "child" but criminalize intercourse with a "child" at or above a certain age, such as 15. Here, the courts must supply the meaning: a child 15 years or older is any person of 15, 16, or 17 years of age.

10. N.Y. Penal Law § 130.05.

11. Tex. Penal Code Ann. § 21.11.

12. For a general discussion of this dynamic, see Paul H. Robinson and Sarah M. Robinson, *Tragedy, Outrage & Reform: Crimes That Changed Our World* (Rowman & Littlefield 2017).

CHAPTER TWENTY-FOUR

Domestic Violence

The last three decades have seen an enormous shift in public attitudes about domestic violence. The problem of domestic violence was once widely regarded as a private matter between husband and wife—so much so that police would routinely stay out of such incidents as much as possible. Now, however, episodes of domestic violence are considered a matter of public concern to which police are encouraged and even required to aggressively respond.

Much of the shift was sparked by a series of horrific cases in which husbands would regularly and severely beat their wives, often with local police standing by, as occurred in the case of Tracey Thurman. But in 1985, Thurman sued the Torrington, Connecticut, Police Department and won. Increasing public intolerance of such conduct, combined with the momentum of the women's rights movement, have brought about a variety of legal reforms.[1] Two common responses have been the abolition of the marital rape exception and a change in police practice so as to encourage or even require arrest in cases of domestic violence, even where there is no arrest warrant.

Regarding marital rape, the traditional rule before the reforms had been that a husband could not be convicted of raping his wife. His use of physical force might render him liable for assault or even aggravated assault, but the traditional view barred rape liability under the theory that the sexual component of the conduct could not be grounds for a crime if the two people were married.

Today, states no longer provide wholesale immunity to actors who rape their spouses.[2] Still, states remain divided over whether to grant a limited exception to rape liability for a spouse. Fifteen states, shown with a dots overlay on Map 24, have retained a limited exception from liability for raping a spouse in certain situations: Alaska, California, Connecticut, Hawaii, Idaho, Iowa, Maryland, Michigan, Minnesota, Mississippi, New Hampshire, Ohio, Oklahoma, Rhode Island, and South Carolina.[3] The remaining 36 jurisdictions have abolished all forms of the marital rape exception. Indicated without any dots overlay on the map, these jurisdictions are Alabama, Arizona, Arkansas, Colorado, Delaware, District of Columbia, Florida, Georgia, Illinois, Indiana, Kansas, Kentucky, Louisiana, Maine, Massachusetts, Missouri, Montana, Nebraska, Nevada, New Jersey, New Mexico, New York, North Carolina, North Dakota, Oregon, Pennsylvania, South Dakota, Tennessee, Texas, Utah, Vermont, Virginia, Washington, West Virginia, Wisconsin, and Wyoming.[4]

With regard to the changes in domestic violence arrest policy, the states are split. See the categories represented on Map 24. Twenty states have adopted a mandatory arrest policy.[5] In these states, an officer is required to arrest if the officer has probable cause that the individual has recently committed an act of violence toward a member of the household. (In some states, the act of violence must have actually resulted in at least some harm.[6])

Another seven states have adopted a preferred arrest policy.[7] Where the officer has probable cause to believe that the person has committed domestic violence, these statutes express a preference for an arrest, even in the absence of a judicial arrest warrant. (In some states, this preference takes the form of a presumption: officers must presume that arrest is the appropriate response, but the presumption is rebuttable by special circumstances.[8]) Officers in such circumstances can still lawfully forgo an arrest—for example, they might be persuaded by a victim's plea that it would be better from the victim's point of view if there were no arrest.

The remaining 24 states have left their policy as one of discretionary arrest,[9] which is the standard policy for most offenses: if the officer has probable cause to believe the person committed domestic violence, the officer can make an arrest but has the discretion not to do so, perhaps preferring, for example, to perform the arrest at a later time under a judicial warrant. (Even in discretionary arrest states, an officer may be required to make an arrest where the suspect has violated a protective order, or where serious injury or a deadly weapon is involved.[10])

Map 24 shows how each state deals with each of these issues. The darker the shading, the less aggressive the state has been in promoting reforms on the arrest issue. A dots overlay indicates that the jurisdiction has retained some form of the limited marital rape exception.

No Marital Rape Exception, Mandatory Arrest

Most aggressive in addressing the problem of domestic violence are the 15 jurisdictions shown with light shading and no dots—Arizona, Colorado, District of Columbia, Kansas, Louisiana, Maine, Nevada, New Jersey, New York, Oregon, South Dakota, Utah, Virginia, Washington, and Wisconsin. These jurisdictions have abolished any form of a marital rape exception and have adopted a rule requiring mandatory arrest.

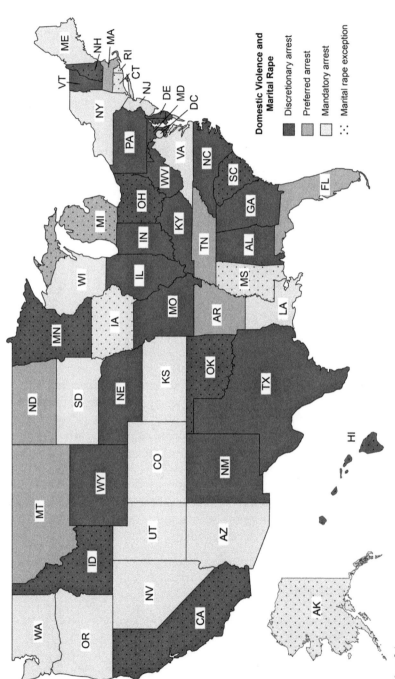

Domestic Violence and Marital Rape

- Discretionary arrest
- Preferred arrest
- Mandatory arrest
- ∴ Marital rape exception

Map 24

Limited Marital Rape Exception, Mandatory Arrest

Five states identified with light shading but with dots—Alaska, Connecticut, Iowa, Mississippi, and Rhode Island—similarly have a mandatory arrest rule but retain some limited form of a marital rape exception.

No Marital Rape Exception, Presumptive Arrest

Six states, those with medium shading and no dots—Arkansas, Florida, Massachusetts, Montana, North Dakota, and Tennessee—have abolished any form of a marital rape exception and take the middle position of encouraging but not requiring arrests in cases of domestic violence.

Limited Marital Rape Exception, Presumptive Arrest

One state, Michigan, takes this position of presumptive arrest in cases of domestic violence and retains some limited marital rape exception.

No Marital Rape Exception, Discretionary Arrest

Fifteen states, the other large grouping in addition to the first group, have abolished any marital rape exception but have not altered their arrest rules for domestic violence cases, leaving the arrest decision at the discretion of the officers. These states are shown in darker shading with no dots—Alabama, Delaware, Georgia, Illinois, Indiana, Kentucky, Missouri, Nebraska, New Mexico, North Carolina, Pennsylvania, Texas, Vermont, West Virginia, and Wyoming.

Limited Marital Rape Exception, Discretionary Arrest

Nine states, identified with darker shading and dots—California, Hawaii, Idaho, Maryland, Minnesota, New Hampshire, Ohio, Oklahoma, and South Carolina—have neither abolished a marital rape exception nor altered their domestic violence arrest rules to require anything more than the usual discretionary arrest practice.

Observations and Speculations

The depth and the speed of the reforms to the marital rape exception and to the domestic violence arrest policies demonstrate just how powerful changes in social norms can be in influencing criminal law and justice policy. There will always be political points of friction on a variety of fronts, but when public attitudes do shift the criminal justice system is typically quick to follow.

Which is as it should be. Especially with the changing influence of other social institutions to educate and convey cultural norms, the criminal law remains a vital and one of the only shared moral authorities in describing what is truly condemnable in our diverse society.

The need for the criminal law to keep up with society's changing norms is not only essential to promote and propagate those norms but also essential for the effective operation of the criminal justice system. As empirical studies have shown,[11] people are less likely to assist, support, and defer to a criminal law that they see as out of step, that seems unreliable as a moral authority of what is and is not truly condemnable. A system without moral credibility with the community it governs is a system more likely to encourage resistance and subversion.

Perhaps most importantly, a system without moral credibility is one that can play little role in helping a community to meet the needs of its changing culture. If the criminal law is perceived as authoritative in judging what is and what is not condemnable, then social reformers can harness that authority when they seek to reform the community's norms—on issues from domestic violence or date rape, to drunk driving or downloading music without a license. But where the criminal law is out of touch with social norms and thus lacks this moral credibility, its announcements and directives about one sort of conduct or another are easily ignored by the community as just one more instance in which the law is misguided.

Ultimately, then, criminal law must keep up with changing social norms not only to help propagate those norms but also to protect its ability to be a player in changing those and other norms in the future.[12]

Notes

1. See Paul H. Robinson & Sarah M. Robinson, *Tragedy, Outrage & Reform: Crimes That Changed Our World*, Chapter 1983 (Rowman & Littlefield 2018).

2. Note, however, that states do generally permit actors to engage in sexual acts with a person under the age of consent, where the person is the actor's spouse. This sort of marital exception is not the subject of this chapter.

3. Alaska Stat. Ann. § 11.41.432; Alaska Stat. Ann. § 11.41.410; Alaska Stat. Ann. § 11.41.420; Cal. Penal Code § 261; Cal. Penal Code § 262; Conn. Gen. Stat. Ann. § 53a-67; Conn. Gen. Stat. Ann. § 53a-73a; Haw. Rev. Stat. Ann. § 707-733; Idaho Code Ann. § 18-6101; Idaho Code Ann. § 18-6107; Iowa Code Ann. § 709.1A; Iowa Code Ann. § 709.4; Md. Code Ann., Crim. Law § 3-318; Md. Code Ann., Crim. Law § 3-303; Md. Code Ann., Crim. Law § 3-304; Md. Code Ann., Crim. Law § 3-307; Md. Code Ann., Crim. Law § 3-308; Mich. Comp. Laws Ann. § 750.520l; Minn. Stat. Ann. § 609.344; Minn. Stat. Ann. § 609.349; Miss. Code. Ann. § 97-3-99; N.H. Rev. Stat. Ann. § 632-A:2; N.H. Rev. Stat. Ann. § 632-A:5; Ohio Rev. Code Ann. § 2907.02; Ohio Rev. Code Ann. § 2907.03; Okla.

Stat. Ann. tit. 21, § 1111; 11 R.I. Gen. Laws Ann. § 11-37-2; 11 R.I. Gen. Laws Ann. § 11-37-4; S.C. Code Ann. § 16-3-615; S.C. Code Ann. § 16-3-658; S.C. Code Ann. § 16-3-654; S.C. Code Ann. § 16-3-652; S.C. Code Ann. § 16-3-653.

In Connecticut and Hawaii, the limited marital rape exception applies only to offenses involving "sexual contact," which includes contact beyond sexual penetration. See Conn. Gen. Stat. Ann. § 53a-67; Conn. Gen. Stat. Ann. § 53a-73a; Haw. Rev. Stat. Ann. § 707-733.

In Rhode Island, the limited marital rape exception applies only to offenses involving penetration, not sexual contact. See 11 R.I. Gen. Laws Ann. § 11-37-2; 11 R.I. Gen. Laws Ann. § 11-37-4. Perhaps this suggests that the spouse-actor in a case of unlawful sexual penetration would be prosecuted under the statute forbidding nonconsensual sexual contact.

In Virginia, though there is no limited marital rape exception as defined in this chapter, trial courts have limited discretion to place the defendant on probation with counseling eventually leading to dismissal of charges, where the court finds that "such action will promote maintenance of the family unit and be in the best interest of the [victim]." See Va. Code Ann. § 18.2-61.

4. Indeed, some states have expressly repealed the common-law marital rape exception. See, e.g., D.C. Code Ann. § 22-3019.

5. Alaska Stat. Ann. § 18.65.530; Ariz. Rev. Stat. Ann. § 13-3601; Colo. Rev. Stat. Ann. § 18-6-803.6; Conn. Gen. Stat. Ann. § 46b-38b; D.C. Code Ann. § 16-1031; Iowa Code Ann. § 236.12; Kan. Stat. Ann. § 22-2307; La. Stat. Ann. § 46:2140; Me. Rev. Stat. tit. 19-A, § 4012; Miss. Code. Ann. § 99-3-7; Nev. Rev. Stat. Ann. § 171.137; N.J. Stat. Ann. § 2C:25-21; N.Y. Crim. Proc. Law § 140.10; Or. Rev. Stat. Ann. § 133.055; 12 R.I. Gen. Laws Ann. § 12-29-3; S.D. Codified Laws § 23A-3-2.1; Utah Code Ann. § 78B-7-113; Va. Code Ann. § 19.2-81.3; Wash. Rev. Code Ann. § 10.31.100; Wis. Stat. Ann. § 968.075.

6. See, e.g., Iowa Code Ann. § 236.12.

7. Ark. Code Ann. § 16-81-113; Fla. Stat. Ann. § 741.29; Fla. Stat. Ann. § 901.15; Mass. Gen. Laws Ann. ch. 209A, § 6; Mass. Gen. Laws Ann. ch. 209A, § 1; Mich. Comp. Laws Ann. § 776.22; Mich. Comp. Laws Ann. § 764.15a; Mont. Code Ann. § 46-6-311; N.D. Cent. Code Ann. § 14-07.1-10; Tenn. Code Ann. § 36-3-619.

8. See, e.g., N.D. Cent. Code Ann. § 14-07.1-10.

9. Ala. Code § 15-10-3; Cal. Penal Code § 836; Del. Code Ann. tit. 11, § 1904; Ga. Code Ann. § 17-4-20; Haw. Rev. Stat. Ann. § 709-906; Idaho Code Ann. § 19-603; Ind. Code Ann. § 35-33-1-1; 725 Ill. Comp. Stat. Ann. 5/107-2; Ky. Rev. Stat. Ann. § 431.005; Md. Code Ann., Crim. Proc. § 2-204; Minn. Stat. Ann. § 629.341; Mo. Ann. Stat. § 455.085; Neb. Rev. Stat. Ann. § 29-404.02; N.H. Rev. Stat. Ann. § 594:10; N.M. Stat. Ann. § 31-1-7; N.C. Gen. Stat. Ann. § 15A-401; N.C. Gen. Stat. Ann. § 50B-1; Ohio Rev. Code Ann. § 2935.032; Okla. Stat. Ann. tit. 22, § 60.16; 18 Pa. Stat. and Cons. Stat. Ann. § 2711; S.C. Code Ann. § 16-25-70; Tex. Crim. Proc. Code Ann. § 14.03; Vt. R. Crim. P. 3; W. Va. Code Ann. § 48-27-1002; Wyo. Stat. Ann. § 6-2-510; Wyo. Stat. Ann. § 7-20-102.

In Ohio, a police officer has discretion whether to arrest where there is probable cause that a person has committed an act of domestic violence, except where the suspect caused serious bodily harm or used a deadly weapon, in which case the officer must arrest the suspect. See Ohio Rev. Code Ann. § 2935.032.

10. See, e.g., Ohio Rev. Code Ann. § 2935.032 (requiring arrest where serious bodily injury resulted, or where the suspect used a deadly weapon).

11. Paul H. Robinson, *Intuitions of Justice and the Utility of Desert*, Chapters 8–10 (Oxford 2013).

12. Id. at 196–201.

CHAPTER TWENTY-FIVE

Stalking and Harassment

A strong trend of the last several decades has been the creation of so-called "stalking" or "harassment" offenses. These new offenses go beyond the traditional assault and battery statutes to specially criminalize a repeated or continual course of conduct that either causes, risks, or is intended to cause another person mental or emotional distress, or fear of injury to himself, a close relative, a pet, property, or a business or financial interest.[1] Nearly every state now has a stalking or harassment offense of some kind.[2]

Many states have instituted a variety of different offense grades to reflect the relative seriousness of different kinds of stalking cases—increasing the offense grade, for example, if there was a previous conviction for the offense or if the conduct was in violation of a court protective order. In 36 states the lowest grade of stalking is a misdemeanor,[3] but in 15 states the lowest grade is a felony or at least an offense for which the authorized term of imprisonment is greater than a year.[4]

State stalking statutes take somewhat different approaches in defining the breadth of the offense. Some states require that the stalking conduct actually cause fear or distress in the victim.[5] But some states require only that the defendant intended to or believed his conduct would cause fear or distress, or that a reasonable person in his situation would have believed that it would result in causing fear or distress in the target; no actual fear or distress by the victim need be shown.[6]

Map 25 indicates the position that each state takes with regard to these issues.

Requires Actual Fear or Distress, Punished as a Misdemeanor

In 15 states, identified with no shading and no dots on the map—Alabama, Alaska, Connecticut, Georgia, Kentucky, Michigan, Montana, Nebraska, Nevada, Ohio, Oklahoma, Oregon, South Carolina, Tennessee, and

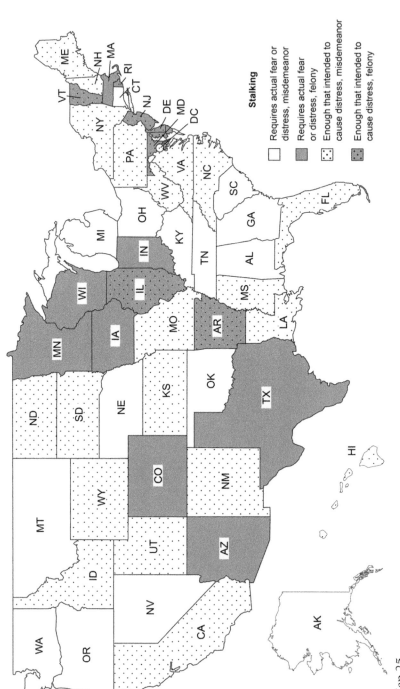

Stalking

☐ Requires actual fear or distress, misdemeanor

▨ Requires actual fear or distress, felony

⦂ Enough that intended to cause distress, misdemeanor

▨⦂ Enough that intended to cause distress, felony

Map 25

Washington[7]—to be convicted of the lowest grade of stalking, the offender's victim must have actually experienced some mental or emotional harm, broadly defined to include any fear, anguish, distress, terror, fright, intimidation, or worry. Generally any mental harm will do, but the victim must have actually experienced the mental harm. These 15 states punish the offense as a misdemeanor.

Requires Actual Fear or Distress, Punished as a Felony

In eight states, shown with shading and no dots on the map—Arizona, Colorado, Indiana, Iowa, Massachusetts, Minnesota, Texas, and Wisconsin[8]—the stalking offense requires actual fear or distress, as with the group above, but is punished as a felony. This group includes states that label their stalking offense a misdemeanor but actually provide a maximum sentence of greater than one year imprisonment (the traditional basis for the felony-misdemeanor distinction).

Enough That Intended or Believed Would Cause Distress, Punished as a Misdemeanor

In 21 jurisdictions, shown with no shading but with dots on the map—California, District of Columbia, Florida, Hawaii, Idaho, Kansas, Louisiana, Maine, Mississippi, Missouri, New Hampshire, New Mexico, New York, North Carolina, North Dakota, Pennsylvania, South Dakota, Utah, Virginia, West Virginia, and Wyoming[9]—a defendant can be convicted of the lowest grade of stalking even if he or she did not cause the victim to have experienced mental or emotional harm or distress of any kind. In these states the offense generally requires only that the actor intended or believed that his conduct would cause fear or distress, or acted in such a way that a reasonable victim would have felt fear or distress from his actions. These 21 states punish the offense as a misdemeanor.

Enough That Intended or Believed Would Cause Distress, Punished as a Felony

Seven states, identified on the map with shading and dots—Arkansas, Delaware, Illinois, Maryland, New Jersey, Rhode Island, and Vermont[10]—provide for convictions of defendants who intended or believed or should have known that their conduct would cause distress. But in these states, the lowest grade of the stalking offense is a felony—that is, it carries a maximum sentence of more than one year.

Observations and Speculations

The creation of stalking and harassment offenses recognizes that what might normally be conduct too trivial to warrant the condemnation of criminal conviction—such as staring at a person across the street—can be something quite serious if done repeatedly or continuously for some length of time. Thus, states were right to create this new offense to fill a gap in current law.

As often happens with the recognition of new offenses, however, it is easy to go a bit too far. The public attention and upset that trigger the legislative action can often create a momentum toward excess that turns a good idea into a source of future injustice.[11] This is most evident in the second and fourth groups above, which punish stalking or harassment as a felony.

Remember that every American criminal code already has offenses that punish assault, battery, aggravated assault, and a host of other offenses against the person. Each of these offenses is calibrated to carry a maximum punishment that reflects the seriousness of the offense, typically tied to the extent of the harm caused: for example, the offense grade would be greater for causing only fear of bodily injury versus causing bodily injury, and even greater for causing serious bodily injury, and so on. Typically only the more serious injuries are likely to move an offense out of the category of misdemeanor into the category of felony. Yet, the jurisdictions in the second and fourth groups above have set their lowest grade of the stalking or harassment offense as a felony even though no physical injury of any sort has occurred.

Perhaps even more objectionable are the jurisdictions in the fourth group. Not only do they not require any actual physical injury of any kind, they provide for felony liability even if there is no showing of even a fear of injury. The victim can be entirely unaffected by the stalking conduct, can suffer no fear or distress of any kind, yet the defendant's offense, even under the jurisdiction's lowest grade of stalking, will carry a felony penalty.

If one believes in the importance of doing justice, one must also believe in the importance of avoiding injustice. The principle of proportionality—between the seriousness of the offense and the seriousness of the penalty—is central to the notion of justice. The creation of stalking offenses was an appropriate and even important expansion of criminal liability, but like all other criminal law enactments, it must avoid disproportionality or risk endangering the criminal law's moral credibility with the community.

Notes

1. We exclude from our analysis various "special means" stalking statutes, such as cyberstalking statutes. We also exclude statutes that do not require a repeated or continual course of conduct, such as pure harassment statutes.

2. Mississippi's statute permits a single threat to count as stalking and so technically does not meet the "repeated or continual course of conduct" requirement, but is included in our analysis. Miss. Code. Ann. § 97-3-107; see also Nicholson on Behalf of Gollott v. State, 672 So. 2d 744, 753 (Miss. 1996) (holding, in dicta, that a single, credible threat against a victim constitutes "stalking" under the Mississippi statute).

3. Ala. Code § 13A-6-90.1; Alaska Stat. Ann. § 11.41.270; Cal. Penal Code § 646.9; Conn. Gen. Stat. Ann. § 53a-181e; D.C. Code Ann. § 22-3133; D.C. Code Ann. § 22-3134; Fla. Stat. Ann. § 784.048; Ga. Code Ann. § 16-5-90; Haw. Rev. Stat. Ann. § 711-1106.5; Idaho Code Ann. § 18-7906; Kan. Stat. Ann. § 21-5427; Ky. Rev. Stat. Ann. § 508.150; La. Rev. Stat. Ann. § 14:40.2; Me. Rev. Stat. tit. 17-A, § 210-A; Me. Rev. Stat. tit. 17-A, § 1252; Mich. Comp. Laws Ann. § 750.411h; Miss. Code. Ann. § 97-3-107; Mo. Ann. Stat. § 565.227; Mont. Code Ann. § 45-5-220; Neb. Rev. Stat. Ann. § 28-311.03; Neb. Rev. Stat. Ann. § 28-311.04; Nev. Rev. Stat. Ann. § 200.575; N.H. Rev. Stat. Ann. § 633:3-a; N.M. Stat. Ann. § 30-3A-3; N.Y. Penal Law § 120.45; N.C. Gen. Stat. Ann. § 14-277.3A; N.D. Cent. Code Ann. § 12.1-17-07.1; Ohio Rev. Code Ann. § 2903.211; Okla. Stat. Ann. tit. 21, § 1173; Or. Rev. Stat. Ann. § 163.732; 18 Pa. Stat. and Cons. Stat. Ann. § 2709.1; S.C. Code Ann. § 16-3-1700; S.C. Code Ann. § 16-3-1710; S.D. Codified Laws § 22-19A-1; Tenn. Code Ann. § 39-17-315; Tenn. Code Ann. § 40-35-111; Utah Code Ann. § 76-5-106.5; Va. Code Ann. § 18.2-60.3; Wash. Rev. Code Ann. § 9A.46.110; W. Va. Code Ann. § 61-2-9a; Wyo. Stat. Ann. § 6-2-506. In Maine, the lowest graded stalking offense is classified a Class D crime, which results in imprisonment not to exceed one year. Me. Rev. Stat. tit. 17-A, § 1252.

4. Ariz. Rev. Stat. Ann. § 13-2923; Ark. Code Ann. § 5-71-229 (stalking in the second degree is a felony); Colo. Rev. Stat. Ann. § 18-3-602; Del. Code Ann. tit. 11, § 1312; 720 Ill. Comp. Stat. Ann. 5/12-7.3; Ind. Code Ann. § 35-45-10-5; Iowa Code Ann. § 708.11; Iowa Code Ann. § 903.1; Md. Code Ann., Crim. Law § 3-802; Mass. Gen. Laws Ann. ch. 265, § 43; Minn. Stat. Ann. § 609.749; N.J. Stat. Ann. § 2C:12-10; N.J. Stat. Ann. § 2C:43-6; 11 R.I. Gen. Laws Ann. § 11-59-2; Tex. Penal Code Ann. § 42.072; Vt. Stat. Ann. tit. 13, § 1061; Vt. Stat. Ann. tit. 13, § 1062; Wis. Stat. Ann. § 940.32.

In Iowa, the lowest graded stalking offense is classified an aggravated misdemeanor, which may result in imprisonment not to exceed two years. Iowa Code Ann. § 903.1. In Maryland, the offense is classified as a misdemeanor but results in imprisonment not exceeding five years. Md. Code Ann., Crim. Law § 3-802. In New Jersey, the lowest graded stalking offense is classified a crime of the fourth degree, which results in imprisonment not exceeding 18 months. N.J. Stat. Ann. § 2C:43-6.

In Arkansas, the lowest graded "stalking" offense is stalking in the third degree, a misdemeanor. However, under this third degree stalking offense, the actor needs only to commit a single act for conviction, and so does not meet the "repeated or continual course of conduct" requirement. See Ark. Code Ann. § 5-71-229.

5. Ala. Code § 13A-6-90.1; Ala. Code § 13A-6-92; Alaska Stat. Ann. § 11.41.270; Ariz. Rev. Stat. Ann. § 13-2923; Colo. Rev. Stat. Ann. § 18-3-602;

Conn. Gen. Stat. Ann. § 53a-181e; Ga. Code Ann. § 16-5-90; Ind. Code Ann. § 35-45-10-5; Ind. Code Ann. § 35-45-10-2; Iowa Code Ann. § 708.11; Ky. Rev. Stat. Ann. § 508.150; Mass. Gen. Laws Ann. ch. 265, § 43; Mich. Comp. Laws Ann. § 750.411h; Minn. Stat. Ann. § 609.749; Mont. Code Ann. § 45-5-220; Neb. Rev. Stat. Ann. § 28-311.02; Neb. Rev. Stat. Ann. § 28-311.03; Nev. Rev. Stat. Ann. § 200.575; Ohio Rev. Code Ann. § 2903.211; Okla. Stat. Ann. tit. 21, § 1173; Or. Rev. Stat. Ann. § 163.732; S.C. Code Ann. § 16-3-1700; Tenn. Code Ann. § 39-17-315; Tex. Penal Code Ann. § 42.072; Wash. Rev. Code Ann. § 9A.46.110; Wis. Stat. Ann. § 940.32.

6. Ark. Code Ann. § 5-71-229; Ark. Code Ann. § 5-71-208; Cal. Penal Code § 646.9; Del. Code Ann. tit. 11, § 1312; D.C. Code Ann. § 22-3133; D.C. Code Ann. § 22-3132; Fla. Stat. Ann. § 784.048; Haw. Rev. Stat. Ann. § 711-1106.5; Idaho Code Ann. § 18-7906; 720 Ill. Comp. Stat. Ann. 5/12-7.3; Kan. Stat. Ann. § 21-5427; La. Stat. Ann. § 14:40.2; Me. Rev. Stat. tit. 17-A, § 210-A; Md. Code Ann., Crim. Law § 3-802; Md. Code Ann., Crim. Law § 3-801; Miss. Code. Ann. § 97-3-107; Mo. Ann. Stat. § 565.225; Mo. Ann. Stat. § 565.227; N.H. Rev. Stat. Ann. § 633:3-a; N.J. Stat. Ann. § 2C:12-10; N.M. Stat. Ann. § 30-3A-3; N.Y. Penal Law § 120.45; N.C. Gen. Stat. Ann. § 14-277.3A; N.D. Cent. Code Ann. § 12.1-17-07.1; 18 Pa. Stat. and Cons. Stat. Ann. § 2709.1; 11 R.I. Gen. Laws Ann. § 11-59-2; 11 R.I. Gen. Laws Ann. § 11-59-1; S.D. Codified Laws § 22-19A-1; S.D. Codified Laws § 22-19A-4; S.D. Codified Laws § 22-19A-5; S.D. Codified Laws § 22-19A-6; Utah Code Ann. § 76-5-106.5; Vt. Stat. Ann. tit. 13, § 1061; Va. Code Ann. § 18.2-60.3; W. Va. Code Ann. § 61-2-9a; Wyo. Stat. Ann. § 6-2-506.

7. See supra notes 3 and 5.

8. See supra notes 4 and 5.

9. See supra notes 3 and 6.

10. See supra notes 4 and 6.

11. See, e.g., Paul H. Robinson and Sarah M. Robinson, *Tragedy, Outrage, and Reform: Crimes That Changed Our World*, Chapters 1932, 1962, 1993 (Rowman & Littlefield 2018) (the federalization of criminal law, drug laws, three strikes).

CHAPTER TWENTY-SIX

Child Neglect

All American jurisdictions have in place criminal offenses that punish a parent or guardian who fails to obtain care or treatment for a child's physical injury or for a child suffering physical pain. But beyond that, there is considerable diversity among the states in terms of their identification of other actions (or lack of actions) that constitute a child neglect offense, as Map 26 illustrates. The darker the shading on the map, the broader and more demanding the criminal neglect offense.

Criminalize Only Neglect of General Health or Welfare

Fourteen jurisdictions, shown without shading on the map—Arizona, Colorado, Connecticut, District of Columbia, Illinois, Indiana, Maine, Massachusetts, Oregon, Rhode Island, Tennessee, Vermont, Washington, and West Virginia[1]—criminalize neglect harmful to the "health" or "physical health" of the child, or criminalize failure to provide appropriate or necessary "care." These jurisdictions do not specifically criminalize "mental" or "emotional" neglect, or "education" neglect.[2]

Also Criminalize Neglect of "Education"

Three states, identified with dots and no shading on the map—Alaska, Hawaii, and New Mexico[3]—also criminalize, in addition to the general health and welfare coverage above, failure to generally "educate" or to provide "education" necessary for a child's welfare. (This category does not account for laws that criminalize a parent's failure to ensure a child's presence in school, or "education as required by law.")

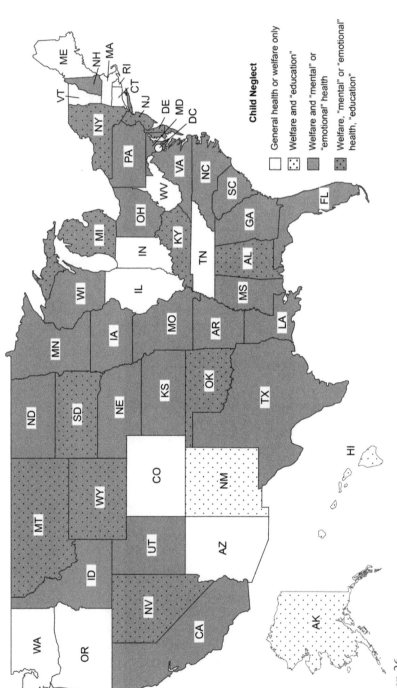

Child Neglect

☐ General health or welfare only

▢ Welfare and "education"

▨ Welfare and "mental" or "emotional" health

▨ Welfare, "mental" or "emotional" health, "education"

Map 26

Also Criminalize Neglect of "Mental" or "Emotional" Health

Twenty-three states, designated on the map with medium shading and no dots—Arkansas, California, Florida, Georgia, Idaho, Iowa, Kansas, Louisiana, Maryland, Minnesota, Mississippi, Missouri, Nebraska, New Hampshire, North Carolina, North Dakota, Ohio, Pennsylvania, South Carolina, Texas, Utah, Virginia, and Wisconsin[4]—punish physical neglect but also criminalize acts or omissions that result in harm to a child's mental or emotional welfare. Often the statutes use the language of "emotional health," "mental health," "mental pain," or "mental suffering."

Also Criminalize Neglect of "Mental" or "Emotional" Health, "Education"

Eleven states, those with medium shading and dots on the map—Alabama, Delaware, Kentucky, Michigan, Montana, Nevada, New Jersey, New York, Oklahoma, South Dakota, and Wyoming[5]—criminalize everything covered by the three categories above.

Observations and Speculations

It is easy to agree that parents should provide not only the support necessary for physical health and safety but also provide the support necessary for mental and emotional health as well as a sound education. But the issue here is somewhat different: in what circumstances should a parent be criminally liable for a failure to provide the support needed to achieve these desirable goals?

There can be little surprise that every jurisdiction will criminalize a parent's failure to provide for the health and safety of the child. In many respects, this criminalization logically follows from the criminalization of endangerment generally. (See Chapter 22, concerning endangerment and risking catastrophe.) If the state is going to criminalize the creation of danger to the health or safety of strangers, it should have no hesitation to do so for parents who endanger children.

That unanimity breaks down, however, as soon as the one crosses the line to mental or emotional health—the shaded jurisdictions on the map—or to criminal liability for failing to assure minimal educational opportunities—the jurisdictions with dots on the map. Notice that most of the jurisdictions that go so far as to criminalize failure to provide minimal educational opportunity are jurisdictions that already also provide criminal liability for failing to protect mental or emotional health. Only New Mexico, Alaska, and Hawaii—with dots and no shading on the map—criminalize the former (failure to provide minimal educational opportunity) but not the latter (failure to protect mental or emotional health). In contrast 11 jurisdictions—with shading and dots on the map—provide both the former and the latter.

In other words, failure to provide adequate educational opportunities—14 jurisdictions—seems to be the minority view on the high side, just as criminalizing only failure to protect health and welfare—14 jurisdictions—is the majority view on the low side, with protecting physical and mental or emotional health as the majority middle ground.

Why the disagreement among the jurisdictions? Why don't all jurisdictions criminalize child neglect of all of the types? Aren't these laudable goals that ought to be encouraged in all parents even, if necessary, by criminalizing the neglect? One might speculate that what is spooking some legislatures is a possibility that not all parents will have the capacity to provide the support covered by the child neglect offense. For example, a parent's financial limitations, as well as his or her own mental or emotional limitations, may seem to create a significant risk that criminal liability might be imposed in situations that are more tragic than condemnable.

But the truth is that these potential problems can be easily solved and are in fact fully avoided by a well-drafted criminal code. For example, Model Penal Code section 2.01, subsections (1) and (3), set out a general rule for liability for any offense based on an omission. Among other things, subsection (1) bars liability for an omission unless the defendant was "physically capable" of performing the act required by the omission offense. A better approach would be to require proof that the defendant was "capable" (rather than "*physically* capable") of performing the conduct required by the offense, so as to include in the defense cases of mental or emotional incapacity.

In addition, most modern American criminal codes have a collection of justification defenses that also can play an important role here. Thus, for example, where the parent has money that could be used to promote the child's mental or emotional health or education, but is the same source of funds that is needed to buy food (and thereby to protect the child's physical health), the lesser evils defense, such as that in Model Penal Code section 3.02, would protect the parent from criminal liability for spending the money on food when he was "capable" of spending it on emotional health or education. He has a defense for his failure to spend it on emotional health or education because he was faced with a choice of evils and properly picked the lesser of the two evils. (See Chapter 14, concerning the lesser evils defense.)

The conclusion, then, is that legislatures could feel more comfortable in expanding their child neglect statutes if they put in place a well-constructed system of principles for omission liability, justification defenses, and excuse defenses. Unfortunately, as the review of state criminal codes in other chapters has made clear, the status of such general liability principles in American criminal codes is quite mixed.

Notes

1. Ariz. Rev. Stat. Ann. § 13-3613; Ariz. Rev. Stat. Ann. § 13-3612; Ariz. Rev. Stat. Ann. § 8-201; Ariz. Rev. Stat. Ann. § 13-3619; Ariz. Rev. Stat. Ann. § 13 3623; Colo. Rev. Stat. Ann. § 18-6-401; Conn. Gen. Stat. Ann. § 53-20; Conn. Gen. Stat. Ann. § 53-21; D.C. Code Ann. § 22-1101; D.C. Code Ann. § 22-1102; 720 Ill. Comp. Stat. Ann. 5/12C-5; 720 Ill. Comp. Stat. Ann. 5/12C-10; 720 Ill. Comp. Stat. Ann. 5/12C-25; Ind. Code Ann. § 35-46-1-1; Ind. Code Ann. § 35-46-1-4; Ind. Code Ann. § 35-46-1-5; Me. Rev. Stat. tit. 17-A, § 554; Mass. Gen. Laws Ann. ch. 265, § 13J; Or. Rev. Stat. Ann. § 163.545; Or. Rev. Stat. Ann. § 163.577; Or. Rev. Stat. Ann. § 163.200; Or. Rev. Stat. Ann. § 163.205; 11 R.I. Gen. Laws Ann. § 11-9-5; Tenn. Code Ann. § 39-15-401; Vt. Stat. Ann. tit. 13, § 1303; Vt. Stat. Ann. tit. 13, § 1304; Vt. Stat. Ann. tit. 13, § 1305; Wash. Rev. Code Ann. § 9A.42.010; W. Va. Code Ann. § 61-8D-1.

2. Except as occasionally provided by compulsory school attendance laws, statutes that we have ignored for purposes of this chapter.

3. Alaska Stat. Ann. § 11.51.120; Haw. Rev. Stat. Ann. § 709-903; Haw. Rev. Stat. Ann. § 709-904; N.M. Stat. Ann. § 30-6-1.

4. Ark. Code Ann. § 5-27-207; Ark. Code Ann. § 5-27-209; Cal. Penal Code § 270; Cal. Penal Code § 271; Cal. Penal Code § 273a; Fla. Stat. Ann. § 827.03; Fla. Stat. Ann. § 827.04; Ga. Code Ann. § 16-5-70; Ga. Code Ann. § 16-5-72; Idaho Code Ann. § 18-1501; Iowa Code Ann. § 726.6; Kan. Stat. Ann. § 21-5601; Kan. Stat. Ann. § 21-5603; Kan. Stat. Ann. § 38-2202; La. Stat. Ann. § 14:92.1; La. Stat. Ann. § 14:93; State v. Moran, 400 So. 2d 1359, 1363 (La. 1981); La. Child. Code Ann. art. 603; Md. Code Ann., Crim. Law § 3-602.1; Minn. Stat. Ann. § 609.378; Miss. Code. Ann. § 97-5-39; Mo. Ann. Stat. § 568.045; Mo. Ann. Stat. § 568.060; Neb. Rev. Stat. Ann. § 28-707; Neb. Rev. Stat. Ann. § 28-710; Neb. Rev. Stat. Ann. § 28-711; N.H. Rev. Stat. Ann. § 639:3; State v. Yates, 152 N.H. 245, 255, 876 A.2d 176, 185 (2005); N.H. Rev. Stat. Ann. § 169-C:3; N.H. Rev. Stat. Ann. § 169-C:3; N.C. Gen. Stat. Ann. § 14-316.1; N.C. Gen. Stat. Ann. § 7B-101; N.D. Cent. Code Ann. § 12.1-17-03; N.D. Cent. Code Ann. § 14-09-22.1; Ohio Rev. Code Ann. § 2151.414; 18 Pa. Stat. and Cons. Stat. Ann. § 4304; 42 Pa. Stat. and Cons. Stat. Ann. § 6302; Com. v. Barnhart, 345 Pa. Super. 10, 18, 497 A.2d 616, 619–21 (1985); Com. v. Barnhart, 345 Pa. Super. 10, 18, 497 A.2d 616, 619–21 (1985); S.C. Code Ann. § 63-5-70; Tex. Penal Code Ann. § 22.04; Tex. Penal Code Ann. § 22.041; Utah Code Ann. § 76-5-109; Va. Code Ann. § 16.1-228; Wis. Stat. Ann. § 948.01; Wis. Stat. Ann. § 948.03; Wis. Stat. Ann. § 948.04; Wis. Stat. Ann. § 939.22.

5. Ala. Code § 13A-13-6; Ala. Code § 12-15-102; Ala. Code § 12-15-301; Ala. Code § 12-15-301; Del. Code Ann. tit. 10, § 901; Del. Code Ann. tit. 11, § 1100; Del. Code Ann. tit. 11, § 1102; Del. Code Ann. tit. 11, § 1103; Ky. Rev. Stat. Ann. § 508.090; Ky. Rev. Stat. Ann. § 508.100; Ky. Rev. Stat. Ann. § 508.110; Ky. Rev. Stat. Ann. § 508.120; Ky. Rev. Stat. Ann. § 530.060; Ky. Rev. Stat. Ann. § 600.020; Mich. Comp. Laws Ann. § 750.136b; Mich. Comp. Laws Ann. § 750.145; Mich.

Comp. Laws Ann. § 712A.2; Mont. Code Ann. § 45-5-622; Mont. Code Ann. § 45-5-628; Mont. Code Ann. § 41-3-102; Nev. Rev. Stat. Ann. § 200.508; Nev. Rev. Stat. Ann. § 432B.140; N.J. Stat. Ann. § 2C:24-4; N.J. Stat. Ann. § 9:6-1; N.J. Stat. Ann. § 9:6-8.21; N.Y. Penal Law § 260.10; N.Y. Fam. Ct. Act § 1012; N.Y. Fam. Ct. Act § 1012; Okla. Stat. Ann. tit. 21, § 858.1; Okla. Stat. Ann. tit. 21, § 858.3; Okla. Stat. Ann. tit. 10A, § 1-1-105; S.D. Codified Laws § 26-9-1; S.D. Codified Laws § 26-8A-2; Wyo. Stat. Ann. § 6-4-403; Wyo. Stat. Ann. § 14-3-202.

CHAPTER TWENTY-SEVEN

Deceptive Business Practices

Across cultures, people share an intuition that the core of wrongdoing includes acts of physical aggression and the taking of another's property without consent. But social psychologists suggest that there is a third piece of this core of wrongdoing: deception in exchanges. In theft, the person takes your property when you aren't looking. But the criminal intent and the resulting injury are the same in instances where you are essentially tricked out of your property, like the classic case of the butcher who puts a thumb on the scale to exaggerate the weight of the meat being sold.

One of the central offenses designed to criminalize such deception is "deceptive business practices," which usually includes five types of conduct:

A. use or possession of false weight or measure ("false measure"),
B. taking more in quantity than what a person represented to the seller,
C. giving less in quantity than what a person represented to the buyer,
D. selling or offering adulterated or mislabeled commodities,
E. making a false statement in an advertisement addressed to the public or some substantial number of people ("false advertising").[1]

Most or all these practices may result in criminal liability through some broader statute punishing fraud or false pretenses. For instance, in Oklahoma, a person is liable for misdemeanor criminal fraud when the person:

> with intent to . . . defraud, . . . obtain[s] from any person . . . any money [or] property . . . , by means . . . of any . . . deception, or false or fraudulent representation or statement. . . .[2]

The "deceptive business practices" statutes are intended to reach further by softening the mens rea requirements and by extending attempt liability to

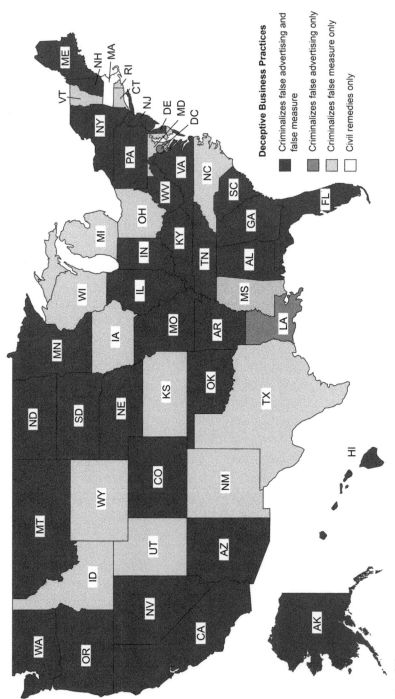

Deceptive Business Practices

- Criminalizes false advertising and false measure
- Criminalizes false advertising only
- Criminalizes false measure only
- Civil remedies only

Map 27

earlier acts beyond mere preparation.[3] Thus, instead of having to prove that it was the actor's intention—his purpose, his conscious object—to obtain money or property through deception, it is enough to show that the actor knew his conduct deceived the victim or was aware of a substantial risk that his conduct deceived the victim. Further, the deceptive business practices offense only requires proof of the deceptive conduct, such as using false weights or publishing a misleading advertisement, not proof that any particular person was actually defrauded out of money or property as a result. In practice, then, it is the deceptive business practices statute, rather than the general fraud statute, that is the daily workhorse in the battle against defrauding consumers.

As Map 27 makes clear, almost all states have an offense that criminalizes deceptive business practices. Nonetheless, there exists some diversity from jurisdiction to jurisdiction as to the breadth of the criminal offense.

Criminalizes False Advertising and False Measure

Thirty-two states, designated with dark shading—Alabama, Alaska, Arizona, Arkansas, California, Colorado, Delaware, Florida, Georgia, Hawaii, Illinois, Indiana, Kentucky, Maine, Minnesota, Missouri, Montana, Nebraska, Nevada, New Hampshire, New Jersey, New York, North Dakota, Oklahoma, Oregon, Pennsylvania, South Carolina, South Dakota, Tennessee, Virginia, Washington, and West Virginia[4]—specifically criminalize both false advertising and the use in commerce of false or incorrect weights or measures.

The false advertising statutes specifically prohibit making false or misleading statements in advertising or other communications addressed to the public or to a substantial number of people. The false measure statutes specifically prohibit the possession or use in commerce of a device that misrepresents the weight or quantity of a commodity for sale. Some of these statutes specifically criminalize possession or use of a device that fails to meet state standards.

Criminalizes False Advertising Only

In two jurisdictions—the District of Columbia and Louisiana[5]—shown on the map with medium shading, false advertising is criminalized, but the possession or use of a false measure results only in a civil fine. As noted above however, the possession or use of a false measure may still be subject to criminal sanction through a broader fraud statute with more demanding requirements. Additionally, while the District of Columbia does not specifically criminalize the possession of a false measure as most other states do, it does specifically criminalize the related offense of exaggerating or understating the weight, measure, or quantity of "any commodity" as seller or buyer, respectively, even where no transaction is completed.

Criminalizes False Measure Only

In 16 states, identified on the map with light shading—Connecticut, Idaho, Iowa, Kansas, Maryland, Michigan, Mississippi, New Mexico, North Carolina, Ohio, Rhode Island, Texas, Utah, Vermont, Wisconsin, and Wyoming[7]—false measures are criminalized but false advertising per se is not criminalized and generally results only in a civil fine.[8] As noted above, false advertising may still result in criminal liability that meets the more demanding requirements of a broader fraud statute.

Civil Remedies Only

In Massachusetts, neither false measure nor false advertising per se is criminalized, but these deceptive practices may result in civil fines, other civil liability, or criminal sanction through a broader, more demanding fraud statute.[9]

Observations and Speculations

An obvious question raised by the legal analysis above is why a significant number of jurisdictions would fail to criminalize deceptive business practices of one kind or another. Given the increasing sensitivity to the need for consumer protection, one would have thought that the criminalization of such clearly deceptive practices would be a popular legislative priority. Note for example the recent creation of the Consumer Financial Protection Bureau, an independent federal agency responsible for consumer protection in the financial sector.[10]

One might initially speculate that in the area of deceptive practices criminal law has simply not caught up with popular sentiment. Legislatures seem to increasingly appreciate how easily these deceptions can be perpetrated and how helpless consumers are to detect and avoid them. That is, one might speculate that some of the states simply didn't realize that they need the coverage of such deceptive business practices statutes.

But that explanation for the current situation does not really work. The Model Penal Code, which was promulgated in 1962 and is the basis for three-quarters of the state criminal codes, criminalizes a full basket of different forms of deceptive business practices, as summarized at the beginning of the chapter. Many of the jurisdictions that have deceptive business practices offenses narrower than that of the Model Code have them because they have affirmatively rejected some pieces of the Model Code's offense.

Presumably, this approach—trimming the breadth of the Model Penal Code offense—was a move pressed by business groups or legislators with special sympathies for such groups, perhaps on the theory that civil liability was always available to undo cheating or misrepresentation in a business context.

However, as a practical matter, that simply is not so. Few noncommercial victims are going to have the financial means to bring a civil lawsuit. More importantly, even if the victim is well financed, such civil litigation would make no economic sense. The butcher can feel free to put a thumb on the scale 100 times a day comforted in the knowledge that no victim would rationally endure the cost of a lawsuit to collect the few dollars he or she has cheated them out of.

The entire point of the deceptive business practices offense—made available even though a more demanding general fraud statute may already cover the conduct—is to make the threat of criminal prosecution sufficiently clear and meaningful that violators cannot hide behind undue burdens for prosecution.

The Model Penal Code statute and the statutes of a majority of American jurisdictions typically provide an appropriate balance of interests: the requirements for criminal liability are sufficiently demanding such that criminal liability is imposed only on those who engage in clear wrongdoing, yet effective prosecution is feasible, albeit producing liability only in the misdemeanor range.

Notes

1. Model Penal Code § 224.7.
2. Okla. Stat. Ann. tit. 21, § 1541.1.
3. See Model Penal Code Commentary § 224.7.
4. Ala. Code § 13A-9-41; Ala. Code § 13A-9-42; Alaska Stat. Ann. § 11.46.710; Ariz. Rev. Stat. Ann. § 13-2202; Ariz. Rev. Stat. Ann. § 44-1481; Cal. Bus. & Prof. Code § 17500; Cal. Bus. & Prof. Code § 12020; Colo. Rev. Stat. Ann. § 18-5-301; Del. Code Ann. tit. 11, § 906; Fla. Stat. Ann. § 817.06; Fla. Stat. Ann. § 817.41; Fla. Stat. Ann. § 817.44; Fla. Stat. Ann. § 817.45; Fla. Stat. Ann. § 531.50; Ga. Code Ann. § 10-1-420; Ga. Code Ann. § 10-1-421; Haw. Rev. Stat. Ann. § 708-870; Haw. Rev. Stat. Ann. § 708-871; 720 Ill. Comp. Stat. Ann. 5/17-1; 720 Ill. Comp. Stat. Ann. 5/17-5.7; 225 Ill. Comp. Stat. Ann. 470/56; Ind. Code Ann. § 35-43-5-3; Ind. Code Ann. § 24-6-3-11; Ind. Code Ann. § 24-6-3-15; Ky. Rev. Stat. Ann. § 517.030; Ky. Rev. Stat. Ann. § 517.020; Me. Rev. Stat. tit. 17-A, § 901; Minn. Stat. Ann. § 325F.67; Minn. Stat. Ann. § 239.23; Mo. Ann. Stat. § 570.140; Mont. Code Ann. § 45-6-318; Neb. Rev. Stat. Ann. § 89-197; Neb. Rev. Stat. Ann. § 89-1,101; Neb. Rev. Stat. Ann. § 87-302; Neb. Rev. Stat. Ann. § 87-303.08; Nev. Rev. Stat. Ann. § 207.171; Nev. Rev. Stat. Ann. § 207.175; Nev. Rev. Stat. Ann. § 598.0915; Nev. Rev. Stat. Ann. § 598.0999; Nev. Rev. Stat. Ann. § 581.445; Nev. Rev. Stat. Ann. § 581.415; N.H. Rev. Stat. Ann. § 638:6; N.J. Stat. Ann. § 2C:21-7; N.Y. Agric. & Mkts. Law § 186; N.Y. Gen. Bus. Law § 396-b; N.D. Cent. Code Ann. § 51-12-01; N.D. Cent. Code Ann. § 51-12-02; N.D. Cent. Code Ann. § 51-12-08; N.D. Cent. Code Ann. § 51-12-13; N.D. Cent. Code Ann. § 64-03-01; N.D. Cent. Code Ann. § 64-03-09; Okla. Stat. Ann. tit. 21, § 1551; Okla. Stat. Ann. tit. 21, § 1502; Or. Rev. Stat. Ann. § 646.608; Or. Rev. Stat. Ann. § 616.992;

Or. Rev. Stat. Ann. § 618.991; Or. Rev. Stat. Ann. § 618.096; 18 Pa. Stat. and Cons. Stat. Ann. § 4107; S.C. Code Ann. § 39-1-20; S.C. Code Ann. § 39-9-208; S.C. Code Ann. § 39-9-200; S.D. Codified Laws § 37-24-6; S.D. Codified Laws § 37-21-18; Tenn. Code Ann. § 39-14-127; Va. Code Ann. § 18.2-216; Va. Code Ann. § 3.2-5645; Wash. Rev. Code Ann. § 9.04.010; Wash. Rev. Code Ann. § 9.45.124; W. Va. Code Ann. § 32A-1-2; W. Va. Code Ann. § 47-1-23. Note, Missouri's "false advertising" statute is overbroad, targeting any misleading statement, even ones not addressed to the public or a substantial number of people. Mo. Ann. Stat. § 413.105 ("A person commits the crime of false or misleading advertising if, in connection with the promotion of the sale of . . . any commodity or service . . . , he or she recklessly makes . . . any statement . . . which . . . tends to mislead . . . a person.").

5. D.C. Code Ann. § 37-201.07; D.C. Code Ann. § 37-201.32; D.C. Code Ann. § 22-1511; La. Stat. Ann. § 51:411; La. Stat. Ann. § 3:4612; La. Stat. Ann. § 3:4624.

6. D.C. Code Ann. § 37-201.07.

7. Conn. Gen. Stat. Ann. § 43-9; Idaho Code Ann. § 71-305; Iowa Code Ann. § 215.6; Iowa Code Ann. § 189.21; Kan. Stat. Ann. § 83-219; Kan. Stat. Ann. § 83-220; Md. Code Ann., Agric. § 11-208; Md. Code Ann., Agric. § 12-101; Mich. Comp. Laws Ann. § 750.561; Mich. Comp. Laws Ann. § 750.218; Mich. Comp. Laws Ann. § 290.631; Miss. Code. Ann. § 75-27-59; N.M. Stat. Ann. § 57-17-18; N.C. Gen. Stat. Ann. § 81A-29; Ohio Rev. Code Ann. § 1327.61; Ohio Rev. Code Ann. § 1327.99; 47 R.I. Gen. Laws Ann. § 47-3-3; Tex. Penal Code Ann. § 32.42; Utah Code Ann. § 76-6-507; Vt. Stat. Ann. tit. 9, § 2761; Wis. Stat. Ann. § 98.26; Wyo. Stat. Ann. § 40-10-132; Wyo. Stat. Ann. § 40-10-133.

8. In Wyoming, false advertising is a criminal misdemeanor but may result in a fine only.

9. Mass. Gen. Laws Ann. ch. 94, § 177 (providing civil fines for use of false measure); Mass. Gen. Laws Ann. ch. 266, § 91 (providing civil fines for false advertising); Mass. Gen. Laws Ann. ch. 266, § 91A (criminalizing a limited kind of false advertising).

10. Ross Colvin, *Obama Signs Sweeping Wall Street Overhaul into Law,* Reuters (July 21, 2010, 9:23 p.m.), http://www.reuters.com/article/us-financial-regulation -obama/obama-signs-sweeping-wall-street-overhaul-into-law-idUSTRE66 K1QR20100722.

CHAPTER TWENTY-EIGHT

Extortion

If you force someone to hand over to you his or her property upon a threat of immediate physical injury, you have committed a serious offense in all jurisdictions in the United States: robbery. But if you coerce the victim to give you property by the threat of some *future* harm, the offense is most often called "extortion" or "theft by extortion,"[1] or sometimes "coercion"[2] or "intimidation."[3] The extortion offense is broader than robbery, both in the broader range of the offender's threats that it criminalizes, and in the broader range of the victim's coerced conduct that it covers.

The extortion offense may cover either obtaining property, or compelling the victim to do certain things or refrain from doing certain things.[4] The modern offense also covers what was once treated separately as blackmail: threats to hurt the victim's reputation, expose a secret, or accuse the victim of a crime, accompanied by a demand.[5] Perhaps most interesting, the extortion offense may make criminal a threat to do something that the actor has a lawful right to do, such as reveal certain embarrassing information. This breadth of the offense has made extortion a favorite puzzle for criminal law theorists. (More on this later in the chapter.)

At the same time, there are important limits on the offense. No jurisdiction wants to include within the offense simple "hard bargaining," where, for example, you threaten not to sign a contract unless the other person agrees to provide certain additional property.[6]

There turns out to be a good deal of diversity among the states in formulating the crime of extortion, especially on the issue of the kinds of threats that will constitute the offense and the actual effects the threats must bring about, as Map 28 shows.

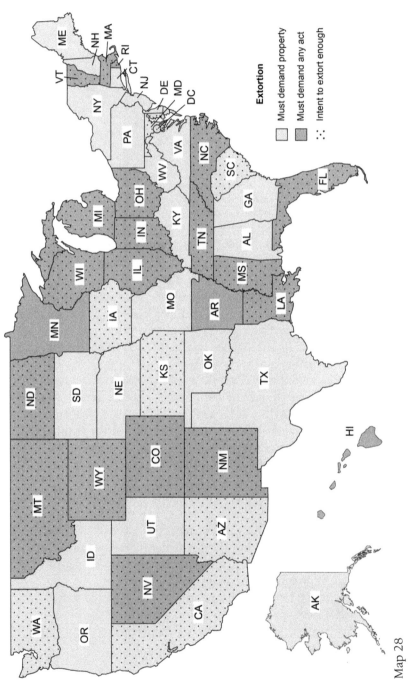

Extortion

☐ Must demand property

☐ Must demand any act

∴ Intent to extort enough

Map 28

Offender Must Demand Property

Twenty-nine states, identified with light shading on the map—Alabama, Alaska, Arizona, California, Connecticut, Delaware, District of Columbia, Georgia, Idaho, Iowa, Kansas, Kentucky, Maine, Maryland, Missouri, Nebraska, New Hampshire, New Jersey, New York, Oklahoma, Oregon, Pennsylvania, South Carolina, South Dakota, Texas, Utah, Virginia, Washington, and West Virginia[7]—require that the actor's demand must be for property or something of value, including labor or services. For instance, in Iowa, the actor must obtain "anything of value, tangible or intangible, including labor or services."[8] In Missouri, the actor must obtain the "property or services of another."[9]

Offender May Demand Any Act

The remaining 22 states, designated with medium shading on the map—Arkansas, Colorado, Florida, Hawaii, Illinois, Indiana, Louisiana, Massachusetts, Michigan, Minnesota, Mississippi, Montana, Nevada, New Mexico, North Carolina, North Dakota, Ohio, Rhode Island, Tennessee, Vermont, Wisconsin, and Wyoming[10]—permit virtually any demand to suffice, such as the demand that the victim "engage in conduct from which [the victim] has a legal right to abstain, or to abstain from engaging in conduct in which the [victim] has a legal right to engage."[11]

Effect of Threat Must Be to Actually Extort

Twenty-four states, those without a dots overlay on the map—Alabama, Alaska, Arkansas, Connecticut, Delaware, Georgia, Hawaii, Idaho, Kentucky, Maine, Minnesota, Missouri, Nebraska, New Hampshire, New Jersey, New York, Oklahoma, Oregon, Pennsylvania, South Dakota, Texas, Utah, Virginia, and West Virginia[12]—define the offense as containing a result element: requiring that the offender actually obtained or exercised control over the victim's property, or successfully compelled, induced, or coerced the victim to act.

Enough That the Offender Intends to Extort

The remaining 27 states, those with a dots overlay on the map—Arizona, California, Colorado, District of Columbia, Florida, Illinois, Indiana, Iowa, Kansas, Louisiana, Maryland, Massachusetts, Michigan, Mississippi, Montana, Nevada, New Mexico, North Carolina, North Dakota, Ohio, Rhode Island, South Carolina, Tennessee, Vermont, Washington, Wisconsin, and Wyoming[13]—do not contain a result element; they merely require that the actor intend to cause the result. For instance, in Arizona, the offense of extortion is defined as "knowingly obtaining or *seeking to obtain* property or services by means of a threat. . . ."[14]

Observations and Speculations

This significant diversity among the states may in part be a reflection of the fact that extortion is a rather peculiar offense in some respects. It criminalizes making a threat to do something that would not itself be a crime to do. It would not be a crime for Jones to report his neighbor Smith's affair to his wife, for example, but the offense of extortion makes it a crime if Jones gives Smith an opportunity to avoid the secret being revealed by asking for something in return for his restraint. Smith might well very much prefer satisfying the condition that the blackmailer sets—for example, that Smith move his noisy swimming pool pump away from Jones's property line—rather than having the secret revealed. Why, then, should the law care about what Jones has done? Why should the law care that the "victim" is being given an opportunity that he apparently wants?

It is probably this somewhat odd nature of the offense that helps provide its diversity in formulation. Some states will criminalize Jones's conduct because it is meant to coerce an act, while other states would not criminalize it because it is not a demand for property. Some states would criminalize it because Jones actually got the performance he demanded, while other states would not criminalize it if Smith refused the demand. How can states have such different views of the proper scope of the offense?

Part of the problem is that even the criminal law theorists cannot agree among themselves about the nature of blackmail and its underlying rationale. As one of us has detailed elsewhere,[15] there are more than half a dozen different theories of blackmail. If the proper underlying theory is this unclear to the scholars, it is perhaps no surprise to see that the different jurisdictions also disagree.

The diversity among the American jurisdictions and among the scholars does provide an interesting opportunity for the social psychologists: if empirical researchers tested ordinary people's intuitions of justice regarding a variety of different blackmail scenarios, could the research results identify which theories and which statutory formulations best tracked the shared intuitions of ordinary people on the subject?

Such a study was done and came to these conclusions:

> [L]ay intuitions seem to accord with the position that blackmail amounts to extortion because of the blackmailer's bad faith or improper motivations. The blackmailer's central interest is to benefit himself, and his means of pursuing that interest displays his willingness to wrong the other person, either by forcing that person to sacrifice money (or something else) or by

subjecting that person to the harm the blackmailer knows the threatened act will cause.

At the same time, however, . . . lay intuitions seem to view some demands as objectively legitimate even if their subjective motivation in a given case is improper. Thus a person whose demand seeks to vindicate a valid legal or societal interest . . . is not seen as engaging in blackmail even if his underlying motivation is to harm the recipient rather than to advance the legitimate interest.[16]

The study was able to suggest a particular formulation of the blackmail offense that would track community views:

Criminal Coercion

1. A person commits criminal coercion if he demands money or other valuable consideration as a condition of refraining from any act he intends or knows would cause harm to another person.

2. For purposes of subsection 1, "harm" may include physical injury, financial deprivation, or substantial psychological stress.

3. Exception. It is not an offense under subsection 1 if the actor believed his demand to be justified as a means of advancing a legitimate legal or societal interest.[17]

Part of what this demonstrates is that legislatures can look to researchers to determine the shared judgments of justice of their constituents on criminal law liability and punishment issues. For reasons discussed in Chapter 1, there is great practical crime control value in building the criminal law's moral credibility by having it reflect the community's shared judgments of justice. We see here that such tracking is possible, even where the underlying theoretical rationales are disputed.

Notes

1. Many states treat extortion under a statute that consolidates all theft offenses. See, e.g, Idaho Code Ann. § 18-2403 (treating theft "by extortion" as a subsection of the theft statute).

2. Mo. Ann. Stat. § 570.030.

3. Mont. Code Ann. § 45-5-203.

4. The legal survey here covers statutes of general applicability, not the variety of extortion statutes that target only specific classes of people or a narrow range of demands. See, e.g., Mich. Comp. Laws Ann. § 750.213a (targeting extortion where the offender intends to cause a woman to have an abortion against her will); Mich. Comp. Laws Ann. § 750.214 (targeting extortion by public

officers); Nev. Rev. Stat. Ann. § 197.170 (targeting extortion by public officers); Okla. Stat. Ann. tit. 21, § 1484 (targeting extortion by public officers). The survey does not cover offenses that do not contain both the threat and demand elements, such as statutes targeting threats generally. See, e.g., Vt. Stat. Ann. tit. 13, § 1702 (prohibiting, under a "criminal threatening" statute, threats that place another person in reasonable apprehension of death or serious bodily injury).

5. Some states continue to treat blackmail and extortion as separate offenses. See, e.g., D.C. Code Ann. § 22-3251; D.C. Code Ann. § 22-3252; Kan. Stat. Ann. § 21-5428; Kan. Stat. Ann. § 21-6501; N.C. Gen. Stat. Ann. § 14-118.4; N.C. Gen. Stat. Ann. § 14-118; Okla. Stat. Ann. tit. 21, § 1483; Okla. Stat. Ann. tit. 21, § 1488; Wis. Stat. Ann. § 943.30; Wis. Stat. Ann. § 943.31.

6. Paul H. Robinson and Michael T. Cahill, *Criminal Law,* 2nd ed. §15.7 (Wolters Kluwer 2012).

7. Ala. Code § 13A-8-13; Ala. Code § 13A-8-14; Ala. Code § 13A-8-15; Ala. Code § 13A-8-1; Alaska Stat. Ann. § 11.41.520; Ariz. Rev. Stat. Ann. § 13-1804; Cal. Penal Code § 518; Cal. Penal Code § 519; Cal. Penal Code § 522; Cal. Penal Code § 523; Conn. Gen. Stat. Ann. § 53a-119; Del. Code Ann. tit. 11, § 846; D.C. Code Ann. § 22-3251; D.C. Code Ann. § 22-3252; D.C. Code Ann. § 22-3201; Ga. Code Ann. § 16-8-16; Idaho Code Ann. § 18-2403; Iowa Code Ann. § 711.4; Kan. Stat. Ann. § 21-5428; Kan. Stat. Ann. § 21-6501; Ky. Rev. Stat. Ann. § 514.080; Me. Rev. Stat. tit. 17-A, § 355; Md. Code Ann., Crim. Law § 3-701; Md. Code Ann., Crim. Law § 3-705; Md. Code Ann., Crim. Law § 3-706; Mo. Ann. Stat. § 570.010; Mo. Ann. Stat. § 570.030; Neb. Rev. Stat. Ann. § 28-513; Neb. Rev. Stat. Ann. § 28-509; N.H. Rev. Stat. Ann. § 637:5; N.J. Stat. Ann. § 2C:20-5; N.Y. Penal Law § 155.05; Okla. Stat. Ann. tit. 21, § 1481; Okla. Stat. Ann. tit. 21, § 1482; Okla. Stat. Ann. tit. 21, § 1483; Okla. Stat. Ann. tit. 21, § 1488; Or. Rev. Stat. Ann. § 164.075; 18 Pa. Stat. and Cons. Stat. Ann. § 3923; S.C. Code Ann. § 16-17-640; S.D. Codified Laws § 22-30A-4; Tex. Penal Code Ann. § 31.01; Tex. Penal Code Ann. § 31.02; Tex. Penal Code Ann. § 31.03; Utah Code Ann. § 76-6-406; Va. Code Ann. § 18.2-59; Wash. Rev. Code Ann. § 9A.56.110; Wash. Rev. Code Ann. § 9A.56.120; Wash. Rev. Code Ann. § 9A.56.130; Wash. Rev. Code Ann. § 9A.04.110; W. Va. Code Ann. § 61-2-13. In Kansas and Oklahoma, while the broader extortion statute requires a demand for property, both states' blackmail-specific statutes permit a threat with intent to cause the other person to engage in any act. See Kan. Stat. Ann. § 21-5428; Okla. Stat. Ann. tit. 21, § 1488.

8. Iowa Code Ann. § 711.4.

9. Mo. Ann. Stat. § 570.030.

10. Ark. Code Ann. § 5-13-208; Colo. Rev. Stat. Ann. § 18-3-207; Fla. Stat. Ann. § 836.05; Haw. Rev. Stat. Ann. § 707-764; 720 Ill. Comp. Stat. Ann. 5/12-6; Ind. Code Ann. § 35-45-2-1; La. Stat. Ann. § 14:66; Mass. Gen. Laws Ann. ch. 265, § 25; Mich. Comp. Laws Ann. § 750.213; Minn. Stat. Ann. § 609.27; Miss. Code. Ann. § 97-3-82; Mont. Code Ann. § 45-5-203; Nev. Rev. Stat. Ann. § 205.320; N.M. Stat. Ann. § 30-16-9; N.C. Gen. Stat. Ann. § 14-118.4; N.C. Gen. Stat. Ann. § 14-118; N.D. Cent. Code Ann. § 12.1-23-10; N.D. Cent. Code Ann. § 12.1-17-06; Ohio Rev. Code Ann. § 2905.11; 11 R.I. Gen. Laws Ann. § 11-42-2;

Tenn. Code Ann. § 39-14-112; Vt. Stat. Ann. tit. 13, § 1701; Wis. Stat. Ann. § 943.30; Wis. Stat. Ann. § 943.31; Wyo. Stat. Ann. § 6-2-402. Louisiana, Mississippi, and North Carolina permit the demand for an "advantage" to satisfy the statute. See La. Stat. Ann. § 14:66; Miss. Code. Ann. § 97-3-82; N.C. Gen. Stat. Ann. § 14-118.4; N.C. Gen. Stat. Ann. § 14-118. This broad language would certainly extend extortion to cover more than demands for property or things of value. Cf. State v. Felton, 339 So. 2d 797, 799 (La. 1976) (interpreting "advantage" under extortion statute to include "[a]ny state, condition, circumstance, opportunity, or means specially favorable to success, prosperity, interest, reputation, or any desired end," including in this case sexual acts of the victim). North Dakota's extortion statute permits any act to satisfy the demand element, but the state's broader theft-by-threat statute requires that the demand be the "property of another." See N.D. Cent. Code Ann. § 12.1-23-02.

11. Ark. Code Ann. § 5-13-208.

12. Ala. Code § 13A-8-13; Ala. Code § 13A-8-14; Ala. Code § 13A-8-15; Ala. Code § 13A-8-1; Alaska Stat. Ann. § 11.41.520; Ark. Code Ann. § 5-13-208; Conn. Gen. Stat. Ann. § 53a-119; Del. Code Ann. tit. 11, § 846; Ga. Code Ann. § 16-8-16; Haw. Rev. Stat. Ann. § 707-764; Idaho Code Ann. § 18-2403; Ky. Rev. Stat. Ann. § 514.080; Me. Rev. Stat. tit. 17-A, § 355; Minn. Stat. Ann. § 609.27; Mo. Ann. Stat. § 570.010; Mo. Ann. Stat. § 570.030; Neb. Rev. Stat. Ann. § 28-513; Neb. Rev. Stat. Ann. § 28-509; N.H. Rev. Stat. Ann. § 637:5; N.J. Stat. Ann. § 2C:20-5; N.Y. Penal Law § 155.05; Okla. Stat. Ann. tit. 21, § 1481; Okla. Stat. Ann. tit. 21, § 1482; Okla. Stat. Ann. tit. 21, § 1483; Okla. Stat. Ann. tit. 21, § 1488; Or. Rev. Stat. Ann. § 164.075; 18 Pa. Stat. and Cons. Stat. Ann. § 3923; S.D. Codified Laws § 22-30A-4; Tex. Penal Code Ann. § 31.01; Tex. Penal Code Ann. § 31.02; Tex. Penal Code Ann. § 31.03; Utah Code Ann. § 76-6-406; Va. Code Ann. § 18.2-59; W. Va. Code Ann. § 61-2-13. In Idaho, if the threat is to libel the victim, intent will satisfy. See Idaho Code Ann. § 18-4809. In Kansas and Oklahoma, while the broader extortion statute requires that the actor actually extorts the property, both states' blackmail-specific statutes permit intent to satisfy. See Kan. Stat. Ann. § 21-5428; Okla. Stat. Ann. tit. 21, § 1488.

13. Ariz. Rev. Stat. Ann. § 13-1804; Cal. Penal Code § 518; Cal. Penal Code § 519; Cal. Penal Code § 522; Cal. Penal Code § 523; Colo. Rev. Stat. Ann. § 18-3-207; D.C. Code Ann. § 22-3251; D.C. Code Ann. § 22-3252; D.C. Code Ann. § 22-3201; Fla. Stat. Ann. § 836.05; 720 Ill. Comp. Stat. Ann. 5/12-6; Ind. Code Ann. § 35-45-2-1; Iowa Code Ann. § 711.4; Kan. Stat. Ann. § 21-5428; Kan. Stat. Ann. § 21-6501; La. Stat. Ann. § 14:66; State v. Felton, 339 So. 2d 797, 799 (La. 1976) (interpreting "advantage" under extortion statute to include "[a]ny state, condition, circumstance, opportunity, or means specially favorable to success, prosperity, interest, reputation, or any desired end," including voluntary sexual acts of the victim); Md. Code Ann., Crim. Law § 3-701; Md. Code Ann., Crim. Law § 3-705; Md. Code Ann., Crim. Law § 3-706; Mass. Gen. Laws Ann. ch. 265, § 25; Mich. Comp. Laws Ann. § 750.213; Miss. Code. Ann. § 97-3-82; Mont. Code Ann. § 45-5-203; Nev. Rev. Stat. Ann. § 205.320; N.M. Stat. Ann. § 30-16-9; N.C. Gen. Stat. Ann. § 14-118.4; N.C. Gen. Stat. Ann. § 14-118; N.D. Cent. Code Ann. § 12.1-23-10;

N.D. Cent. Code Ann. § 12.1-17-06; Ohio Rev. Code Ann. § 2905.11; 11 R.I. Gen. Laws Ann. § 11-42-2; S.C. Code Ann. § 16-17-640; Tenn. Code Ann. § 39-14-112; Vt. Stat. Ann. tit. 13, § 1701; Wash. Rev. Code Ann. § 9A.56.110; Wash. Rev. Code Ann. § 9A.56.120; Wash. Rev. Code Ann. § 9A.56.130; Wash. Rev. Code Ann. § 9A.04.110; Wis. Stat. Ann. § 943.30; Wis. Stat. Ann. § 943.31; Wyo. Stat. Ann. § 6-2-402. In North Dakota, the extortion statute permits intent to satisfy, but the state's broader theft-by-threat statute requires that the actor actually obtain the "property of another." See N.D. Cent. Code Ann. § 12.1-23-02.

14. Ariz. Rev. Stat. Ann. § 13-1804.

15. Paul H. Robinson et al., *Competing Theories of Blackmail: An Empirical Research Critique of Criminal Law Theory,* 89 Texas Law Review 291, 295–308 (2010).

16. Id. at 348.

17. Id.

PART 8

Public Order and Decency Offenses

CHAPTER TWENTY-NINE

Adultery

"A married person who has sexual intercourse with a person not his spouse or an unmarried person who has sexual intercourse with a married person" commits the offense of adultery.[1] A U.S. Supreme Court ruling in 2003 invalidated antisodomy statutes[2] and appeared to put privacy interests of the individual above legislative criminalization of social prohibitions, yet the criminalization of adultery had been upheld as constitutional.[3] Still, while adultery was once punished with severe penalties, most Western countries have now decriminalized it.

As Map 29 indicates, decriminalization of adultery has taken place across much of the United States as well. Nonetheless, a minority of states still have statutes on their books providing for some form of punishment for adultery-related offenses.

Repealed by 1995

Nineteen states, those with no shading on the map—Alaska, Arkansas, California, Connecticut, Hawaii, Iowa, Louisiana, Maine, Montana, Nevada, New Mexico, Oregon, Pennsylvania, South Dakota, Tennessee, Texas, Vermont, Washington, and Wyoming[4]—either never had such an offense or repealed it before 1995. But this means that as recently as 1995 the legal landscape looked quite different for adultery than it is today: 32 of 51 jurisdictions—about two-thirds—did recognize adultery as a crime.

Repealed after 1995

Twelve jurisdictions, marked with light shading on the map—Colorado, Delaware, District of Columbia, Indiana, Kentucky, Missouri, Nebraska, New Hampshire, New Jersey, North Dakota, Ohio, and West Virginia[5]—criminalized

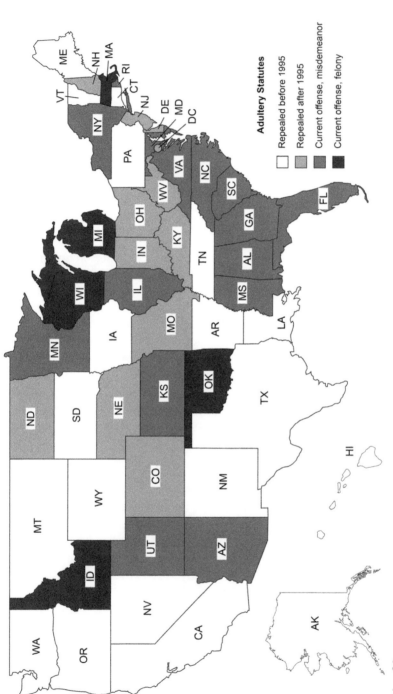

WA
OR
CA
NV
ID
MT
WY
UT
AZ
CO
NM
ND
SD
NE
KS
OK
TX
MN
IA
MO
AR
LA
WI
IL
MI
IN
OH
KY
TN
MS
AL
GA
FL
SC
NC
VA
WV
PA
NY
VT
ME
NH
MA
RI
CT
NJ
DE
MD
DC
AK
HI
Adultery Statutes
Repealed before 1995
Repealed after 1995
Current offense, misdemeanor
Current offense, felony

Map 29

adultery as of 1995 but have since repealed it. Thus, 31 of 51 jurisdictions have now decriminalized adultery, reversing the situation from 1995 to make this now the two-thirds majority position.

Current Offense, Misdemeanor

Fifteen states, designated with medium shading on the map—Alabama, Arizona, Florida, Georgia, Illinois, Kansas, Maryland, Minnesota, Mississippi, New York, North Carolina, Rhode Island, South Carolina, Utah, and Virginia[6]—currently criminalize adultery and categorize it as a misdemeanor. Notice the geographic patterns revealed by the map: the southern states are well represented in this group, joined by a number of other states known for their strong religious norms.

Current Offense, Felony

Five states, identified with dark shading on the map—Idaho, Massachusetts, Michigan, Oklahoma, and Wisconsin[7]—currently criminalize adultery and categorize it as a felony. Together with the states in the group above, this makes adultery an offense today in 20 states, a significant minority.

Observations and Speculations

Although adultery remains on the books in many states, it is rarely prosecuted. The 2003 conviction of John R. Bushey Jr. under Virginia's adultery statute generated national attention, due in part to the irregularity of such prosecutions.[8] Many people may see this situation—prohibition without enforcement—as having some significant practical value. While adultery is rarely prosecuted, it remains on the books as an official source of moral condemnation of the conduct. Decriminalizing adultery might be seen as approving it; thus such action ought to be avoided.

But the prohibition-without-enforcement approach raises several problems. First, it mistakes the proper role of criminal law. There are a number of social institutions in the business of building or reinforcing social norms—churches are a prime example—but criminal law has a more limited role. It seeks to identify that wrongdoing that is so condemnable that it deserves the label of crime and the punishment that follows. There are many sorts of conduct that may be socially and even morally objectionable, such as lying to a spouse about an important matter or cutting in line to get scarce concert tickets. But just because they are wrong, it does not follow that their wrongfulness rises to the level of criminality.

Criminalizing adultery when it is judged insufficiently serious to deserve actual prosecution and punishment is to dilute the power of the "criminal" label. By representing adultery to be an offense, when in practice it really is not, is to risk having people assume that other offenses in the criminal code are similarly just "pretend" offenses. Creating that kind of ambiguity tends to undermine the social influence of the criminal prohibition generally.

Further, the criminalization of conduct that is not necessarily meant by the legislature to be prosecuted essentially shifts the criminalization power to prosecutors rather than keeping it within the more democratic legislative branch where it belongs. If the rate of prosecution is the true test of whether conduct is truly criminally condemnable, then the prosecutor's power to define crimes trumps that of the legislature's.

Further, to create offenses whose violation are not regularly prosecuted is to vest prosecutors with an unhealthy discretionary power, for it gives the prosecutor the ability to resurrect the rarely used statute—that may have never been intended to be used, but was meant only to serve only a symbolic function—in order to persecute a disfavored defendant.

To protect its moral credibility and its fair application, the criminal law ought to say what it means and mean what it says. That is, it ought to be careful to define as criminal only the conduct that deserves the sanction of criminal liability and punishment and, when such conduct occurs, it ought to normally prosecute violations to the extent feasible, unless some special circumstances of the case justify nonprosecution.

Notes

1. See, e.g., Mass. Gen. Laws Ann. ch. 272 § 14.

2. Lawrence v. Texas, 539 U.S. 558 (2003).

3. See, e.g., Com. v. Stowell, 389 Mass. 171, 449 N.E.2d 357 (1983) (upholding a Massachusetts criminal adultery statute as constitutional, challenged by a defendant awaiting trial); Oliverson v. W. Valley City, 875 F. Supp. 1465 (D. Utah 1995) (upholding Utah's criminal adultery statute as constitutional).

4. See Richard A. Posner and Katharine B. Silbaugh, *A Guide to America's Sex Laws*, 103–10 (University of Chicago Press 1996).

5. Id.

6. Ala. Code § 13A-13-2; Ariz. Rev. Stat. Ann. § 13-1408; Fla. Stat. Ann. § 798.01; Ga. Code Ann. § 16-6-19; 720 Ill. 5/11-35; Kan. Stat. Ann. § 21-5511; Maryland § 10-501; Minn. Stat. Ann. § 609.36; Miss. Code Ann. § 97-29-1; New York § 255.17; N.C. Gen. Stat. § 14-184; R.I. Gen. Laws § 11-6-2; S.C. Code Ann. § 16-15-60; Utah Code Ann. § 76-7-103; Va. Code Ann. § 18.2-365.

7. Idaho Code Ann. § 18-6601; Mass. Gen. Laws Ann. Ch. 272 § 14; Mich. Stat. Ann. § 750.30; Okla. Stat. § 21-872; Wis. Stat. Ann. § 944.16.

8. See John F. Kelly, *Va. Adultery Case Roils Divorce Industry,* Wash. Post (Dec. 1, 2003), https://www.washingtonpost.com/archive/local/2003/12/01/va-adultery -case-roils-divorce-industry/84ff5ce8-f69b-410e-9a2f-d1bae148993a/.

CHAPTER THIRTY

Criminal Obscenity

U.S. Supreme Court case law has long made clear that the free-speech protections of the First Amendment do not apply to "obscenity."[1] Exactly what "obscenity" is, however, is harder to pin down. The most famous expression of the indeterminacy of the category came when Justice Potter Stewart, taking the view that the Constitution does not protect "hard-core pornography," was unable to further define that term except to say, "I know it when I see it."[2] In the 1973 case of *Miller v. California*, the Court articulated three criteria for assessing obscenity:

> (a) whether the average person, applying contemporary community standards would find that the work, taken as a whole, appeals to the prurient interest . . . ; (b) whether the work depicts or describes, in a patently offensive way, sexual conduct specifically defined by the applicable state law; and (c) whether the work, taken as a whole, lacks serious literary, artistic, political, or scientific value.[3]

With the exception of Maryland and the District of Columbia, which do not define obscenity in their statute, every state offense banning promotion or distribution of obscene material to adults defines obscenity to include at least the first and third elements of the *Miller* criteria: the material must appeal to the "prurient interest" in sex, and it must lack "serious literary, artistic, political, or scientific value." States differ, however, in their inclusion of the second criterion, that the material must be "patently offensive." Additionally, a number of states have extended their obscenity offenses to cover so-called obscene "devices." The different approaches to defining obscenity adopted by different states are presented in Map 30.

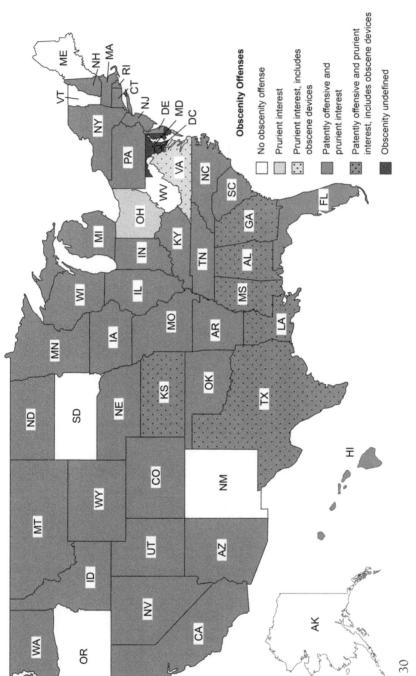

Obscenity Offenses

- ☐ No obscenity offense
- ☐ Prurient interest
- ⊡ Prurient interest, includes obscene devices
- ▨ Patently offensive and prurient interest
- ▨ Patently offensive and prurient interest, includes obscene devices
- ■ Obscenity undefined

Map 30

No Obscenity Offense

Seven jurisdictions, shown with no shading on the map—Alaska, Maine, New Mexico, Oregon, South Dakota, Vermont, and West Virginia[4]—do not have an obscenity offense—that is, a statute that would criminalize the promotion, distribution, or display of obscene material to consenting adults. (As a separate matter, the states may have offenses that criminalize the promotion, distribution, or display of obscenity *to minors*, or the possession of material that *depicts minors* or children.[5])

Defines Obscenity as Lacks Serious Value and Prurient Interest

One jurisdiction, Ohio, identified with light shading on the map, defines obscenity as material that appeals to the "prurient interest" and "lacks serious . . . value," but the statute does not contain the other element of the *Miller* test, requiring that the matter be "patently offensive."[6]

Defines Obscenity as Lacks Serious Value and Prurient Interest, Also Prohibits Devices

One jurisdiction, Virginia, shown on the map with light shading and dots, similarly defines obscenity as material that appeals to the "prurient interest" and "lacks serious . . . value," without reference to a "patently offensive" requirement,[7] as with Ohio above. Virginia differs from Ohio, however, in that it also criminalizes the sale of obscene devices, such as those designed or marketed as useful primarily for the stimulation of human genital organs.

Defines Obscenity as Lacks Serious Value, Prurient Interest, and Patently Offensive

Thirty-four jurisdictions, shown with medium shading on the map—Arizona, Arkansas, California, Colorado, Connecticut, Delaware, Florida, Hawaii, Idaho, Illinois, Indiana, Iowa, Kentucky, Massachusetts, Michigan, Minnesota, Missouri, Montana, Nebraska, Nevada, New Hampshire, New Jersey, New York, North Carolina, North Dakota, Oklahoma, Pennsylvania, Rhode Island, South Carolina, Tennessee, Utah, Washington, Wisconsin, and Wyoming[8]—define obscenity to follow the Supreme Court's language in *Miller*, which includes material that appeals to the "prurient interest" and which portrays sexual conduct in a "patently offensive" way.

Defines Obscenity as Lacks Serious Value, Prurient Interest, and Patently Offensive, Also Prohibits Devices

Six additional states, marked on the map with medium shading and dots—Alabama, Georgia, Kansas, Louisiana, Mississippi, and Texas[9]—define obscenity to follow the Supreme Court's language in *Miller*, which includes material that appeals to the "prurient interest" and portrays sexual conduct in a "patently offensive" way, but go further than the group above and also criminalize the sale of obscene devices.

Obscenity Offense but Leaves Obscenity Undefined

Two jurisdictions shaded black on the map—District of Columbia and Maryland[10]—have obscenity offenses but do not define what is "obscene." As a practical matter, they must apply the Supreme Court's limit in *Miller v. California*, described above. Arguably, these statutes may be interpreted broadly to include obscene devices.

Observations and Speculations

What may be most interesting about the diversity among the states and their definitions of "obscenity" is that these differences are as a practical matter legally irrelevant. Under the 1973 *Miller* Supreme Court opinion, states may not criminalize obscene speech unless it satisfies all three parts of the *Miller* test, quoted at the start of the chapter. As the analysis above suggests, however, many states adopt an abbreviated definition modeled after the Court's 1957 opinion in *Roth v. United States*.[11] There the Court held that obscenity is "material which deals with sex in a manner appealing to prurient interest"—that is, "material having a tendency to excite lustful thoughts."[12]

Obviously the *Roth* definition is overbroad, and in the 16 years separating *Roth* and *Miller*, the Court struggled to narrow the reach of obscenity statutes. In *Memoirs v. Massachusetts*,[13] the Court held that obscenity appeals to the prurient interest, is patently offensive, and "is utterly without redeeming social value."[14] The Court's 1973 decision in *Miller* refined and replaced the *Memoirs* standard, and survives today. In practice, obscenity convictions will not stand if the prosecution fails to show that the defendant's speech satisfies the *Miller* standard.

One difference among the states that is of practical importance is whether the state extends its obscenity prohibition to include the sale of obscene devices, typically defined as objects useful primarily for the stimulation of human genital organs. Of the seven states criminalizing the sale of obscene devices—Alabama, Georgia, Kansas, Louisiana, Mississippi, Texas, and

Virginia—nearly all are southern states, suggesting that these communities take a special interest in sanctioning obscenity.[15] Interestingly enough, bans on obscene devices are not mere vestiges of an earlier age. For instance, Alabama actually amended its obscenity statute in 1998 to extend to devices.[16]

Obscenity laws remain relevant today and are occasionally enforced, despite evidence that a substantial share of Americans consume obscene material in the form of Internet pornography.[17] Since 2003, federal and state prosecutors have brought charges in dozens of cases, sometimes resulting in serious penalties for offenders.[18] For instance, in 2008, Paul Little was convicted of 10 counts of violating federal obscenity statutes, leading to a 46-month prison sentence.[19] In 2006, Ronald Crump was convicted of three counts of promoting obscenity, resulting in a three-year prison sentence that was ultimately suspended.[20] And Beatrice Villarreal received a six-month prison sentence for violating Texas's statute prohibiting the sale of obscene devices, arising out of her 2004 sale of a vibrating dildo to an undercover police officer.[21] In nearly every case where convictions are challenged, courts have upheld the statutes as constitutional.[22]

At a time when Americans' moral views are perhaps more "permissive" than ever,[23] what accounts for the survival of obscenity statutes? Some argue in favor of the continuing criminalization of obscenity on the view that consumption of obscene material is harmful to individuals and society.[24] And there are certainly legal academics who argue that adult pornography may be harmful to women or exploitative, and thus a proper subject of criminal law.[25] However, where there may be little political impetus to modify or repeal such statutes, some state legislatures may have simply failed to revisit the issue.

Notes

1. See, e.g., Roth v. United States, 354 U.S. 476 (1957); Chaplinsky v. New Hampshire, 315 U.S. 568, 571–572 (1942); see generally Paul H. Robinson and Michael T. Cahill, *Criminal Law*, 2nd ed. §13.3 (Wolters Kluwer 2012). Note that mere private possession of obscene matters cannot constitutionally be criminalized. See Stanley v. Georgia, 394 U.S. 557, 559 (1969).

2. Jacobellis v. Ohio, 378 U.S. 184, 197 (1964) (Stewart, J., concurring).

3. Miller v. California, 413 U.S. 15, 24–25 (1973) (internal quotations and citations omitted).

4. Alaska and Oregon do not have obscenity offenses. Maine, New Mexico, South Dakota, Vermont, and West Virginia criminalize distributing or exhibiting obscene material to minors. See Me. Rev. Stat. tit. 17, § 2911 (criminalizing only distributing or exhibiting obscene matters to minors); N.M. Stat. Ann. § 30-37-2 (same); S.D. Codified Laws § 22-24-29 (same); Vt. Stat. Ann. tit. 13, § 2802 (same); W. Va. Code Ann. § 61-8A-2 (same).

5. For an examination of child pornography statutes, see Chapter 31.

6. Ohio Rev. Code Ann. § 2907.01; Ohio Rev. Code Ann. § 2907.32.

7. Va. Code Ann. § 18.2-372; Va. Code Ann. § 18.2-373; Va. Code Ann. § 18.2-374.

8. Ariz. Rev. Stat. Ann. § 13-3501; Ariz. Rev. Stat. Ann. § 13-3502; Ark. Code Ann. § 5-68-302; Ark. Code Ann. § 5-68-303; Cal. Penal Code § 311; Cal. Penal Code § 311.5; Colo. Rev. Stat. Ann. § 18-7-101; Colo. Rev. Stat. Ann. § 18-7-102; Conn. Gen. Stat. Ann. § 53a-193; Conn. Gen. Stat. Ann. § 53a-194; Del. Code Ann. tit. 11, § 1364; Del. Code Ann. tit. 11, § 1361; Fla. Stat. Ann. § 847.001; Fla. Stat. Ann. § 847.011; Haw. Rev. Stat. Ann. § 712-1210; Haw. Rev. Stat. Ann. § 712-1214; Haw. Rev. Stat. Ann. § 712-1211 (see below); Idaho Code Ann. § 18-4101; Idaho Code Ann. § 18-4103; 720 Ill. Comp. Stat. Ann. 5/11-20; Ind. Code Ann. § 35-49-2-1; Ind. Code Ann. § 35-49-3-1; Iowa Code Ann. § 728.1; Iowa Code Ann. § 728.4; Ky. Rev. Stat. Ann. § 531.010; Ky. Rev. Stat. Ann. § 531.020; Mass. Gen. Laws Ann. ch. 272, § 31; Mass. Gen. Laws Ann. ch. 272, § 29; Mich. Comp. Laws Ann. § 752.362; Mich. Comp. Laws Ann. § 752.364; Mich. Comp. Laws Ann. § 752.365; Minn. Stat. Ann. § 617.241; Mo. Ann. Stat. § 573.010; Mo. Ann. Stat. § 573.020; Mont. Code Ann. § 45-8-201; Neb. Rev. Stat. Ann. § 28-807; Neb. Rev. Stat. Ann. § 28-813; Nev. Rev. Stat. Ann. § 201.235; Nev. Rev. Stat. Ann. § 201.249; N.H. Rev. Stat. Ann. § 650:1; N.H. Rev. Stat. Ann. § 650:2; N.J. Stat. Ann. § 2C:34-2; N.Y. Penal Law § 235.00; N.Y. Penal Law § 235.05; N.C. Gen. Stat. Ann. § 14-190.1; N.D. Cent. Code Ann. § 12.1-27.1-01; Okla. Stat. Ann. tit. 21, § 1024.1; Okla. Stat. Ann. tit. 21, § 1021; 18 Pa. Stat. and Cons. Stat. Ann. § 5903; 11 R.I. Gen. Laws Ann. § 11-31-1; S.C. Code Ann. § 16-15-305; Tenn. Code Ann. § 39-17-901; Tenn. Code Ann. § 39-17-902; Utah Code Ann. § 76-10-1201; Utah Code Ann. § 76-10-1203; Utah Code Ann. § 76-10-1204; Wash. Rev. Code Ann. § 7.48A.010; Wash. Rev. Code Ann. § 9.68.140; Wis. Stat. Ann. § 944.21; Wyo. Stat. Ann. § 6-4-301; Wyo. Stat. Ann. § 6-4-302. Note that, perhaps due to drafting error, Hawaii's offense of displaying indecent material does not include "prurient interest" or "patently offensive" formulations. See Haw. Rev. Stat. Ann. § 712-1211. However, Hawaii's general offense of promoting "pornography" incorporates both formulations. See Haw. Rev. Stat. Ann. § 712-1214; Haw. Rev. Stat. Ann. § 712-1210.

9. Ala. Code § 13A-12-200.1; Ala. Code § 13A-12-200.2; Ga. Code Ann. § 16-12-80; Kan. Stat. Ann. § 21-6401; La. Stat. Ann. § 14:106; Miss. Code. Ann. § 97-29-103; Miss. Code. Ann. § 97-29-101; Miss. Code. Ann. § 97-29-105; Tex. Penal Code Ann. § 43.21; Tex. Penal Code Ann. § 43.22; Tex. Penal Code Ann. § 43.23. Note that the District of Columbia's obscenity offense arguably includes obscene devices. See D.C. Code Ann. § 22-2201 (forbidding the marketing of "any article, thing, or device which is intended for or represented as being for indecent or immoral use"). Likewise, Maryland's may as well. See Md. Code Ann., Crim. Law § 11-202 (forbidding marketing of "obscene matter").

10. D.C. Code Ann. § 22-2201; Md. Code Ann., Crim. Law § 11-202. Note that these jurisdictions are, as other jurisdictions, bound by the U.S. Supreme Court decision in Miller v. California, which held that obscenity may be

criminalized only where the material appeals to the "prurient interest," portrays sexual conduct in a "patently offensive way," and "do[es] not have serious literary, artistic, political, or scientific value." Miller, 413 U.S. at 24. See, e.g., Retzer v. United States, 363 A.2d 307, 309 (D.C. 1976) (adopting Miller test as the law of the District of Columbia).

Note also that D.C. law forbids marketing "any article, thing, or device which is intended for or represented as being for indecent or immoral use," D.C. Code Ann. § 22-2201, which arguably includes "obscene" devices such as those designed or marketed as useful primarily for the stimulation of human genital organs. Likewise, Maryland forbids marketing any "obscene matter." Md. Code Ann., Crim. Law § 11-202.

11. 354 U.S. 476 (1957).

12. Roth, 354 U.S. at 487.

13. 383 U.S. 413 (1966).

14. Memoirs, 383 U.S. at 418.

15. Cf. Jennifer M. Kinsley, *The Myth of Obsolete Obscenity*, 33 Cardozo Arts & Ent. L.J. 607 (2015) (suggesting that southern "Bible Belt" states are "much more likely to pursue obscenity charges outright," while northern states generally pursue obscenity charges in tandem with other offenses, such as child pornography).

16. See Karthik Subramanian, *It's A Dildo in 49 States, but It's a Dildon't in Alabama: Alabama's Anti-Obscenity Enforcement Act and the Assault on Civil Liberty and Personal Freedom*, 1 Ala. C.R. & C.L.L. Rev. 111 (2011) (discussing the recent history of obscenity laws targeting obscene devices, especially Alabama's 1998 law).

17. See Mark Regnerus et al., *Documenting Pornography Use in America: A Comparative Analysis of Methodological Approaches*, 53 J. Sex Research 873 (2015) (finding that 46 percent of American men and 16 percent of American women between the ages of 18 and 39 intentionally viewed pornography in a given week). Cf. Cody Harper & David C. Hodgins, *Examining Correlates of Problematic Internet Pornography Use Among University Students*, 5 J. Behavior Addiction 179 (2016) (finding, in a study of university students in Calgary, Canada, that only 5 percent of male students indicated that they did not "use [Internet pornography] for masturbation at all").

18. In Kinsley, supra note 15, the author documents at least 25 state prosecutions of obscenity violations across at least seven jurisdictions since 2003. See Kinsley, supra note 15, at 615–38. "[O]bscenity prosecutions are still very much occurring on both the federal and state levels." Kinsley at 615.

19. See United States v. Little, 365 F. App'x 159, 161 (11th Cir. 2010).

20. See State v. Crump, 223 S.W.3d 915, 915 (Mo. Ct. App. 2007).

21. See Villarreal v. State, 267 S.W.3d 204, 206 (Tex. App. 2008).

22. See, e.g., Ex parte Dave, 220 S.W.3d 154 (Tex. App. 2007); Varkonyi v. State, 276 S.W.3d 27 (Tex. App. 2008); Williams v. Morgan, 478 F.3d 1316, 1323 (11th Cir. 2007); 1568 Montgomery Highway, Inc. v. City of Hoover, 45 So. 3d 319 (Ala. 2010); United States v. Little, 365 F. App'x 159, 161 (11th Cir. 2010);

State v. Crump, 223 S.W.3d 915, 915 (Mo. Ct. App. 2007); Villarreal v. State, 267 S.W.3d 204, 206 (Tex. App. 2008).

23. Jeffrey M. Jones, *Americans Hold Record Liberal Views on Most Moral Issues*, Gallup.com (May 11, 2017), http://www.gallup.com/poll/210542/americans-hold -record-liberal-views-moral-issues.aspx.

24. For instance, in a law review article encouraging prosecution of obscenity, U.S. Senator Orrin G. Hatch argues that obscenity, including hard-core pornography, is damaging to individuals and communities. Citing studies over the last three decades, Hatch argues that some pornography is associated with aggressive behavior toward women as well as other social maladies, such as violence. See Orrin G. Hatch, *Fighting the Pornification of America by Enforcing Obscenity Laws*, 23 Stan. L. & Pol'y Rev. 1, 17 (2012).

25. See, e.g., Catherine MacKinnon, *Pornography, Civil Rights, and Speech*, 20 Harv. C.R.-C.L. L. Rev. 1, 18 (1985) (arguing that pornography "sexualizes inequality" and "institutionalizes the sexuality of male supremacy," and as such should be carefully regulated through a kind of obscenity statute).

CHAPTER THIRTY-ONE

Child Pornography

As a practical matter, the obscenity offenses discussed in the previous chapter are only occasionally prosecuted and typically garner minor penalties. Far more important, in terms of the number of prosecutions and the magnitude of the sanctions, are the numerous criminal code provisions focusing on child pornography. All 52 jurisdictions within the United States categorize the possession, distribution, and production of child pornography as serious crimes. To qualify for the offense, the material typically must depict a minor engaged in sexual conduct, or must contain a "lewd" exhibition of the genitals or female breasts of the minor, or must contain a visual depiction of such exhibition "for purposes of sexual stimulation of the viewer."[1] (As a matter of federal constitutional law, an image does not have to satisfy the legal definition of obscenity to qualify as child pornography.[2])

The most significant distinctions among the states concern two issues. First, states adopt different views on how young the child must be to trigger the child pornography *possession* offense. As Map 31 shows, the age cutoffs range from 16 to 18. A second distinction among the states is whether mere possession of material is punished the same as its production or distribution.

Person Depicted Must Be under 16 Years Old

Six states—Connecticut, Maine, Maryland, Nevada, New York, and Vermont[3]—use 16 as the cutoff age. Note that some states may treat the child's age differently in criminalizing possession as opposed to production or distribution of child pornography.

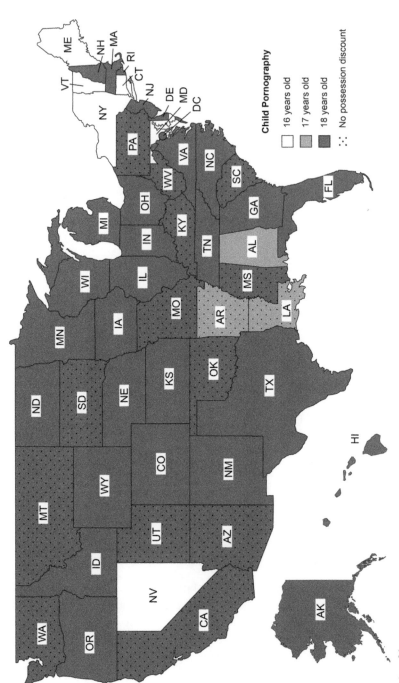

Child Pornography

- ☐ 16 years old
- ☐ 17 years old
- ☐ 18 years old
- ∴ No possession discount

Map 31

Person Depicted Must Be under 17 Years Old

Three other states, identified with medium shading on the map—Alabama, Arkansas, and Louisiana[4]—set the cutoff age at 17 years old. That is, in these states, for purposes of criminal possession of child pornography, a "child" is any individual below the age of 17.

Person Depicted Must Be under 18 Years Old

The vast majority of jurisdictions, designated on the map with dark shading—Alaska, Arizona, California, Colorado, Delaware, District of Columbia, Florida, Georgia, Hawaii, Idaho, Illinois, Indiana, Iowa, Kansas, Kentucky, Massachusetts, Michigan, Minnesota, Mississippi, Missouri, Montana, Nebraska, New Hampshire, New Jersey, New Mexico, North Carolina, North Dakota, Ohio, Oklahoma, Oregon, Pennsylvania, Rhode Island, South Carolina, South Dakota, Tennessee, Texas, Utah, Virginia, Washington, West Virginia, Wisconsin, and Wyoming[5]—provide for child pornography charges if the subject of the material is less than 18 years old.

Possession Punished the Same as Production or Distribution

Most states treat mere possession of child pornography as a less serious offense than either of the more "involved" offenses of production or distribution.[6] But 15 states, those with an overlay of dots on the map—Arizona, Arkansas, California, Kentucky, Louisiana, Mississippi, Missouri, Montana, Oklahoma, Pennsylvania, South Carolina, South Dakota, Utah, Washington, and West Virginia[7]—do not make this distinction. In these states, the lowest-level offense for mere possession of child pornography will result in the same punishment as either the lowest-level offense for production, the lowest-level offense for distribution, or both.

Observations and Speculations

Multiple possible rationales exist for criminalizing possession of child pornography. The most obvious rationale is that it causes harm to those depicted in the material; where material depicts minors, those subjects are unable to give valid consent to sexual activity. Under this rationale, the mere possessor of child pornography—even if he or she had no role in creating the material—may be considered an accomplice because he or she provided material support. (Such support would not satisfy the usual modern rules of complicity, however, as it comes after the fact.[8])

Another argument for criminalizing the possession of child pornography is that such possession makes one more likely to commit sexual offenses against children, making anti-child pornography legislation a sort of risk-prevention measure akin to an endangerment offense.[9] The federal Child Pornography Prevention Act of 1996, which banned possession of images whose subjects even "appear" to be minors engaging in sexual conduct, suggests this rationale.[10] But the empirical support for the claim that consumption of pornography leads to sexually abusive behavior is mixed.[11]

Yet another possibility is that such possession is simply considered immoral or indecent and criminalized on that basis.[12] Of course, this rationale runs into the standard arguments against criminalizing so-called private immorality, as discussed in the previous two chapters concerning adultery and obscenity.

The availability of all forms of pornography on the Internet means that the potential for possession is easy and could be widespread; potential offenders are no longer a few zealots who have gone to great lengths to obtain forbidden images, as may have been the case in the past. Technological advances have thus created both the possibility for more violations as well as the possibility for inadvertent violations that will trigger serious penalties.

Note the striking geographic distribution of the nine "outlier" states that permit possession of at least some pornography where the image depicts a child under 18 years of age—shown with light and medium shading on the map. Of the six most-permissive states, which allow possession of pornography in cases where the subject is at least 16 years old, five of these are geographically northeastern. On the other hand, the only three states that permit possession where the child is 17 years old—Alabama, Arkansas, and Louisiana—are clustered southern states. Perhaps the clustered distribution of the outlier states suggests regional influences, such as different perspectives on age and responsibility, or the criminality or wrongfulness of sexual conduct with children near the cusp of adulthood.

Is there anything principled about the various positions taken by the states? A comparison with the states' policies on the age of consent in Chapter 23 may be enlightening. For example, a large number of states would permit an 18-year-old to have sex with a 16-year-old partner but not to possess nude images of that partner. New York, on the other hand, would permit an 18-year-old to possess nude images of a 16-year-old partner, but would not permit him to have sex with that partner. Some states, however, are more consistent: Connecticut, Maine, Maryland, Nevada, and Vermont have set the age of consent at 16 and permit possession of pornography where the child is 16 years old. Louisiana, one of the three states permitting possession of pornography where the child is 17, sets the age of consent at 17 as well.

Like the subjects of some other chapters in this book, child pornography offenses highlight an important issue: that the degree of a person's blameworthiness often rises and falls along a continuum, such that abrupt cutoffs for assigning criminal liability—such as those that arise from sharp age cutoffs—yield unsatisfactory results. An 18-year-old who possesses a pornographic image of his 17-year-old partner commits an offense just as serious as the 30-year-old who possesses the same image, even as the community would assign far different levels of blameworthiness to their conduct. The patent injustice of abrupt cutoffs has gradually led to reform in the statutory rape context, as the majority of states have adopted close-in-age exceptions.[13] The states generally have not done the same in the child pornography context—a serious oversight, given the culture of digital image-sharing that prevails among youths today.

Child pornography offenses are also unusually susceptible to a familiar problem in criminal law: the tendency of legislatures to gradually increase the severity or punishment for certain offenses until they are grossly out of proportion to the offense seriousness. As one author notes, 30 states have increased the penalties for child pornography since criminalizing it, and 19 of those increases came between the years 2005 and 2011. The result is that mere possession in many cases leads to a longer sentence than actual sexual abuse of children.[14]

Notes

1. For three different approaches to defining the offense, see, e.g., Ala. Code § 13A-12-192 (covering possession of "any obscene matter that contains a visual depiction of a person under the age of 17 years engaged in any act of sadomasochistic abuse, sexual intercourse, sexual excitement, masturbation, breast nudity, genital nudity, or other sexual conduct"); Alaska Stat. Ann. § 11.41.455 (defining child pornography to include depiction of a child under 18 years of age "engaged in . . . sexual penetration[,] the lewd touching of another person's genitals, anus, or breast[,] the lewd touching by another person of the child's genitals, anus, or breast[,] masturbation[,] bestiality[,] the lewd exhibition of the child's genitals[,] or sexual masochism or sadism"); Ariz. Rev. Stat. Ann. § 13-3551; Ariz. Rev. Stat. Ann. § 13-3553 (covering possession of any visual depiction of a minor where there is "exhibition of the genitals or pubic or rectal areas of any person for the purpose of sexual stimulation of the viewer," or where the minor is "engaged in . . . sexual conduct").

2. See New York v. Ferber, 458 U.S. 747 (1982).

3. Conn. Gen. Stat. Ann. § 53a-193; Conn. Gen. Stat. Ann. § 53a-196f; Conn. Gen. Stat. Ann. § 53a-196g; Me. Rev. Stat. tit. 17-A, § 284; Md. Code Ann., Crim. Law § 11-208; Nev. Rev. Stat. Ann. § 200.730; N.Y. Penal Law § 263.16; N.Y. Penal Law § 263.11; Vt. Stat. Ann. tit. 13, § 2827; Vt. Stat. Ann. tit. 13, § 2821.

4. Ala. Code § 13A-12-190; Ala. Code § 13A-12-192; Ark. Code Ann. § 5-27-302; Ark. Code Ann. § 5-27-602; La. Stat. Ann. § 14:81.1.

5. Alaska Stat. Ann. § 11.61.127; Alaska Stat. Ann. § 11.41.455; Ariz. Rev. Stat. Ann. § 13-3553; Ariz. Rev. Stat. Ann. § 13-3551; Cal. Penal Code § 311.11; Colo. Rev. Stat. Ann. § 18-6-403; Del. Code Ann. tit. 11, § 1100; Del. Code Ann. tit. 11, § 1111; D.C. Code Ann. § 22-3101; D.C. Code Ann. § 22-3102; Fla. Stat. Ann. § 847.001; Fla. Stat. Ann. § 847.011; Ga. Code Ann. § 16-12-100; Haw. Rev. Stat. Ann. § 707-752; Idaho Code Ann. § 18-1507; 720 Ill. Comp. Stat. Ann. 5/11-20.1; Ind. Code Ann. § 35-42-4-4; Iowa Code Ann. § 728.1; Iowa Code Ann. § 728.12; Kan. Stat. Ann. § 21-5510; Ky. Rev. Stat. Ann. § 531.335; Mass. Gen. Laws Ann. ch. 272, § 29C; Mich. Comp. Laws Ann. § 750.145c; Minn. Stat. Ann. § 617.246; Minn. Stat. Ann. § 617.247; Miss. Code. Ann. § 97-5-31; Miss. Code. Ann. § 97-5-33; Mo. Ann. Stat. § 573.037; Mont. Code Ann. § 45-5-625; State v. Dasen, 2007 MT 87, 337 Mont. 74, 155 P.3d 1282, 1284 (interpreting "child" to be a person under 18 years old); Neb. Rev. Stat. Ann. § 28-1463.02; N.H. Rev. Stat. Ann. § 649-A:3; N.H. Rev. Stat. Ann. § 649-A:2; N.J. Stat. Ann. § 2C:24-4; N.M. Stat. Ann. § 30-6A-3; N.C. Gen. Stat. Ann. § 14-190.17A; N.C. Gen. Stat. Ann. § 14-190.13; N.D. Cent. Code Ann. § 12.1-27.2-05; N.D. Cent. Code Ann. § 12.1-27.2-04.1; Ohio Rev. Code Ann. § 2907.01; Ohio Rev. Code Ann. § 2907.323; Okla. Stat. Ann. tit. 21, § 1021.2; Or. Rev. Stat. Ann. § 163.665; Or. Rev. Stat. Ann. § 163.686; 18 Pa. Stat. and Cons. Stat. Ann. § 6312; 11 R.I. Gen. Laws Ann. § 11-9-1.3; S.C. Code Ann. § 16-15-375; S.C. Code Ann. § 16-15-410; S.D. Codified Laws § 22-24A-3; S.D. Codified Laws § 22-24A-2; Tenn. Code Ann. § 39-17-1003; Tenn. Code Ann. § 39-17-1002; Tex. Penal Code Ann. § 43.26; Utah Code Ann. § 76-5b-103; Utah Code Ann. § 76-5b-201; Va. Code Ann. § 18.2-374.1:1; Va. Code Ann. § 18.2-374.1; Wash. Rev. Code Ann. § 9.68A.011; Wash. Rev. Code Ann. § 9.68A.070; W. Va. Code Ann. § 61-8C-3; W. Va. Code Ann. § 61-8C-1; Wis. Stat. Ann. § 948.12; Wis. Stat. Ann. § 948.01; Wyo. Stat. Ann. § 6-4-303.

6. *Production* is usually defined as causing a child, directly or indirectly, to be the subject or a participant in child pornography. *Distribution* is usually defined as disseminating the images or transferring their possession, with or without remuneration.

7. Ariz. Rev. Stat. Ann. § 13-3552; Ariz. Rev. Stat. Ann. § 13-3553; Ark. Code Ann. § 5-27-602; Ark. Code Ann. § 5-27-605; Cal. Penal Code § 311.11; Cal. Penal Code § 311.3; Cal. Penal Code § 311.2; Ky. Rev. Stat. Ann. § 531.335; Ky. Rev. Stat. Ann. § 531.340; La. Stat. Ann. § 14:81.1; Miss. Code. Ann. § 97-5-35; Mo. Ann. Stat. § 573.035; Mo. Ann. Stat. § 573.023; Mont. Code Ann. § 45-5-625; Okla. Stat. Ann. tit. 21, § 1040.8; 18 Pa. Stat. and Cons. Stat. Ann. § 6312; S.C. Code Ann. § 16-15-410; S.C. Code Ann. § 16-15-405; S.D. Codified Laws § 22-24A-3; S.D. Codified Laws § 22-24A-2; Utah Code Ann. § 76-5b-201; Wash. Rev. Code Ann. § 9.68A.070; Wash. Rev. Code Ann. § 9.68A.060; Wash. Rev. Code Ann. § 9.68A.050; Wash. Rev. Code Ann. § 9.68A.040; W. Va. Code Ann. § 61-8C-3; W. Va. Code Ann. § 61-8C-2. Note that some states distinguish between production of child pornography for private use and production for commercial use or remuneration. See, e.g., Cal. Penal Code § 311.4 (specifying a higher penalty for commercial production).

8. For discussion of complicity liability, see Paul H. Robinson and Michael T. Cahill, *Criminal Law,* 2nd ed. §6.1.

9. For discussion of endangerment offenses, see Robinson and Cahill, *Criminal Law,* 2nd ed. §15.4.

10. This federal ban on so-called "virtual" child pornography, which does not in fact involve the use of children in its production, was held unconstitutional by the U.S. Supreme Court in Ashcroft v. Free Speech Coal., 535 U.S. 234 (2002).

11. See, e.g., Ian O'Donnell & Claire Milner, *Child Pornography: Crime, Computers and Society,* 75 (Routledge 2007) ("There is much debate . . . as to whether the use of child pornography stimulates sexual fantasies of children, relieves impulses to commit offenses, or leads to a desire to act out those fantasies."); Dean D. Knudsen, *Child Abuse and Pornography: Is There a Relationship?* 3 J. Family Violence 253, 261 (1988) ("The degree to which child sexual abuse is related to the availability of child pornography is extremely difficult to establish.").

12. For discussion of offenses against public values, see Chapter 18.

13. See Chapter 23, "Statutory Rape."

14. See Carissa Byrne Hessick, *Disentangling Child Pornography from Child Sex Abuse,* 88 Wash. U.L. Rev. 853, 860 (2011).

PART 9

Offenses against the Community

CHAPTER THIRTY-TWO

Drug Offenses

Drug offenses have become a point of significant controversy and disagreement among the states. At the lowest end of the seriousness continuum, some states have decriminalized the possession of small amounts of marijuana for recreational use, while other states still consider it a serious offense for which jail time is authorized. Map 32 shows the position of each state on the issue. (Some of the states that continue to criminalize marijuana use have carved out from their offense a special exemption for medical use.[1])

For more serious drug offenses criminalized by all jurisdictions, there is disagreement over the harshness of the penalties to be imposed. With a dots or a diagonal lines overlay, Map 32 indicates those states that authorize life or even life without parole on the defendant's first conviction for certain serious drug offenses.

Thus, the states with the darker shading and an overlay are states that are harsh throughout—for both marijuana and more serious drug offenses. States like Alaska, Nebraska, and Nevada, which have overlays but do not have shading or have very light shading, are states that take very different approaches to marijuana and more serious drug offenses—they essentially decriminalize marijuana but impose harsh sentences for nonviolent serious drug offenses.

Marijuana Decriminalized

In nine states, those with no shading on the map—Alaska, California, Colorado, District of Columbia, Maine, Massachusetts, Nevada, Oregon, and Washington[2]—the possession of a small amount of marijuana is permitted by law for recreational use.

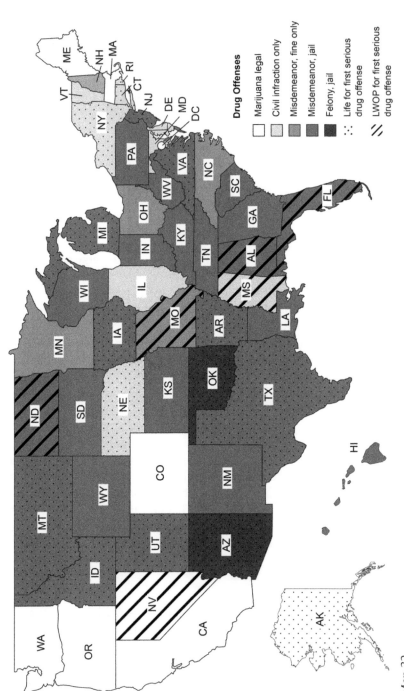

Drug Offenses

☐ Marijuana legal
⬚ Civil infraction only
▨ Misdemeanor, fine only
▦ Misdemeanor, jail
▩ Felony, jail
⬛ Life for first serious drug offense
⸬ Life for first serious drug offense
╱ LWOP for first serious drug offense

Map 32

Marijuana a Civil Infraction Only

In another nine states, designated with the lightest shading on the map—Connecticut, Delaware, Illinois, Maryland, Mississippi, Nebraska, New York, Rhode Island, and Vermont[3]—possession of a small amount of marijuana for recreational use will result in a civil fine (much like a traffic ticket) but not in criminal liability.

Misdemeanor, Fine Only

In five states, marked with the second lightest shading on the map—Minnesota, Missouri, New Hampshire, North Carolina, and Ohio[4]—first-offense possession is a misdemeanor crime, but no jail sentence is permitted.

Misdemeanor, Jail

In a bare majority of states (26), designated with medium shading on the map—Alabama, Arkansas, Florida, Georgia, Hawaii, Idaho, Indiana, Iowa, Kansas, Kentucky, Louisiana, Michigan, Montana, New Jersey, New Mexico, North Dakota, Pennsylvania, South Carolina, South Dakota, Tennessee, Texas, Utah, Virginia, West Virginia, Wisconsin, and Wyoming[5]—the defendant's first offense for possession of a small amount of marijuana for recreational use is a misdemeanor offense for which imprisonment is authorized.

Felony, Jail

The darkest shading on the map identifies two states—Arizona and Oklahoma[6]—wherein the defendant's first offense for possession of a small amount of marijuana for recreational use can be a felony offense and can result in imprisonment. In Arizona, the first-time offense carries a maximum of 18 months, unless aggravating factors apply, in which case the maximum sentence is two years' imprisonment. In Oklahoma, first-time possession within 1,000 feet of a school is a felony. (Otherwise, the first-time offense is a misdemeanor.)

Life Imprisonment for Serious Nonviolent Drug Offense

Sixteen states, designated on Map 32 with a dots overlay—Alaska, Arizona, Arkansas, Connecticut, Idaho, Iowa, Michigan, Montana, Nebraska, New Jersey, New York, Oklahoma, Rhode Island, Texas, Utah, and Virginia[7]—authorize life imprisonment on the first conviction for at least one of their nonviolent drug offenses. The offenses here are generally serious drug offenses, such as manufacture or sale of large quantities of cocaine, heroin, or marijuana; engaging in large-scale drug-trafficking enterprises; manufacture of illegal drugs in a school zone; or distribution of drugs to minors.

Life without Parole for Serious Nonviolent Drug Offense

Six jurisdictions, shown on the map with a diagonal lines overlay—Alabama, Florida, Mississippi, Missouri, Nevada, and North Dakota[8]—go even further and provide life imprisonment without the possibility of parole on the first conviction for certain serious nonviolent drug offenses, such as those offenses described for the group above.

Observations and Speculations

It seems clear that public views relating to some drug offenses are changing. And if it is to reflect shared community views, as it should,[9] criminal law must change accordingly. But it may also be the case that community views in this instance are leading society into a danger zone. Would society be better off if marijuana, and perhaps other drugs, were decriminalized? Or would this lead to increased suffering and dysfunction? Only time will tell.

But what we can say now is that ordinary people would normally assess the seriousness of many drug offenses to be dramatically less serious than current punishments provide. Empirical research has shown that current drug offense punishments are out of line with community norms.[10] We also know that significant conflicts between the criminal law and community views can seriously undermine the moral credibility of the criminal law and thereby undermine its power to gain compliance through social influence and the internalization of norms.[11]

A relevant example here is the experience of American Prohibition in the 1920s. The law prohibited the use of alcohol, but that prohibition conflicted with the judgment of a large sector of society, and alcohol consumption was common and often public, even by government officials. Alcohol-related prosecutions proliferated in this period. But, interestingly, what is not as well known is that non-alcohol-related crimes also increased significantly. The criminal law's prohibition of alcohol so conflicted with community views that it undermined the law's moral credibility generally and thereby reduced the law's crime control effectiveness.[12]

The law's criminalization of marijuana today, some have argued, is in some ways parallel to American Prohibition. Marijuana use is officially prohibited but commonly occurs, and is frequently ignored by authorities—just the kind of conflict between community views and the criminal law that one saw in Prohibition. On the other hand, in many respects the cases are not comparable. First, the extent of flouting the law in Prohibition was significantly greater than today with marijuana. Second, citizens today have never experienced a time when marijuana was legal and generally accepted, the way alcohol was at the time it was criminalized by Prohibition. Third, it simply is not clear that there is the level of public acceptance of marijuana use today that there was for alcohol use before Prohibition.

Indeed, one could argue that decriminalizing marijuana today would in many parts of the country create a significant conflict between criminal law and community views that does not now exist. Thus, the decriminalization of marijuana use, when it is seen as condemnable conduct, would undermine the criminal law's moral credibility rather than reinforce it.

The point illustrates the challenges for criminal law in tracking community views when on some issues—think abortion and the death penalty—the community simply disagrees among itself. What is a criminal law to do if it seeks to maximize its moral credibility by tracking community views? The answer, of course, is that it must suffer some loss in deference and respect from some portion of the community—which simply points out how important it is to build up its moral credibility whenever it can, whenever there is community consensus, which fortunately includes the vast majority of the issues that criminal code drafters must deal with.[13]

In the long run, what will help criminal law most in dealing with this potentially dangerous area of unsettled views is the American tradition of the 50 states as "laboratories of democracy" in which statewide communities can test out new approaches. Thus, if the nine states on Map 32 that decriminalize marijuana show success—few detrimental effects, greater individual freedom, and greater respect for the law—their success may well shift the community views in other states, who may then join in the experiment. On the other hand, if the experiment goes badly—producing more dysfunction and suffering, less respect for the law, and more crime—then other states will have been saved from the detrimental effects that a national experiment would have brought.

In this instance, one might say about the dramatic differences among the states: *Vive la différence!*

Notes

1. See, e.g., N.M. Stat. Ann. § 26-2B-4 (permitting marijuana use for medical reasons); Ariz. Rev. Stat. Ann. § 36-2811 (same).

2. Alaska Stat. Ann. § 17.38.020; Cal. Health & Safety Code § 11362.1; Colo. Const. art. XVIII, § 16; D.C. Code Ann. § 48-904.01; Mass. Gen. Laws Ann. ch. 94G, § 7; Me. Rev. Stat. tit. 7, § 2452; Or. Rev. Stat. Ann. § 475B.260; Wash. Rev. Code Ann. § 69.50.4013. In 2016, Nevada adopted a ballot measure to legalize marijuana for recreational use. *See Nevada Marjiana Legalization, Question 2 (2016)*, Ballotpedia (last accessed June 24, 2017), https://ballotpedia.org/Nevada

_Marijuana_Legalization,_Question_2_(2016). The measure will be active only after the Nevada legislature determines how sales will be regulated.

3. Conn. Gen. Stat. Ann. § 21a-279; Conn. Gen. Stat. Ann. § 21a-279a; Del. Code Ann. tit. 16, § 4764; Del. Code Ann. tit. 16, § 4701; 720 Ill. Comp. Stat. Ann. 550/4; Md. Code Ann., Crim. Law § 5-601; Miss. Code. Ann. § 41-29-139; Neb. Rev. Stat. Ann. § 28-416; N.Y. Penal Law § 221.05; 21 R.I. Gen. Laws Ann. § 21-28-4.01; Vt. Stat. Ann. tit. 18, § 4230a.

4. Minn. Stat. Ann. § 152.027; Minn. Stat. Ann. § 152.01; Mo. Ann. Stat. § 579.015; Mo. Ann. Stat. § 558.002; Mo. Ann. Stat. § 558.011; N.H. Rev. Stat. Ann. § 318-B:26; N.C. Gen. Stat. Ann. § 90-95; N.C. Gen. Stat. Ann. § 15A-1340.23; Ohio Rev. Code Ann. § 2925.11.

5. Ala. Code Ann. §13A-12-214; Ala. Code Ann. §13A-5-7; Ark. Code Ann. § 5-64-419; Fla. Stat. Ann. § 893.13; Ga. Code Ann. § 16-13-30; Ga. Code Ann. § 16-13-2; Haw. Rev. Stat. § 712-1249; Haw. Rev. Stat. §706-663; Idaho Code Ann. § 37-2732; Ind. Code Ann. § 35-48-4-11; Iowa Code Ann. § 124.401; Kan. Stat. Ann. § 21-5706; Ky. Rev. Stat. Ann. § 218A.1421; La. Stat. Ann. § 40:966; Mich. Comp. Laws Ann. § 333.7403; Mont. Code Ann. § 45-9-102; N.J. Stat. Ann. § 2C:35-10; N.M. Stat. Ann. § 30-31-23; N.D. Cent. Code Ann. § 19-03.1-23; 35 Pa. Stat. Ann. § 780-113; S.C. Code Ann. § 44-53-370; S.D. Codified Laws § 22-42-6; Tenn. Code Ann. § 39-17-418; Tex. Health & Safety Code Ann. § 481.121; Utah Code Ann. § 58-37-8; Va. Code Ann. § 18.2-250.1; W. Va. Code Ann. § 60A-4-401; Wis. Stat. Ann. § 961.41; Wyo. Stat. Ann. § 35-7-1031.

6. Ariz. Rev. Stat. Ann. § 13-3405; Ariz. Rev. Stat. Ann. § 13-702; Okla. Stat. Ann. tit. 63, § 2-402.

7. See Caitlin Lee Hall, *Good Intentions: A National Survey of Life Sentences for Nonviolent Offenses,* 16 N.Y.U. J. Leg. Pub. Pol'y. 1101, 1159-84 (2013) (surveying state laws punishing nonviolent drug offenses).

8. Id.

9. See the Chapter 1 discussion of the crime control benefits of criminal law enhancing its moral credibility with community.

10. See, e.g., Paul H. Robinson, *Intuitions of Justice and Utility of Desert,* 113–14, 120–28 (Oxford 2013).

11. See Robinson, Intuitions of Justice and Utility of Desert, at Chapter 9.

12. See Paul H. Robinson and Sarah M. Robinson, *Pirates, Prisoners, and Lepers: Lessons from Life Outside the Law,* Chapter 8 (Potomac Books 2015).

13. See Robinson, *Intuitions of Justice and Utility of Desert,* Chapters 1–4.

CHAPTER THIRTY-THREE

Firearms Possession Offenses

The U.S. Supreme Court has recognized that the Second Amendment generally gives individuals a right to possess certain firearms.[1] In *District of Columbia v. Heller*, the Court invalidated the nation's most restrictive gun law, the District of Columbia's handgun ban, which totally banned handgun possession in the home and required lawful owners of other guns to disassemble or lock guns, rendering them inoperable.[2] The individual right recognized in *Heller* was extended to cover state and local bans, such as Chicago's restrictions on gun ownership.[3] However, courts have permitted a variety of restrictions on gun ownership, upholding laws banning possession by felons, violent misdemeanants, domestic abusers, and others.[4]

Federal law prohibits felons from possessing firearms, where the felony is any crime that could lead to greater imprisonment than a year.[5] Federal law also prohibits certain others from possessing firearms, including people who use illegal drugs, people who have been declared mentally ill or have been institutionalized for mental illness, illegal aliens generally, and people who are subject to restraining orders related to domestic violence or who have been convicted of any domestic violence offense.[6]

As a practical matter, however, it is local police and prosecutors who generally discover and decide whether to prosecute unlawful gun possession. Federal authorities may charge 5,000 people a year with unlawful firearms possession while state authorities charge almost 200,000 people a year.[7] Thus, it is state rather than federal law that actually controls the scope and enforcement of unlawful gun laws. As Map 33 makes clear, state law governing unlawful possession often, but not always, differs from federal law.

The darker the shading and the more overlays for a state on the map, the more restrictive their gun possession laws.

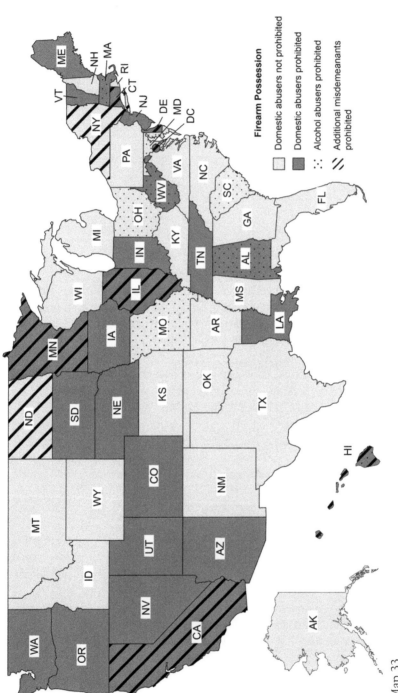

Firearm Possession

☐ Domestic abusers not prohibited

■ Domestic abusers prohibited

∴ Alcohol abusers prohibited

∥ Additional misdemeanants prohibited

Map 33

Domestic Abusers Prohibited

Twenty-five jurisdictions, designated on the map with medium shading—Alabama, Arizona, California, Colorado, Connecticut, Delaware, District of Columbia, Hawaii, Illinois, Indiana, Iowa, Louisiana, Maine, Massachusetts, Minnesota, Nebraska, Nevada, New Jersey, Oregon, South Dakota, Tennessee, Utah, Vermont, Washington, and West Virginia[8]—specifically prohibit gun possession by people who have been convicted of the state's lowest-level domestic violence offense, in effect following the federal standard. Note, however, that some jurisdictions limit the length of this prohibition to a term of years following the conviction.[9]

Justification for such a limitation on gun ownership is often based on concerns about the relation between guns and domestic violence homicides: Bureau of Criminal Justice Statistics data suggest that firearms are used in about half of homicides in which the victim is a member of the offender's immediate family.[10]

Domestic Abusers Not Prohibited

The remaining jurisdictions, identified with light shading on the map—Alaska, Arkansas, Florida, Georgia, Idaho, Kansas, Kentucky, Maryland, Michigan, Mississippi, Missouri, Montana, New Hampshire, New Mexico, New York, North Carolina, North Dakota, Ohio, Oklahoma, Pennsylvania, Rhode Island, South Carolina, Texas, Virginia, Wisconsin, and Wyoming—do not specifically prohibit people convicted of crimes of domestic violence from possessing firearms. This is significant because, although convicted domestic abusers are prohibited under federal law from such possession, as a practical matter these charges are rarely brought by federal prosecutors.[11]

In many of these jurisdictions, domestic abusers may be barred from possession if a court issues a protective order against the abuser. (Such orders do not typically issue automatically upon a domestic abuse conviction.)

Alcohol Abusers Prohibited

Eight states, marked with a dots overlay on the map—Alabama, Hawaii, Maryland, Massachusetts, Missouri, Ohio, South Carolina, and West Virginia[12]—generally prohibit firearm possession by those who are addicted to or abuse alcohol. In some jurisdictions, the prohibition applies to "habitual drunkard[s]," while in others the prohibition is triggered by a relevant event, such as treatment or counseling for alcohol addiction or dependence.[13]

Possession Prohibited by Other Specified Misdemeanors

Nine states, designated on the map with a diagonal lines overlay—California, Connecticut, Delaware, District of Columbia, Hawaii, Illinois, Minnesota, New York, and North Dakota[14]—go beyond federal law to prohibit people who have been convicted of certain other misdemeanor offenses not involving domestic abuse or drug use. For instance, in Connecticut, a person convicted of misdemeanor reckless endangerment is prohibited from possessing a firearm.[15]

Observations and Speculations

The law governing firearm possession is particularly interesting because of the state-federal overlap in jurisdiction. The U.S. Constitution gives the states, not the federal government, the general police power. Federal jurisdiction to prosecute any crime, even the most serious, typically is limited to instances where there is a special federal interest. For example, murder is not a federal crime, unless it involves some special federal interest such as murdering certain federal officials or murdering on a place of exclusive federal jurisdiction such as on some military bases. One can debate whether possession of a firearm by a person convicted of domestic violence has a sufficient federal interest to justify federal jurisdiction.

As noted above, however, even where there is federal jurisdiction for an offense within a state, it may have limited practical effect because there simply is no federal police force to speak of. Federal agencies like the FBI, ATF, and DEA have their own special missions, typically strictly focused on criminality that specially threatens federal interests.

Nonetheless, federal statutes sometimes create apparently broad federal jurisdiction in a wide range of situations in which it is never exercised but presumably could be. The existence of such rarely used federal jurisdiction is not necessarily consistent with our democratic values or the rule of law. It creates enormous discretion in federal prosecutors to decide for themselves what offenses will and will not be prosecuted. It allows for dramatic changes in enforcement and prosecution practices without legislative consultation or involvement. Nor does it give the legislature any role in shaping the selection criteria that federal executive authorities will use in selecting the particular cases that it will choose to prosecute.

A better approach might be to respect the Constitution's assignment of the police powers to the states and to limit the creation of federal offenses to those instances in which there is a sufficiently compelling federal interest such that law enforcement authorities really will use the jurisdiction that they are given.

Notes

1. See District of Columbia v. Heller, 554 U.S. 570 (2008).
2. See Heller, 554 U.S. 570, 628 (2008).
3. See McDonald v. City of Chicago, 561 U.S. 742 (2010).
4. See, e.g., Lewis v. United States, 445 U.S. 55, 66 (1980) (upholding federal law prohibiting a felony from knowingly possessing a firearm); Binderup v. Attorney Gen. United States of Am., 836 F.3d 336 (3d Cir. 2016) (holding that violent offenders are "unvirtuous citizens [who] lack Second Amendment rights").
5. See 18 U.S.C.A. § 922(g)(1).
6. See 18 U.S.C.A. § 922(g)(2)-(9). The law distinguishes between "carrying" and "possession." The law also distinguishes between "handguns" (or "pistols," or "any gun capable of being concealed on the person"), and "long guns." For purposes of this chapter, "firearms" is used to refer to all guns that are generally subject to restrictions.
7. State and local authorities arrested an estimated 190,600 people, while federal authorities arrested or referred 4,907 people in the same year, 1998. Caroline Wolf Harlow, *Firearm Use by Offenders,* Bureau of Justice Statistics at 4 (Nov. 2001), https://bjs.gov/content/pub/pdf/fuo.pdf.
8. Ala. Code § 13A-11-72; Ariz. Rev. Stat. Ann. § 13-3101; Cal. Penal Code § 29805; Cal. Penal Code § 243; Colo. Rev. Stat. Ann. § 18-6-801; Conn. Gen. Stat. Ann. § 53a-217; Del. Code Ann. tit. 11, § 1448; D.C. Code Ann. § 22-4503; Haw. Rev. Stat. Ann. § 134-7; Haw. Rev. Stat. Ann. § 134-1; 430 Ill. Comp. Stat. Ann. 65/8; Ind. Code Ann. § 35-47-4-6; Iowa Code Ann. § 724.26; La. Stat. Ann. § 14:95.10; Me. Rev. Stat. tit. 15, § 393; Me. Rev. Stat. tit. 17-A, § 207-A; Mass. Gen. Laws Ann. ch. 140, § 129C; Mass. Gen. Laws Ann. ch. 140, § 129B; Minn. Stat. Ann. § 609.224; Minn. Stat. Ann. § 609.2242; Neb. Rev. Stat. Ann. § 28-1206; Nev. Rev. Stat. Ann. § 202.360; N.J. Stat. Ann. § 2C:39-7; Or. Rev. Stat. Ann. § 166.255; S.D. Codified Laws § 22-14-15.2; Tenn. Code Ann. § 39-13-111; Utah Code Ann. § 76-10-503; Vt. Stat. Ann. tit. 13, § 4017; Vt. Stat. Ann. tit. 13, § 5301; Vt. Stat. Ann. tit. 13, § 1042; Wash. Rev. Code Ann. § 9.41.040; W. Va. Code Ann. § 61-7-7; W. Va. Code Ann. § 61-2-28.
9. See, e.g., D.C. Code Ann. § 22-4503 (prohibiting possession for five years); Neb. Rev. Stat. Ann. § 28-1206 (prohibiting possession for seven years); S.D. Codified Laws § 22-14-15.2 (prohibiting possession for one year).
10. For instance, in 2002, 50.1 percent of such homicides involved a firearm. See Matthew R. Durose et al., *Family Violence Statistics,* Bureau of Justice Statistics (June 2005), https://www.bjs.gov/content/pub/pdf/fvs.pdf.
11. According to a February 13, 2013, report published by the Transactional Records Access Clearinghouse, which studies data obtained through FOIA requests, in the period 2008–2012, there were just 244 prosecutions under 18 U.S.C.A. § 922(g)(9), the federal statute prohibiting possession by convicted domestic abusers. See *Federal Weapons Enforcement: A Moving Target,* Transactional Records Access Clearinghouse (Feb. 13, 2013), http://trac.syr.edu/tracreports/crim/307.

12. Ala. Code § 13A-11-72 ("habitual drunkard"); Haw. Rev. Stat. Ann. § 134-7 ("has been under treatment or counseling for addiction to, abuse of, or dependence upon any . . . intoxicating liquor"); MD PUBLIC SAFETY § 5-133 ("habitual drunkard"); Mass. Gen. Laws Ann. ch. 140, § 129B ("has been . . . committed to any hospital or institution for . . . alcohol or substance abuse"); Mo. Ann. Stat. § 571.070 ("habitually in an intoxicated or drugged condition"); Ohio Rev. Code Ann. § 2923.13 ("chronic alcoholic"); S.C. Code Ann. § 16-23-30 ("habitual drunkard"); W. Va. Code Ann. § 61-7-7 ("habitually addicted to alcohol"). Note that Alabama prohibits alcoholics from possessing handguns but does not generally prohibit them from possessing other firearms. See Ala. Code § 13A-11-72.

13. See supra note 12 (listing the states' formulations). Note, as a separate matter, some states specifically prohibit transfers of firearms to people who are intoxicated at the time of transfer. See, e.g., Alaska Stat. Ann. § 11.61.200.

14. Cal. Penal Code § 29805; Conn. Gen. Stat. Ann. § 53a-217; Del. Code Ann. tit. 11, § 1448; Del. Code Ann. tit. 11, § 4391; D.C. Code Ann. § 7-2502.03; D.C. Code Ann. § 22-404; Haw. Rev. Stat. Ann. § 134-7; Haw. Rev. Stat. Ann. § 134-1; 430 Ill. Comp. Stat. Ann. 65/14; 430 Ill. Comp. Stat. Ann. 65/2; 430 Ill. Comp. Stat. Ann. 65/8; 720 Ill. Comp. Stat. Ann. 5/12-3; Minn. Stat. Ann. § 609.224; N.Y. Penal Law § 265.00; N.D. Cent. Code Ann. § 62.1-02-01.

15. See Conn. Gen. Stat. Ann. § 53a-217; Conn. Gen. Stat. Ann. § 53a-63. In Hawaii, a person convicted of any offense that involves injury or threat of injury is prohibited from possessing a firearm. See Haw. Rev. Stat. Ann. § 134-7; Haw. Rev. Stat. Ann. § 134-1.

CHAPTER THIRTY-FOUR

Predatory Pricing

By the 1850s, some businessmen had learned to use the power of capital to stifle competition, in order to maximize profits and accumulate wealth. In that era, industrialists like Rockefeller, Carnegie, Gould, and Frick developed a variety of schemes that today would be prohibited under various modern antitrust statutes.

Some schemes employed by the so-called robber barons of yesteryear involved what is commonly called "predatory pricing." While small companies with limited capital must set prices according to the actual costs of goods or services in a particular marketplace, larger companies are able to set prices at whatever level is required to destroy competition, offsetting temporary losses with profits from other marketplaces. Modern economic policy seeks to protect competition and long-term price stability by prohibiting these kinds of schemes. Thus, a large number of states criminalize predatory pricing.

The statutes target two kinds of anticompetitive practices: sales below cost and price discrimination.[1] Prohibitions on *sales below cost* date to early-15th-century England. A company sets the price below the company's actual costs, taking on temporary losses as it destroys competition. Once the company drives out competitors, it is able to recoup the losses by returning prices to a profitable level. In the United States, states began to adopt below-cost statutes in 1902. Commenting on the purpose of such statutes, the U.S. Supreme Court wrote in *Safeway Stores, Inc. v. Oklahoma Retail Grocers Association, Inc.* that the selling of selected goods at a loss in order to lure customers into the store is not only "a destructive means of competition," but also a deceptive tactic that "plays on the gullibility of customers by leading them to expect what generally is not true, namely, that a store which offers such an amazing bargain is full of other such bargains."[2]

The other kind of predatory pricing is *price discrimination*. In the early 1900s, states began to adopt *territorial* price discrimination statutes, which

Criminal Predatory Pricing

No criminal predatory pricing

:·: Sales below cost

∕∕ Price discrimination

Map 34

prohibit selling goods in one area at a lower price, in order to eliminate competition in that area. Generally, firms recoup losses in the one area by retaining the higher prices where there is little or no competition.

Most states that target price discrimination have adopted such territorial price discrimination statutes, but a handful of states have adopted statutes modeled on the federal Robinson-Patman Act of 1936, which prohibits "discriminat[ion] in price between different purchasers of commodities of like grade and quality, . . . where the effect of such discrimination may be substantially to lessen competition or tend to create a monopoly in any line of commerce, or to injure, destroy, or prevent competition."[3] This prohibition of price discrimination at the *purchaser* level is meant to "provide some measure of protection to small independent retailers and their independent suppliers from what was thought to be unfair competition from vertically integrated, multi-location chain stores."[4] Or as the U.S. Supreme Court noted, the Robinson-Patman amendment was "motivated principally by congressional concern over the impact upon secondary line competition of the burgeoning of mammoth purchasers, notably chain stores."[5]

Map 34 indicates the position of each of the states with regard to these two kinds of predatory pricing. The more overlays, the broader the predatory pricing criminalization.

No Criminalization of Either Form of Predatory Pricing

Twenty-eight states, those with shading on the map—Alabama, Alaska, Arizona, Connecticut, District of Columbia, Georgia, Hawaii, Idaho, Illinois, Indiana, Kansas, Maine, Michigan, Mississippi, Missouri, Nevada, New Hampshire, New Jersey, New Mexico, New York, North Carolina, Ohio, Oregon, South Carolina, Texas, Vermont, Virginia, and Washington[6]—have not adopted criminal statutes prohibiting either species of predatory pricing, sales below cost or price discrimination. However, some of these states have adopted civil statutes prohibiting predatory pricing.

Criminalizes Sales Below Cost

Of the states that do criminalize some kind of predatory pricing, 15 states, those with a dots overlay on the map—Arkansas, California, Colorado, Kentucky, Massachusetts, Minnesota, Montana, Nebraska, North Dakota, Oklahoma, Pennsylvania, Rhode Island, Tennessee, West Virginia, and Wyoming[7]—have adopted criminal statutes specifically prohibiting sales below cost, the practice of selling or marketing products or services at less than their cost to the vendor, for the purpose of injuring or destroying competition.

Criminalizes Price Discrimination

Seventeen states, those with diagonal lines on the map—Arkansas, California, Colorado, Delaware, Florida, Iowa, Kentucky, Louisiana, Maryland, Minnesota, Montana, Nebraska, North Dakota, Oklahoma, South Dakota, Utah, and Wisconsin[8]—have adopted criminal statutes specifically prohibiting price discrimination, the practice of selling identical or nearly identical goods at different prices to similarly situated buyers or in similarly situated communities with the purpose of injuring or destroying competition.

Observations and Speculations

It is interesting to consider what it is exactly about predatory pricing that merits the condemnation of the criminal sanction. "Low prices" are generally thought to be a *good* thing. A common reaction among laypersons to criminal sales-below-cost statutes is puzzlement: How could there be such a thing as a bargain price too low?

Only on further examination does one realize a deeper function of predatory pricing statutes, beyond economic efficiency concerns, which is to sanction conduct that violates the community's moral assessment. Note, again, the expression of the U.S. Supreme Court in *Safeway Stores*, regarding the predatory practice of sales below cost: not only are sales below cost "destructive" of competition, a harm to the general welfare, but they are *dishonest*, "play[ing] on the gullibility of customers by leading them to expect what . . . is not true, . . . that a store which offers such an amazing bargain is full of other such bargains."[9] Further, predatory pricing is not only dishonest about the worth of the goods or services provided, but it also *hides an agenda* from the consumer, one that may not ultimately be in the consumer's interest—namely, the destruction of another businessperson's ability to make an honest living. On yet another view, the chief wrong of predatory pricing consists in the predation itself, and analytically the offense belongs in the class of offenses against property. It's what one court called the "malevolent purpose of driving [a] competitor out of business," which "in its moral quality may be no better than highway robbery."[10]

More often, such statutes are defended on general welfare grounds. The purpose of predatory pricing statutes is to "safeguard the public" by preventing ruinous competition,[11] which threatens to "[drive] smaller merchants out of business."[12] Particularly in the 1930s, when new statutes targeted predatory pricing, the welfare rationale was apparent to consumers, many of whom loathed the influx of large retailers into their communities. However, this public welfare rationale is not without scholarly criticism. For instance, some have cast doubt on the contention that sales below cost can actually eliminate competition. In most cases, such sales are ultimately unprofitable. "The predator loses money during the period of predation," so the argument goes, and "if he tries to recoup it later by raising his price, new entrants will be attracted," and the predator will be undersold.[13] The debate suggests that a better rationale of predatory pricing statutes lies in fairness and moral concerns, noted above.

Much has changed since the early predatory pricing statutes were adopted, including important shifts in the way that consumers purchase most goods and services. Large, national retailers control a larger share of the market. For instance, one study found that CVS and Walgreens together control between 50 and 75 percent of the drugstore market in the nation's largest metropolitan areas.[14] Consumers are now able to purchase goods online, allowing quick and easy comparisons of price, and generally forestalling the possibility of territorial price discrimination. Despite these important changes, the states' predatory pricing statutes largely remain unchanged. As retail habits continue to evolve in the 21st century, it's an open question whether predatory pricing statutes will continue to be relevant.

Notes

1. See William J. Haynes Jr., State Antitrust Laws 183 (1989).

2. Safeway Stores, Inc. v. Oklahoma Retail Grocers Ass'n, Inc., 360 U.S. 334, 340 (1959).

3. 15 U.S.C. § 13.

4. Donald S. Clark, Secretary of the Fed. Trade Comm'n, *The Robinson-Patman Act: Annual Update,* The Robinson-Patman Act Committee, Section of Antitrust Law, Forty-Sixth Annual Spring Meeting (Apr. 2, 1998), https://www.ftc.gov/es/public-statements/1998/04/robinson-patman-act-annual-update.

5. F.T.C. v. Anheuser-Busch, Inc., 363 U.S. 536, 543–44, 80 S. Ct. 1267, 1271, 4 L. Ed. 2d 1385 (1960).

6. Though a slight majority of states do not have criminal statutes targeting predatory pricing, some states have adopted civil statutes. Civil liability for price discrimination—Conn. Gen. Stat. Ann. § 35-45; Haw. Rev. Stat. Ann. § 481-1; Idaho Code Ann. § 48-202; Kan. Stat. Ann. § 50-149; Miss. Code. Ann. § 75-21-3; N.M. Stat. Ann. § 57-14-3; Or. Rev. Stat. Ann. § 646.040; Va. Code Ann. § 59.1-9.7. Civil liability for sales below cost—Haw. Rev. Stat. Ann. § 481-3; Idaho Code Ann. § 48-404; La. Stat. Ann. § 51:422; Me. Rev. Stat. tit. 10, § 1204-A; Md. Code Ann., Com. Law § 11-404; S.C. Code Ann. § 39-3-150; Wis. Stat. Ann. § 100.30.

7. Ark. Code Ann. § 4-75-209; Cal. Bus. & Prof. Code § 17043; Cal. Bus. & Prof. Code § 17100; Colo. Rev. Stat. Ann. § 6-2-105; Colo. Rev. Stat. Ann. § 6-2-116; Ky. Rev. Stat. Ann. § 365.030; Ky. Rev. Stat. Ann. § 365.990; Mass. Gen. Laws Ann. ch. 93, § 14F; Minn. Stat. Ann. § 325D.04; Minn. Stat. Ann. § 325D.071; Mont. Code Ann. § 30-14-209; Mont. Code Ann. § 30-14-224 Neb. Rev. Stat. Ann. § 59-805; N.D. Cent. Code Ann. § 51-10-05; Okla. Stat. Ann. tit. 15, § 598.4;

73 Pa. Stat. Ann. § 213; 73 Pa. Stat. Ann. § 214; 6 R.I. Gen. Laws Ann. § 6-13-3; Tenn. Code Ann. § 47-25-205; W. Va. Code Ann. § 47-11A-2; W. Va. Code Ann. § 47-11A-11; Wyo. Stat. Ann. § 40-4-107; Wyo. Stat. Ann. § 40-4-104.

8. Ark. Code Ann. § 4-75-207; Ark. Code Ann. § 4-75-204; Cal. Bus. & Prof. Code § 17040; Cal. Bus. & Prof. Code § 17100; Colo. Rev. Stat. Ann. § 6-2-103; Colo. Rev. Stat. Ann. § 6-2-116; Del. Code Ann. tit. 6, § 2504; Fla. Stat. Ann. § 540.01; Fla. Stat. Ann. § 540.06; Iowa Code Ann. § 551.1; Iowa Code Ann. § 551.2; Iowa Code Ann. § 551.4; Ky. Rev. Stat. Ann. § 365.020; Ky. Rev. Stat. Ann. § 365.990; La. Stat. Ann. § 51:331; La. Stat. Ann. § 51:332; Md. Code Ann., Com. Law § 11-204; Md. Code Ann., Com. Law § 11-212; Mont. Code Ann. § 30-14-207; Mont. Code Ann. § 30-14-208; Mont. Code Ann. § 30-14-224; Neb. Rev. Stat. Ann. § 59-501; Neb. Rev. Stat. Ann. § 59-503; Neb. Rev. Stat. Ann. § 59-505; N.D. Cent. Code Ann. § 51-09-01; N.D. Cent. Code Ann. § 51-09-02; Okla. Stat. Ann. tit. 79, § 204; Okla. Stat. Ann. tit. 79, § 206; S.D. Codified Laws § 37-1-4; S.D. Codified Laws § 37-1-5; S.D. Codified Laws § 37-1-7; Utah Code Ann. § 13-5-3; Utah Code Ann. § 13-5-15; Wis. Stat. Ann. § 133.04.

9. Safeway Stores, 360 U.S. at 340.

10. Tuttle v. Buck, 107 Minn. 145, 151, 119 N.W. 946, 948 (1909). In *Tuttle*, a banker allegedly sought vengeance on a barber by setting up a rival barber shop for the sole purpose of destroying the barber's business. The barber won a civil claim against the banker, which was ultimately upheld on appeal.

11. See, e.g., Cal. Bus. & Prof. Code § 17001; Colo. Rev. Stat. Ann. § 6-2-102; Utah Code Ann. § 13-5-17.

12. Vill. Food & Liquor Mart v. H & S Petroleum, Inc., 2002 WI 92, ¶ 28, 254 Wis. 2d 478, 492, 647 N.W.2d 177, 184.

13. Richard A. Posner, *The Chicago School of Antitrust Analysis,* 127 U. Pa. L. Rev. 925, 927 (1979).

14. Corey Stern, *CVS and Walgreens Are Completely Dominating the US Drugstore Industry,* Business Insider (July 29, 2015, 5:18 PM), http://www.businessinsider.com/cvs-and-walgreens-us-drugstore-market-share-2015-7.

CHAPTER THIRTY-FIVE

Organized Crime

For many decades, traditional criminal liability principles proved generally inadequate to reach the leaders of organized crime. Crime bosses could simply insulate themselves by providing general direction rather than participating in any particular offense and by giving that direction only through a few trusted lieutenants, making it difficult as a practical matter for prosecutors to make a case.

That changed in 1970 with the adoption of the federal Racketeer Influenced and Corrupt Organizations Act (RICO).[1] RICO adopted a new form of criminal liability specifically designed to criminalize certain kinds of organizations and the participation in or leadership of such organizations. Under RICO, it is a crime to "acquire or maintain any interest in or control of an enterprise" or to "conduct, or participate in, any enterprise," where the person does so "through a pattern of racketeering activity." It is also unlawful to "use or invest proceeds derived from racketeering activity to acquire interest in real property or to establish or operate any enterprise."[2]

The distinguishing feature of enterprise crime is its relation to "racketeering activity."[3] Racketeering activity differs under each state statute, but often the term includes dozens of crimes—from violent crimes, such as murder, kidnapping, and robbery; to property offenses, such as theft and trespass; to certain white-collar crimes, such as extortion, bribery, and corruption; to crimes against public health or morality, such as soliciting prostitution, pandering obscenity, and distributing child pornography.[4]

All states with shading on Map 35 have adopted their own RICO statutes. They have done so for a number of reasons. First, states have an independent interest in prosecuting organized crime, and federal authorities necessarily tend to focus their investigation and prosecution resources on the most serious criminal enterprises. Second, state RICO statutes often reach more conduct than the federal Act, not only due to textual differences in the statutes,

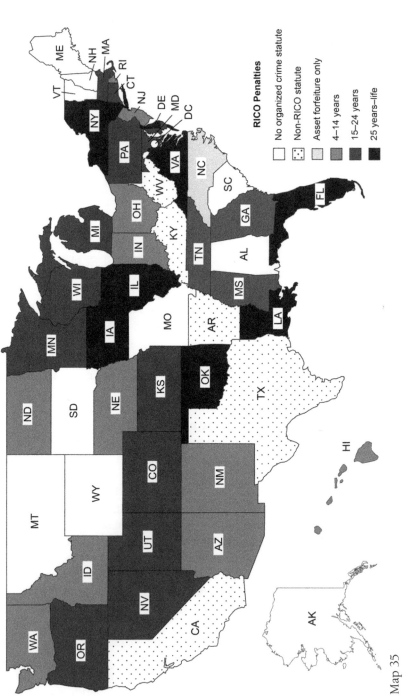

RICO Penalties

- ☐ No organized crime statute
- ⠿ Non-RICO statute
- Asset forfeiture only
- 4–14 years
- 15–24 years
- 25 years–life

Map 35

but also due to some courts' broader construction of them. In addition, many state statutes target patterns of activity involving state law offenses that are outside the scope of the federal statute, such as computer fraud, environmental offenses, and unfair competition.[5] Finally, as a matter of federal constitutional law, the federal RICO statute is only available to prosecute organized crime cases in which there is a federal interest, as with a crime family operating across state borders.

As is clear from Map 35, states take a variety of different views with regard to using RICO against organized crime. Some simply have not created state RICO offenses, while others have adopted RICO statutes but with limited penalties attached. The darker the shading on the map, the more aggressive the state RICO offense.

No Organized Crime Offense

Eleven states, identified with no shading on the map—Alabama, Alaska, District of Columbia, Maine, Missouri, Montana, New Hampshire, South Carolina, South Dakota, Vermont, and Wyoming—have not adopted a statute targeting organized crime. (However, some of these states have adopted statutes targeting specific criminal enterprises, such as street gangs and drug syndicates.[6])

Non-RICO Organized Crime Statutes

Five states, marked with dots—Arkansas, California, Kentucky, Texas, and West Virginia[7]—have not adopted statutes patterned on the comprehensive federal RICO statute but have adopted some kind of statute targeting organized crime. Under these statutes, the state typically must show that the defendant's conduct is related in some specified way to a criminal enterprise.

Arkansas's organized crime statute prohibits "engag[ing] in a continuing criminal gang, organization, or enterprise," which means that the person commits or attempts to commit at least two qualifying offenses as part of a criminal enterprise. Conviction under the organized crime statute results in a felony, the severity of which depends on the underlying offenses.[8]

California's organized crime statute targets anyone who "engage[s] in a pattern of profiteering activity," which under the statute means that the person commits or attempts to commit at least two qualifying offenses, which share a relationship of purpose or method, as part of a criminal enterprise. Upon conviction of the qualifying offenses, the statute permits the state to file a petition of forfeiture before the same court, which holds a hearing to determine whether the state may seize assets related to the defendant's enterprise.[9]

Kentucky's organized crime statute prohibits a range of conduct related to "criminal syndicate[s] or any of [their] activities," including organizing or participating in such an enterprise, providing material aid to it, managing, supervising, or directing its activities, knowingly providing professional services to it, or committing, attempting to commit, or acting as an accomplice to certain qualifying offenses in relation to the criminal syndicate. Only a handful of offenses may satisfy the standard of "criminal syndicate," including extortion, human trafficking, prostitution-related offenses, theft offenses, gambling offenses, drug offenses, and usury.[10]

Texas's statute expressly targets "criminal street gang[s]," but in fact the statute is broad enough to encompass most criminal enterprises. A person is liable under the statute if, "with the intent to establish, maintain, or participate in a combination or in the profits of a combination or as a member of a criminal street gang," the person commits or conspires to commit one or more qualifying offenses. Qualifying offenses range from violent crimes to gambling offenses, felony offenses under the tax code, prostitution-related offenses, drug offenses, obscenity offenses, offenses involving child pornography or exploitation, and others.[11]

West Virginia's statute vaguely prohibits "becom[ing] a member" of an enterprise and "knowingly promot[ing] . . . the commission of any qualifying offense." An enterprise is a group of five or more people "engaging" in one or more qualifying offenses over the course of at least six months. Qualifying offenses include insurance-related offenses, alcohol-related offenses, violent crimes, arson, burglary, theft, forgery, various sexual offenses, and others.[12]

Asset Forfeiture Only

One state, North Carolina, in light shading on the map, has adopted a statute patterned on the federal RICO statute, but the statute does not create any additional criminal liability.[13] Instead, the statute authorizes the government to initiate a separate, civil forfeiture proceeding to show by a preponderance of the evidence that the assets were involved in the criminal enterprise.

RICO with 4 to 14 Years Maximum

Eleven states, shown with medium shading on the map—Arizona, Hawaii, Idaho, Indiana, Nebraska, New Jersey, New Mexico, North Dakota, Ohio, Rhode Island, and Washington[14]—have adopted statutes patterned on the federal RICO Act which provide a maximum sentence of imprisonment on the first offense, where there are no special circumstances, that ranges from 4 years (Nebraska) to 14 years (Idaho).

RICO with 15 to 24 Years Maximum

Fifteen states, designated with dark shading on the map—Colorado, Connecticut, Georgia, Kansas, Maryland, Massachusetts, Michigan, Minnesota, Mississippi, Nevada, Oregon, Pennsylvania, Tennessee, Utah, and

Wisconsin[15]—impose a prison sentence up to some number of years between 15 and 24, inclusive. The maximum sentence is 15 years in Massachusetts, Utah, and Wisconsin, while it is 24 years in Colorado.

RICO with 25 Years to Life Maximum

Eight states, those with black coloring on the map—Delaware, Florida, Illinois, Iowa, Louisiana, New York, Oklahoma, and Virginia[16]—impose a maximum prison sentence of some number of years between 25 to life. In Delaware, Iowa, and New York, the maximum is 25 years. In Oklahoma, an offender may get life in prison on the first offense.

Observations and Speculations

The highly successful federal RICO offense, and the 35 state imitations that followed, can be understood only in the context of 20th-century organized crime in the United States. From 1920 to 1933, when there was a nationwide prohibition on the commercial sale of alcoholic beverages, gangs entered the liquor business and "transformed themselves into sophisticated criminal enterprises, skilled at smuggling, money laundering and bribing police."[17] Chief among them were those gangs that would become the American Mafia, which continued to operate after Prohibition ended. These crime "families" conducted a number of illegal activities alongside legitimate businesses, using tactics such as bribery and criminal threats to increase profits, avoid prosecution, and eliminate business competitors. Profits of organized crime would be used to buy and operate these legitimate businesses, and while law enforcement was sometimes able to prosecute an individual offender, the operation's economic base permitted the syndicate to go on. By the 1950s, there were 24 known criminal enterprises with thousands of associates.[18]

The federal RICO Act, enacted in 1970, was designed to eliminate organized crime by "crippling its financial base."[19] This it does by broadly targeting anyone who "has received any income derived, directly or indirectly, from a pattern of racketeering activity," or "use[s] or invest[s]" the proceeds of such activity to acquire interest in real property, or establishes or operates a prohibited enterprise.[20] The Act permits private parties to bring actions for treble damages, and permits the government to seize assets. It also authorizes severe criminal penalties, up to 20 years imprisonment upon conviction.[21]

States have followed the lead of the federal government. Of the 35 statutes modeled on the federal RICO, all target those who "use" or "invest" proceeds from a criminal enterprise, and all permit the government to seize assets. In addition, many state RICO statutes permit harsh prison sentences for a single offense, as noted above. Eight states set the maximum term of imprisonment at 25 or more years, including Oklahoma, which permits life imprisonment on the first offense.

By the end of 1992, RICO was credited with dismantling much of organized crime. On December 21, 1992, Victor J. Orena, known as the "acting boss of the Colombo crime family," was convicted of racketeering, the third time that year that federal prosecutors obtained a conviction of a Mafia boss in New York City.[22] The author of a 1992 article credited federal RICO in part for "unprecedented success in putting away" members of the Mafia, writing that "[n]ot one of the nation's 24 Mafia families has escaped successful prosecution in recent years, and only a few are left with their leadership intact."[23]

Notes

1. 18 U.S.C. §§ 1961 et seq.

2. 18 U.S.C. § 1962.

3. Every RICO statute uses the term "racketeering activity," except Minnesota ("criminal activity"), New York ("criminal activity"), Ohio ("corrupt activity"), Utah ("unlawful activity"), and Washington ("criminal profiteering activity"). See infra notes 13–16.

4. A few states have adopted similar statutes but have limited the underlying activity to specific criminal enterprises, such as street gangs or drug-trafficking syndicates. See, e.g., Mo. Ann. Stat. § 578.423 (targeting those who "actively [participate] in any criminal street gang with knowledge that its members . . . have engaged in a pattern of criminal street gang activity," defined to include murder, assault, robbery, arson, drug offenses, weapons offenses, and witness tampering). These statutes are excluded from consideration for purposes of this chapter.

5. John E. Floyd, *RICO State by State: A Guide to Litigation Under the State Racketeering Statutes*, 2–10 (ABA1998).

6. See, e.g., Mo. Ann. Stat. § 578.423 (targeting those who "actively [participate] in any criminal street gang with knowledge that its members . . . have engaged in a pattern of criminal street gang activity," defined to include murder, assault, robbery, arson, drug offenses, weapons offenses, and witness tampering).

7. Ark. Code Ann. § 5-74-104; Cal. Penal Code § 186.2; Cal. Penal Code § 186.3; Ky. Rev. Stat. Ann. § 506.120; Tex. Penal Code Ann. § 71.02; W. Va. Code Ann. § 61-13-3.

8. See Ark. Code Ann. § 5-74-104.

9. See Cal. Penal Code § 186.2; Cal. Penal Code § 186.3.

10. See Ky. Rev. Stat. Ann. § 506.120.

11. See Tex. Penal Code Ann. § 71.02.

12. See W. Va. Code Ann. § 61-13-2.

13. N.C. Gen. Stat. Ann. § 75D-4; N.C. Gen. Stat. Ann. § 75D-5.

14. Ariz. Rev. Stat. Ann. § 13-2312; Ariz. Rev. Stat. Ann. § 13-702; Haw. Rev. Stat. Ann. § 842-2; Haw. Rev. Stat. Ann. § 706-660; Idaho Code Ann. § 18-7804; Ind. Code Ann. § 35-45-6-2; Ind. Code Ann. § 35-50-2-6; Neb. Rev. Stat. Ann. § 28-1355; Neb. Rev. Stat. Ann. § 28-1356; Neb. Rev. Stat. Ann. § 28-105; N.J. Stat. Ann. § 2C:41-2; N.J. Stat. Ann. § 2C:41-3; N.J. Stat. Ann. § 2C:43-6; N.M.

Stat. Ann. § 31-18-15; N.D. Cent. Code Ann. § 12.1-06.1-02; N.D. Cent. Code Ann. § 12.1-06.1-03; N.D. Cent. Code Ann. § 12.1-32-01; Ohio Rev. Code Ann. § 2923.32; Ohio Rev. Code Ann. § 2929.14; 7 R.I. Gen. Laws Ann. § 7-15-2; 7 R.I. Gen. Laws Ann. § 7-15-3; Wash. Rev. Code Ann. § 9A.82.060; Wash. Rev. Code Ann. § 9A.82.080; Wash. Rev. Code Ann. § 9A.20.021.

15. Colo. Rev. Stat. Ann. § 18-17-104; Colo. Rev. Stat. Ann. § 18-17-105; Colo. Rev. Stat. Ann. § 18-1.3-401; Conn. Gen. Stat. Ann. § 53-395; Conn. Gen. Stat. Ann. § 53-397; Ga. Code Ann. § 16-14-4; Ga. Code Ann. § 16-14-5; Kan. Stat. Ann. § 21-6329; Kan. Stat. Ann. § 21-6804; Md. Code Ann., Crim. Law § 9-804; Md. Code Ann., Crim. Law § 9-801; Mass. Gen. Laws Ann. ch. 271A, § 2; Mich. Comp. Laws Ann. § 750.159i; Mich. Comp. Laws Ann. § 750.159j; Minn. Stat. Ann. § 609.903; Minn. Stat. Ann. § 609.904; Miss. Code. Ann. § 97-43-5; Miss. Code. Ann. § 97-43-7; Nev. Rev. Stat. Ann. § 207.400; Or. Rev. Stat. Ann. § 166.720; Or. Rev. Stat. Ann. § 161.605; 18 Pa. Stat. and Cons. Stat. Ann. § 911; 18 Pa. Stat. and Cons. Stat. Ann. § 1103; Tenn. Code Ann. § 39-12-204; Tenn. Code Ann. § 39-12-205; Tenn. Code Ann. § 40-35-112; Utah Code Ann. § 76-10-1603; Utah Code Ann. § 76-10-1603.5; Utah Code Ann. § 76-3-203; Wis. Stat. Ann. § 946.83; Wis. Stat. Ann. § 946.84; Wis. Stat. Ann. § 939.50.

16. Del. Code Ann. tit. 11, § 1503; Del. Code Ann. tit. 11, § 1504; Del. Code Ann. tit. 11, § 4205; Fla. Stat. Ann. § 895.03; Fla. Stat. Ann. § 895.04; Fla. Stat. Ann. § 775.082; 720 Ill. Comp. Stat. Ann. 5/33G-4; 720 Ill. Comp. Stat. Ann. 5/33G-5; Iowa Code Ann. § 706A.2; Iowa Code Ann. § 706A.4; Iowa Code Ann. § 902.9; La. Stat. Ann. § 15:1353; La. Stat. Ann. § 15:1354; N.Y. Penal Law § 460.20; N.Y. Penal Law § 70.00; Okla. Stat. Ann. tit. 22, § 1403; Okla. Stat. Ann. tit. 22, § 1404; Okla. Stat. Ann. tit. 21, § 62.1; Va. Code Ann. § 18.2-514; Va. Code Ann. § 18.2-515.

17. *Mafia in the United States,* History.com (2009), http://www.history.com /topics/mafia-in-the-united-states.

18. Id. For additional history of federal RICO and the Italian American Mafia, see Miranda Lievsay, *Containing the Uncontainable: Drawing Rico's Border with the Presumption against Extraterritoriality,* 84 Fordham L. Rev. 1735, 1739 (2016). See also Benjamin Levin, *American Gangsters: Rico, Criminal Syndicates, and Conspiracy Law as Market Control,* 48 Harv. C. R.-C. L. L. Rev. 105, 109 (2013); Lesley Suzanne Bonney, *The Prosecution of Sophisticated Urban Street Gangs: A Proper Application of RICO,* 42 Cath. U. L. Rev. 579 (1993).

19. Bonney, *The Prosecution of Sophisticated Urban Street Gangs,* at 580.

20. 18 U.S.C.A. § 1962.

21. See 18 U.S.C.A. § 1963.

22. Arnold H. Lubasch, *Acting Crime Boss Is Convicted of Murder and Racketeering,* N.Y. Times (Dec. 22, 1992), http://www.nytimes.com/1992/12/22/nyregion /acting-crime-boss-is-convicted-of-murder-and-racketeering.html.

23. Ron Nordland, *The 'Velcro Don': Wiseguys Finish Last,* Newsweek (Apr. 12, 1992), http://www.newsweek.com/velcro-don-wiseguys-finish-last-197190.

CHAPTER THIRTY-SIX

Fixing Sporting Events

Thirty-eight states—Alabama, Alaska, Arizona, California, Colorado, Connecticut, Delaware, Florida, Hawaii, Illinois, Iowa, Kansas, Kentucky, Louisiana, Maine, Massachusetts, Michigan, Minnesota, Mississippi, Missouri, Nebraska, Nevada, New Hampshire, New Jersey, New York, North Carolina, North Dakota, Oklahoma, Pennsylvania, Rhode Island, South Carolina, South Dakota, Texas, Utah, Vermont, Virginia, Washington, and Wisconsin[1]—have a general offense criminalizing commercial bribery. Commercial bribery is bribery in the private sector and specifically includes the corrupt influence of employees or other agents in relation to the employer's or principal's affairs, such as where a third party induces an employee to violate a fiduciary duty without the employer's knowledge. Think of the procurement officer who uses his employer's funds to purchase the more expensive supply, not because the supply is a better grade or quality, but because the employee has been promised a secret payment from the supplier.

Depending on the factual context and the language of the statute, commercial bribery can include bribery in sports and public contests. For instance, certain statutes broaden the scope of liability to include inducements to violate virtually any professional duty, such as Alaska's statute, which specifically prohibits such inducement of a "purportedly disinterested adjudicator or referee."[2]

Problems arise, however, where corruption lies beyond the reach of general commercial bribery statutes. In the unique context of public contests, corrupt influence not only undermines trust among officials and participants, but also the viewing public, where no contractual or fiduciary relationship may exist. Such conduct is worthy of the criminal sanction but requires special treatment in a state's criminal code if it is to be subject to liability. For example, general commercial bribery statutes in most cases do not extend to bribes intended to cause players or participants to fail to give their "best efforts" in an athletic contest, or to limit their team's margin of victory, where, strictly speaking, no professional duty is violated. Nor do commercial bribery statutes extend to bribes in amateur sports, where the players typically have no contractual or agency relationship with anyone.

Consider, for example, Arizona's general commercial bribery statute: it applies only in the context of an employer-employee relationship, where the corruption results in actual economic loss to the employer.[3] Arizona's sports-bribery statute, in contrast, covers bribes of participants and officials where the intent is "to influence [the player] to lose or try to lose or cause to be lost or to limit his or his team's margin of victory or defeat, or in the case of a referee or other official to affect his decisions or the performance of his duties in any way."[4]

Not all sports fixing involves bribery. Much of it falls under a special kind of corruption called sports tampering. These broadly written statutes cover tampering with persons, animals, or things in a manner inconsistent with the rules of the contest, and the conduct need not involve any officials or participants. For instance, a third party may be liable for criminal tampering where he sneaks into a locker room and deflates the game ball below league standards, with the intent that one team's performance be improperly enhanced or another's inhibited. Here, prosecutors may rely on specific tampering statutes to punish condemnable practices that, though not involving bribery, undermine the integrity of high-profile social institutions.

Map 36 indicates the position of each of the states with regard specific criminal prohibitions against sports bribery and sports tampering. The darker the shading on the map, the greater the coverage.

Criminalizes Bribery of Officials or Participants

Thirty-seven states, identified on the map with dark shading—Alabama, Arizona, California, Colorado, Connecticut, Delaware, District of Columbia, Florida, Hawaii, Illinois, Iowa, Kansas, Kentucky, Louisiana, Maine, Maryland, Michigan, Minnesota, Montana, Nebraska, Nevada, New Hampshire, New Jersey, New York, North Carolina, North Dakota, Ohio, Oklahoma, Oregon, Pennsylvania, Rhode Island, South Carolina, Tennessee, Texas, Utah, Washington, and Wyoming[5]—have adopted criminal statutes specifically prohibiting bribery of both officials and participants in professional and amateur sports as well as other public contests.

A sports participant includes any person whose role is to advance a particular player or team, such as players, coaches, managers, and trainers. Bribery of a participant is nearly always framed in terms of conferring a benefit on the participant in exchange for his agreement to try to lose or diminish his performance, or to fail to put forth his best efforts.

A sports official includes any person whose role is to be neutral and whose role would ordinarily permit the person to influence the outcome or result of a competition, such as a judge, referee, or umpire. Bribery of an official is

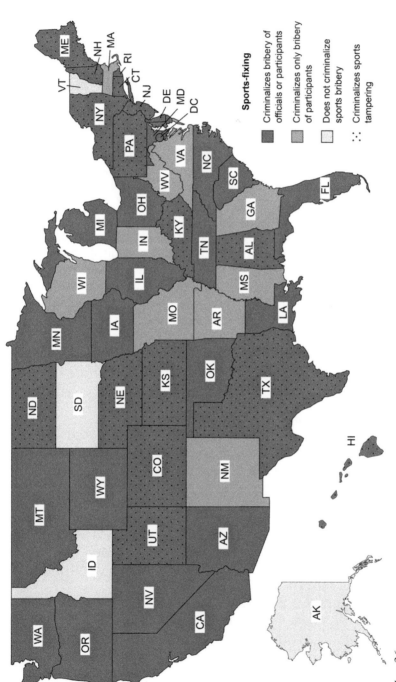

Sports-fixing

- Criminalizes bribery of officials or participants
- Criminalizes only bribery of participants
- Does not criminalize sports bribery
- ∴ Criminalizes sports tampering

Map 36

framed in terms of inducing the official to perform her duties improperly. It is not required that the participant or official successfully alter the course or result of the contest.

Many statutes, in addition to criminalizing sports bribery, also create an affirmative duty to report such bribery.[6] In other words, a failure to "blow the whistle" on a corrupt official or participant may itself lead to liability for sports bribery.

Criminalizes Only Bribery of Participants

Ten states, shown with medium shading on the map—Arkansas, Georgia, Indiana, Massachusetts, Mississippi, Missouri, New Mexico, Virginia, West Virginia, and Wisconsin[7]—have adopted criminal statutes targeting sports bribery of participants only.

Does Not Criminalize Sports Bribery

Four states, designated with light shading on the map—Alaska, Idaho, South Dakota, and Vermont—do not have special criminal statutes targeting bribery of sports participants or officials. In these states, the criminal law can only address instances of sports bribery if the conduct at issue falls under the prohibitions of the state's general commercial bribery statute.

Criminalizes Sports Tampering

Fifteen states, shown with a dots overlay on the map—Alabama, Colorado, Connecticut, Hawaii, Kansas, Kentucky, Maine, Nebraska, New Hampshire, New Jersey, New York, North Dakota, Pennsylvania, Texas, and Utah[8]—have adopted criminal statutes that criminalize "tampering" with people, animals, things, such as equipment, with the intent to prevent a public contest to be held according to the rules of play. For instance, these statutes would prohibit the deflating of footballs with the intent to confer an inappropriate advantage, or the poisoning, injuring, or drugging of a competition horse or dog with the intent to confer an inappropriate advantage or disadvantage.[9]

Observations and Speculations

Setting aside Idaho, which appears to have neither a general commercial bribery statute nor a specific sports bribery or tampering offense, every jurisdiction has some relevant offense. The differences among the states really come down to how much detail they want in order to assure that the offense will cover the possible versions of sports fixing.

It should be no surprise, then, to see that many if not most of the states with the most detailed approach—darkest shading with a dots overlay, indicating both a sports tampering and a sports bribery offense including both officials and participants—are states with active sports agendas, such as New York, Pennsylvania, and New Jersey, as well as horse-racing Kentucky and football-obsessed Alabama and Texas. There are, however, other states with active sports cultures, professional or amateur, that do not have this full coverage.

Why shouldn't a sports bribery offense cover not only corrupt participants but also corrupt officials? Why shouldn't sports tampering be specifically criminalized, in addition to sports bribery, especially since such tampering is the kind of activity that the general commercial bribery statute is less likely to capture? In the states with limited coverage, it may be simply a matter of legislative inertia. Until a major scandal breaks, the legislature may not focus on the risk of incomplete coverage or the greater difficulties of prosecuting sports fixing under their general commercial bribery statute.

Notes

1. Ala. Code § 13A-11-120; Ala. Code § 13A-11-121; Alaska Stat. Ann. § 11.46.660; Alaska Stat. Ann. § 11.46.670; Ariz. Rev. Stat. Ann. § 13-2605; Cal. Penal Code § 641.3; Colo. Rev. Stat. Ann. § 18-5-401; Conn. Gen. Stat. Ann. § 53a-160; Conn. Gen. Stat. Ann. § 53a-161; Del. Code Ann. tit. 11, § 881; Del. Code Ann. tit. 11, § 882; Fla. Stat. Ann. § 838.15; Fla. Stat. Ann. § 838.16; Haw. Rev. Stat. Ann. § 708-880; 720 Ill. Comp. Stat. Ann. 5/29A-1; 720 Ill. Comp. Stat. Ann. 5/29A-2; Iowa Code Ann. § 722.10; Kan. Stat. Ann. § 21-6506; Ky. Rev. Stat. Ann. § 518.020; Ky. Rev. Stat. Ann. § 518.030; La. Stat. Ann. § 14:73; Me. Rev. Stat. tit. 17-A, § 904; Mass. Gen. Laws Ann. ch. 271, § 39; Mich. Comp. Laws Ann. § 750.125; Mich. Comp. Laws Ann. § 750.119; Mich. Comp. Laws Ann. § 750.120; Minn. Stat. Ann. § 609.86; Miss. Code. Ann. § 97-9-10; Miss. Code. Ann. § 97-9-5; Mo. Ann. Stat. § 570.150; Neb. Rev. Stat. Ann. § 28-613; Nev. Rev. Stat. Ann. § 207.295; N.H. Rev. Stat. Ann. § 638:7; N.J. Stat. Ann. § 2C:21-10; N.Y. Penal Law § 180.00; N.Y. Penal Law § 180.03; N.Y. Penal Law § 180.05; N.Y. Penal Law § 180.08; N.C. Gen. Stat. Ann. § 14-353; N.D. Cent. Code Ann. § 12.1-12-08; Okla. Stat. Ann. tit. 21, § 380; Okla. Stat. Ann. tit. 21, § 380.1; Okla. Stat. Ann. tit. 21, § 386; 18 Pa. Stat. and Cons. Stat. Ann. § 4108; 11 R.I. Gen. Laws Ann. § 11-7-3; 11 R.I. Gen. Laws Ann. § 11-7-4; 11 R.I. Gen. Laws Ann. § 11-7-5; S.C. Code Ann. § 16-17-540; S.D. Codified Laws § 22-43-1; S.D. Codified Laws § 22-43-2; Tex. Penal Code Ann. § 32.43; Utah Code Ann. § 76-6-508; Vt. Stat. Ann. tit. 13, § 1108; Va. Code Ann. § 18.2-444; Wash. Rev. Code Ann. § 9A.68.060; Wis. Stat. Ann. § 134.05.

2. Alaska Stat. Ann. § 11.46.660.
3. See Ariz. Rev. Stat. Ann. S 13-2605.
4. Ariz. Rev. Stat. Ann. S 13-2309.

5. Ala. Code § 13A-11-141; Ala. Code § 13A-11-142; Ariz. Rev. Stat. Ann. § 13-2309; Cal. Penal Code § 337b; Cal. Penal Code § 337c; Cal. Penal Code § 337d; Cal. Penal Code § 337e; Colo. Rev. Stat. Ann. § 18-5-402; Conn. Gen. Stat. Ann. § 53a-162; Del. Code Ann. tit. 11, § 881; Del. Code Ann. tit. 11, § 882; D.C. Code Ann. § 22-1713; Fla. Stat. Ann. § 838.12; Haw. Rev. Stat. Ann. § 708-881; 720 Ill. Comp. Stat. Ann. 5/29-1; 720 Ill. Comp. Stat. Ann. 5/29-2; 720 Ill. Comp. Stat. Ann. 5/29-3; Iowa Code Ann. § 722.3; Kan. Stat. Ann. § 21-6507; Ky. Rev. Stat. Ann. § 518.040; Ky. Rev. Stat. Ann. § 518.050; La. Stat. Ann. § 14:118.1; Me. Rev. Stat. tit. 17-A, § 904; Md. Code Ann., Crim. Law § 9-205; Mich. Comp. Laws Ann. § 750.124; Minn. Stat. Ann. § 609.825; Mont. Code Ann. § 45-8-214; Nev. Rev. Stat. Ann. § 207.290; Neb. Rev. Stat. Ann. § 28-614; N.H. Rev. Stat. Ann. § 638:8; N.J. Stat. Ann. § 2C:21-11; N.Y. Penal Law § 180.40; N.Y. Penal Law § 180.45; N.C. Gen. Stat. Ann. § 14-373; N.C. Gen. Stat. Ann. § 14-374; N.C. Gen. Stat. Ann. § 14-375; N.C. Gen. Stat. Ann. § 14-376; N.C. Gen. Stat. Ann. § 14-377; N.D. Cent. Code Ann. § 12.1-12-07; Ohio Rev. Code Ann. § 2915.05; Okla. Stat. Ann. tit. 21, § 399; Okla. Stat. Ann. tit. 21, § 400; Okla. Stat. Ann. tit. 21, § 386; Or. Rev. Stat. Ann. § 165.085; Or. Rev. Stat. Ann. § 165.090; 18 Pa. Stat. and Cons. Stat. Ann. § 4109; 11 R.I. Gen. Laws Ann. § 11-7-9; 11 R.I. Gen. Laws Ann. § 11-7-10; 11 R.I. Gen. Laws Ann. § 11-7-12; S.C. Code Ann. § 16-17-550; Tenn. Code Ann. § 39-17-1103; Tex. Penal Code Ann. § 32.44; Utah Code Ann. § 76-6-514; Wash. Rev. Code Ann. § 9A.82.070; Wyo. Stat. Ann. § 6-3-609. In Louisiana, participant is defined broadly enough to include officials. See La. Stat. Ann. § 14:118.1 (prohibiting "any person . . . who participates . . . , including . . . judges, . . . or special policemen, . . . with the intent to influence him . . . corruptly to affect or influence the result . . .").

6. See, e.g., 11 R.I. Gen. Laws Ann. § 11-7-12; 720 Ill. Comp. Stat. Ann. 5/29-3.

7. Ark. Code Ann. § 5-66-115; Ga. Code Ann. § 16-12-33; Ga. Code Ann. § 16-12-34; Ind. Code Ann. § 35-44.1-1-2; Mass. Gen. Laws Ann. ch. 271, § 39A; Miss. Code. Ann. § 97-29-17; Mo. Ann. Stat. § 578.399; Mo. Ann. Stat. § 578.398; N.M. Stat. Ann. § 30-19-13; Va. Code Ann. § 18.2-442; Va. Code Ann. § 18.2-443; W. Va. Code Ann. § 61-10-22; Wis. Stat. Ann. § 945.08.

8. Ala. Code § 13A-11-143; Colo. Rev. Stat. Ann. § 18-5-402; Conn. Gen. Stat. Ann. § 53a-162; Haw. Rev. Stat. Ann. § 708-881; Kan. Stat. Ann. § 21-6508; Ky. Rev. Stat. Ann. § 518.060; Me. Rev. Stat. tit. 17-A, § 901; Neb. Rev. Stat. Ann. § 28-614; N.H. Rev. Stat. Ann. § 638:8; N.J. Stat. Ann. § 2C:21-11; N.Y. Penal Law § 180.35; N.Y. Penal Law § 180.50; N.Y. Penal Law § 180.51; N.D. Cent. Code Ann. § 12.1-12-07; 18 Pa. Stat. and Cons. Stat. Ann. § 4109; Tex. Penal Code Ann. § 32.44; Utah Code Ann. § 76-6-514.

In Maine, tampering is criminalized only through the state's deceptive business practices statute, which prohibits sponsoring a public contest with the knowledge that the contest has been subject to such tampering. See Me. Rev. Stat. tit. 17-A, S 901.

9. Maine's statute targets only those who knowingly sponsor an event where such tampering has taken place. See Me. Rev. Stat. tit. 17-A, S 901.

PART 10

Procedural Issues

CHAPTER THIRTY-SEVEN

Extradition

After a person commits an offense, especially a serious offense to which serious punishment attaches, it is not uncommon for the person to flee the state. Because it is the states, rather than the federal government, that are given the police power under the Constitution, most offenses are state offenses for which only the state authorities have jurisdiction to prosecute. (Federal offenses are limited to instances of special federal interest, such as assaulting a federal officer or engaging in interstate criminal activity.) Because states are independent sovereigns, the officials of the state pursuing the fugitive cannot simply go to the receiving state and arrest the suspect. They must instead request the other state to capture, detain, and return the person—they must request the fugitive's "extradition" back to the state where the crime occurred.

Whether to agree to such extradition, however, is not left to the discretion of the state to which the fugitive flees. The United States Constitution, in Article IV, Section II, Clause 2 (the Extradition Clause), obliges each state to extradite a fugitive upon the request of a state that has jurisdiction to prosecute.[1] Federal legislation, under 18 U.S.C. § 3182, implements this constitutional provision.[2] The details of the extradition process are often governed by the Uniform Criminal Extradition Act (UCEA), which many states have adopted. These details may be different for different states depending on the implementing legislation adopted by the state.

Federal agents also may get involved in interstate extradition processes through 18 U.S.C. § 1073, which creates the federal crime of Unlawful Flight to Avoid Prosecution (UFAP). The offense is used less as a basis for federal prosecution and more as a basis for federal jurisdiction to return a suspect to the site of the crime without having to use the state extradition process.

The extradition process generally depends on the FBI's fugitive tracking database known as the National Crime Information Center (NCIC). Rather

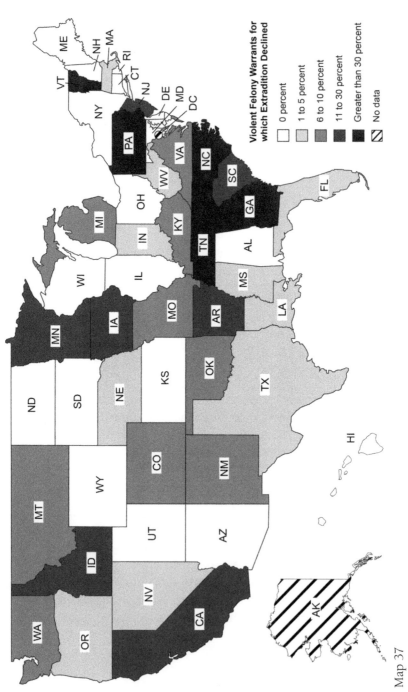

Violent Felony Warrants for which Extradition Declined

- 0 percent
- 1 to 5 percent
- 6 to 10 percent
- 11 to 30 percent
- Greater than 30 percent
- No data

Map 37

than actually chasing after fugitives, states typically simply register their warrant with NCIC, then wait for the fugitive to pop up on the system when some law enforcement agency somewhere has contact with the fugitive.

Interestingly, some states don't want to bother with the expense or the legal hassle of bringing the fugitive back to the state of his or her crime, so they will flag their warrant in the NCIC database as "nonextraditable." This happens even in the case of violent felonies, such as murder, non-negligent manslaughter, forcible rape, robbery, and aggravated assault. One report found, for instance, that police in certain major cities like Philadelphia and Atlanta will not bother to extradite as much as 90 percent or more of their felony suspects. Los Angeles police said they would not extradite 77 people wanted for murder or attempted murder. Among those the police would not pursue: a man accused of attacking his roommate with a machete; a man who allegedly threatened a store manager with a gun in the course of a robbery; and a man identified as one of Pittsburgh's "most wanted" fugitives.[3]

Map 37 presents the percentage of the total warrants for violent crimes of this sort where law enforcement agencies of the state have decided not to pursue extradition. The darker the shading on the map, the greater the percent of fugitive violent felons for which extradition is not requested.

Extradition Sought for All Violent Felony Warrants

Eighteen states, identified on the map with no shading—Alabama, Arizona, Connecticut, Delaware, Hawaii, Illinois, Kansas, Maine, Maryland, North Dakota, New Hampshire, New York, Ohio, Rhode Island, South Dakota, Utah, Wisconsin, and Wyoming[4]—sought extradition for all of their outstanding violent felony warrants.

Extradition Declined for 1 to 5 Percent of Violent Felony Warrants

Ten states, shown with light shading on the map—Florida, Indiana, Louisiana, Massachusetts, Mississippi, Nebraska, Nevada, Oregon, Texas, and West Virginia[5]—declined extradition for 1 to 5 percent of their violent felony warrants.

Extradition Declined for 6 to 10 Percent of Violent Felony Warrants

Nine states, marked with medium shading on the map—Colorado, Kentucky, Michigan, Missouri, Montana, New Mexico, Oklahoma, Virginia, and Washington[6]—declined extradition for between 6 and 10 percent of their violent felony warrants.

Extradition Declined for 11 to 30 Percent of Violent Felony Warrants

Seven states, those with dark shading on the map—Arkansas, California, Idaho, Iowa, Minnesota, New Jersey, and South Carolina[7]—declined extradition for between 11 and 30 percent of their violent felony warrants.

Extradition Declined for Greater Than 30 Percent of Violent Felony Warrants

Five states, those with black shading on the map—Georgia, North Carolina, Pennsylvania, Tennessee, and Vermont[8]—declined extradition for greater than 30 percent of their violent felony warrants.

Observations and Speculations

The practice of listing violent felony warrants on NCIC as "nonextraditable" does seem like a peculiar practice. Not only are these states not pursuing their violent fugitives themselves; they are not bothering to collect them when someone else detains them.

The most obvious troubling aspect of the practice is the apparent indifference to the importance of doing justice that it reveals. If the state has the evidence required to support a felony warrant, doesn't it have at least a moral obligation to pursue the case further? Presumably they would pursue the case if the fugitive happens to be found in their state—if not, presumably they would simply withdraw the warrant altogether—but they can't be bothered if justice involves the inconvenience of returning the fugitive from another state? If the underlying felony offense is really so minor that it does not deserve the pursuit of the fugitive, then perhaps the state ought to reform its criminal codes to drop such offenses from the felony classification.

Also quite unsettling is the message that this practice sends to other states. Apparently, the sending states that are declining extradition are happy to have their fugitives remain in other states. The problem, of course, is that these other states have no legal basis for detaining the dangerous fugitive—only the sending state has that authority—so the state to which the felon has fled must simply tolerate having the dangerous fugitive in their midst until he victimizes someone else, which will give that state the authority to deal with him. This suggests something of a lack of empathy for the citizens and law enforcement of the receiving state.

If one were cynical, one could see such declined-extradition policies as similar to the old Western sheriff telling the gunfighters to "get out of Dodge." The message is: as long as you get out of our state and thus stop victimizing our citizens, we won't pursue you. Especially to hardened professional criminals, this may be a message quickly and easily understood. But the selfish states who send this message and thereby encourage the dangerous to victimize elsewhere, ought to worry about the corollary message: if you want to commit a violent crime and minimize your chances of getting caught and punished, be sure to commit the crime in one of these nonextraditing states, so you can flee without having to worry about being pursued.

A better approach would be for all states to take seriously their moral and legal obligations to do justice, as well as their moral and ethical obligations to other states to pursue all violent felony fugitives.

Notes

1. The Extradition Clause reads:

A person charged in any state with treason, felony, or other crime, who shall flee from justice, and be found in another state, shall on demand of the executive authority of the state from which he fled, be delivered up, to be removed to the state having jurisdiction of the crime.
U.S. Const. art. IV, § 2, cl. 2.

2. It reads as follows:

Whenever the executive authority of any State or Territory demands any person as a fugitive from justice, of the executive authority of any State, District, or Territory to which such person has fled, and produces a copy of an indictment found or an affidavit made before a magistrate of any State or Territory, charging the person demanded with having committed treason, felony, or other crime, certified as authentic by the governor or chief magistrate of the State or Territory from whence the person so charged has fled, the executive authority of the State, District, or Territory to which such person has fled shall cause him to be arrested and secured, and notify the executive authority making such demand, or the agent of such authority appointed to receive the fugitive, and shall cause the fugitive to be delivered to such agent when he shall appear. If no such agent appears within thirty days from the time of the arrest, the prisoner may be discharged.
18 U.S.C.A. § 3182.

3. See Brad Heath, *The Ones That Get Away,* USA Today (Mar. 11, 2014), https://www.usatoday.com/story/news/nation/2014/03/11/fugitives-next-door/6262719.
4. Based on data from the FBI's fugitive tracking database known as the National Crime Information Center. See Heath, supra note 3.
5. Id.
6. Id.
7. Id.
8. Id.

CHAPTER THIRTY-EIGHT

Jurisdiction

Each state commonly has jurisdiction to prosecute only offenses committed within its borders. California generally cannot prosecute a murder committed in Nevada, and vice versa. However, sometimes offenses are committed or have effect in more than one state. For instance, a California murder is planned and organized in Nevada. Or the victim of a Nevada attack flees to California before dying. Or the governor of California is shot while vacationing in Nevada. Does California have jurisdiction in these three cases? As Map 38 makes clear, different states take different approaches to defining the breadth of their criminal jurisdiction. They might define it so as to allow them to prosecute in one or another or all of the examples above. The focus of this chapter is the general issue of how much of an offense, if any, must be committed within a state in order for the state to exercise territorial jurisdiction, at least where no other, more specific rule applies.[1] The darker the shading in the map, the broader the jurisdiction that state claims.

Requires Essential Offense Element

Five states, shown with no shading on the map—Kansas, Maryland, Nebraska, North Carolina, and West Virginia[2]—will exercise territorial jurisdiction over a criminal defendant where an "essential" element or elements of the offense "occurred within" the state. As one Maryland court explained, the law "does not permit prosecution . . . in every jurisdiction in which an element of the offense takes place." Rather, courts "generally [focus] on one element, which is deemed 'essential' or 'key' or 'vital' or the 'gravamen' of the offense, and the offense may be prosecuted only in a jurisdiction where that essential or key element takes place."[3] In practice, which elements are deemed "essential," and which ones nonessential, are matters for the courts of each state.

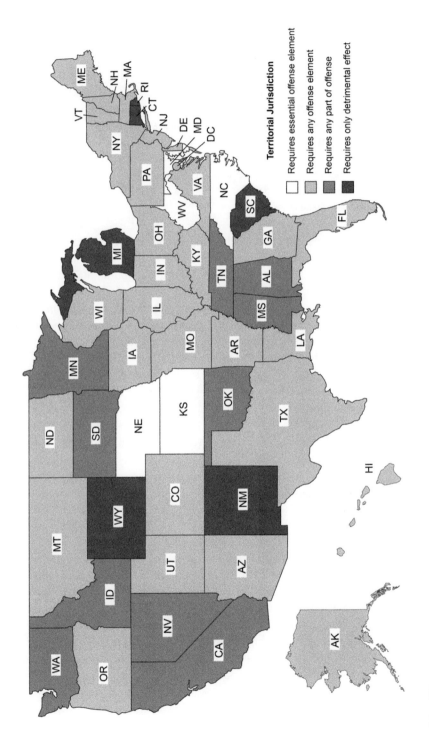

WA
OR
CA
NV
ID
MT
WY
UT
CO
AZ
NM
ND
SD
NE
KS
OK
TX
MN
IA
MO
AR
LA
WI
IL
MI
IN
OH
KY
TN
MS
AL
GA
FL
SC
NC
VA
WV
PA
NY
VT
ME
NH
MA
RI
CT
NJ
DE
MD
DC
AK
HI
Territorial Jurisdiction
Requires essential offense element
Requires any offense element
Requires any part of offense
Requires only detrimental effect

Map 38

The notion that certain elements are crucial for jurisdiction is an old idea, one gradually supplanted by modern statutes asserting broader territorial jurisdiction. At common law, for instance, some courts held that the essential element of homicide is the impact on the victim's body causing the death, not the conduct causing the impact.[4] In bigamy prosecutions, courts held that subsequent cohabitation with the second spouse is not enough for jurisdiction, because the "gist" of the offense is the state where the second marriage was actually solemnized.[5] Gradually, states recognized an interest in punishing defendants where little or no criminal conduct occurred within the state if the harmful impact of the offense was felt there.

Requires Any Offense Element

Thirty jurisdictions, designated with light shading on the map—Alaska, Arizona, Arkansas, Colorado, Delaware, District of Columbia, Florida, Georgia, Hawaii, Illinois, Indiana, Iowa, Kentucky, Louisiana, Maine, Massachusetts, Missouri, Montana, New Hampshire, New Jersey, New York, North Dakota, Ohio, Oregon, Pennsylvania, Texas, Utah, Vermont, Virginia, and Wisconsin[6]—exercise territorial jurisdiction where any element of the offense has occurred within the boundaries of the jurisdiction. In these states, the courts do not attempt to distinguish the more and less "essential" or "material" elements of an offense—the occurrence of any element is sufficient. Twenty-four of these jurisdictions have adopted the Model Penal Code formulation, which permits territorial jurisdiction when "either the conduct that is an element of the offense or the result that is such an element occurs within [the] state."[7] The other six jurisdictions provide that the occurrence of "an[y] element" within the boundaries of the jurisdiction will suffice.[8]

Requires Any Part of Offense

Ten states, marked on the map with medium shading—Alabama, California, Idaho, Minnesota, Mississippi, Nevada, Oklahoma, South Dakota, Tennessee, and Washington[9]—authorize territorial jurisdiction where any part of the offense has occurred within the boundaries of the state, even where a "part" of the offense does not satisfy any offense element. For instance, repeated assaults over a period of hours may result in the death of the victim, even though no single assault is alone sufficient to satisfy the conduct element of homicide. A court might find that any single assault is "part" of the homicide offense and would suffice for jurisdiction. Likewise, a defendant's mere preparations for an offense (short of the conduct that would constitute a criminal attempt) do not satisfy any offense element, but a court may view such preparations as "part" of an offense. Seven states allow criminal liability where the defendant "commit[s], in whole or in part, any crime within" the state.[10] Three states do not use the language of "whole" or "part," but allow jurisdiction when the offense is either "commenced" in the state or is "consummated" there.[11]

Requires Only Detrimental Effect

Six states, with dark shading on the map—Connecticut, Michigan, New Mexico, Rhode Island, South Carolina, and Wyoming[12]—generally permit jurisdiction over a criminal defendant even where no part of the offense itself takes place in the state, provided that the offense at least produces some detrimental effect there. For instance, where an Arizona defendant used a New Mexico victim's personal information without the victim's consent, the defendant may be liable in New Mexico, even where the court does not find that any part of the offense took place there.[13] Or where a diver illegally obtained sponges off the Florida coast and outside the territorial limits of Florida, the state nevertheless may exercise jurisdiction over the criminal offense, because the state "has an interest in the proper maintenance of the sponge fishery."[14]

The far-reaching rule adopted by these states originated in *Strassheim v. Daily*, a 1911 decision in the U.S. Supreme Court, which held that Michigan could convict an Illinois defendant who unlawfully defrauded the government of the State of Michigan, even though the defendant "never had set foot in the state until after the fraud was complete."[15] The Court held that "[a]cts done outside a jurisdiction, but intended to produce and actually producing detrimental effects within it, justify a state in punishing the cause of the harm as if [the defendant] had been present at the effect."[16] Though the decision should be read as expressing the outer limits of a state's constitutional exercise of territorial jurisdiction, several states have effectively adopted the Court's statement,[17] or variations of it,[18] as their general rule.

As broad as it is, the *Strassheim* standard has limits, at least where courts have taken a narrow view of it. For instance, where a Georgia cocaine dealer agreed to deliver cocaine to a Virginia buyer in Georgia, a South Carolina appellate court held that there could be no jurisdiction over the Georgia dealer, even though the dealer might have inferred that the buyers would transport the cocaine through South Carolina after the transaction. The arrest of the buyers in South Carolina was not enough to meet the *Strassheim* standard, which it construed to require defendant's "intent" that the transaction "have a detrimental effect within South Carolina."[19]

Observations and Speculations

Over the course of the 20th century, the law of territorial jurisdiction decisively shifted from one of narrow jurisdiction to broad: many more states today assert jurisdiction where states would not have asserted jurisdiction a century ago. Consider Maryland, a state with an older view of territorial jurisdiction. According to the Maryland court opinion quoted above, state law does not permit prosecution in some cases even where an element of the offense took place within the state. For contrast, consider the extraordinarily broad standard applied in the above Florida case,[20] permitting the state to target offenses that occur entirely outside its boundaries.

The older view represents the historical "strict territorial" principle, under which "only one state could have jurisdiction over a particular crime."[21] Jurisdiction over an offense was a matter of exclusivity. When an offense occurred only in part within the territory, courts had to decide which portion of the offense should control jurisdiction. In theory, there would never be overlapping jurisdiction. The Maryland view limits the power of state law enforcement and harkens back to an era when states would not prosecute homicides except in the state where the mortal wound or blow was inflicted.[22] In the first half of the 20th century, U.S. Supreme Court decisions paved the way for expanded jurisdiction,[23] which states were happy to assert. The Model Penal Code drafters understood the trend,[24] and section 1.03 of the Model Code eventually prompted a majority of states to adopt the "any element" principle.[25]

It remains to be seen whether the trend toward broader territorial jurisdiction will continue. There is certainly room to expand in this direction, for as things stand, only a handful of states have essentially extended territorial jurisdiction to the limits of due process. The Model Penal Code Commentaries acknowledge, for instance, that the provision in section 1.03 fails to reach certain risk-creation offenses, where the only territorial nexus is that the conduct creates the risk within the state, and the risk does not materialize.[26] If the trend toward broader jurisdiction continues, we would expect new codes to assert jurisdiction in such cases.

But even if the trend toward expanded territorial jurisdiction did not continue, the current state of affairs is one that has had a dramatic effect. Unlike the more limited territoriality of the old view, today jurisdiction over many offenses is no longer exclusive but rather overlapping. And overlapping *jurisdiction* between or among states means overlapping *obligations* of potential offenders. A person's sale in Virginia to a buyer in Georgia is subject to the demands of at least three sovereigns: the states of Virginia and Georgia, and the federal government. And if the person's conduct produces a detrimental effect in South Carolina, a fourth body of criminal law may impose yet further demands.[27]

In other words, the modern expanded view of criminal jurisdiction gives greater practical importance to the subject of this volume: the enormous diversity in criminal law among the states. "Since the commands and the excuses of the penal law may vary with the jurisdiction," as this volume makes clear, "there is danger of inconsistent obligations if one's conduct is governed by a multiplicity of legal systems."[28]

While variations across the 50 states may have been primarily a matter of academic and legislative interest under the earlier regime, as state criminal jurisdiction has become more overlapping, the wide array of disagreements documented in this volume creates increasing dangers and difficulties. In the new world of overlapping jurisdiction, perhaps the variations among the states ought to be carefully considered and scrutinized, at least in an effort to reduce the differences to those for which there is some principled and rational explanation.

Notes

1. The law of jurisdiction at first glance is a simple issue: what parts of an offense generally must take place within the state in order for the state to exercise jurisdiction? For instance, the Model Penal Code drafters offer a simple rule in § 1.03(1)(a), that where no more specific rule controls, then there is jurisdiction over an offense where "either the conduct which is an element of the offense or the result which is such an element occurs within th[e] state." No state, however, leaves the matter at that. The issue is made complex by a number of specific rules covering attempts, conspiracies, complicity, and still other specific offenses, such as failure to provide child support. The Model Penal Code does this as well. After the simple rule in § 1.03(1)(a), the remaining provisions under § 1.03 are more specific rules, governing attempts in subsection (1)(b), conspiracies in subsection (1)(c), complicity and inchoate offenses targeting another jurisdiction in subsection (1)(d), omissions in subsection (1)(e), and offenses "which expressly prohibit conduct outside the State" in subsection (1)(f). Further refinements to the rules are provided in subsections (2) through (5). The focus of this chapter, however, is the simple rule in § 1.03(1)(a), and the variations on that rule among the states. (Six states do not have any variation of the rule—that is, no part of an offense needs to have occurred within the state in order for the state to exercise territorial jurisdiction. See infra notes 15–18 and accompanying text.)

2. Kan. Stat. Ann. § 21-5106; West v. State, 369 Md. 150, 161, 797 A.2d 1278, 1284 (2002) (holding that "the offense may be prosecuted only in a jurisdiction where [the] essential or key element [of the offense] takes place," except in rare cases where there are multiple essential elements); State v. Butler, 353 Md. 67, 78, 724 A.2d 657, 662 (1999); State v. Red Kettle, 239 Neb. 317, 327–28, 476 N.W.2d 220, 227 (1991); State v. Hilpert, 213 Neb. 564, 575, 330 N.W.2d 729, 736 (1983) (holding that jurisdiction is available when "an essential element of the crime is committed or occurs in" the state); State v. Lalinde, 231 N.C. App. 308, 311, 750 S.E.2d 868, 871 (2013) (holding that jurisdiction is permitted when "an essential element of [the] crime occurred" in the state); State v. Tucker, 227 N.C. App. 627, 633, 743 S.E.2d 55, 59 (2013); State v. Dennis, 216 W. Va. 331, 346, 607 S.E.2d 437, 452 (2004). Note that Kansas's statute expressly permits the "proximate result" of an act to qualify as a "material" element. See Kan.

Stat. Ann. § 21-5106. Note also that Kansas and West Virginia require a "material" element.

3. West v. State, 369 Md. 150, 161, 797 A.2d 1278, 1284 (2002).

4. See State v. Hall, 114 N.C. 909, 19 S.E. 602, 602 (1894) (holding that North Carolina had no jurisdiction over a North Carolina defendant who fired fatal shots into Tennessee, where the victims died).

5. See Wilson v. State, 16 Okla. Crim. 471, 184 P. 603, 604 (1919).

6. Wheat v. State, 734 P.2d 1007, 1009–10 (Alaska Ct. App. 1987); Ariz. Rev. Stat. Ann. § 13-108; Ark. Code Ann. § 5-1-104; Colo. Rev. Stat. Ann. § 18-1-201; Del. Code Ann. tit. 11, § 204; Dyson v. United States, 848 A.2d 603, 610 (D.C. 2004); United States v. Baish, 460 A.2d 38, 40 (D.C. 1983); Fla. Stat. Ann. § 910.005; Ga. Code Ann. § 17-2-1; Haw. Rev. Stat. Ann. § 701-106; 720 Ill. Comp. Stat. Ann. 5/1-5; Ind. Code Ann. § 35-41-1-1; Iowa Code Ann. § 803.1; Ky. Rev. Stat. Ann. § 500.060; La. Code Crim. Proc. Ann. art. 611; Me. Rev. Stat. tit. 17-A, § 7; Com. v. Armstrong, 73 Mass. App. Ct. 245, 251, 897 N.E.2d 105, 110 (2008); Mo. Ann. Stat. § 541.191; Mont. Code Ann. § 46-2-101; N.H. Rev. Stat. Ann. § 625:4; N.J. Stat. Ann. § 2C:1-3; N.Y. Crim. Proc. Law § 20.20; State v. Tinsley, 325 N.W.2d 177, 179 (N.D. 1982); Ohio Rev. Code Ann. § 2901.11; Or. Rev. Stat. Ann. § 131.215; 18 Pa. Stat. and Cons. Stat. Ann. § 102; Tex. Penal Code Ann. § 1.04; Utah Code Ann. § 76-1-201; State v. Doyen, 165 Vt. 43, 49, 676 A.2d 345, 348 (1996); Romero v. Com., No. 0050-13-4, 2014 WL 1227696, at *10 (Va. Ct. App. Mar. 25, 2014); Wis. Stat. Ann. § 939.03.

7. Model Penal Code § 1.03(1)(a). These states are Alaska, Arizona, Arkansas, Colorado, Delaware, Florida, Georgia, Hawaii, Illinois, Indiana, Iowa, Kentucky, Maine, Missouri, Montana, New Hampshire, New Jersey, New York, Oregon, Pennsylvania, Texas, Utah, Vermont, and Virginia.

8. These jurisdictions are District of Columbia, Louisiana, Massachusetts, North Dakota, Ohio, and Wisconsin.

9. Ala. Code § 15-2-3; Ala. Code § 15-2-4; Cal. Penal Code § 27; Idaho Code Ann. § 18-202; Minn. Stat. Ann. § 609.025; Miss. Code. Ann. § 99-11-15; Miss. Code. Ann. § 99-11-17; Nev. Rev. Stat. Ann. § 194.020; Okla. Stat. Ann. tit. 21, § 151; State v. Winckler, 260 N.W.2d 356, 360 (S.D. 1977); Tenn. Code Ann. § 39-11-103; Wash. Rev. Code Ann. § 9A.04.030.

10. These jurisdictions are California, Idaho, Minnesota, Nevada, Oklahoma, South Dakota, and Washington.

11. These jurisdictions are Alabama, Mississippi, and Tennessee.

12. State v. Ross, 230 Conn. 183, 646 A.2d 1318 (1994); State v. Turner, No. HHDCR09632655, 2011 WL 4424754, at *2 (Conn. Super. Ct. Sept. 6, 2011); Mich. Comp. Laws Ann. § 762.2; State v. Allen, 2014-NMCA-111, ¶ 18, 336 P.3d 1007, 1013–14; State v. Kane, 625 A.2d 1361, 1364 (R.I. 1993); State v. Dudley, 354 S.C. 514, 525, 581 S.E.2d 171, 177 (Ct. App. 2003); Dawes v. State, 2010 WY 113, ¶ 15, 236 P.3d 303, 307 (Wyo. 2010); Rios v. State, 733 P.2d 242, 249 (Wyo. 1987).

13. See State v. Allen, 2014-NMCA-111, ¶ 6, 336 P.3d 1007, 1010. As a practical matter, states that require more to assert jurisdiction could achieve the same result by construing the elements of the statute differently, or by adopting a rule

specific to the identity-theft statute. In the New Mexico case, for instance, the lower court apparently held that the element "without consent" in some sense "occurred" within New Mexico, while the appellate court avoided the problem altogether, holding that a detrimental effect was enough.

14. Skiriotes v. State of Florida, 313 U.S. 69, 75, 61 S. Ct. 924, 928, 85 L. Ed. 1193 (1941). Florida has since adopted the standard supplied in the Model Penal Code. See Fla. Stat. Ann. § 910.005.

15. Strassheim v. Daily, 221 U.S. 280, 285, 31 S. Ct. 558, 560, 55 L. Ed. 735 (1911).

16. Strassheim, 221 U.S. at 285.

17. South Carolina has held that jurisdiction is available for offenses "intended to produce and producing detrimental effects" within the state. State v. Dudley, 354 S.C. 514, 528–29, 581 S.E.2d 171, 178–79 (Ct. App. 2003).

18. New Mexico has interpreted Strassheim to permit jurisdiction where the "crime has a detrimental effect in [the] state." State v. Allen, 2014-NMCA-111, ¶ 18, 336 P.3d 1007, 1013–14. Rhode Island courts have held that jurisdiction is permitted where the offense "produce[d] a detrimental effect within Rhode Island." State v. Kane, 625 A.2d 1361, 1364 (R.I. 1993). Michigan will exercise jurisdiction where the offense produces some harm to the state or people within the state, Mich. Comp. Laws Ann. § 762.2, and Wyoming will do so where the acts "produce an[y] effect within the state." Rios v. State, 733 P.2d 242, 249 (Wyo. 1987). Connecticut will exercise jurisdiction where there is a "factual nexus" between the case and the state, and where the case is "closely tied to public welfare of the state." State v. Ross, 230 Conn. 183, 646 A.2d 1318 (1994).

19. See State v. Dudley, 354 S.C. 514, 533 (Ct. App. 2003).

20. See supra note 17 and accompanying text.

21. State v. Allen, 2014-NMCA-111, ¶ 15, 336 P.3d 1007, 1012.

22. See, e.g., Commonwealth v. Apkins, 148 Ky. 207, 146 S.W. 431, 433 (1912) (holding that, where poison was administered in Ohio but death resulted in Kentucky, Kentucky had no jurisdiction, because "[t]he wrong was done" in Ohio).

23. See supra notes 17 and 18.

24. The Model Penal Code § 1.03 was drafted "[o]n the premise that it is particularly desirable in a federated state to increase jurisdictional options," within the limits of fairness. Model Penal Code and Commentaries § 1.03 at 35 (1985). The code therefore prescribed "broad" jurisdictional bases. Id.

25. See supra notes 9–11 and accompanying text.

26. Model Penal Code and Commentaries § 1.03 cmt. 4, at 52 (1985).

27. Cf. State v. Dudley, 354 S.C. 514, 533 (Ct. App. 2003) (involving a Virginia sale to a buyer in Georgia with detrimental effects in South Carolina).

28. Model Penal Code and Commentaries § 1.03 cmt. 1, at 38 (1985). In contrast, the strict territorial principle "yields some safeguard against the unfair condemnation of conduct that is approved or tolerated by the community in which the acts involved occurred." Id.

Index

Jurisdiction, territorial (*cont.*)
Model Penal Code, 314; overlapping jurisdiction, 314; strict territorial principle, 314; trend toward broader jurisdiction, 312, 314

Jury nullification, 155

Justice. *See* Deontological desert; Desert; Empirical desert; Moral intuitions

Justification defenses, 133; excuses vs., 135–136. *See also* Law enforcement authority; Lesser evils defense; Self-defense

Juveniles. *See* Children

Law enforcement authority, 150–155; deadly force and, 150; deadly force, mistake as to justification, all-or-nothing approach, 151–155; deadly force, mistake as to justification, jury nullification, 155; deadly force, mistake as to justification, principle of proportionality and, 153–155; deadly force, mistake as to justification, sliding-scale approach, 151–155; deadly force, objective formulation, 153–154; deadly force, rule articulation function, 154; deadly force, subjective formulation, 151–154; deadly force, triggering conditions, 150. *See also* Justification defenses

Legal (proximate) causation. *See* Causation

Legality principle, 36–40; common law offenses, 36, 39; ex post facto laws, 36; fair notice, 39, 88, 211; rule of lenity, 36; vague statutes, 36

Lenity, rule of, 36. *See also* Legality principle

Lesser evils defense, 131–137; child neglect and, 230; imminence requirement, 133–135; majority formulation, 136. *See also* Justification defenses

Mafia. *See* Organized crime

Manslaughter, voluntary, 45–49; at common law (provocation), 45–49; continuum of blameworthiness, 49; extreme emotional disturbance, 47; limits on availability of mitigation, 47–49; limits on availability of mitigation, acts vs. mere words, 48–49; limits on availability of mitigation, cooling off period, 47; limits on availability of mitigation, provocative acts, 48–49; Model Penal Code, 47

Mapp v. Ohio, 189. *See also* Exclusionary rule

Marital rape exception, 214–218; limited exception, 214–217; reforms, 214, 217–218; reforms, traditional rule, 214. *See also* Domestic violence; Rape

Memoirs v. Massachusetts, 256

Mens rea. *See* Culpability requirements

Mental illness: death penalty and, 31; extreme mental disturbance, 47; negating culpability, 92–97; negating culpability, general intent, 94; negating culpability, recklessness, 93; negating culpability, specific intent, 93; post-traumatic stress syndrome, 92. *See also* Insanity defense

Mental illness negating offense element (MINOE). *See* Mental illness

Miller v. California, 253–256. *See also* Obscenity offenses

Mistake as to justification, 141–147. *See also* Law enforcement authority; Self-defense

M'Naghten test, 161–162, 166–167. *See also* Insanity defense

Model Penal Code: complicity, 113–114; death penalty, 30; deceptive business practices,

Risking catastrophe, 203–204. *See* Risk creation
Roth v. United States, 256
Rummel v. Estelle, 21

Sadomasochism, 88. *See also* Consent
Safeway Stores, Inc. v. Oklahoma Retail Grocers Assn., Inc., 283
Second Amendment. *See* Firearms possession
Seduction, 88
Self-defense, 141–147; majority formulation, 144–145; mistake as to justification, all-or-nothing approach, 142–143, 146–147; mistake as to justification, Model Penal Code, 143; mistake as to justification, sliding-scale approach, 142–143, 146–147; necessity requirement, 141, 146; proportionality requirement, 141, 146; triggering conditions, 143–147. *See also* Justification defenses
Sexual devices. *See* Obscenity offenses
Sexual offenses. *See* Adultery; Child pornography; Marital rape exception; Obscenity; Statutory rape
Social norms: adultery, 251; child pornography, age of subjects of, 264; differing by region, 211; domestic violence, 214, 217–218; enforcement of, 85, 217–218, 251; marital rape exception, 214, 217–218; responsiveness to, 217–218; sexual conduct and children, 207, 264; statutory rape, 207. *See also* Empirical desert
Social preferences, criminal law as expression of, 88, 251
Sports bribery, 296–300. *See also* Sports fixing

Sports fixing, 296–300; bribery, 296–300; commercial bribery compared, 296; coverage gaps, 296–297, 300; omission liability, 299; rationale, 296–297; tampering, 297–299
Sports tampering, 297–299. *See also* Sports fixing
Stalking, 221–224; defined, 221; grading, 221–224; harm, significance of resulting, 224; repeated conduct requirement, 221; result element, 221–224
Statute of limitations, 181–185; cost to law's moral credibility, 185; declining popularity, 181, 184; public controversy, 181; rationale, 184–185
Statutory rape, 207–211; close-in-age exception, 207–211; ineffective consent, 207; rationale, 207; relationship of authority, 209; social norms, 207, 211. *See also* Children
Strassheim v. Daily, 313
Strict construction, Rule of, 36. *See also* Legality principle
Suicide, assisting, 87. *See also* Consent
Symbolic offenses: adultery and, 88, 251–252; costs of, 88, 251–252; prosecutorial discretion and, 252; seduction and, 88

Tattooing, 88. *See also* Consent
Termination defense, 121–123
Territorial jurisdiction. *See* Jurisdiction, territorial
Theft by extortion. *See* Extortion
Three-strikes statutes. *See* Habitual offender statutes
Thurman, Tracey, 214
Transferred intent. *See* Imputing culpability

About the Authors

Paul H. Robinson is the Colin S. Diver Professor of Law at the University of Pennsylvania Law School and one of the world's leading criminal law scholars. A prolific writer and lecturer, Robinson has lectured in more than 100 cities in 33 states and 27 countries and has had his writings appear in 13 languages. He served as counsel for the U.S. Senate Subcommittee on Criminal Laws and Procedures and was the lone dissenter when the U.S. Sentencing Commission promulgated the current federal sentencing guidelines. He is the author or editor of 15 books, including the standard lawyer's reference on criminal law defenses, three Oxford monographs on criminal law theory, and a highly regarded criminal law treatise. Robinson has worked on a dozen criminal code reform projects in the United States and abroad, including the first modern Islamic penal code, and is currently commissioned to draft criminal codes for Delaware and Somalia.

Tyler Scot Williams is an associate at a law firm in Washington, D.C., and a member of the D.C. Bar. He holds five academic degrees, including the juris doctor from the University of Pennsylvania Law School, and master's degrees in philosophy, medical ethics, and theology.